My Little Monster

1

Robico

CONTENTS

Chapter 1 ... My Classmate Yoshida-kun   4

Chapter 2 ... I Don't Hate You   49

Chapter 3 ... Weird   89

Chapter 4 ... Nuisance   131

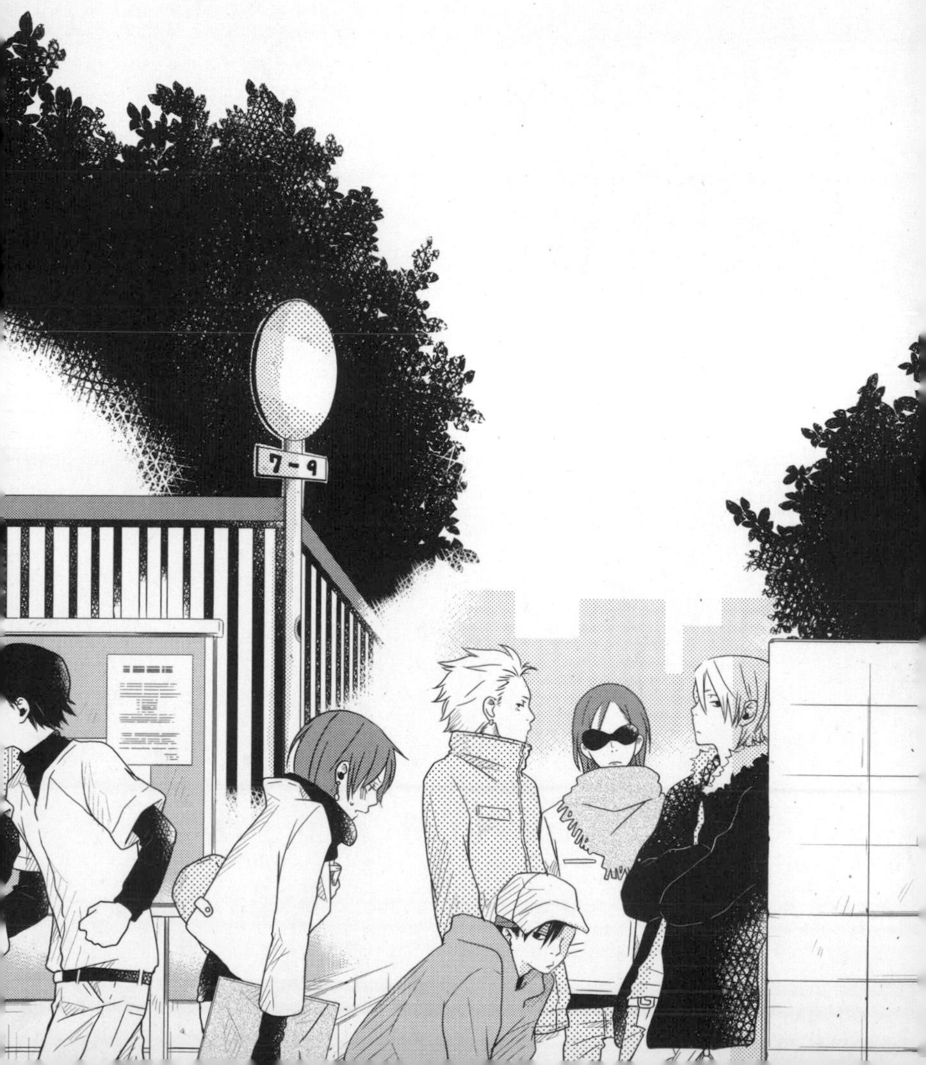
7 - 9

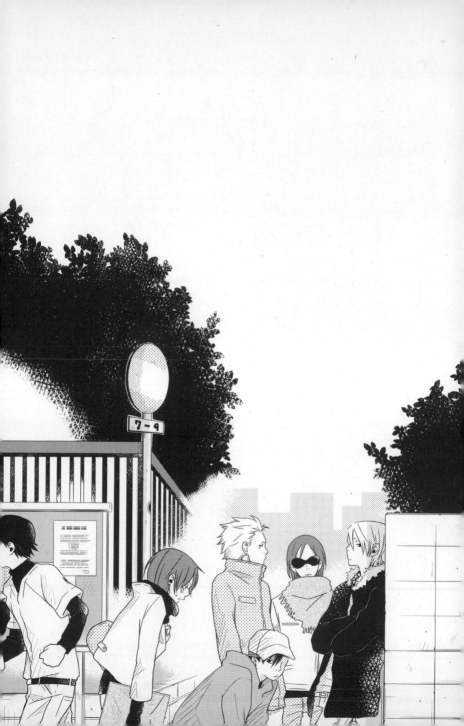

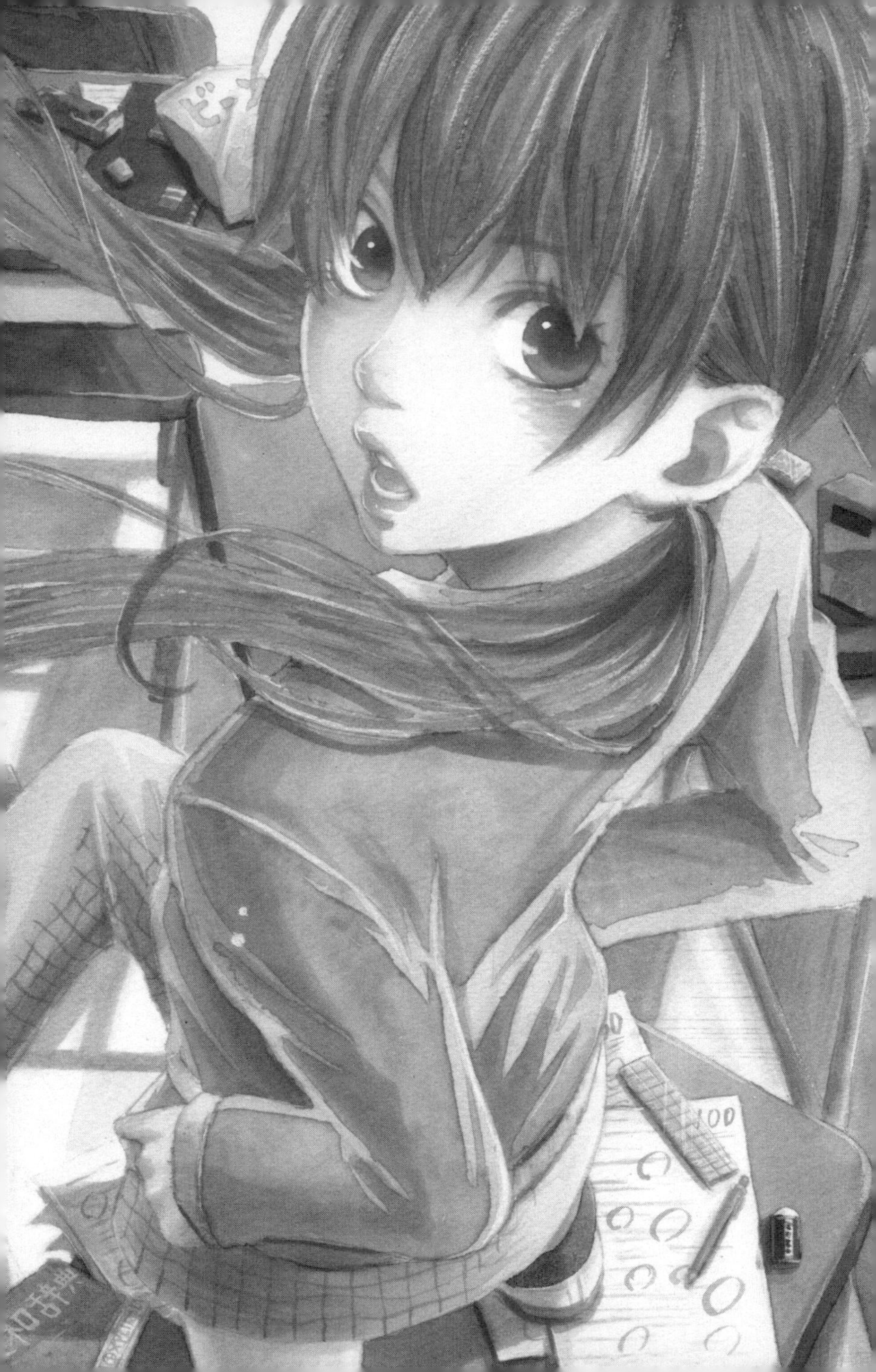
100

Chapter 1 My Classmate Yoshida-kun

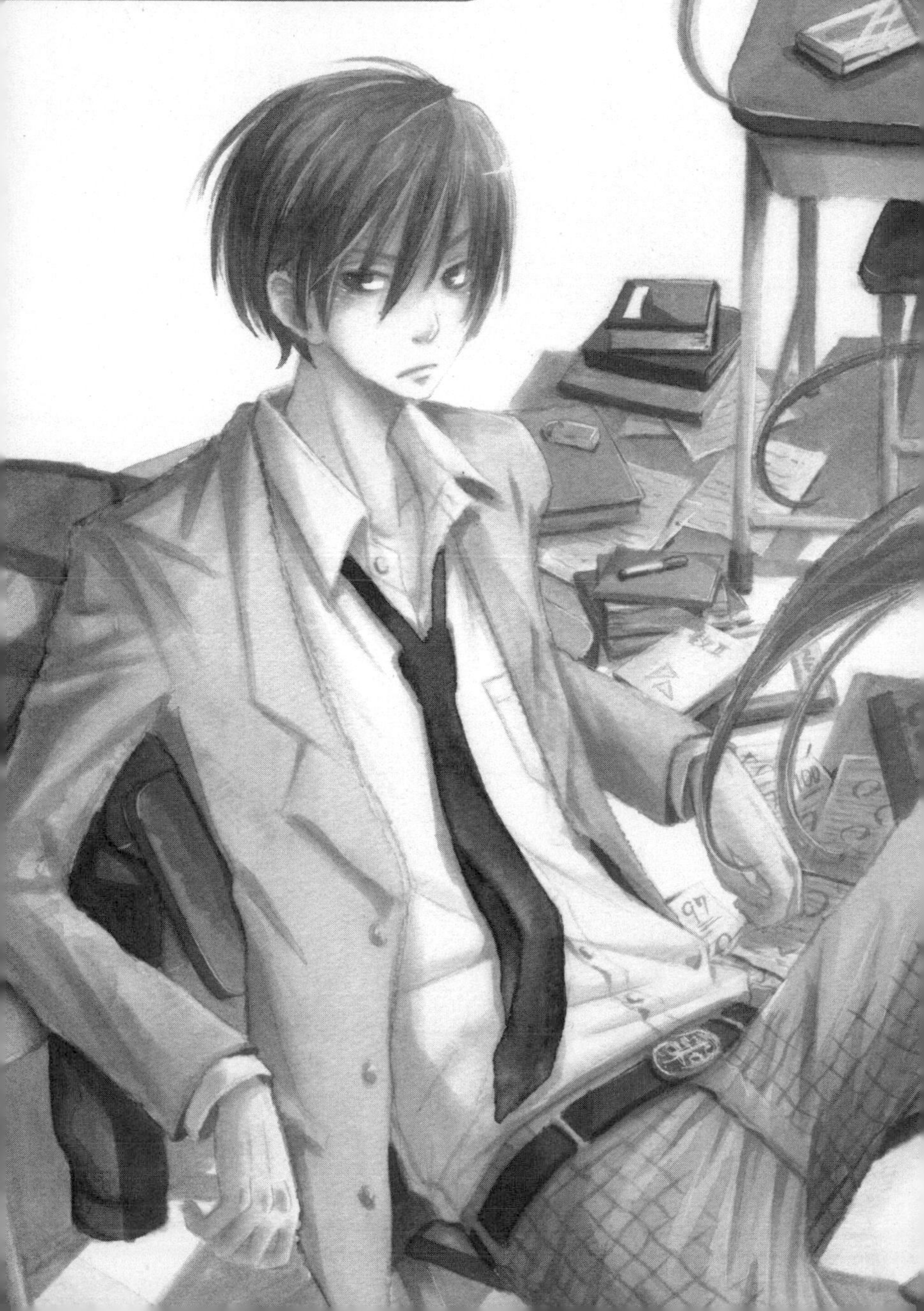

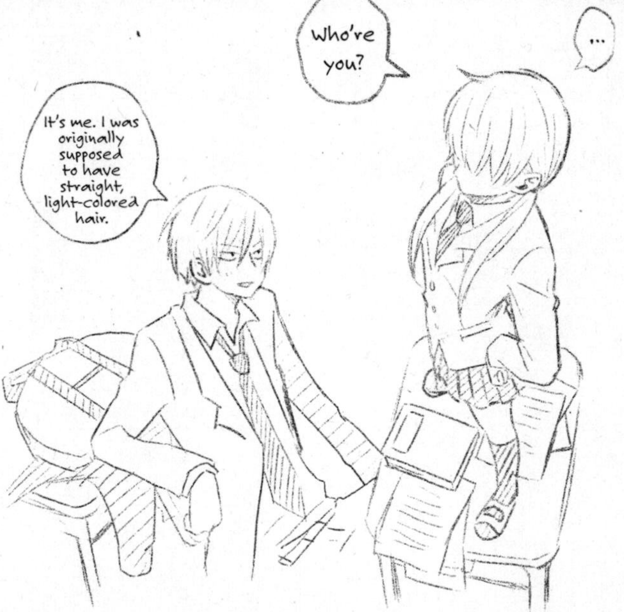
...
Who're you?
It's me. I was originally supposed to have straight, light-colored hair.

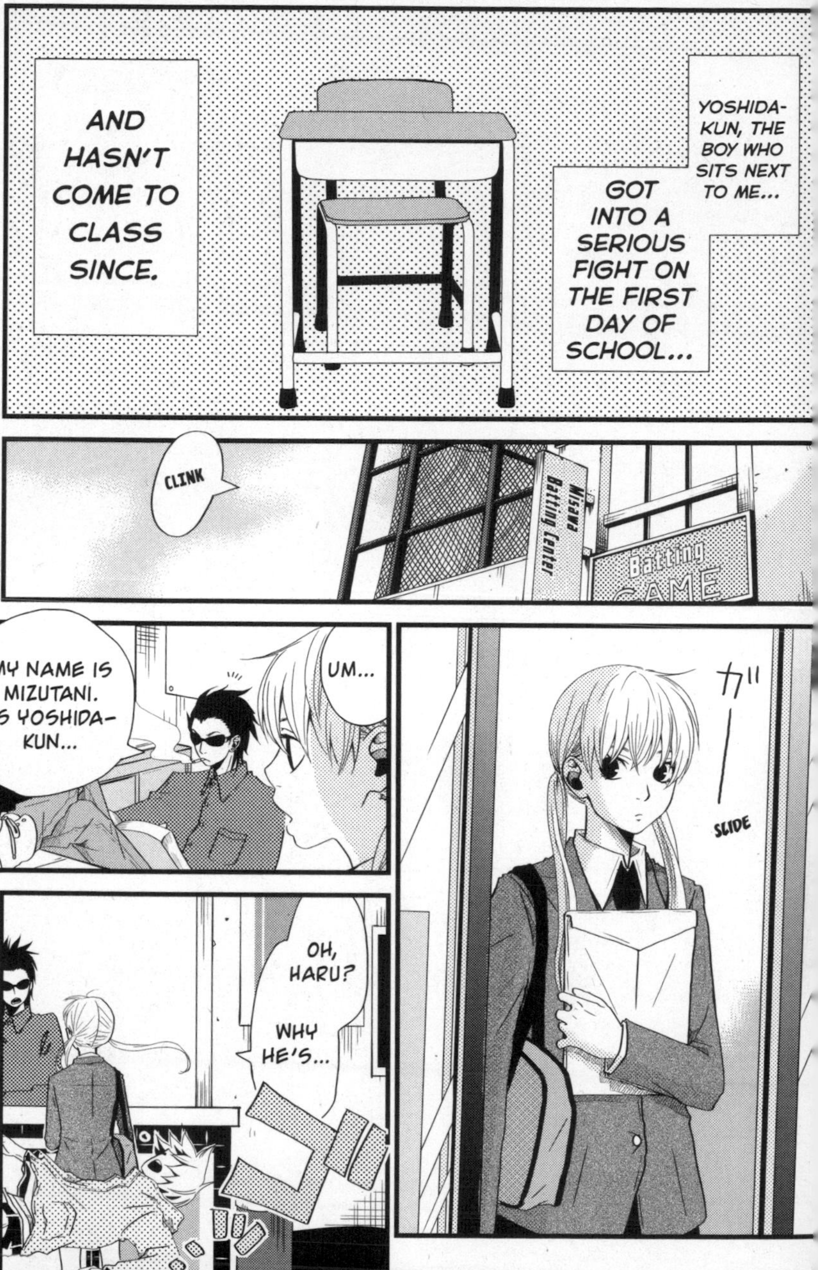
YOSHIDA-KUN, THE BOY WHO SITS NEXT TO ME...
GOT INTO A SERIOUS FIGHT ON THE FIRST DAY OF SCHOOL...
AND HASN'T COME TO CLASS SINCE.
CLINK
Misawa Batting Center
Batting GAME
ガー
SLIDE
UM...
MY NAME IS MIZUTANI. IS YOSHIDA-KUN...
OH, HARU?
WHY HE'S...
THUD

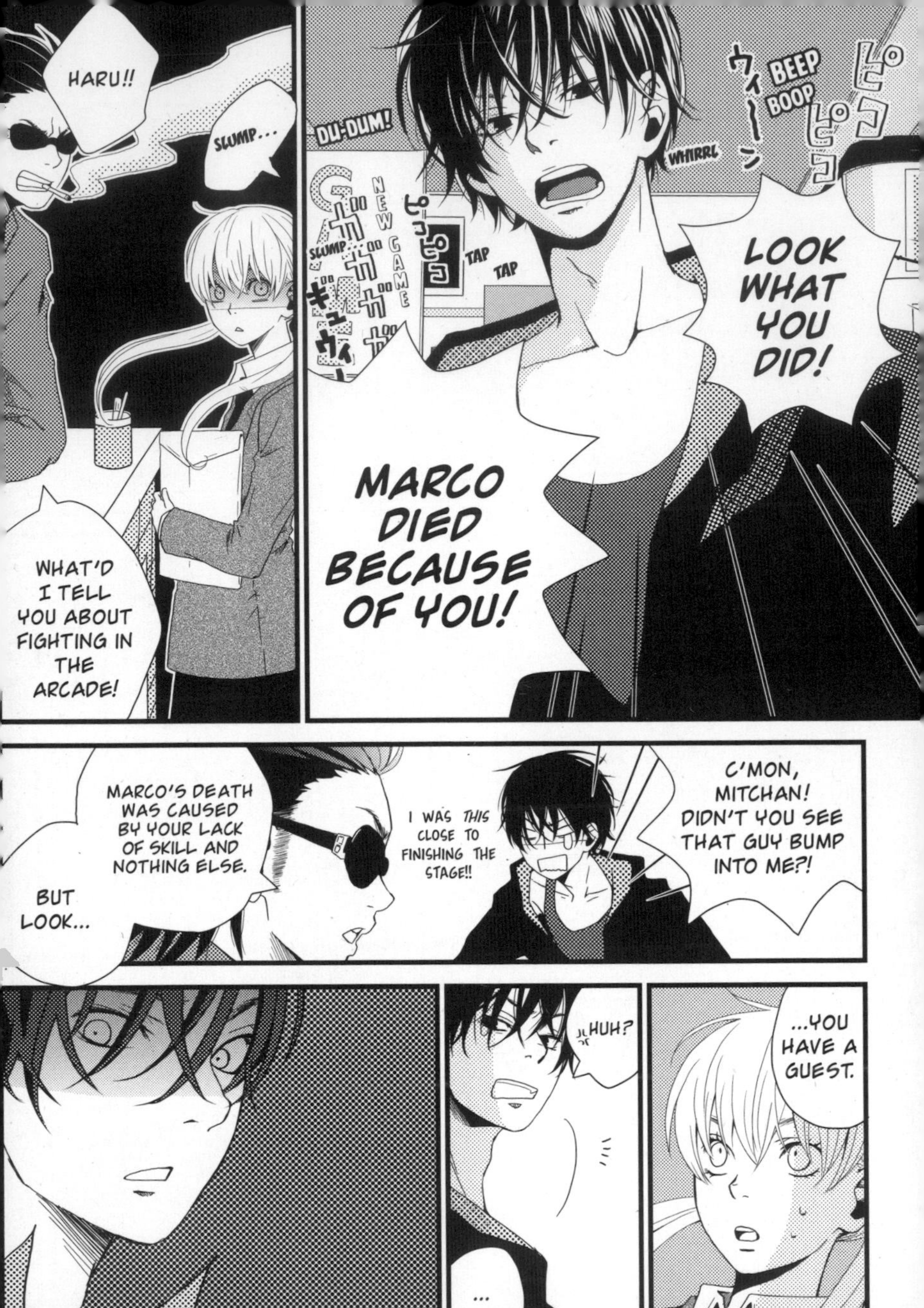
ピコピコ
BEEP BOOP
ウィーン
WHIRRL
LOOK WHAT YOU DID!
DU-DUM!
TAP TAP
NEW GAME
SLUMP...
MARCO DIED BECAUSE OF YOU!
HARU!!
SLUMP...
WHAT'D I TELL YOU ABOUT FIGHTING IN THE ARCADE!
C'MON, MITCHAN! DIDN'T YOU SEE THAT GUY BUMP INTO ME?!
I WAS THIS CLOSE TO FINISHING THE STAGE!!
MARCO'S DEATH WAS CAUSED BY YOUR LACK OF SKILL AND NOTHING ELSE.
BUT LOOK...
...YOU HAVE A GUEST.
HUH?
...

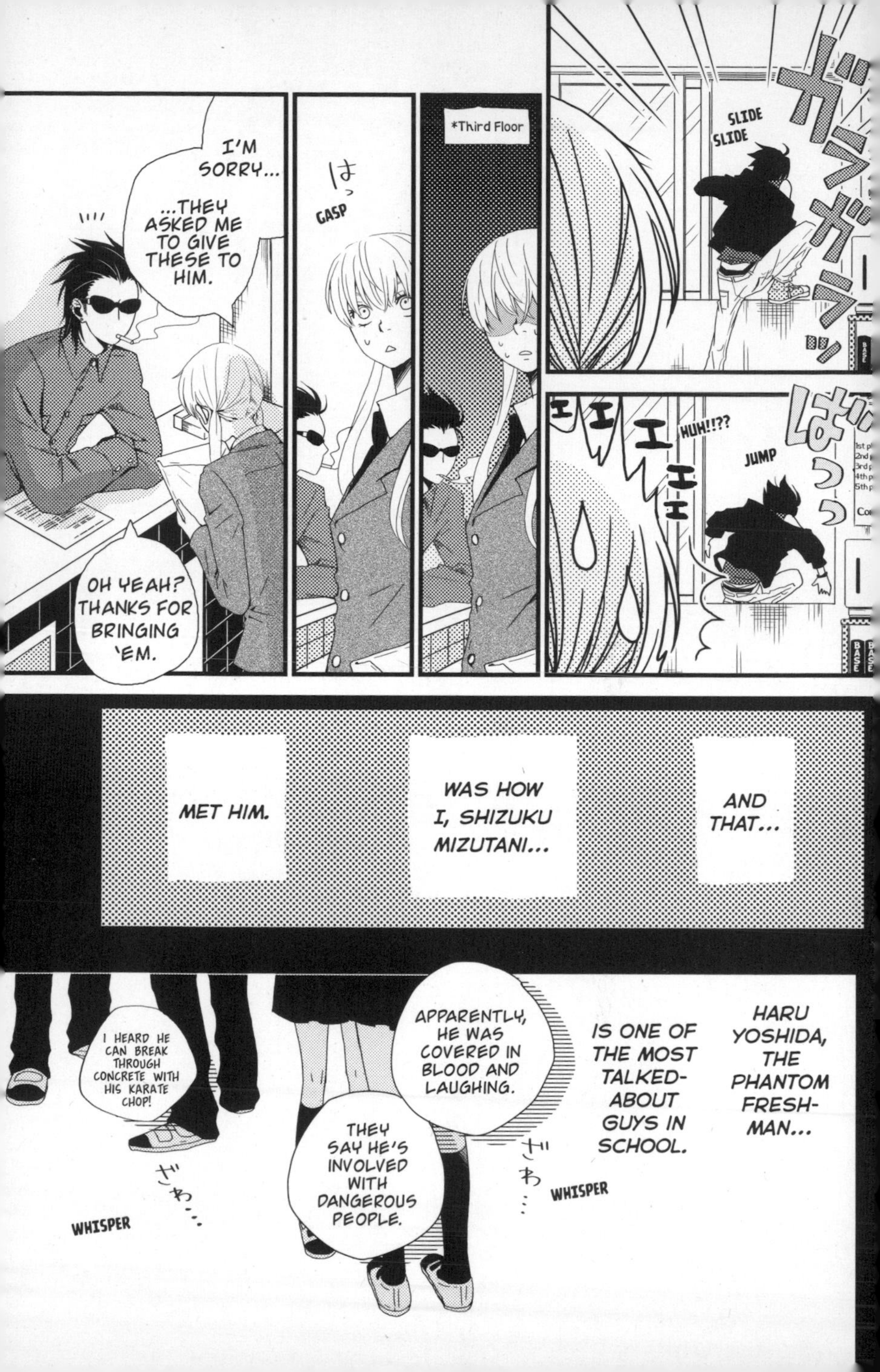
ガラガラッ
SLIDE SLIDE
ばっ
JUMP
エエエエエ
HUH!!??
*Third Floor
はっ
GASP
I'M SORRY...
...THEY ASKED ME TO GIVE THESE TO HIM.
OH YEAH? THANKS FOR BRINGING 'EM.
AND THAT...
WAS HOW I, SHIZUKU MIZUTANI...
MET HIM.
HARU YOSHIDA, THE PHANTOM FRESH-MAN...
IS ONE OF THE MOST TALKED-ABOUT GUYS IN SCHOOL.
ざわ...
WHISPER
APPARENTLY, HE WAS COVERED IN BLOOD AND LAUGHING.
THEY SAY HE'S INVOLVED WITH DANGEROUS PEOPLE.
I HEARD HE CAN BREAK THROUGH CONCRETE WITH HIS KARATE CHOP!
ざわ...
WHISPER

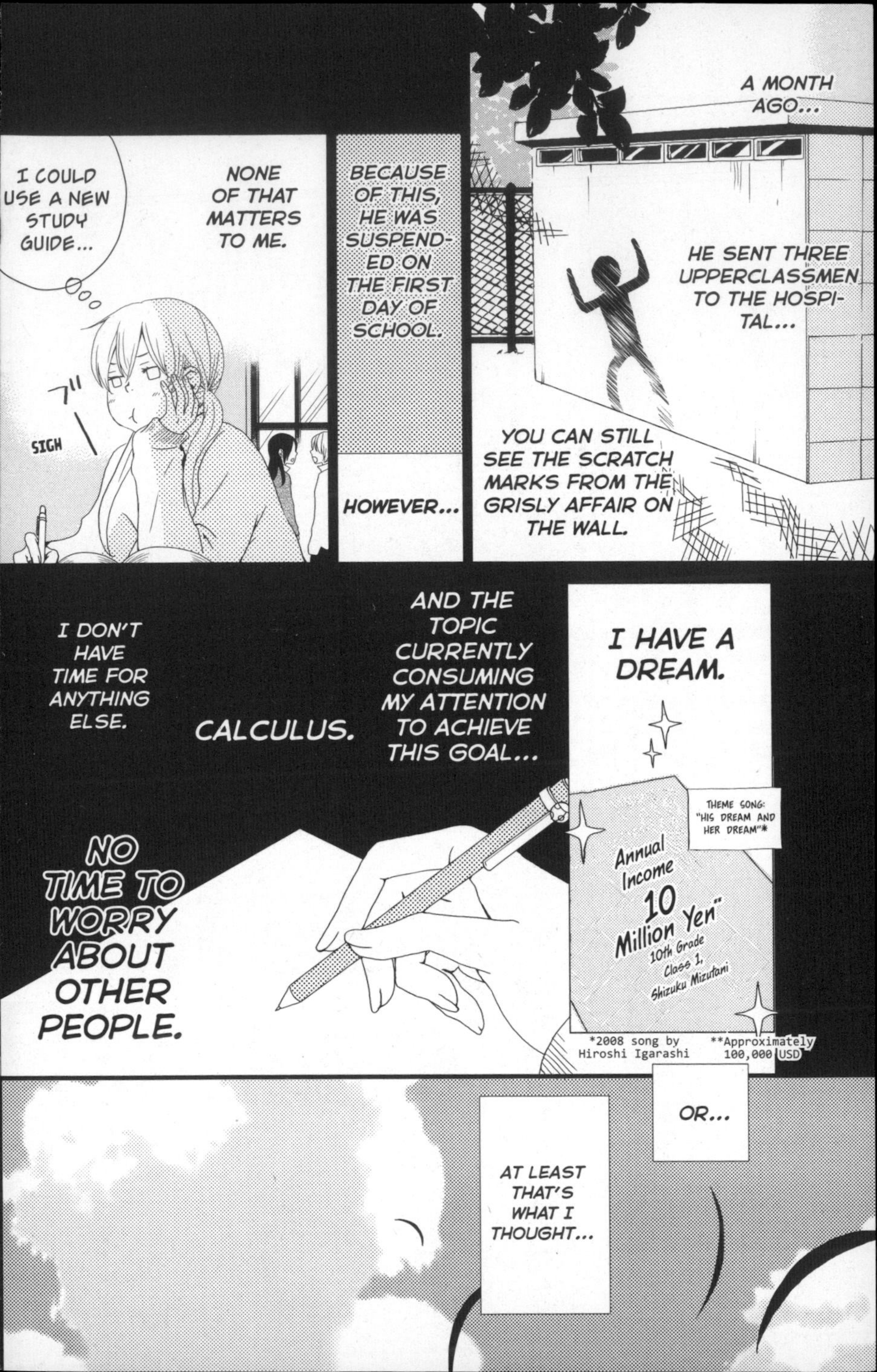
A MONTH AGO...
HE SENT THREE UPPERCLASSMEN TO THE HOSPITAL...
YOU CAN STILL SEE THE SCRATCH MARKS FROM THE GRISLY AFFAIR ON THE WALL.
BECAUSE OF THIS, HE WAS SUSPENDED ON THE FIRST DAY OF SCHOOL.
HOWEVER...
NONE OF THAT MATTERS TO ME.
I COULD USE A NEW STUDY GUIDE...
SIGH
I HAVE A DREAM.
THEME SONG: "HIS DREAM AND HER DREAM"*
Annual Income 10 Million Yen**
10th Grade Class 1, Shizuku Mizutani
*2008 song by Hiroshi Igarashi
**Approximately 100,000 USD
AND THE TOPIC CURRENTLY CONSUMING MY ATTENTION TO ACHIEVE THIS GOAL...
CALCULUS.
I DON'T HAVE TIME FOR ANYTHING ELSE.
NO TIME TO WORRY ABOUT OTHER PEOPLE.
OR...
AT LEAST THAT'S WHAT I THOUGHT...

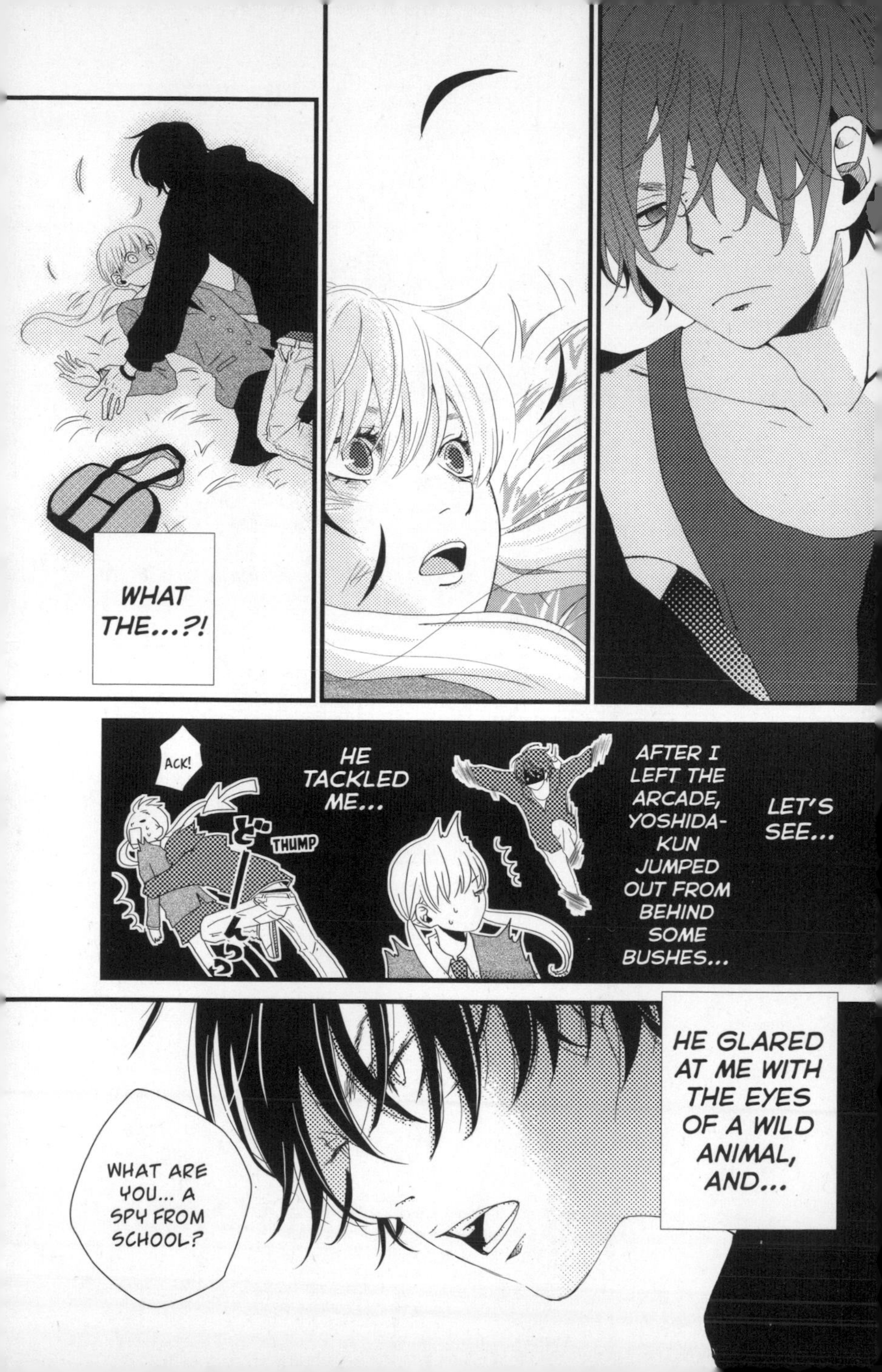
WHAT THE...?!
LET'S SEE...
AFTER I LEFT THE ARCADE, YOSHIDA-KUN JUMPED OUT FROM BEHIND SOME BUSHES...
HE TACKLED ME...
ACK!
THUMP
HE GLARED AT ME WITH THE EYES OF A WILD ANIMAL, AND...
WHAT ARE YOU... A SPY FROM SCHOOL?

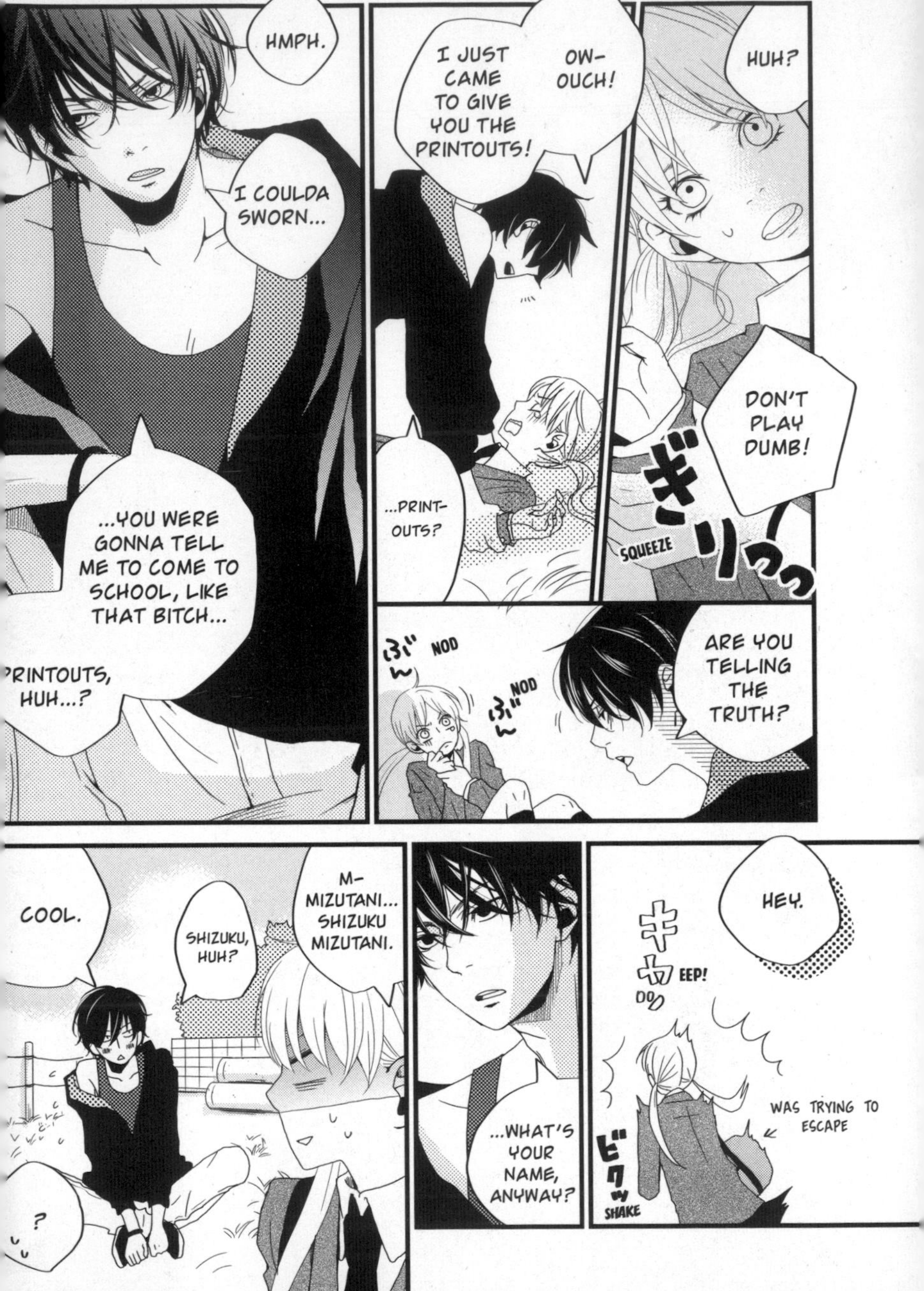
HUH?
DON'T PLAY DUMB!
ギリッ
SQUEEZE
OW-OUCH!
I JUST CAME TO GIVE YOU THE PRINTOUTS!
...PRINT-OUTS?
ARE YOU TELLING THE TRUTH?
ぶん NOD
ぶん NOD
HMPH.
I COULDA SWORN...
...YOU WERE GONNA TELL ME TO COME TO SCHOOL, LIKE THAT BITCH...
PRINTOUTS, HUH...?
HEY.
キャ EEP!
ビクッ SHAKE
WAS TRYING TO ESCAPE
...WHAT'S YOUR NAME, ANYWAY?
M-MIZUTANI... SHIZUKU MIZUTANI.
SHIZUKU, HUH?
COOL.
?

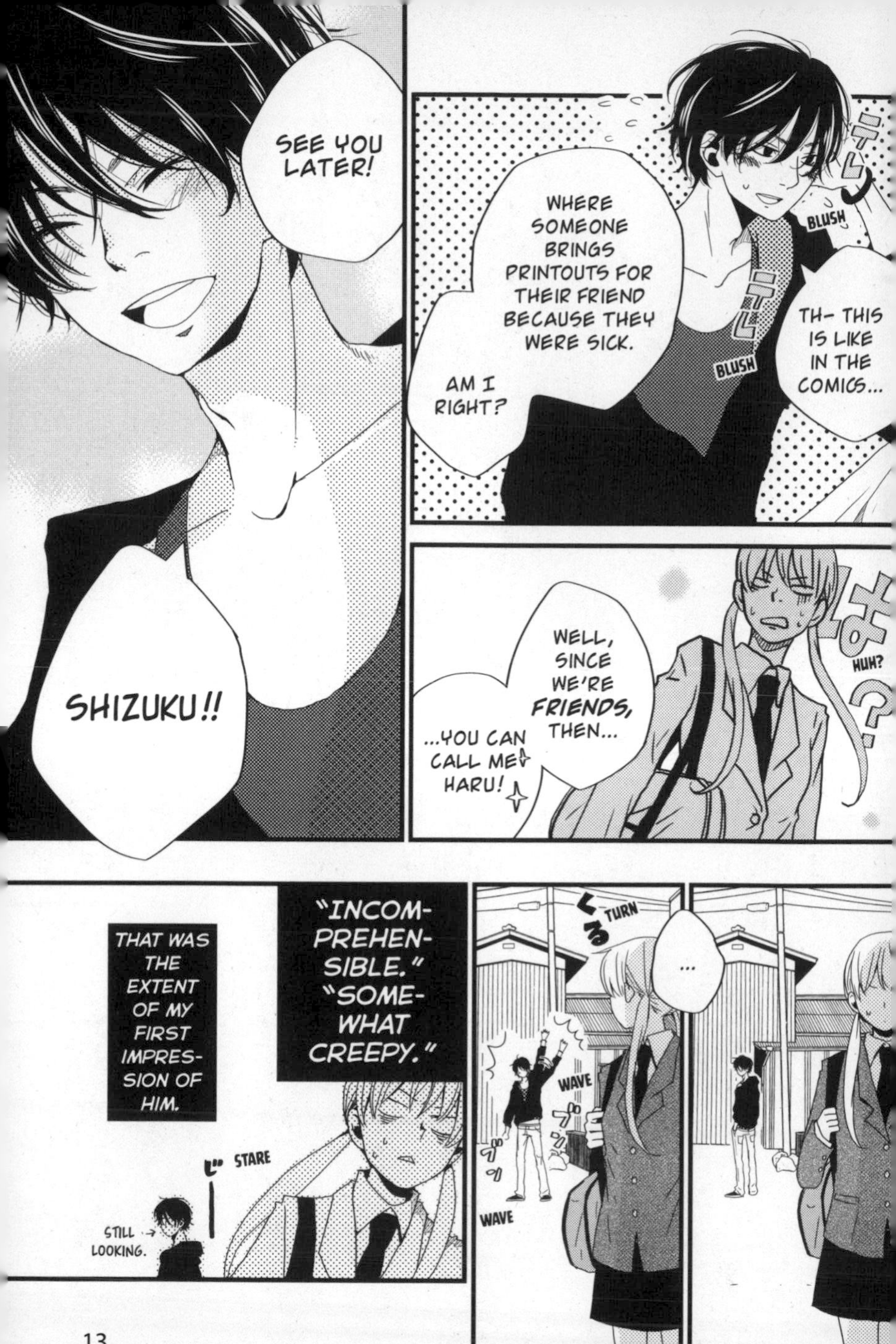
BLUSH
TH- THIS IS LIKE IN THE COMICS...
BLUSH
WHERE SOMEONE BRINGS PRINTOUTS FOR THEIR FRIEND BECAUSE THEY WERE SICK.
AM I RIGHT?
HUH?
WELL, SINCE WE'RE FRIENDS, THEN...
...YOU CAN CALL ME HARU!
SEE YOU LATER!
SHIZUKU!!
...
TURN
WAVE
WAVE
"INCOMPREHENSIBLE." "SOMEWHAT CREEPY."
THAT WAS THE EXTENT OF MY FIRST IMPRESSION OF HIM.
STARE
STILL LOOKING.

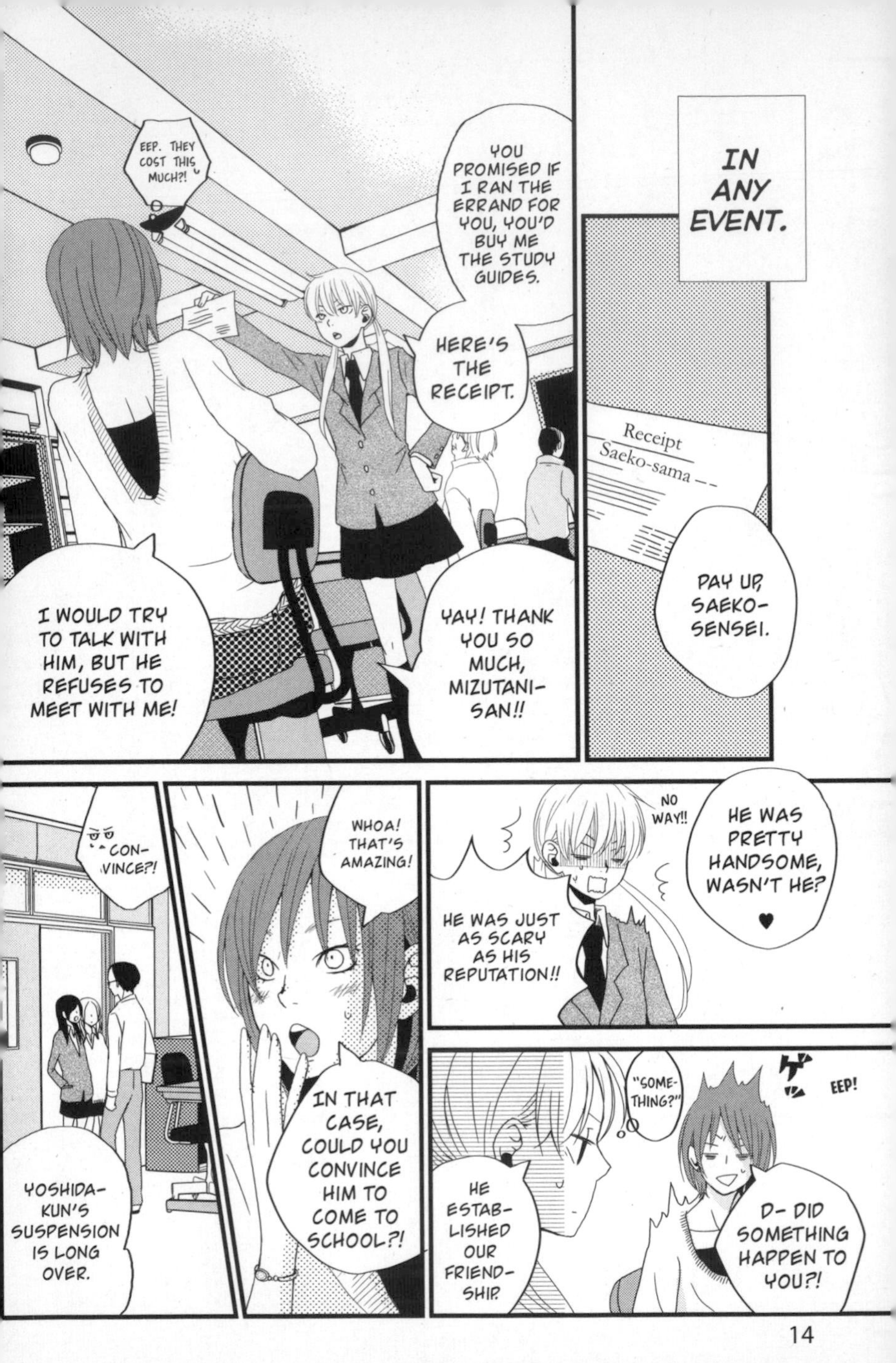
IN ANY EVENT.
Receipt
Saeko-sama
PAY UP, SAEKO-SENSEI.
YOU PROMISED IF I RAN THE ERRAND FOR YOU, YOU'D BUY ME THE STUDY GUIDES.
HERE'S THE RECEIPT.
EEP. THEY COST THIS MUCH?!
YAY! THANK YOU SO MUCH, MIZUTANI-SAN!!
I WOULD TRY TO TALK WITH HIM, BUT HE REFUSES TO MEET WITH ME!
HE WAS PRETTY HANDSOME, WASN'T HE? ♥
NO WAY!!
HE WAS JUST AS SCARY AS HIS REPUTATION!!
EEP!
D- DID SOMETHING HAPPEN TO YOU?!
"SOMETHING?"
HE ESTABLISHED OUR FRIENDSHIP.
WHOA! THAT'S AMAZING!
IN THAT CASE, COULD YOU CONVINCE HIM TO COME TO SCHOOL?!
CONVINCE?!
YOSHIDA-KUN'S SUSPENSION IS LONG OVER.

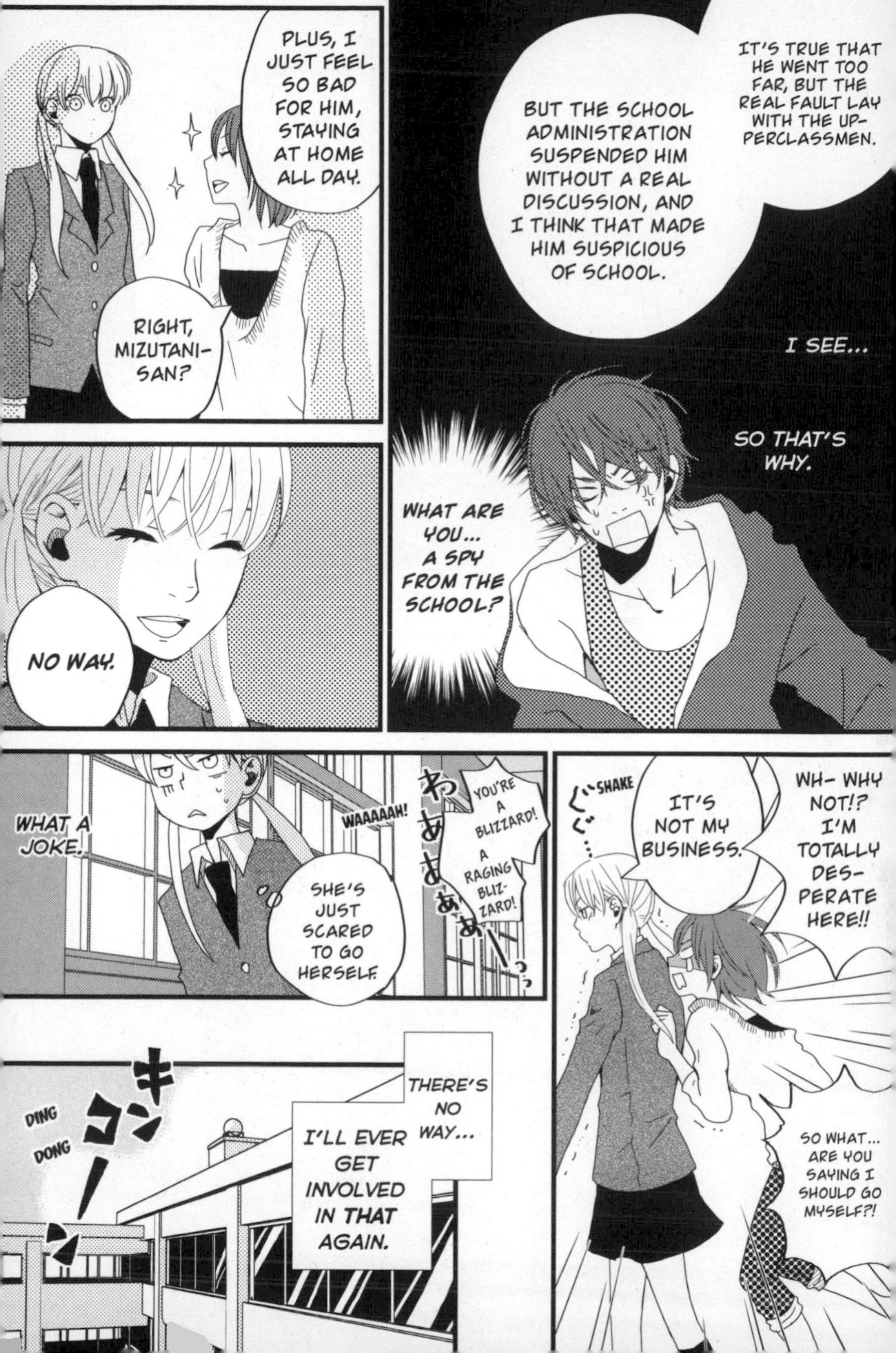
IT'S TRUE THAT HE WENT TOO FAR, BUT THE REAL FAULT LAY WITH THE UP-PERCLASSMEN.
BUT THE SCHOOL ADMINISTRATION SUSPENDED HIM WITHOUT A REAL DISCUSSION, AND I THINK THAT MADE HIM SUSPICIOUS OF SCHOOL.
I SEE...
SO THAT'S WHY.
WHAT ARE YOU... A SPY FROM THE SCHOOL?
PLUS, I JUST FEEL SO BAD FOR HIM, STAYING AT HOME ALL DAY.
RIGHT, MIZUTANI-SAN?
NO WAY.
WH- WHY NOT!? I'M TOTALLY DES-PERATE HERE!!
SHAKE
IT'S NOT MY BUSINESS.
SO WHAT... ARE YOU SAYING I SHOULD GO MYSELF?!
YOU'RE A BLIZZARD!
A RAGING BLIZ-ZARD!
WAAAAAH!
WHAT A JOKE.
SHE'S JUST SCARED TO GO HERSELF.
キンコーン
DING
DONG
THERE'S NO WAY...
I'LL EVER GET INVOLVED IN THAT AGAIN.

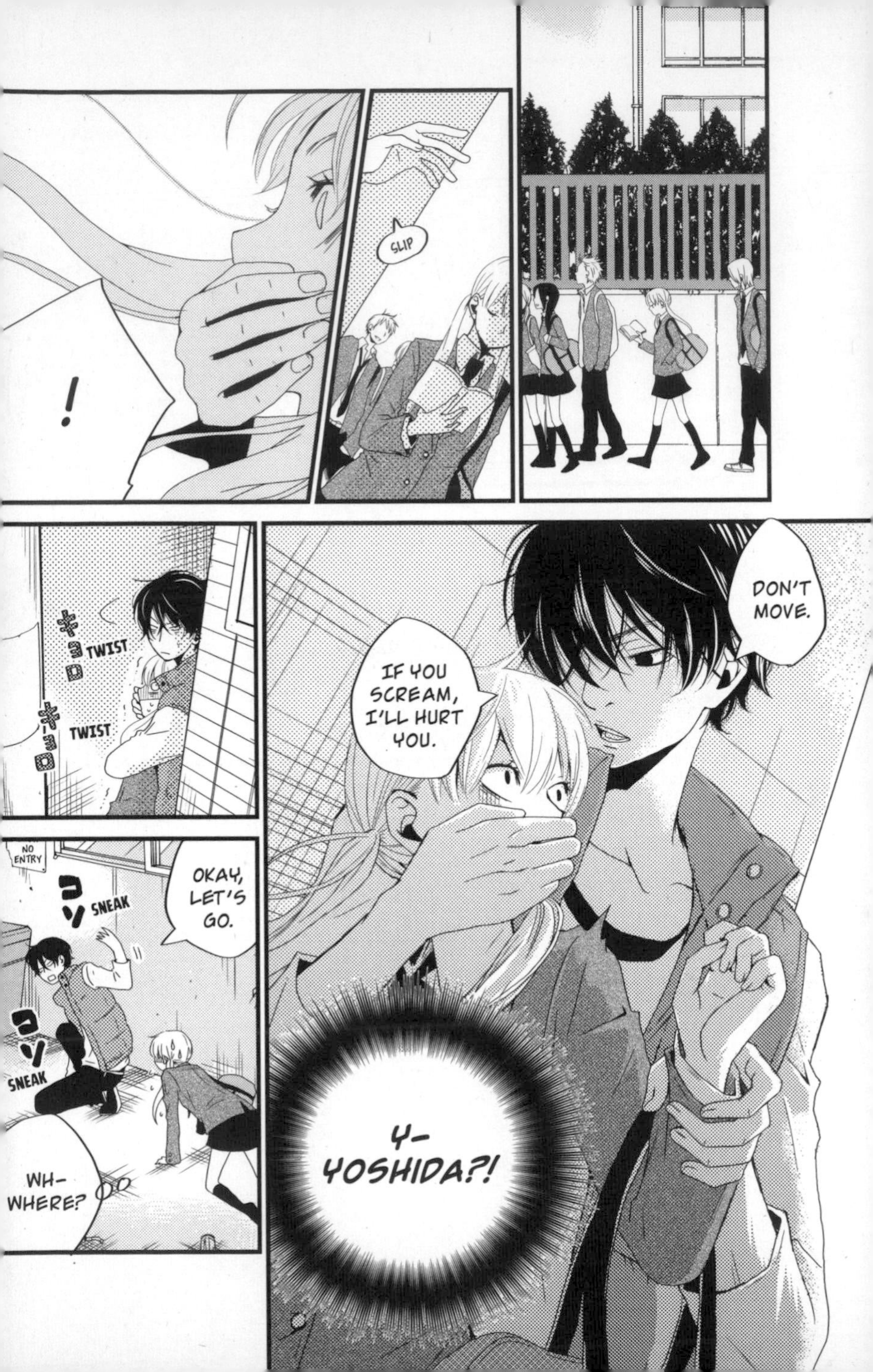
SLIP
!
DON'T MOVE.
IF YOU SCREAM, I'LL HURT YOU.
Y-YOSHIDA?!
キョロ TWIST
キョロ TWIST
NO ENTRY
OKAY, LET'S GO.
コソ SNEAK
コソ SNEAK
WH-WHERE?

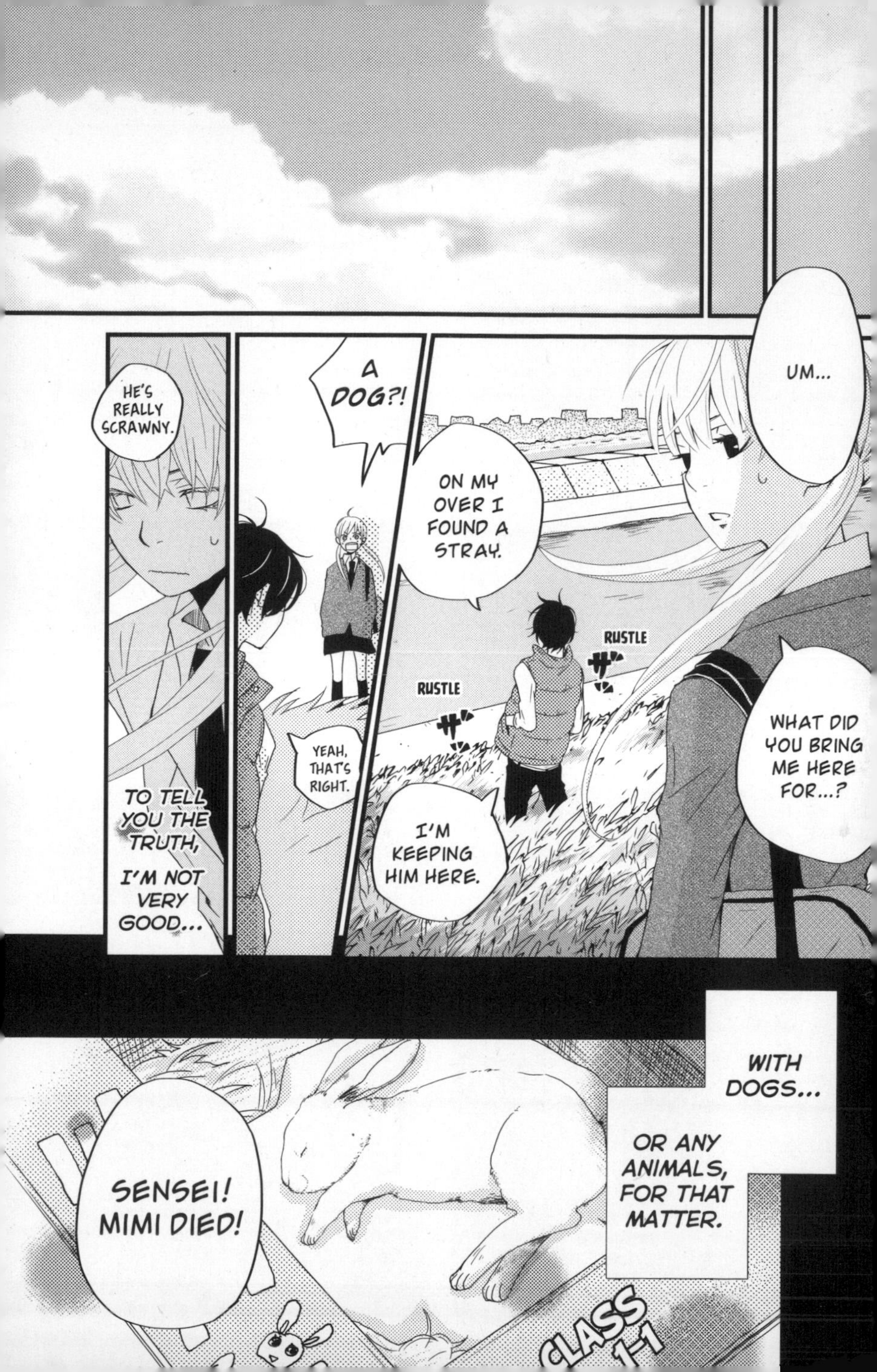
UM...
WHAT DID YOU BRING ME HERE FOR...?
ON MY OVER I FOUND A STRAY.
RUSTLE
RUSTLE
I'M KEEPING HIM HERE.
A DOG?!
YEAH, THAT'S RIGHT.
HE'S REALLY SCRAWNY.
TO TELL YOU THE TRUTH,
I'M NOT VERY GOOD...
WITH DOGS...
OR ANY ANIMALS, FOR THAT MATTER.
SENSEI! MIMI DIED!
CLASS 1-1

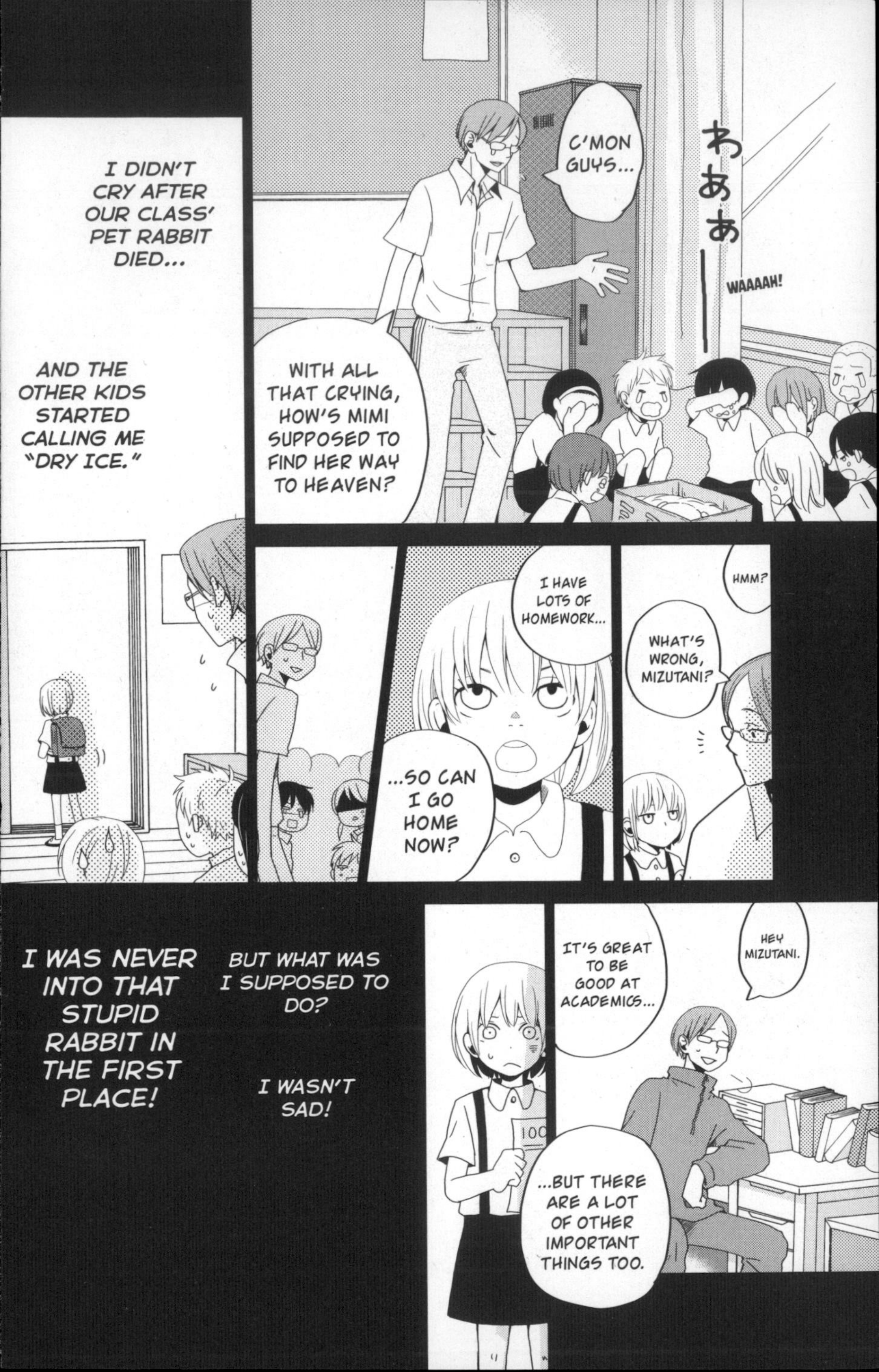
わぁぁー
WAAAAH!
C'MON GUYS...
WITH ALL THAT CRYING, HOW'S MIMI SUPPOSED TO FIND HER WAY TO HEAVEN?
I DIDN'T CRY AFTER OUR CLASS' PET RABBIT DIED...
AND THE OTHER KIDS STARTED CALLING ME "DRY ICE."
HMM?
WHAT'S WRONG, MIZUTANI?
I HAVE LOTS OF HOMEWORK...
...SO CAN I GO HOME NOW?
HEY MIZUTANI.
IT'S GREAT TO BE GOOD AT ACADEMICS...
...BUT THERE ARE A LOT OF OTHER IMPORTANT THINGS TOO.
100
BUT WHAT WAS I SUPPOSED TO DO?
I WASN'T SAD!
I WAS NEVER INTO THAT STUPID RABBIT IN THE FIRST PLACE!

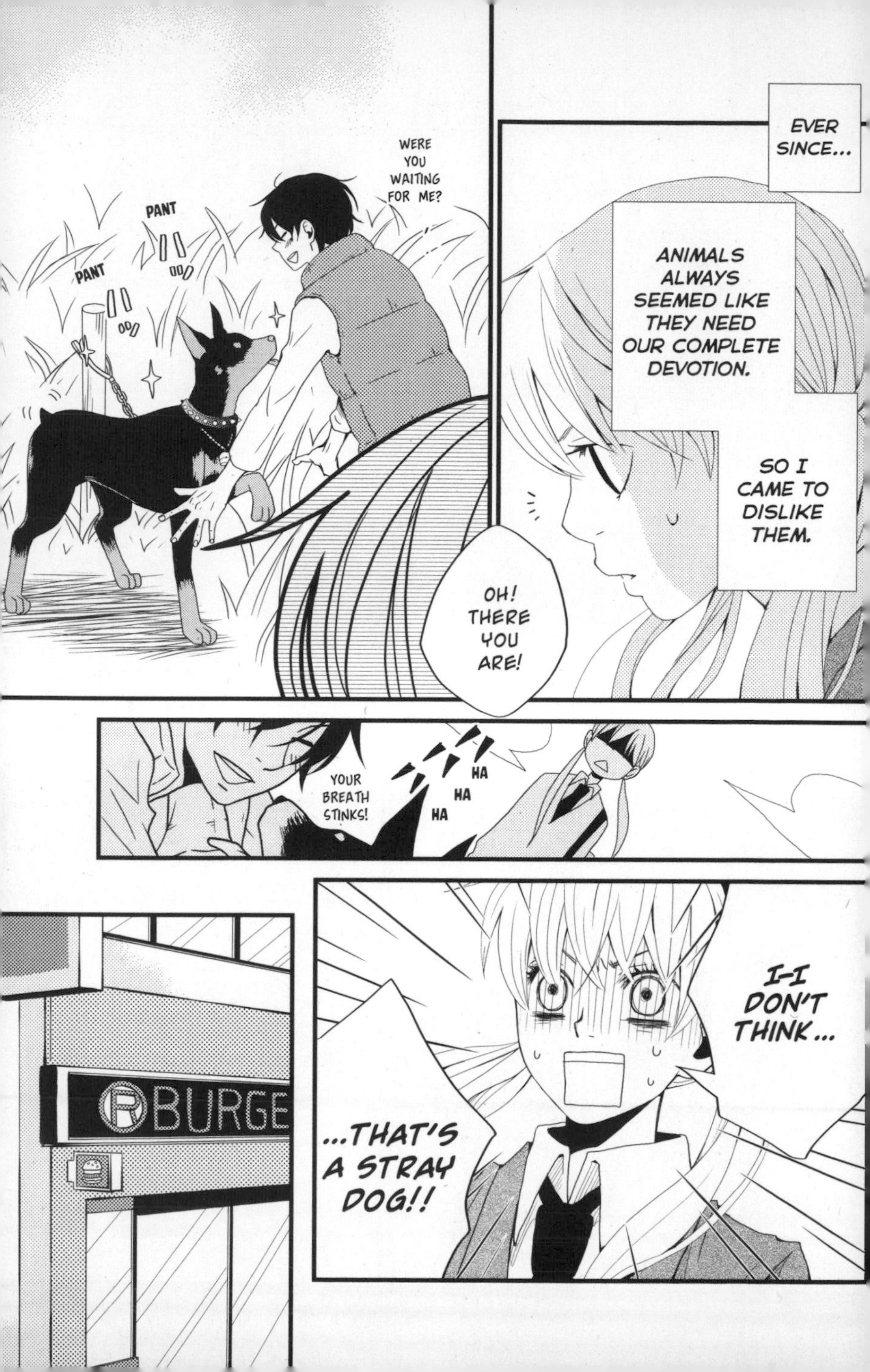
EVER SINCE...
ANIMALS ALWAYS SEEMED LIKE THEY NEED OUR COMPLETE DEVOTION.
SO I CAME TO DISLIKE THEM.
OH! THERE YOU ARE!
WERE YOU WAITING FOR ME?
PANT
PANT
HA HA HA
YOUR BREATH STINKS!
I-I DON'T THINK...
...THAT'S A STRAY DOG!!
BURGE

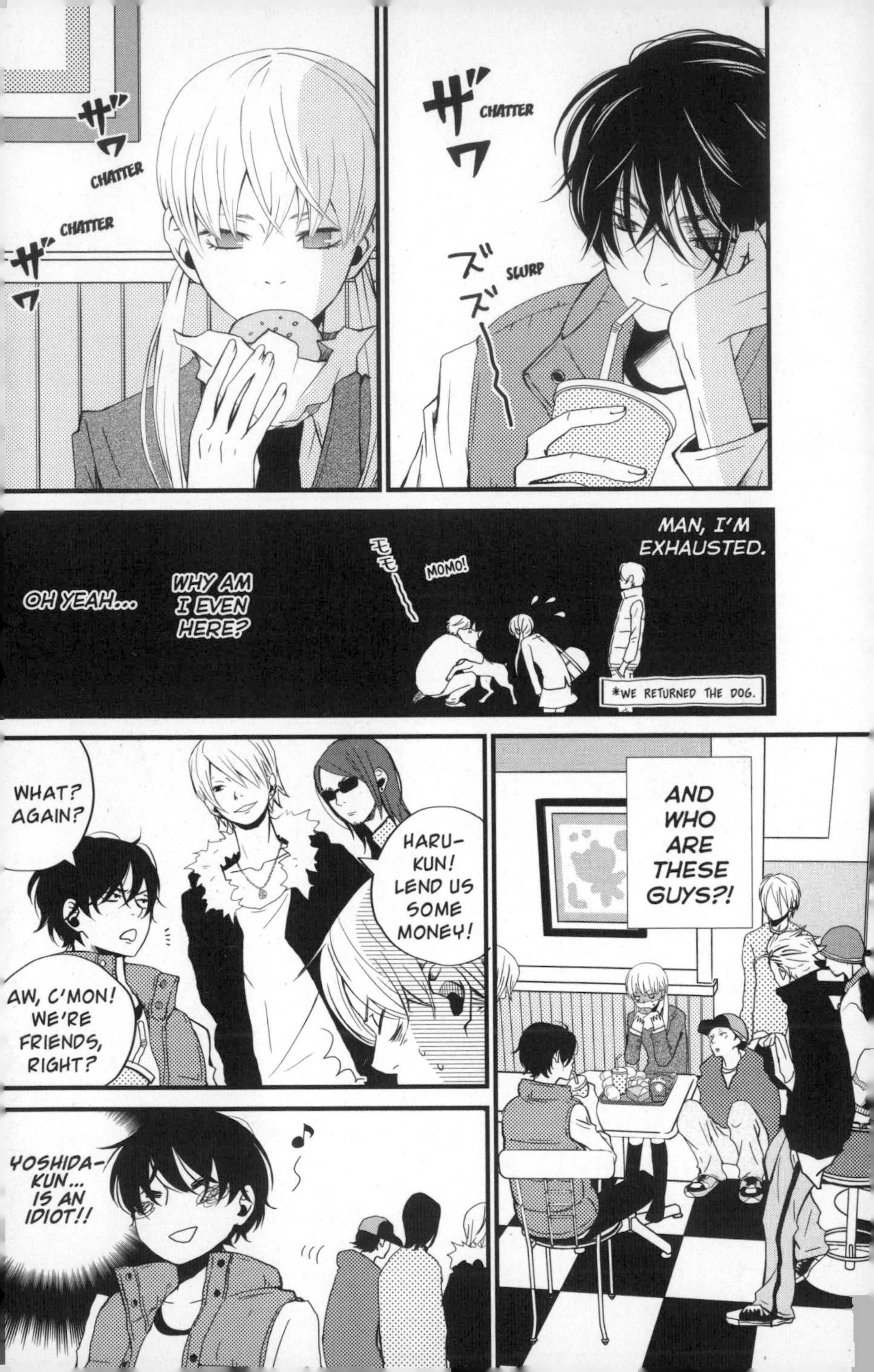
ザワ
CHATTER
ズズー
SLURP
ザワ
CHATTER
ザワ
CHATTER
MAN, I'M EXHAUSTED.
*WE RETURNED THE DOG.
モモー
MOMO!
WHY AM I EVEN HERE?
OH YEAH...
AND WHO ARE THESE GUYS?!
HARU-KUN! LEND US SOME MONEY!
WHAT? AGAIN?
AW, C'MON! WE'RE FRIENDS, RIGHT?
YOSHIDA-KUN... IS AN IDIOT!!

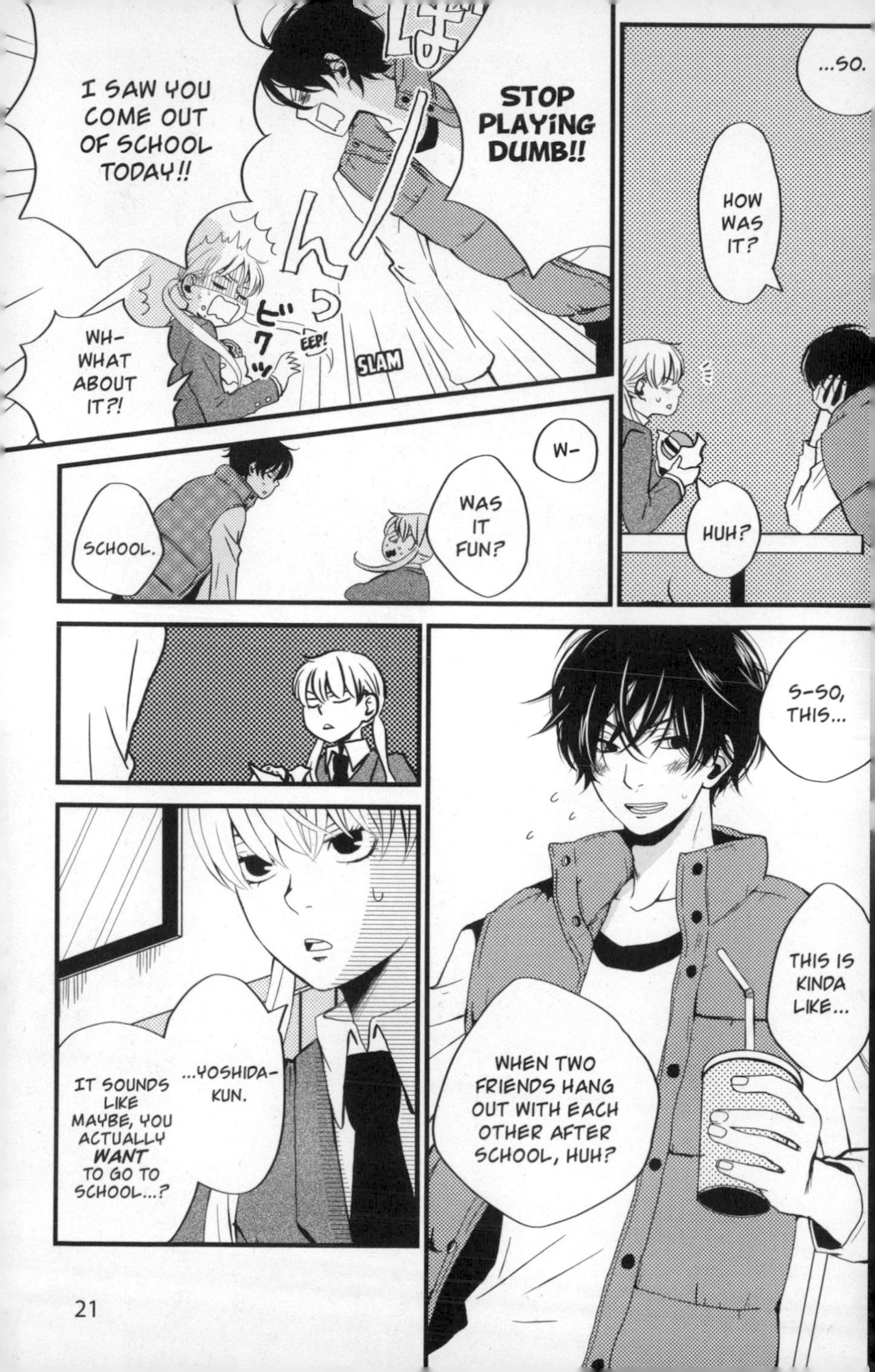
...SO.
HOW WAS IT?
HUH?
STOP PLAYING DUMB!!
I SAW YOU COME OUT OF SCHOOL TODAY!!
SLAM
EEP!
ビクッ
WH- WHAT ABOUT IT?!
W-
WAS IT FUN?
SCHOOL.
S-SO, THIS...
THIS IS KINDA LIKE...
WHEN TWO FRIENDS HANG OUT WITH EACH OTHER AFTER SCHOOL, HUH?
...YOSHIDA-KUN.
IT SOUNDS LIKE MAYBE, YOU ACTUALLY ***WANT*** TO GO TO SCHOOL...?

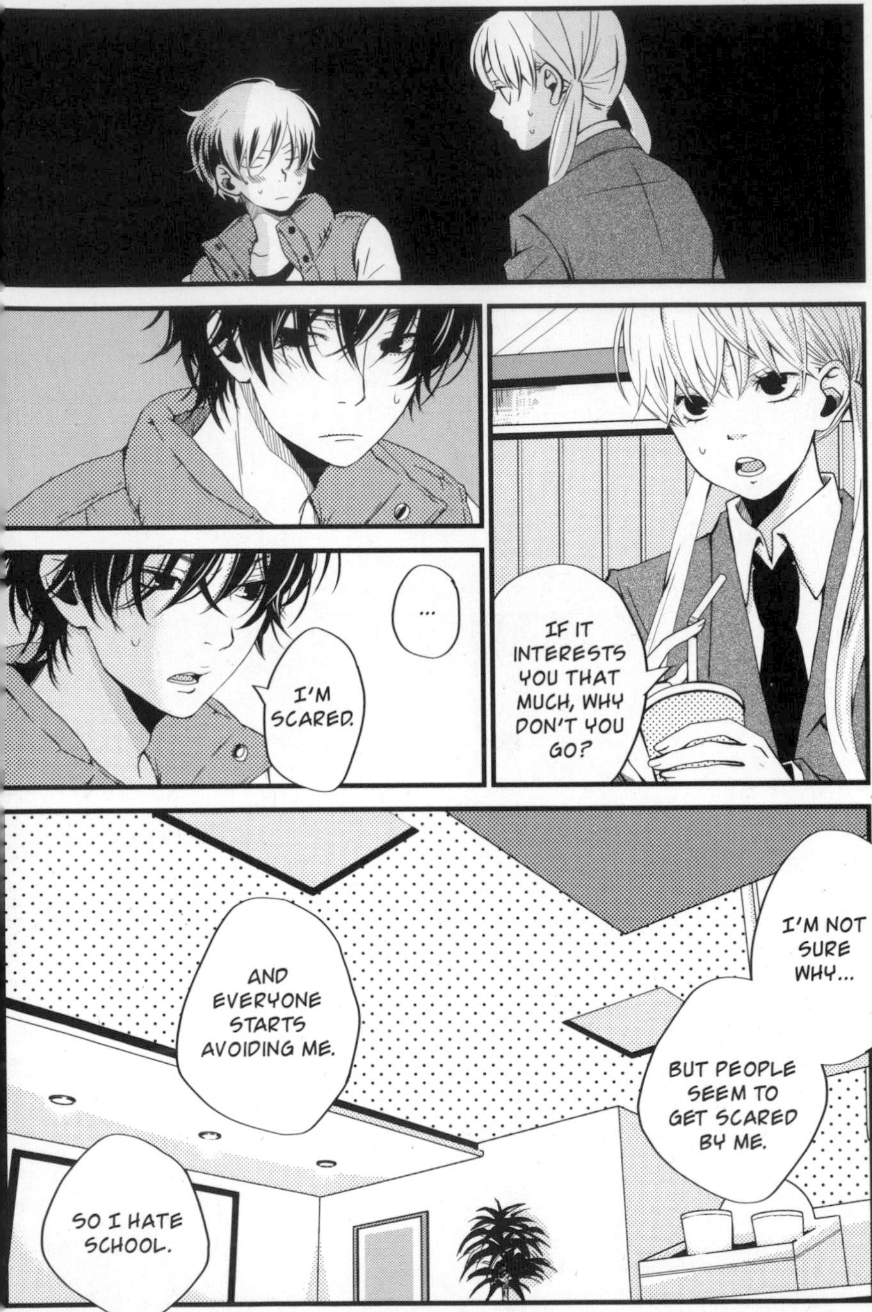
IF IT INTERESTS YOU THAT MUCH, WHY DON'T YOU GO?
...
I'M SCARED.
I'M NOT SURE WHY...
BUT PEOPLE SEEM TO GET SCARED BY ME.
AND EVERYONE STARTS AVOIDING ME.
SO I HATE SCHOOL.

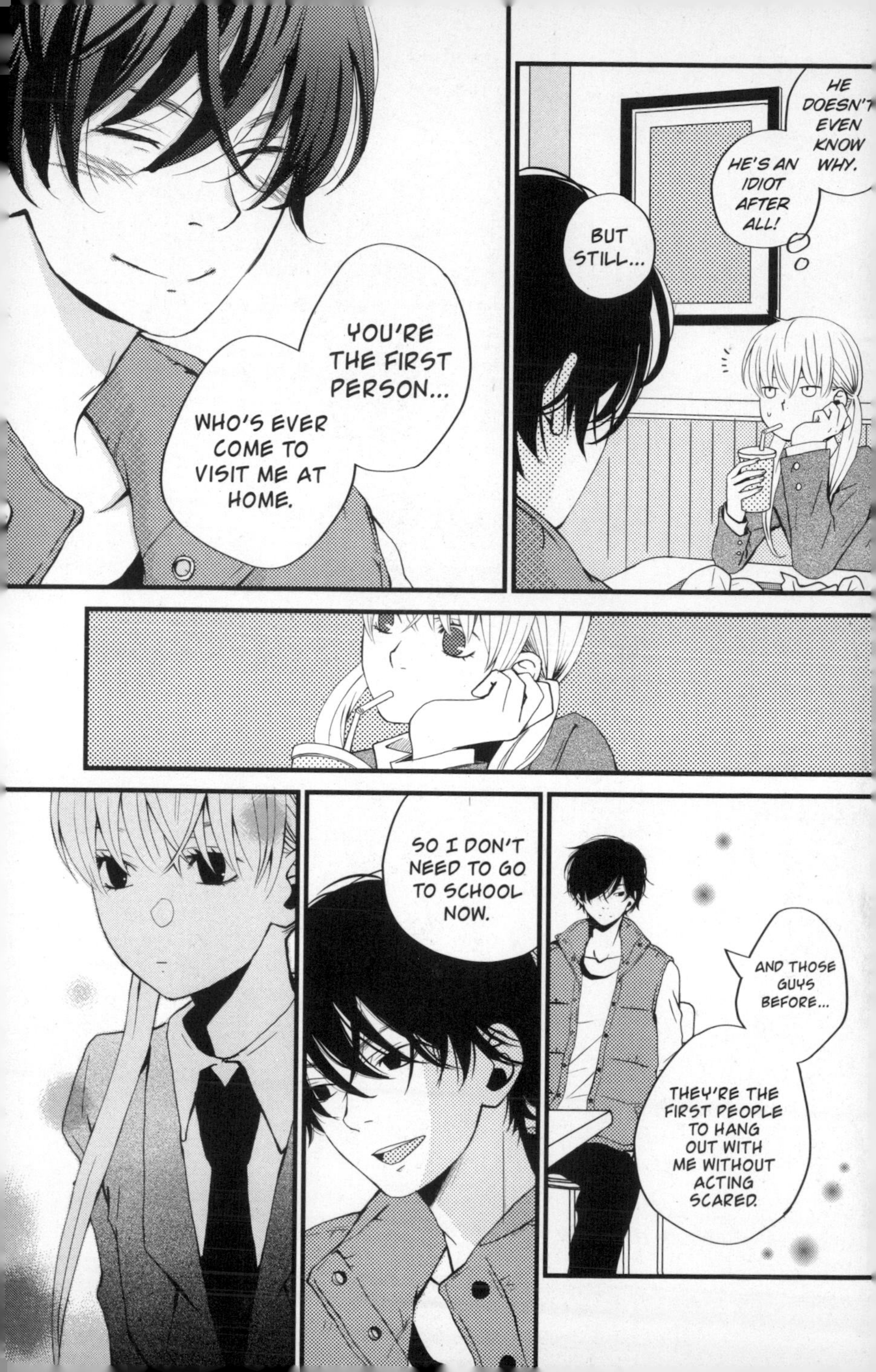
HE DOESN'T EVEN KNOW WHY.
HE'S AN IDIOT AFTER ALL!
BUT STILL...
YOU'RE THE FIRST PERSON...
WHO'S EVER COME TO VISIT ME AT HOME.
AND THOSE GUYS BEFORE...
THEY'RE THE FIRST PEOPLE TO HANG OUT WITH ME WITHOUT ACTING SCARED.
SO I DON'T NEED TO GO TO SCHOOL NOW.

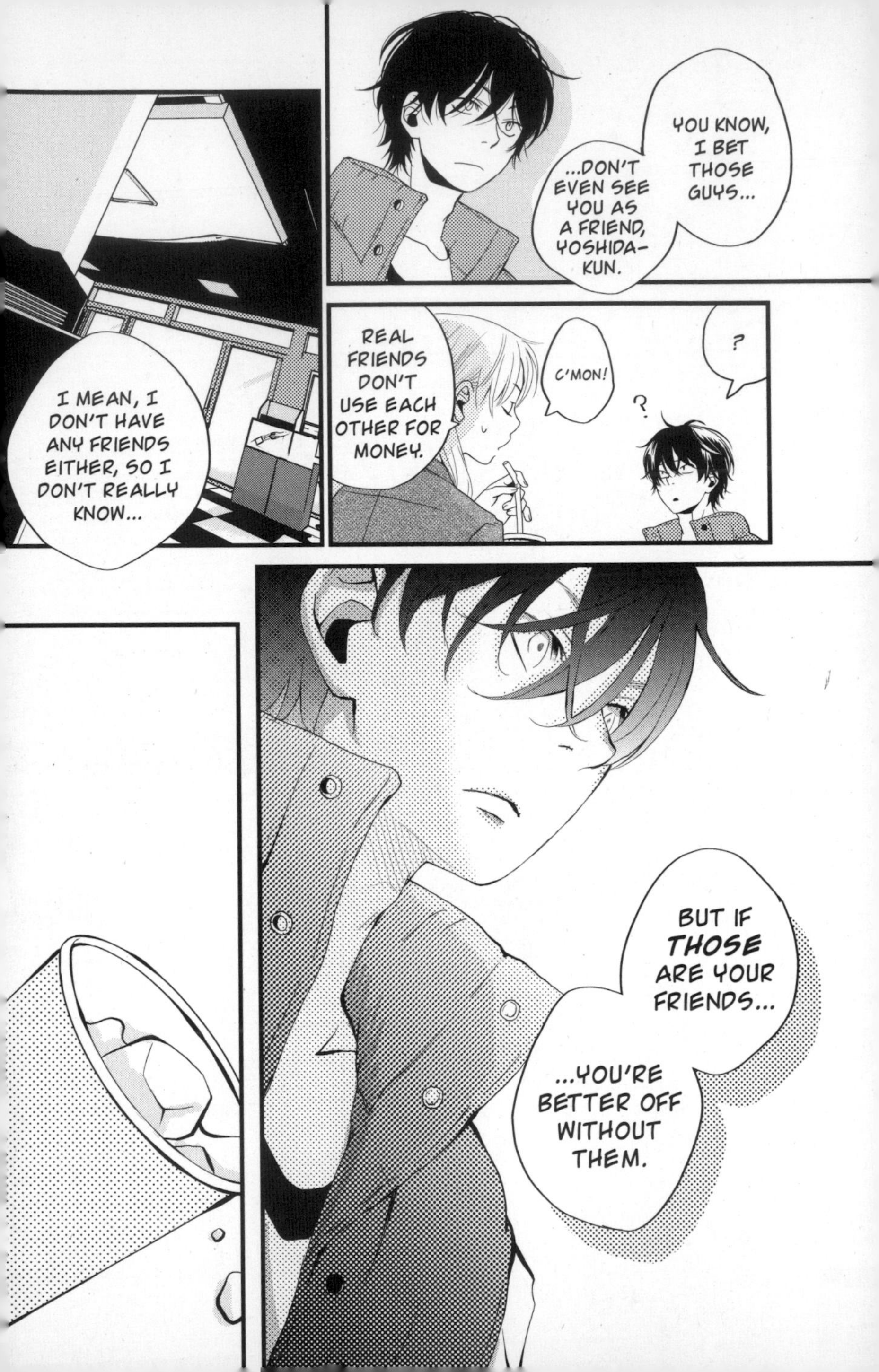
YOU KNOW, I BET THOSE GUYS...
...DON'T EVEN SEE YOU AS A FRIEND, YOSHIDA-KUN.
I MEAN, I DON'T HAVE ANY FRIENDS EITHER, SO I DON'T REALLY KNOW...
?
?
C'MON!
REAL FRIENDS DON'T USE EACH OTHER FOR MONEY.
BUT IF THOSE ARE YOUR FRIENDS...
...YOU'RE BETTER OFF WITHOUT THEM.

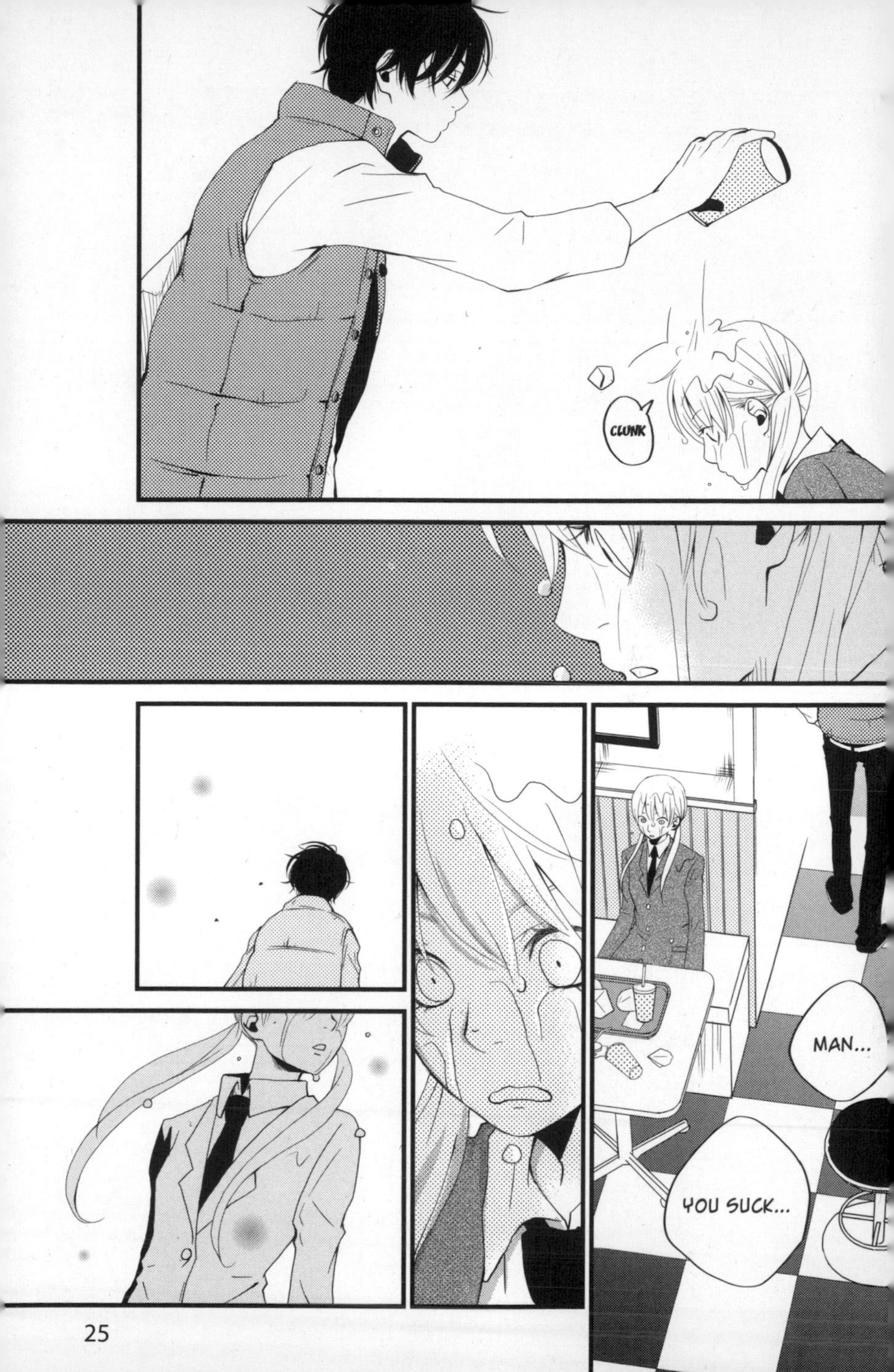
CLUNK
MAN...
YOU SUCK...

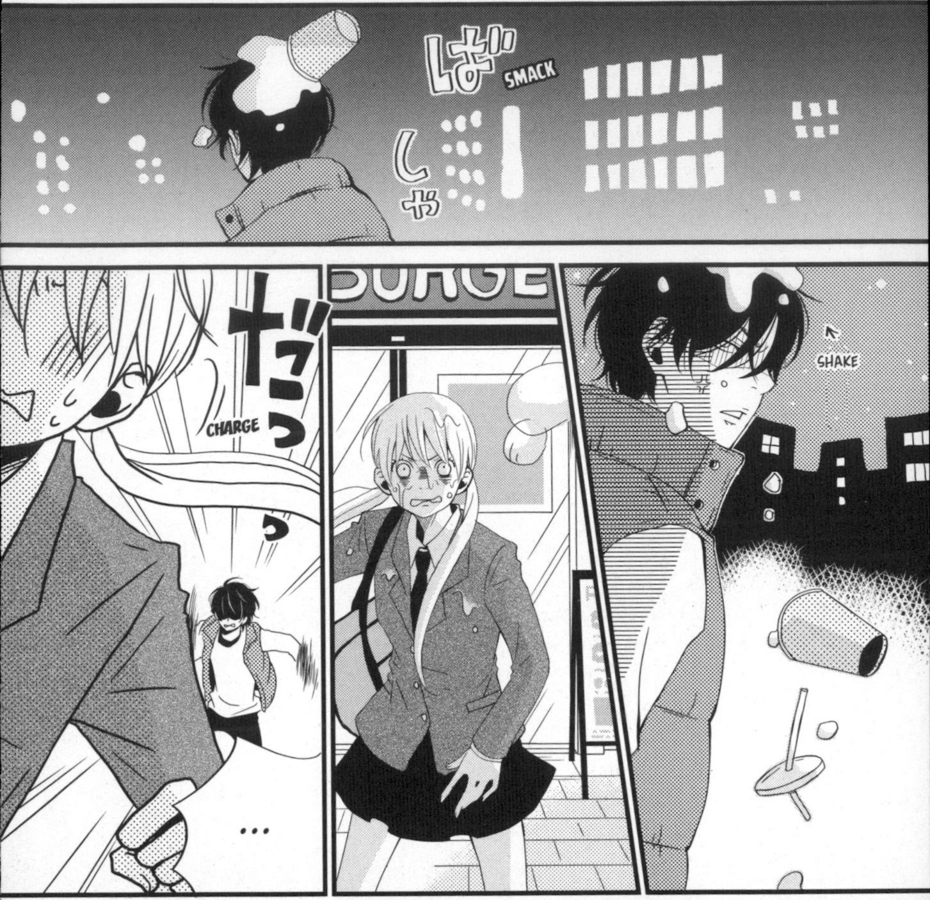
ばしゃ
SMACK
SHAKE
BURGE
だっ
CHARGE
...

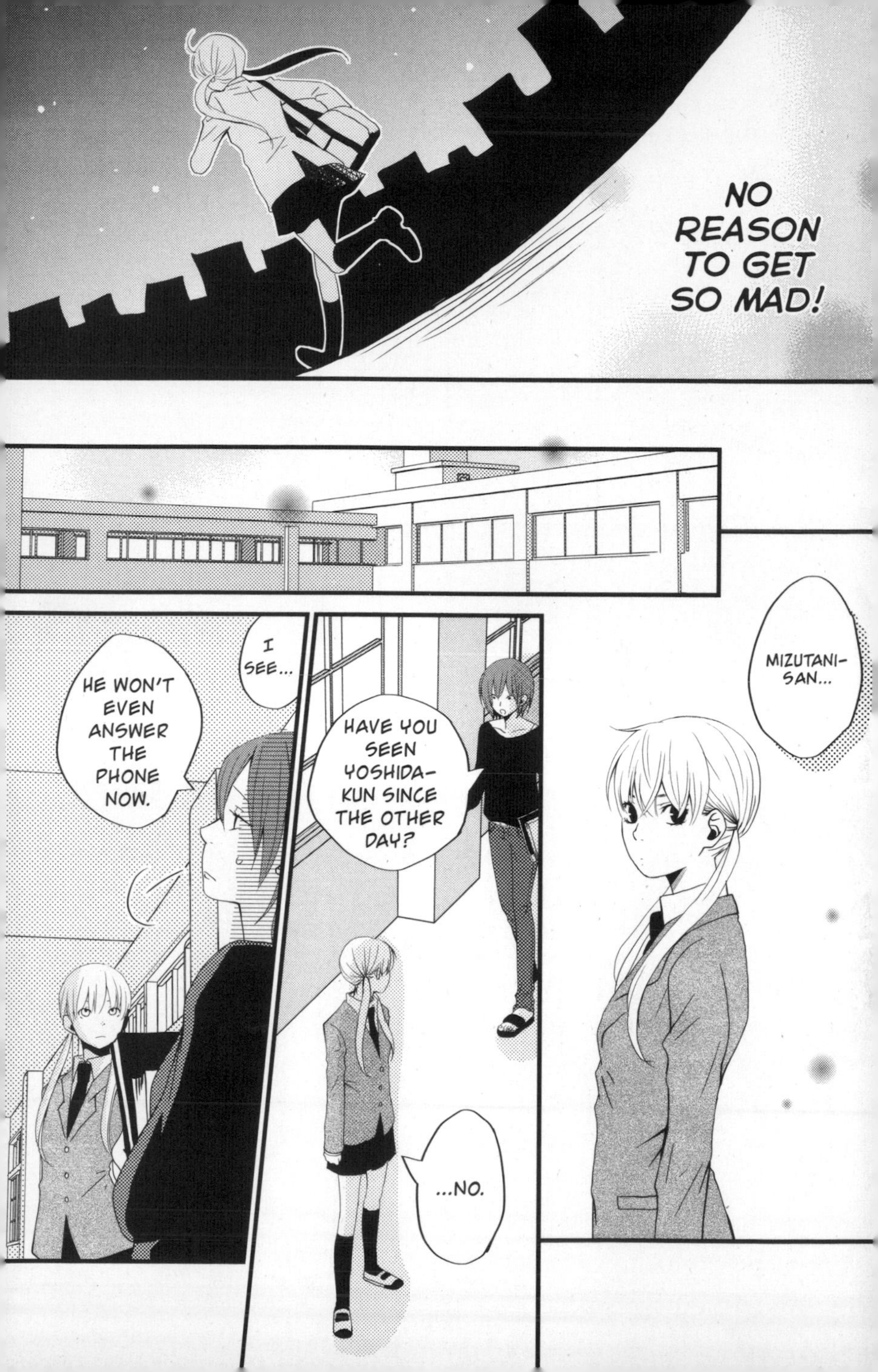
NO REASON TO GET SO MAD!
MIZUTANI-SAN...
HAVE YOU SEEN YOSHIDA-KUN SINCE THE OTHER DAY?
...NO.
I SEE...
HE WON'T EVEN ANSWER THE PHONE NOW.

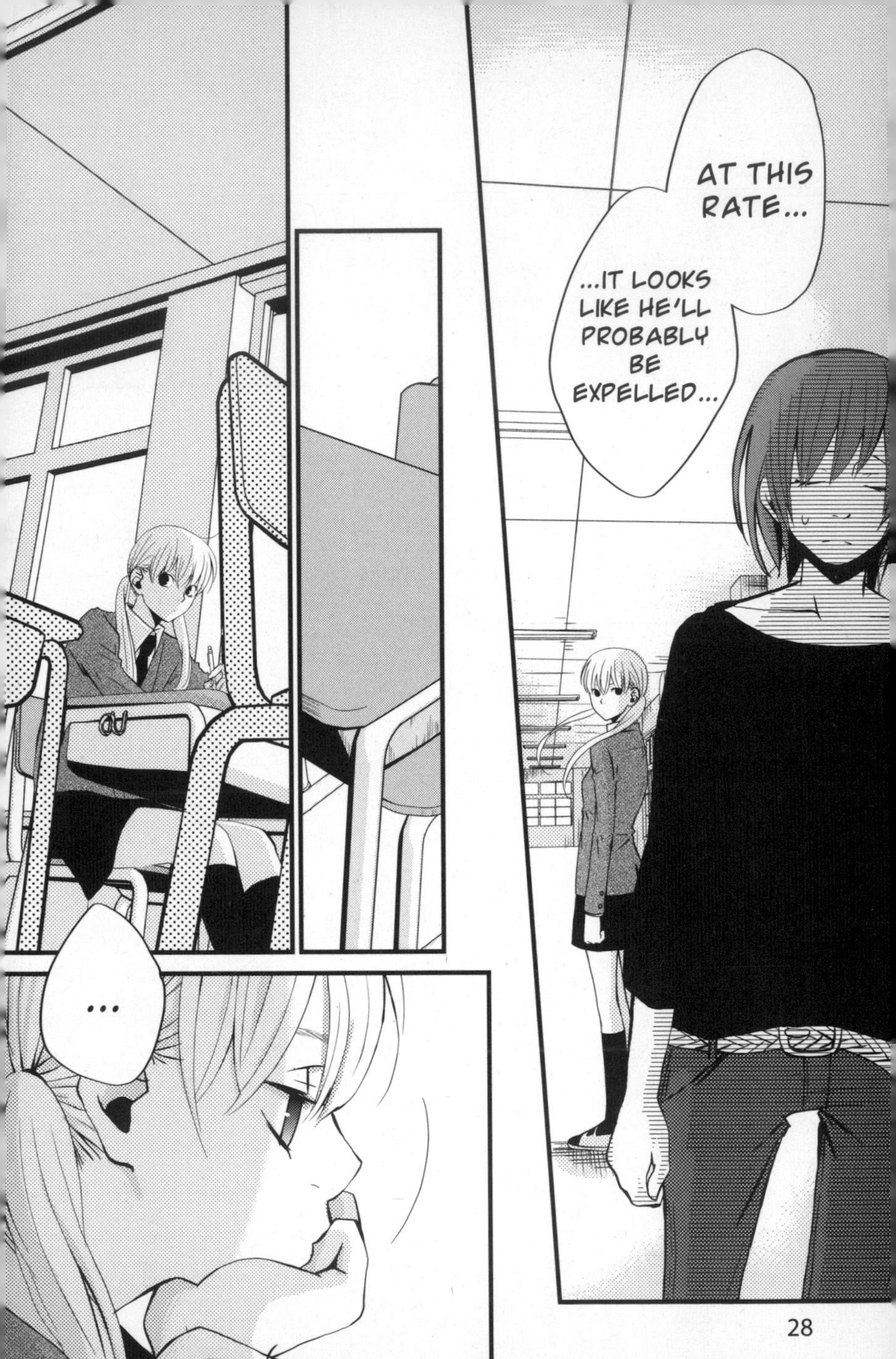
AT THIS RATE...
...IT LOOKS LIKE HE'LL PROBABLY BE EXPELLED...
...

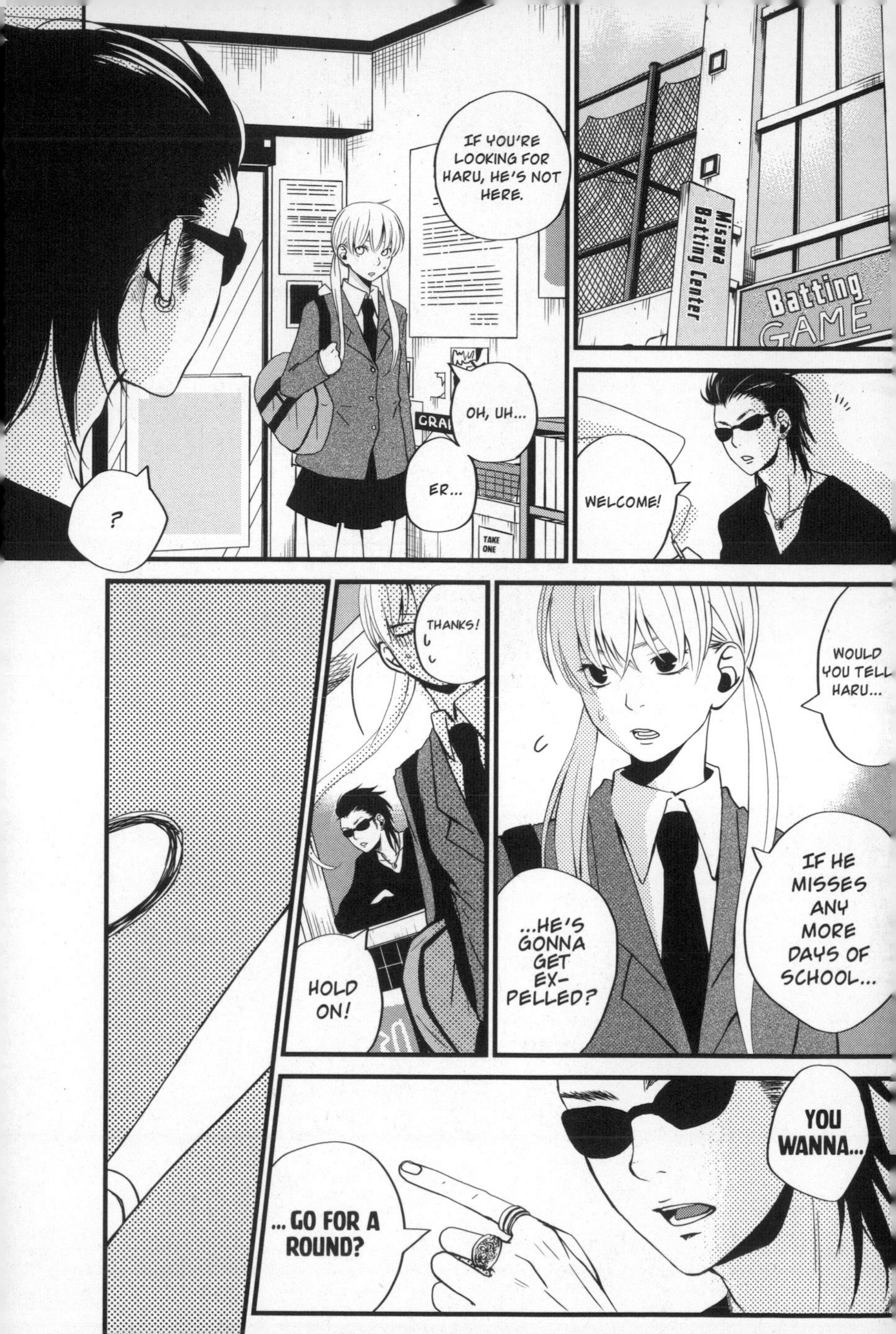
Misawa Batting Center
Batting GAME
WELCOME!
IF YOU'RE LOOKING FOR HARU, HE'S NOT HERE.
OH, UH...
ER...
TAKE ONE
?
WOULD YOU TELL HARU...
IF HE MISSES ANY MORE DAYS OF SCHOOL...
...HE'S GONNA GET EX-PELLED?
THANKS!
HOLD ON!
YOU WANNA...
...GO FOR A ROUND?

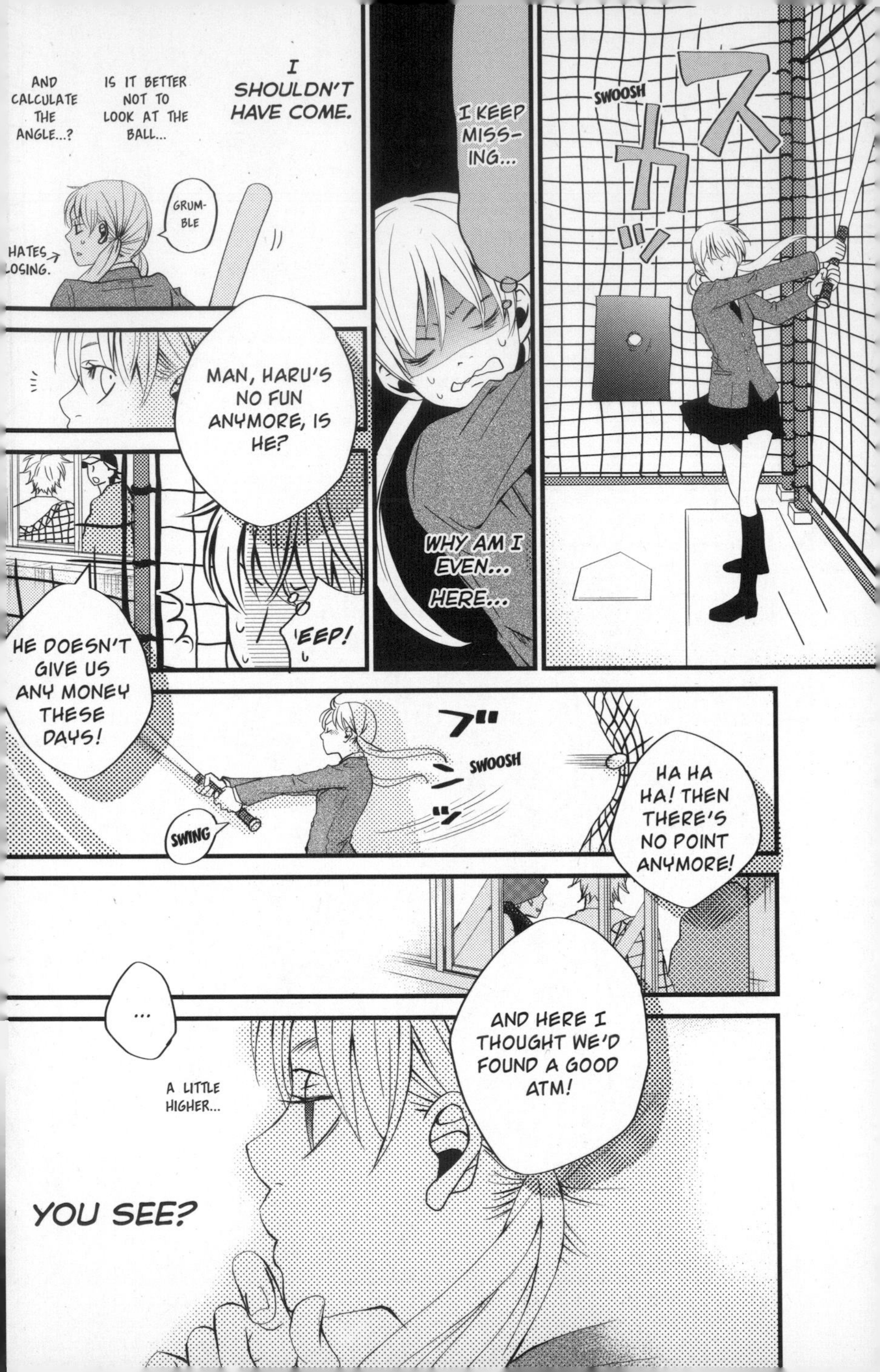
SWOOSH
I KEEP MISSING...
WHY AM I EVEN... HERE...
I SHOULDN'T HAVE COME.
IS IT BETTER NOT TO LOOK AT THE BALL...
AND CALCULATE THE ANGLE...?
GRUMBLE
HATES LOSING.
MAN, HARU'S NO FUN ANYMORE, IS HE?
EEP!
HE DOESN'T GIVE US ANY MONEY THESE DAYS!
HA HA HA! THEN THERE'S NO POINT ANYMORE!
SWOOSH
SWING
AND HERE I THOUGHT WE'D FOUND A GOOD ATM!
...
A LITTLE HIGHER...
YOU SEE?

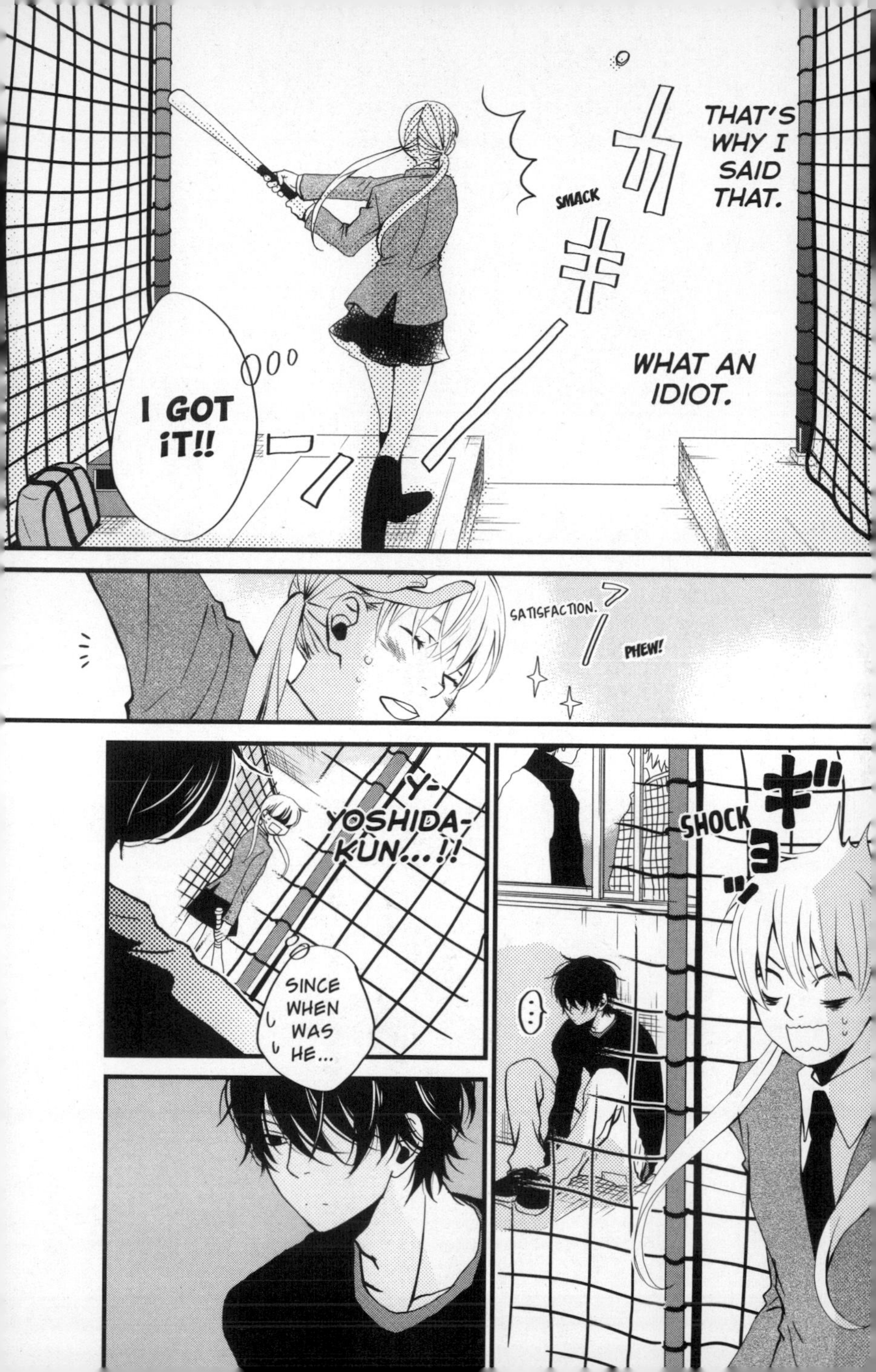
THAT'S WHY I SAID THAT.
SMACK
WHAT AN IDIOT.
I GOT iT!!
SATISFACTION.
PHEW!
SHOCK
...
Y-YOSHIDA-KUN...!!
SINCE WHEN WAS HE...

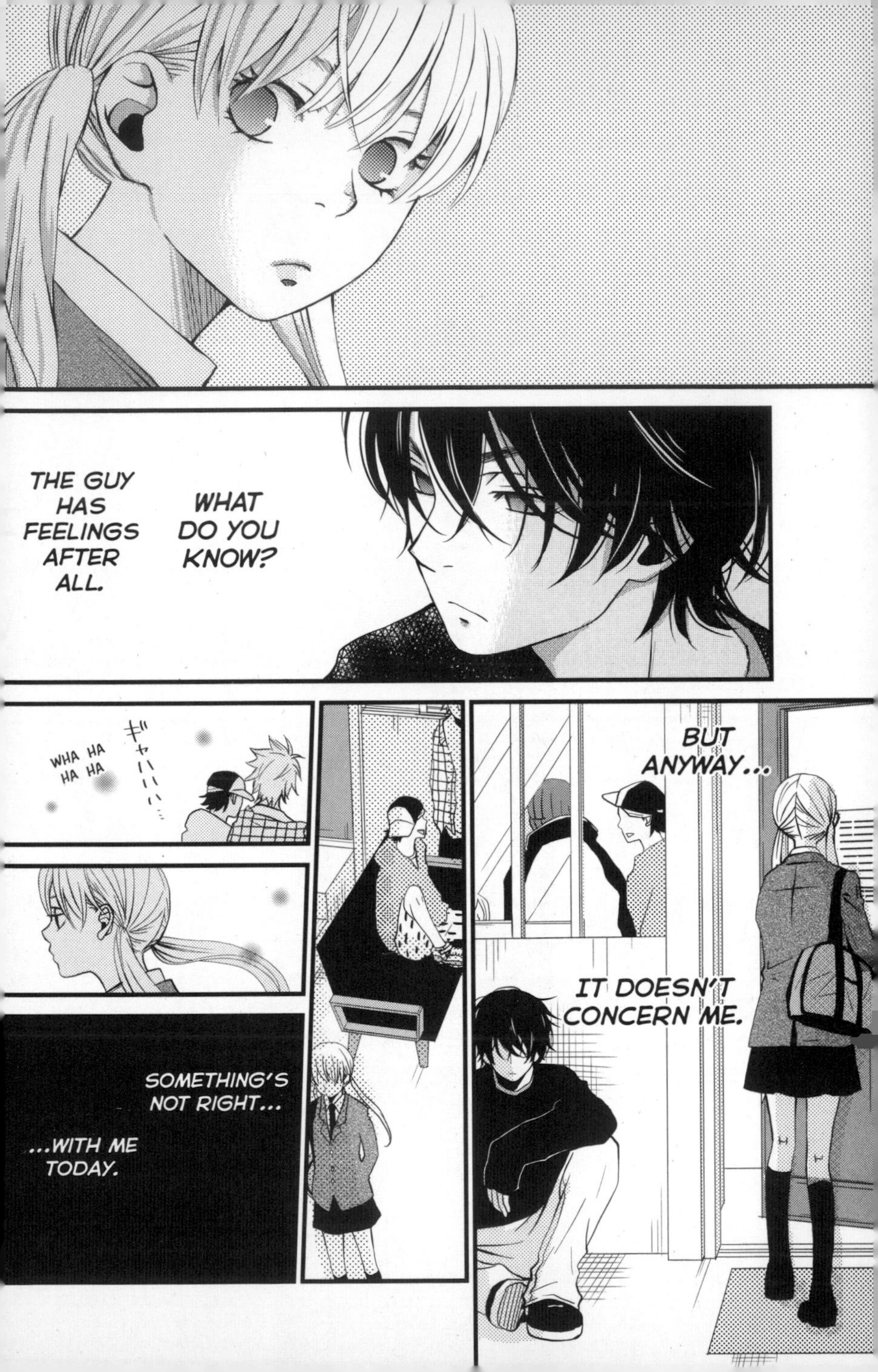
WHAT DO YOU KNOW?
THE GUY HAS FEELINGS AFTER ALL.
BUT ANYWAY...
IT DOESN'T CONCERN ME.
WHA HA HA HA
ギャハハハ…
SOMETHING'S NOT RIGHT...
...WITH ME TODAY.

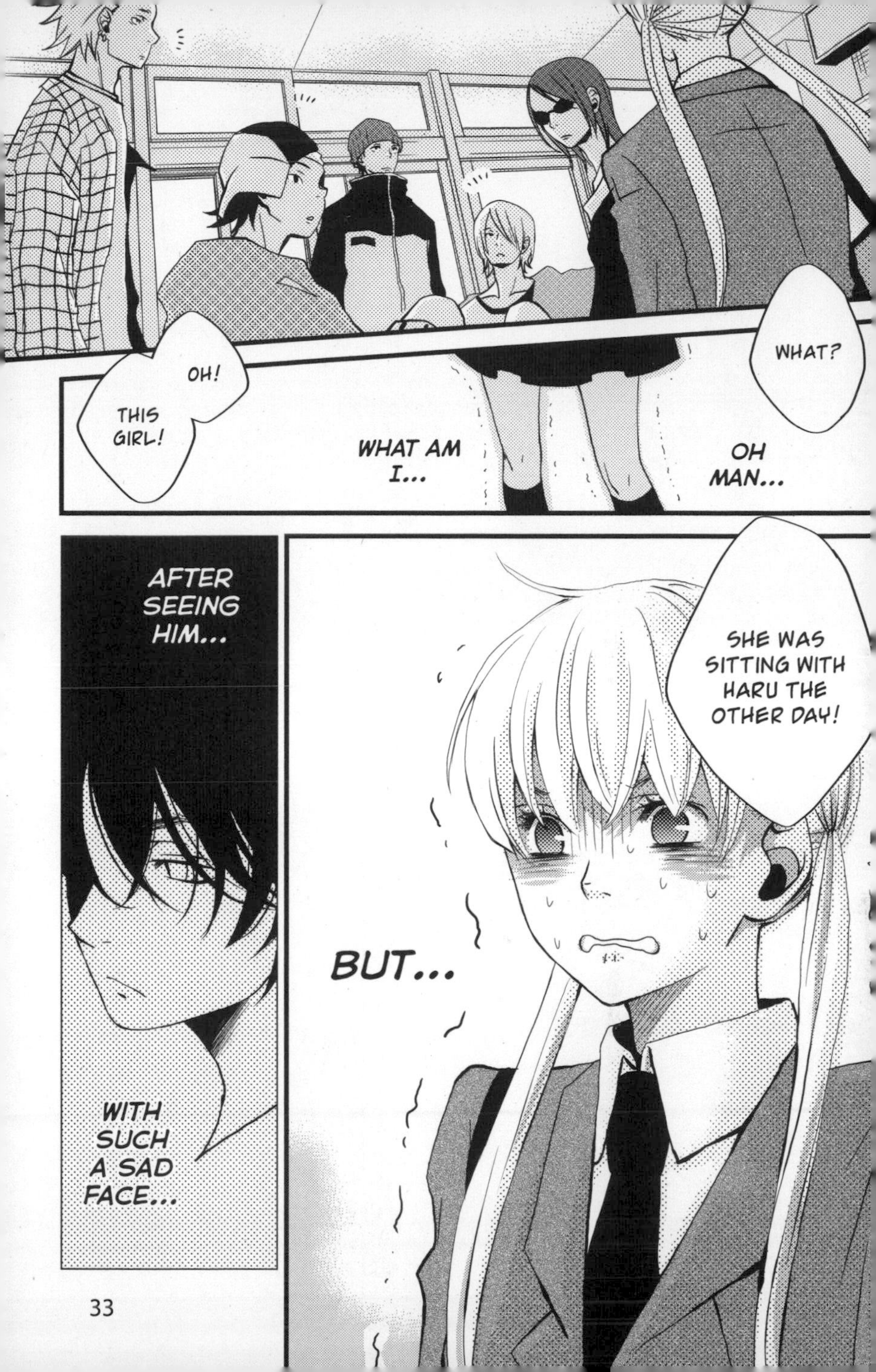
WHAT?
OH MAN...
WHAT AM I...
OH! THIS GIRL!
SHE WAS SITTING WITH HARU THE OTHER DAY!
BUT...
AFTER SEEING HIM...
WITH SUCH A SAD FACE...

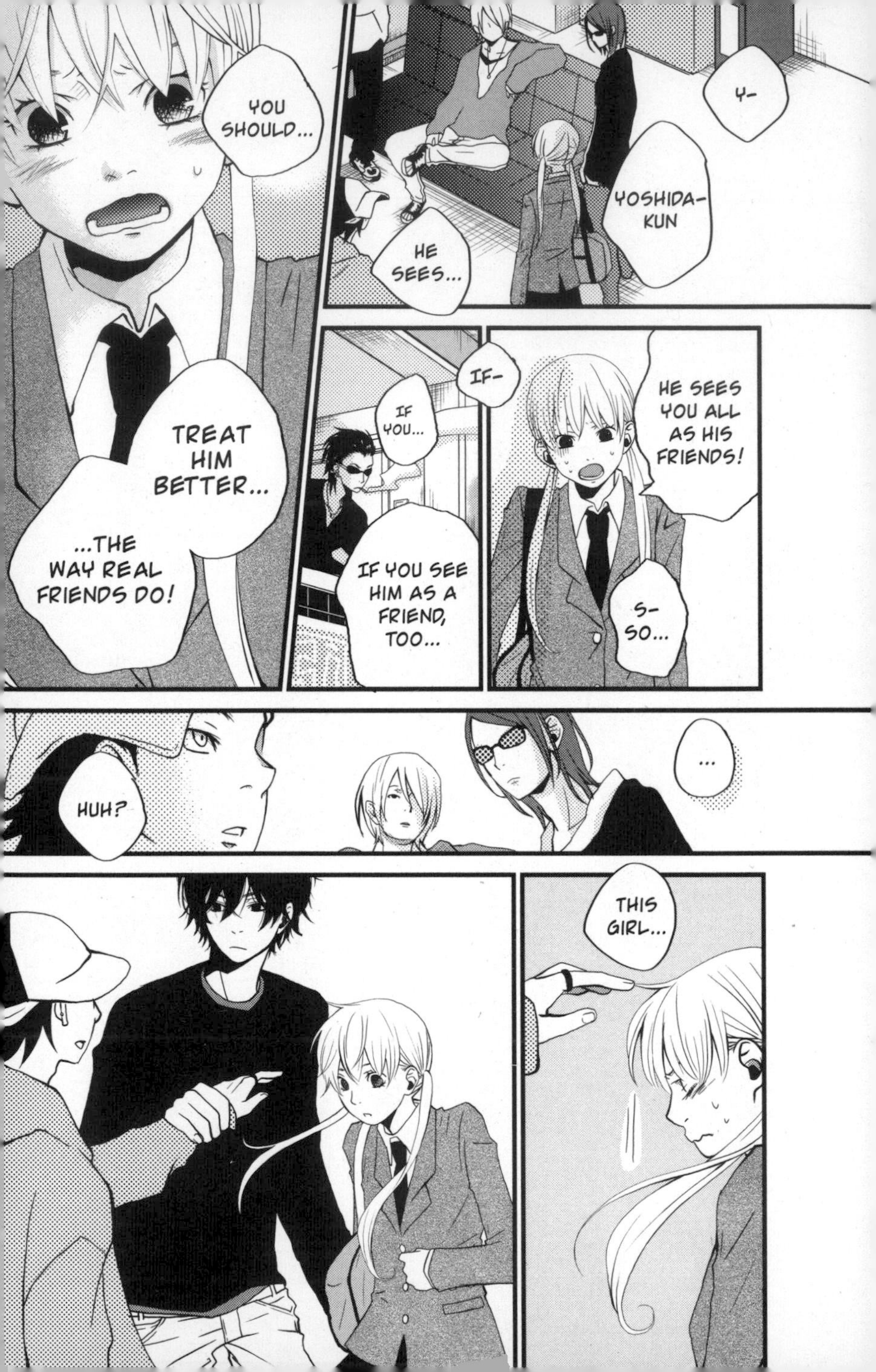
Y-
YOSHIDA-KUN
HE SEES...
HE SEES YOU ALL AS HIS FRIENDS!
S- SO...
IF-
IF YOU...
IF YOU SEE HIM AS A FRIEND, TOO...
YOU SHOULD...
TREAT HIM BETTER...
...THE WAY REAL FRIENDS DO!
...
HUH?
THIS GIRL...

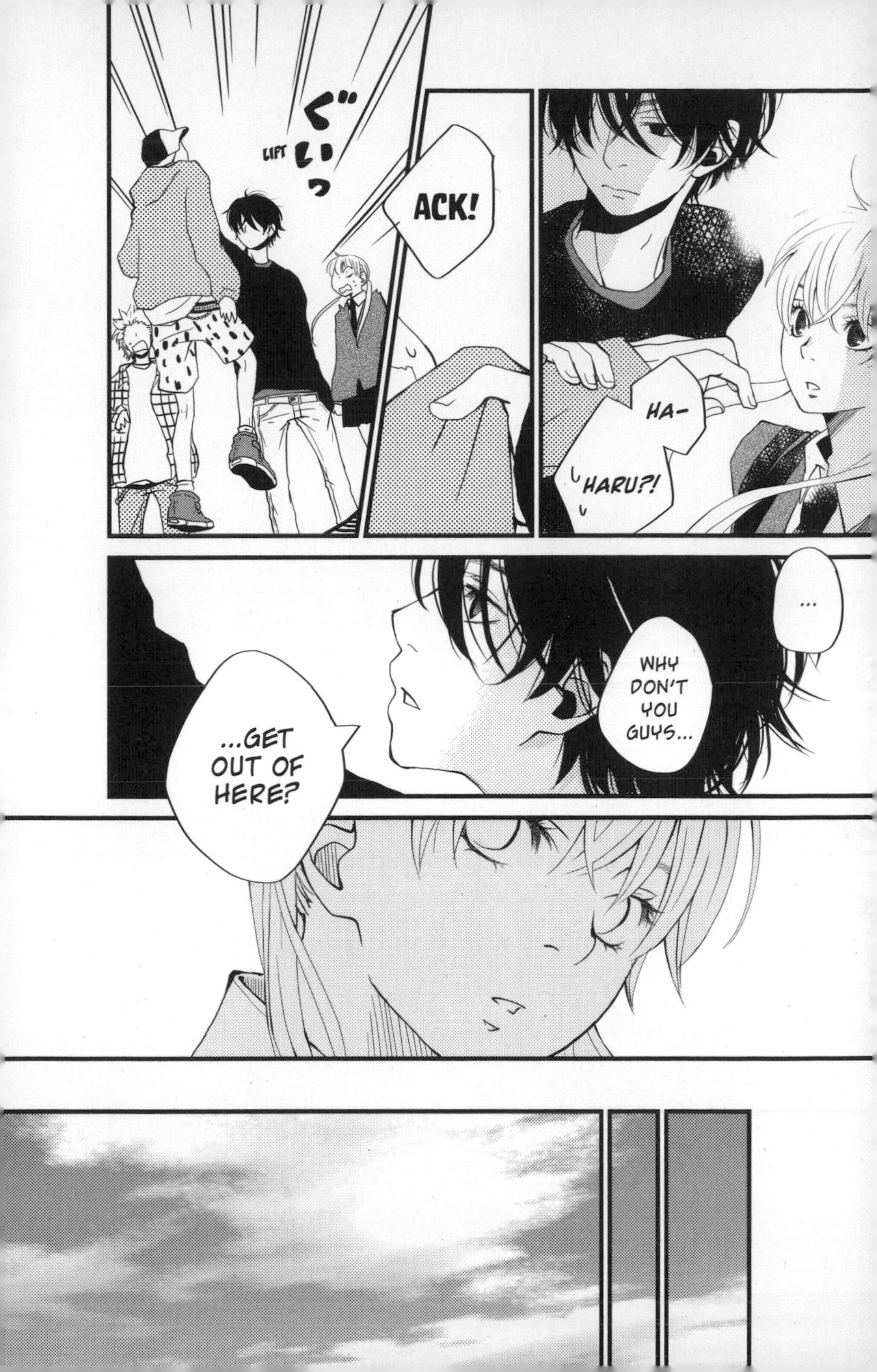
HA-
HARU?!
ACK!
ぐいっ
LIFT
...
WHY DON'T YOU GUYS...
...GET OUT OF HERE?

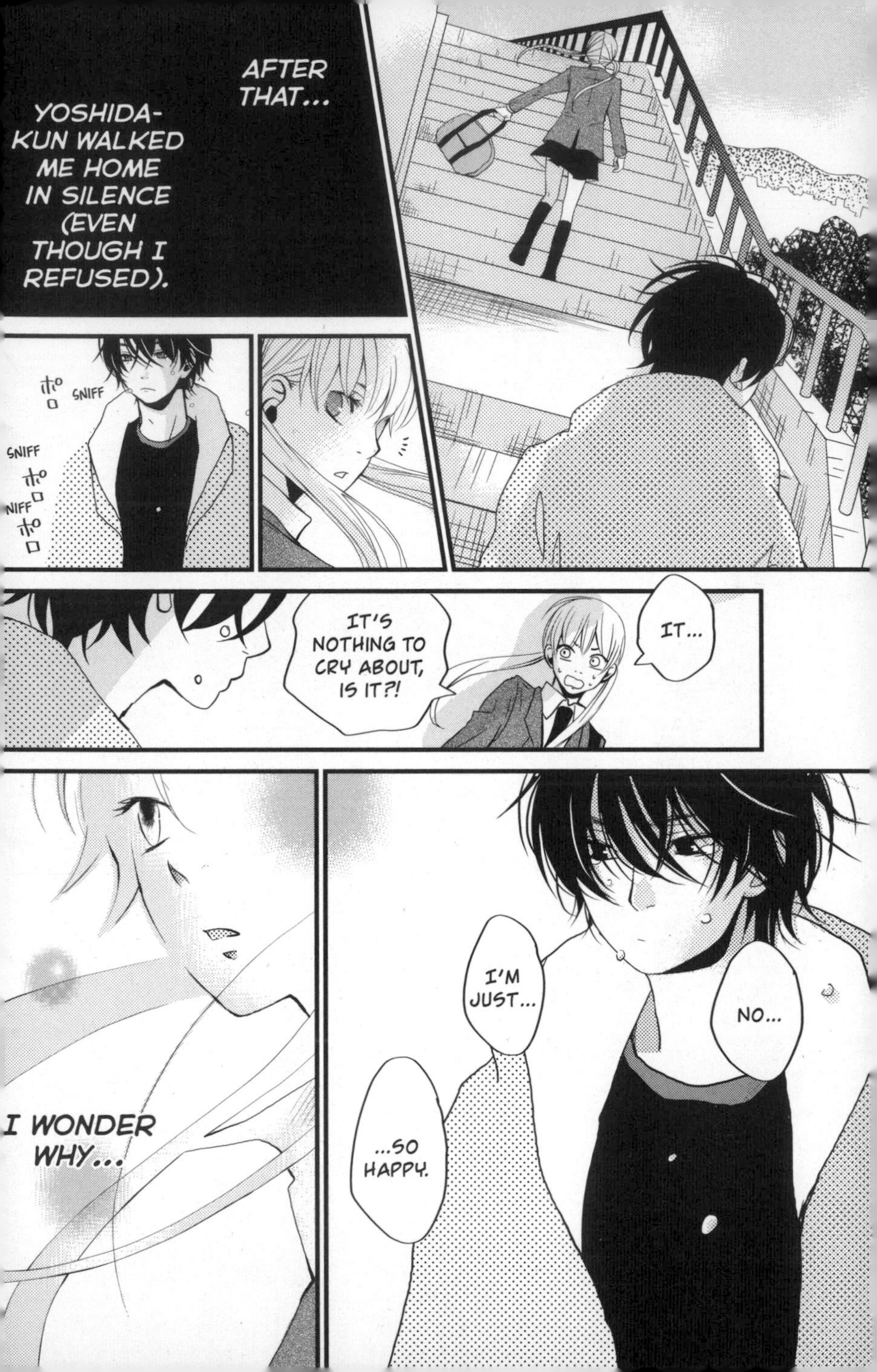
AFTER THAT...
YOSHIDA-KUN WALKED ME HOME IN SILENCE (EVEN THOUGH I REFUSED).
ポロ
SNIFF
SNIFF
ポロ
NIFF
ポロ
IT...
IT'S NOTHING TO CRY ABOUT, IS IT?!
NO...
I'M JUST...
...SO HAPPY.
I WONDER WHY...

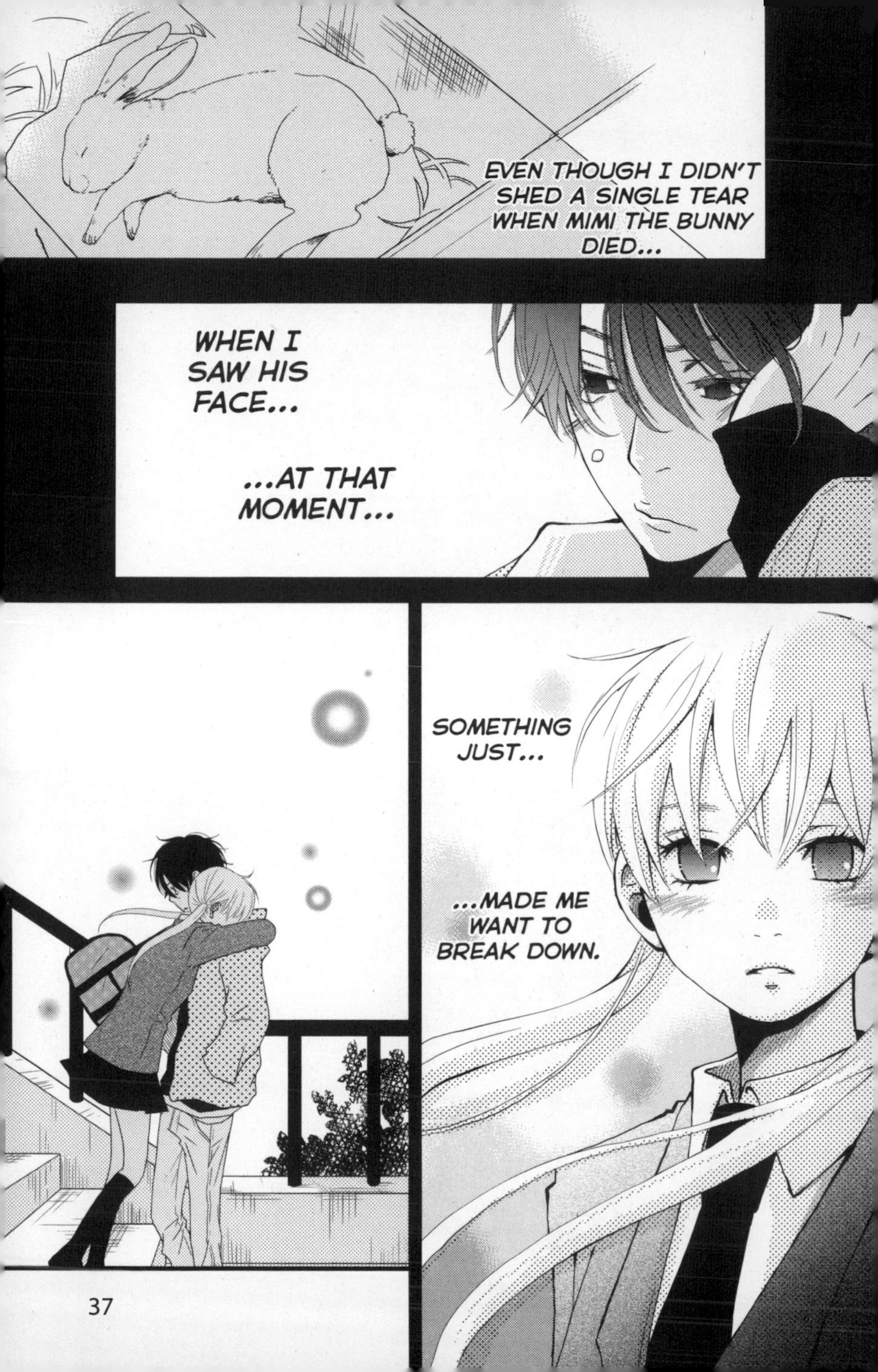
EVEN THOUGH I DIDN'T SHED A SINGLE TEAR WHEN MIMI THE BUNNY DIED...
WHEN I SAW HIS FACE...
...AT THAT MOMENT...
SOMETHING JUST...
...MADE ME WANT TO BREAK DOWN.

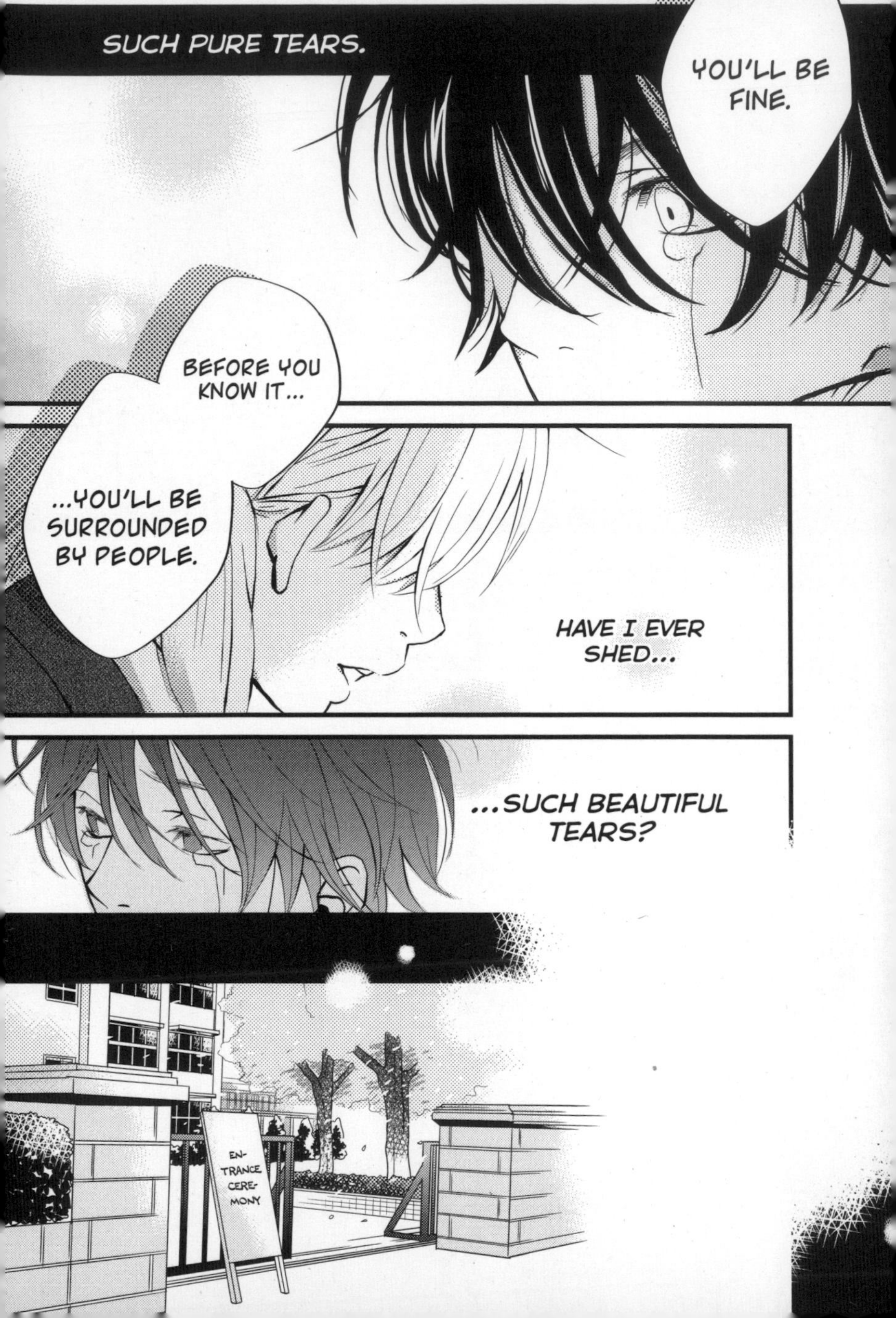
YOU'LL BE FINE.
SUCH PURE TEARS.
BEFORE YOU KNOW IT...
...YOU'LL BE SURROUNDED BY PEOPLE.
HAVE I EVER SHED...
...SUCH BEAUTIFUL TEARS?
EN-TRANCE CERE-MONY

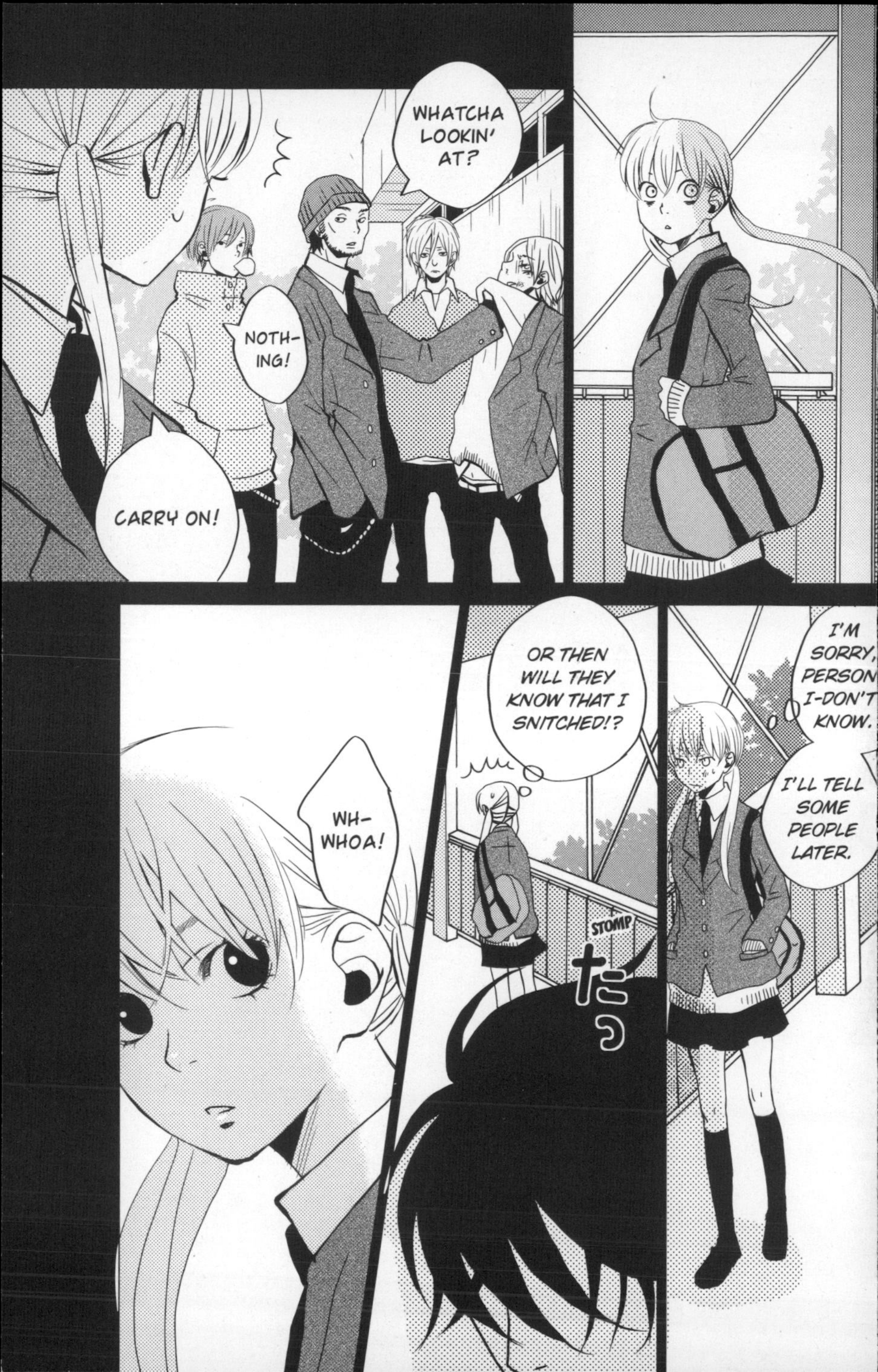
WHATCHA LOOKIN' AT?
NOTH-ING!
CARRY ON!
I'M SORRY, PERSON I-DON'T KNOW.
I'LL TELL SOME PEOPLE LATER.
OR THEN WILL THEY KNOW THAT I SNITCHED!?
STOMP
たっ
WH-WHOA!

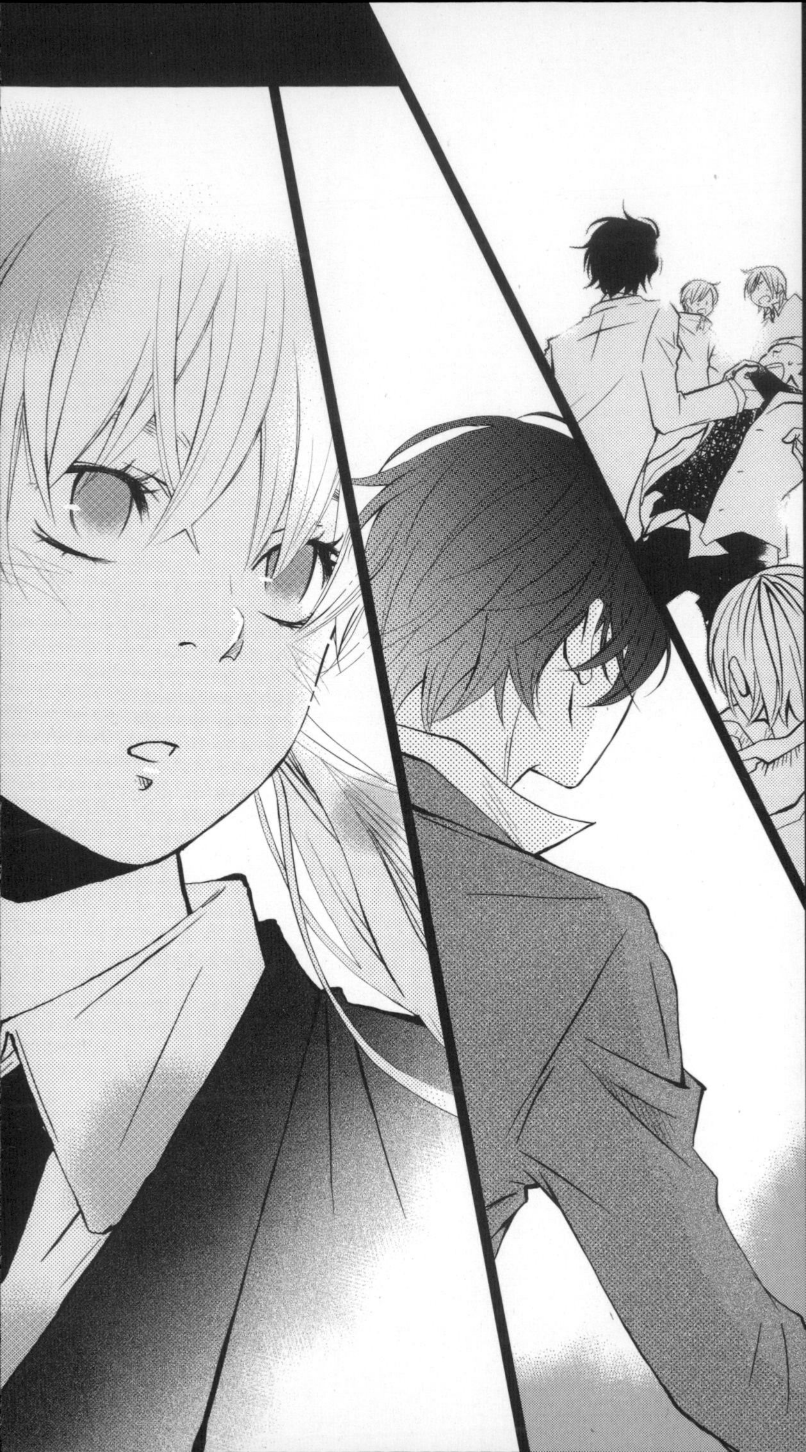

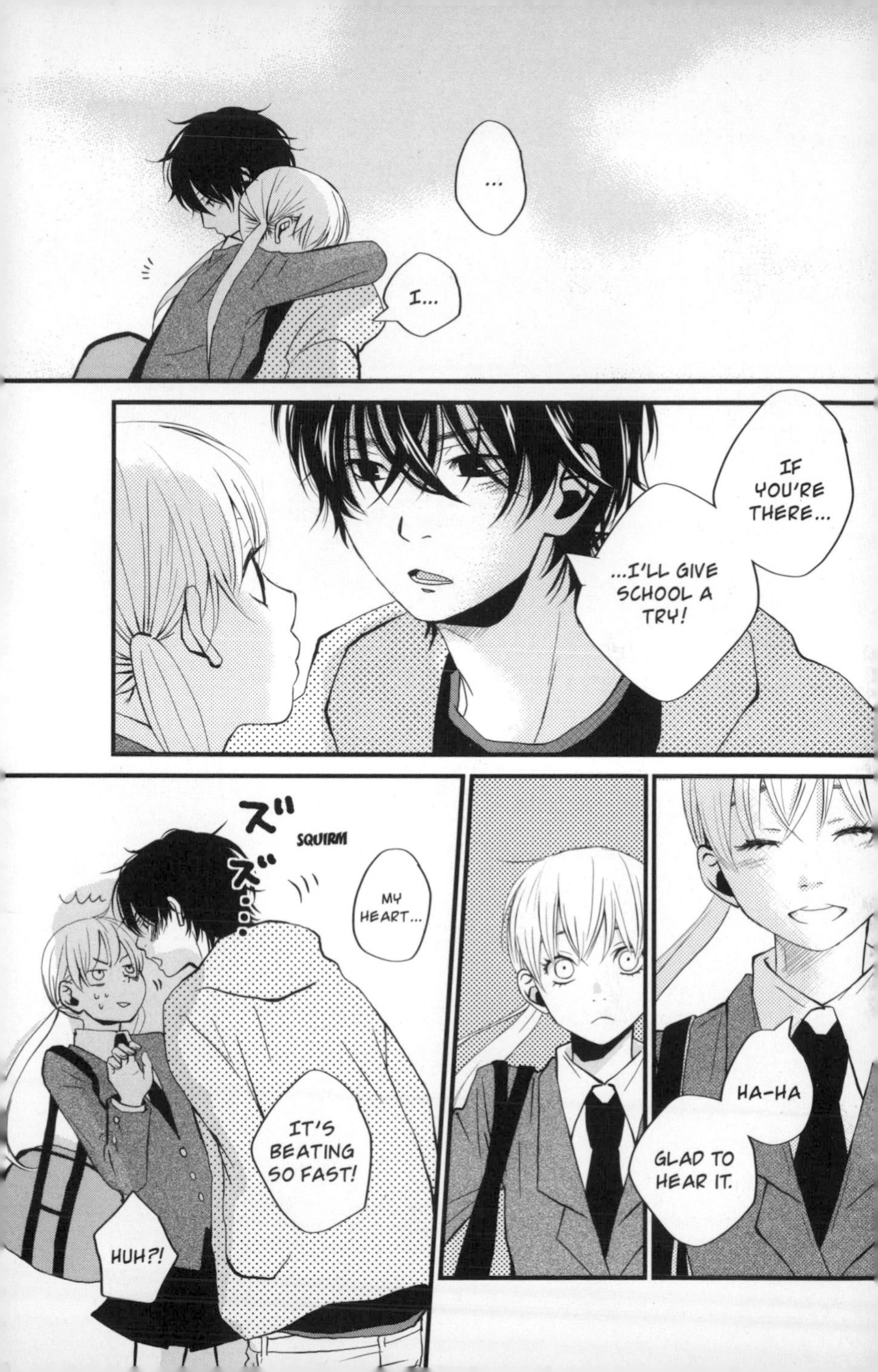
...
I...
IF YOU'RE THERE...
...I'LL GIVE SCHOOL A TRY!
HA-HA
GLAD TO HEAR IT.
MY HEART...
ズズ…
SQUIRM
IT'S BEATING SO FAST!
HUH?!

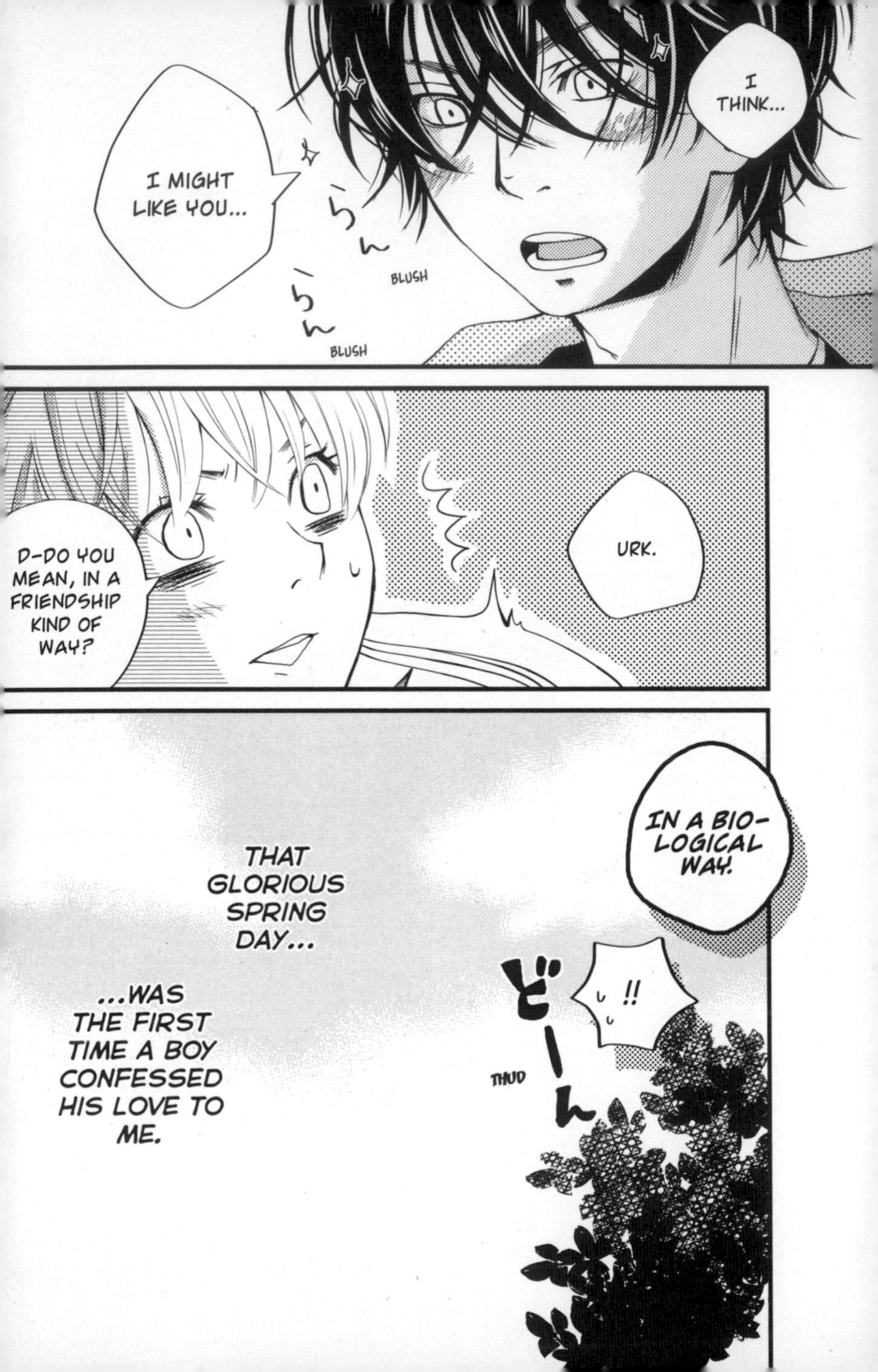
I THINK...
I MIGHT LIKE YOU...
BLUSH
BLUSH
URK.
D-DO YOU MEAN, IN A FRIENDSHIP KIND OF WAY?
IN A BIO-LOGICAL WAY.
!!
THUD
THAT GLORIOUS SPRING DAY...
...WAS THE FIRST TIME A BOY CONFESSED HIS LOVE TO ME.

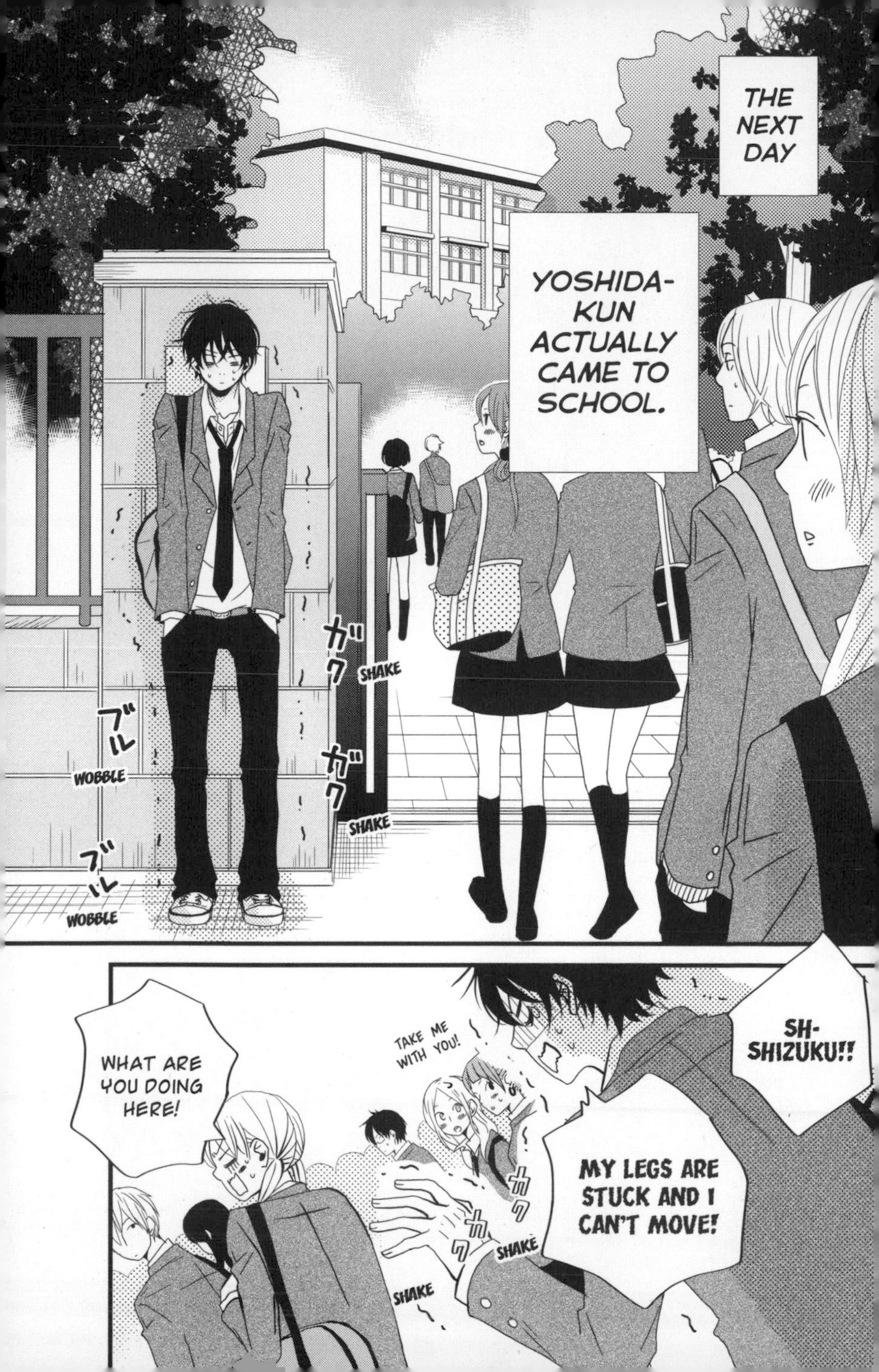
THE NEXT DAY
YOSHIDA-KUN ACTUALLY CAME TO SCHOOL.
ガク SHAKE
ガク SHAKE
ブル WOBBLE
ブル WOBBLE
SH-SHIZUKU!!
MY LEGS ARE STUCK AND I CAN'T MOVE!
TAKE ME WITH YOU!
WHAT ARE YOU DOING HERE!
カク SHAKE
カク SHAKE

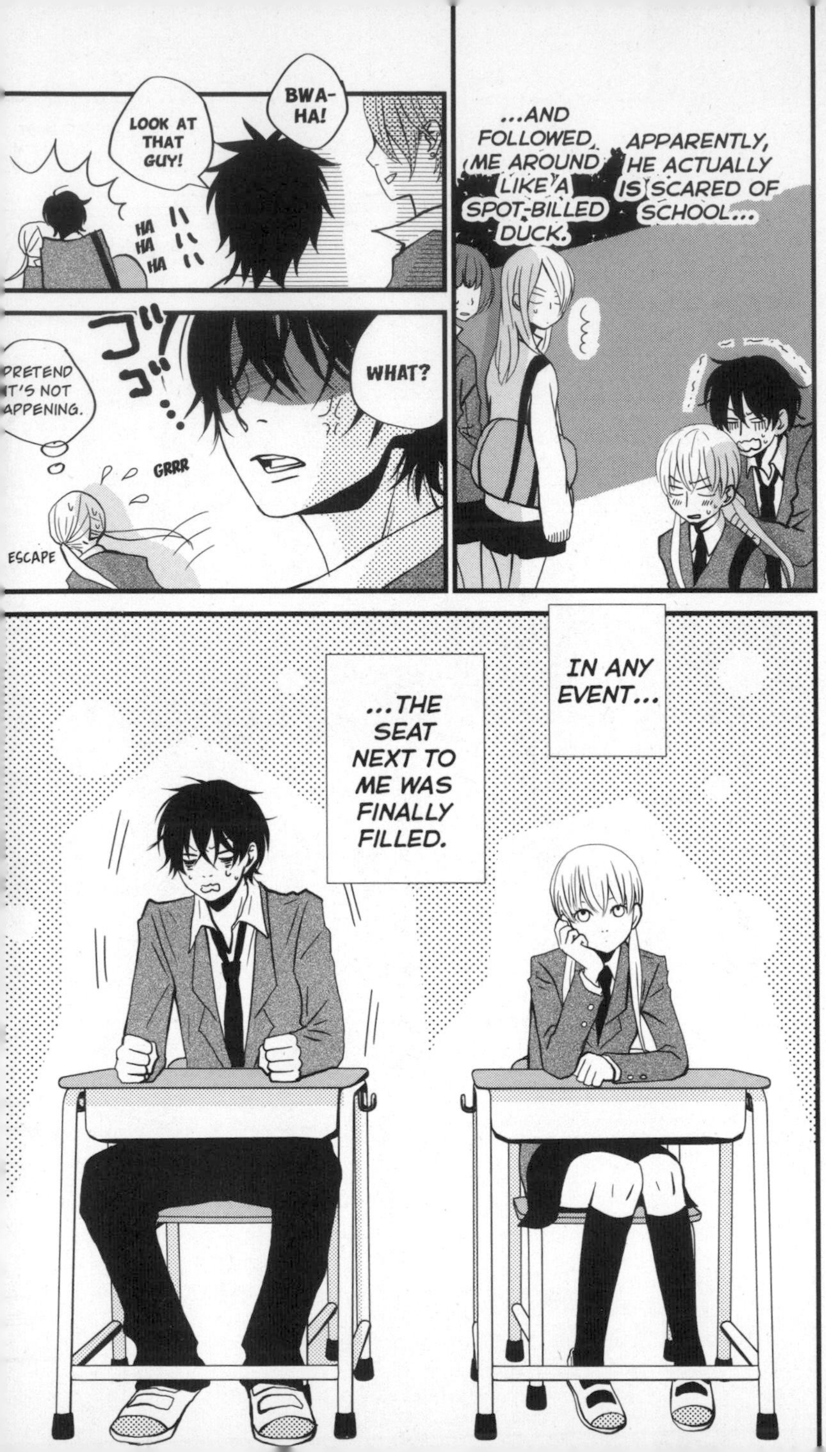
APPARENTLY, HE ACTUALLY IS SCARED OF SCHOOL...
...AND FOLLOWED ME AROUND LIKE A SPOT-BILLED DUCK.
BWA-HA!
LOOK AT THAT GUY!
HA HA HA
WHAT?
GRRR
PRETEND T'S NOT APPENING.
ESCAPE
IN ANY EVENT...
...THE SEAT NEXT TO ME WAS FINALLY FILLED.

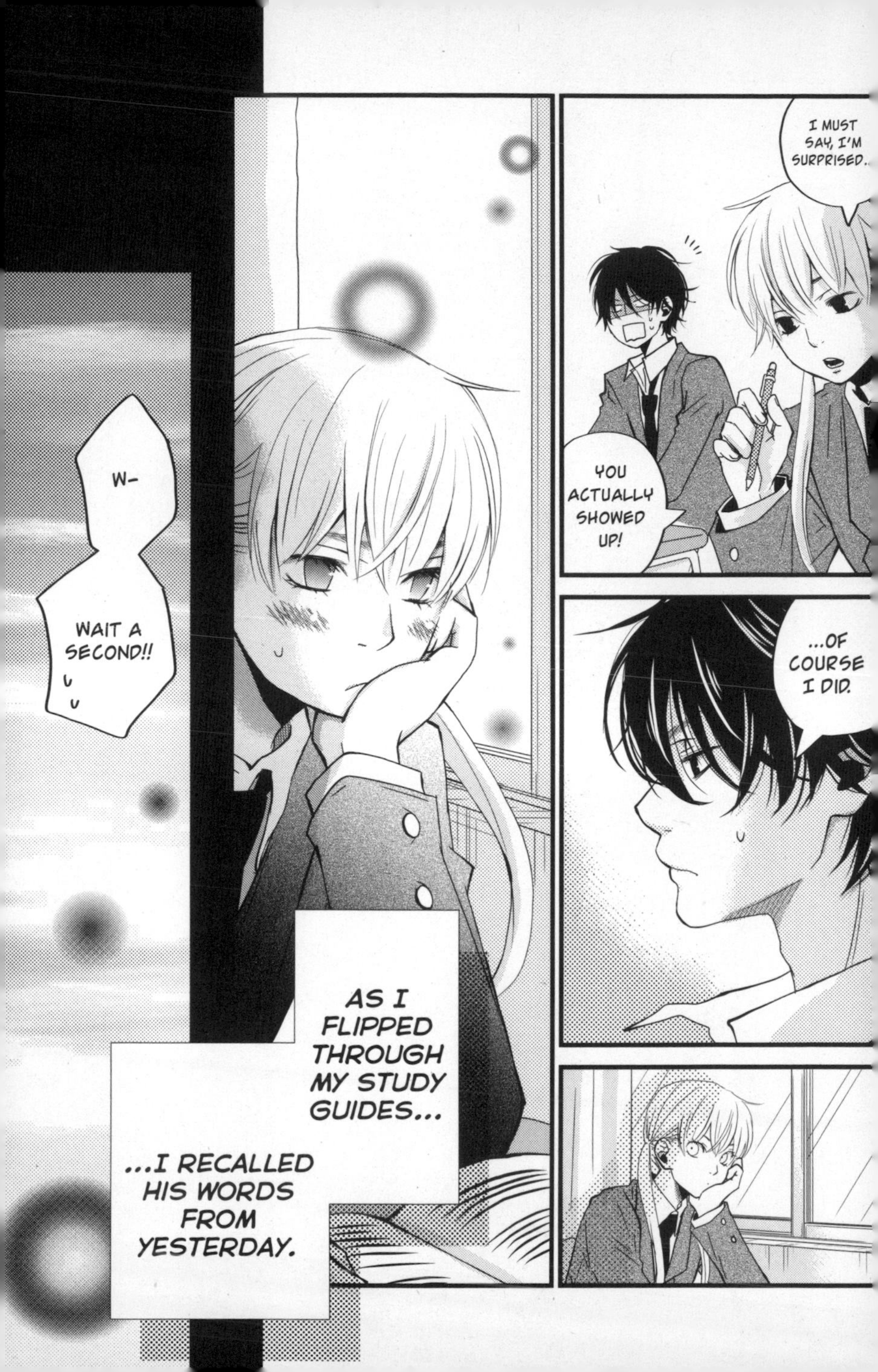
I MUST SAY, I'M SURPRISED..
YOU ACTUALLY SHOWED UP!
...OF COURSE I DID.
AS I FLIPPED THROUGH MY STUDY GUIDES...
...I RECALLED HIS WORDS FROM YESTERDAY.
W-
WAIT A SECOND!!

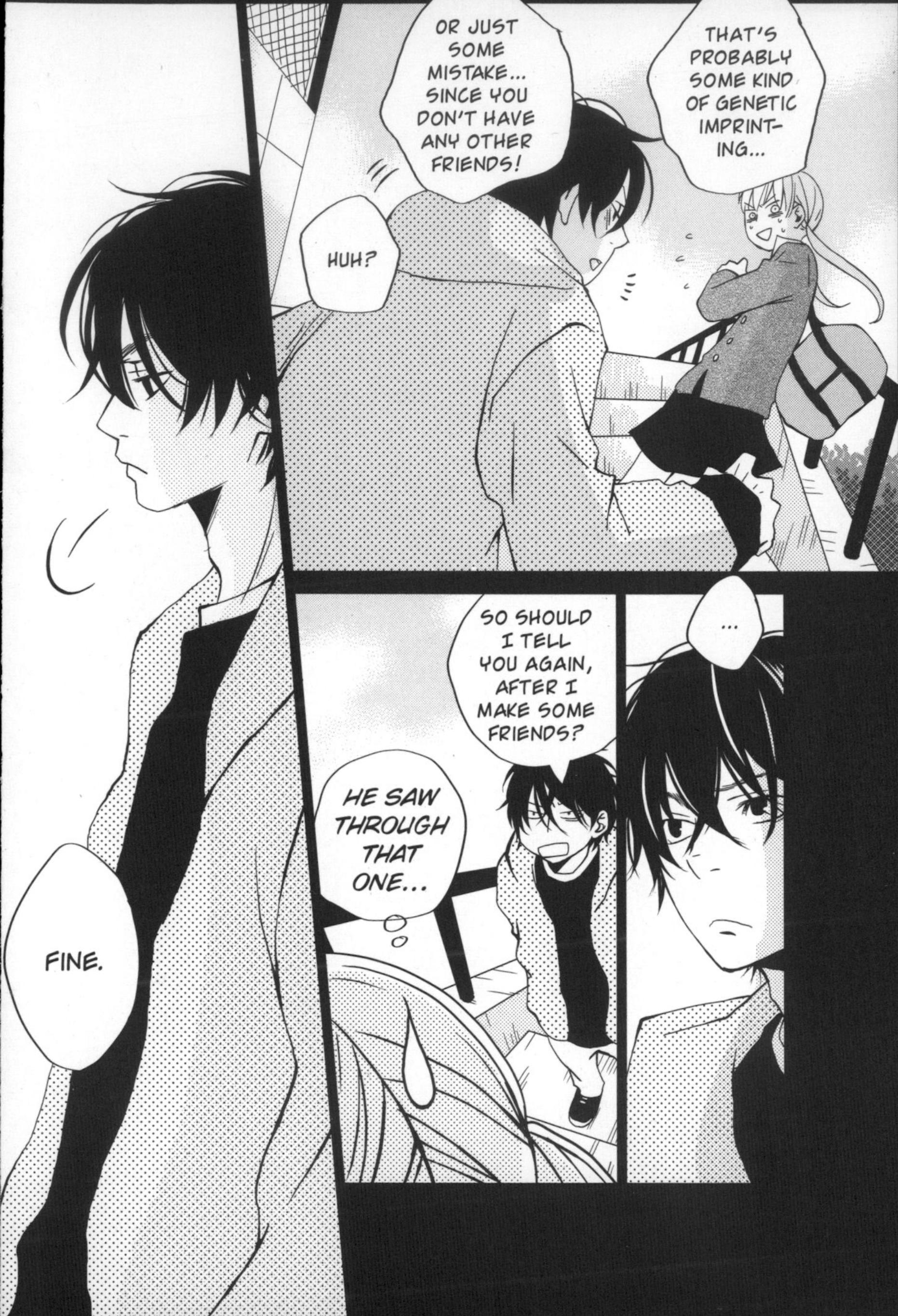
THAT'S PROBABLY SOME KIND OF GENETIC IMPRINT-ING...
OR JUST SOME MISTAKE... SINCE YOU DON'T HAVE ANY OTHER FRIENDS!
HUH?
...
SO SHOULD I TELL YOU AGAIN, AFTER I MAKE SOME FRIENDS?
HE SAW THROUGH THAT ONE...
FINE.

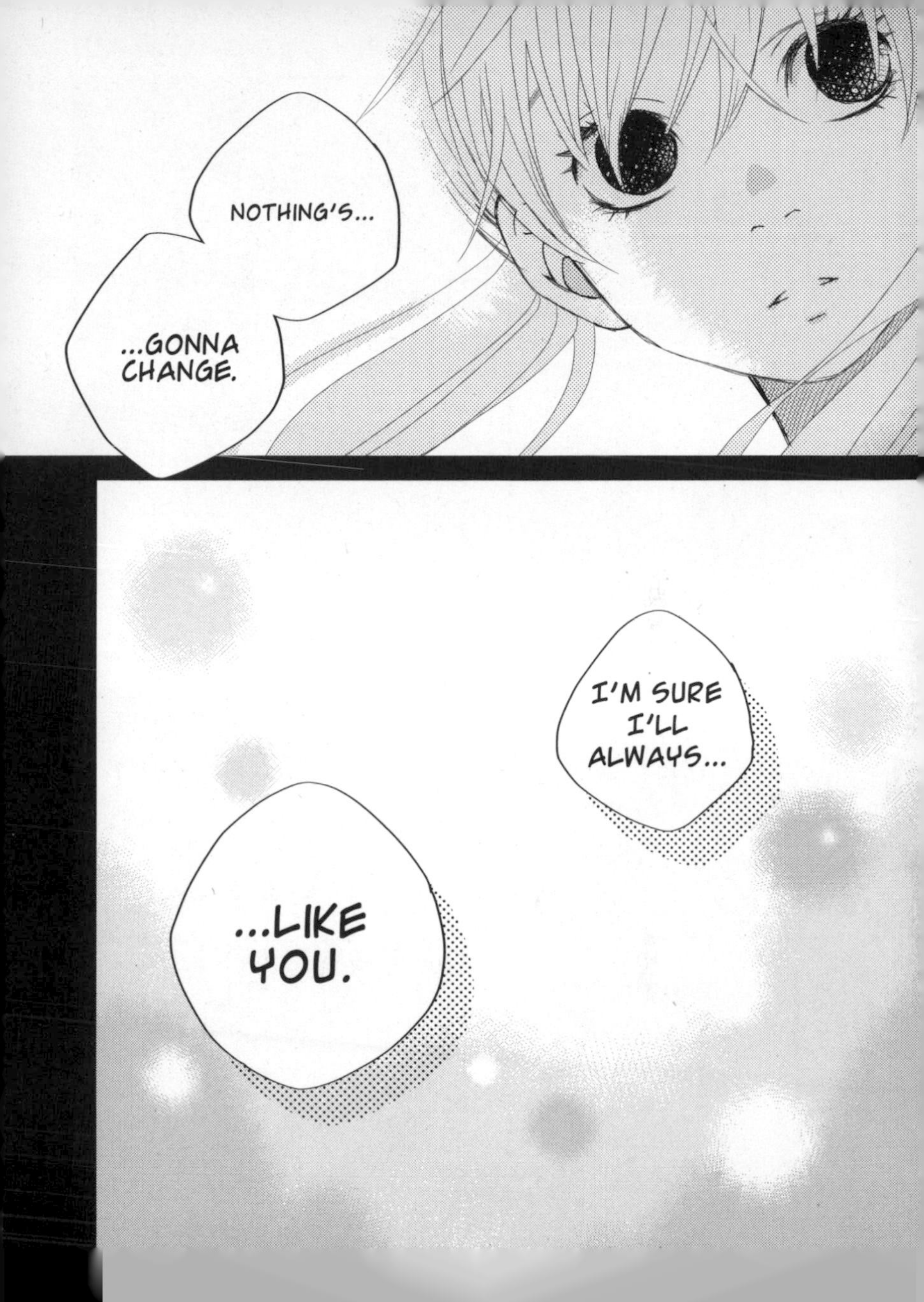
NOTHING'S...
...GONNA CHANGE.
I'M SURE I'LL ALWAYS...
...LIKE YOU.

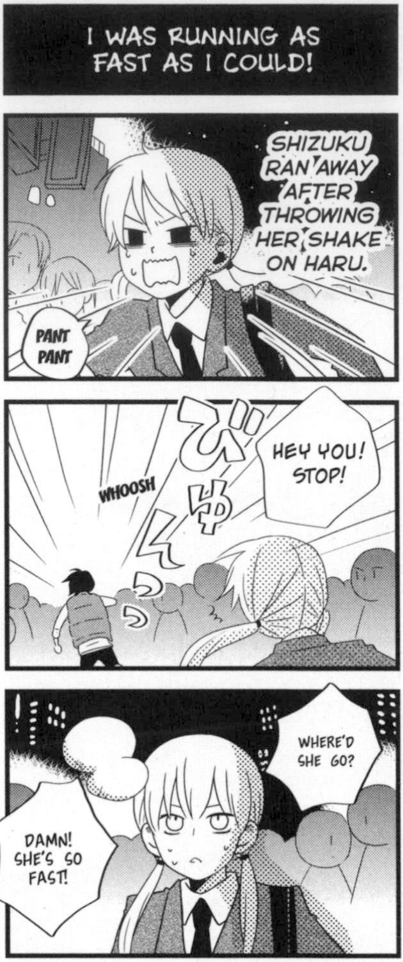
I WAS RUNNING AS FAST AS I COULD!
SHIZUKU RAN AWAY AFTER THROWING HER SHAKE ON HARU.
PANT PANT
HEY YOU! STOP!
びゅん
WHOOSH
WHERE'D SHE GO?
DAMN! SHE'S SO FAST!
SHE WAS RUNNING SO SLOWLY, HE DIDN'T EVEN NOTICE HER.

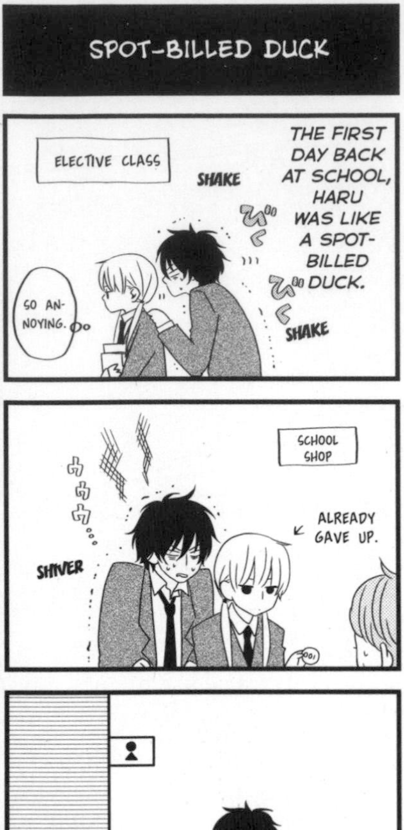
SPOT-BILLED DUCK
THE FIRST DAY BACK AT SCHOOL, HARU WAS LIKE A SPOT-BILLED DUCK.
ELECTIVE CLASS
SHAKE
びく
びく
SHAKE
SO AN-NOYING.
SCHOOL SHOP
ALREADY GAVE UP.
ぅぅぅ
SHIVER
キャー
EEK!
?
YOU DON'T HAVE TO KEEP YOUR PROMISE.

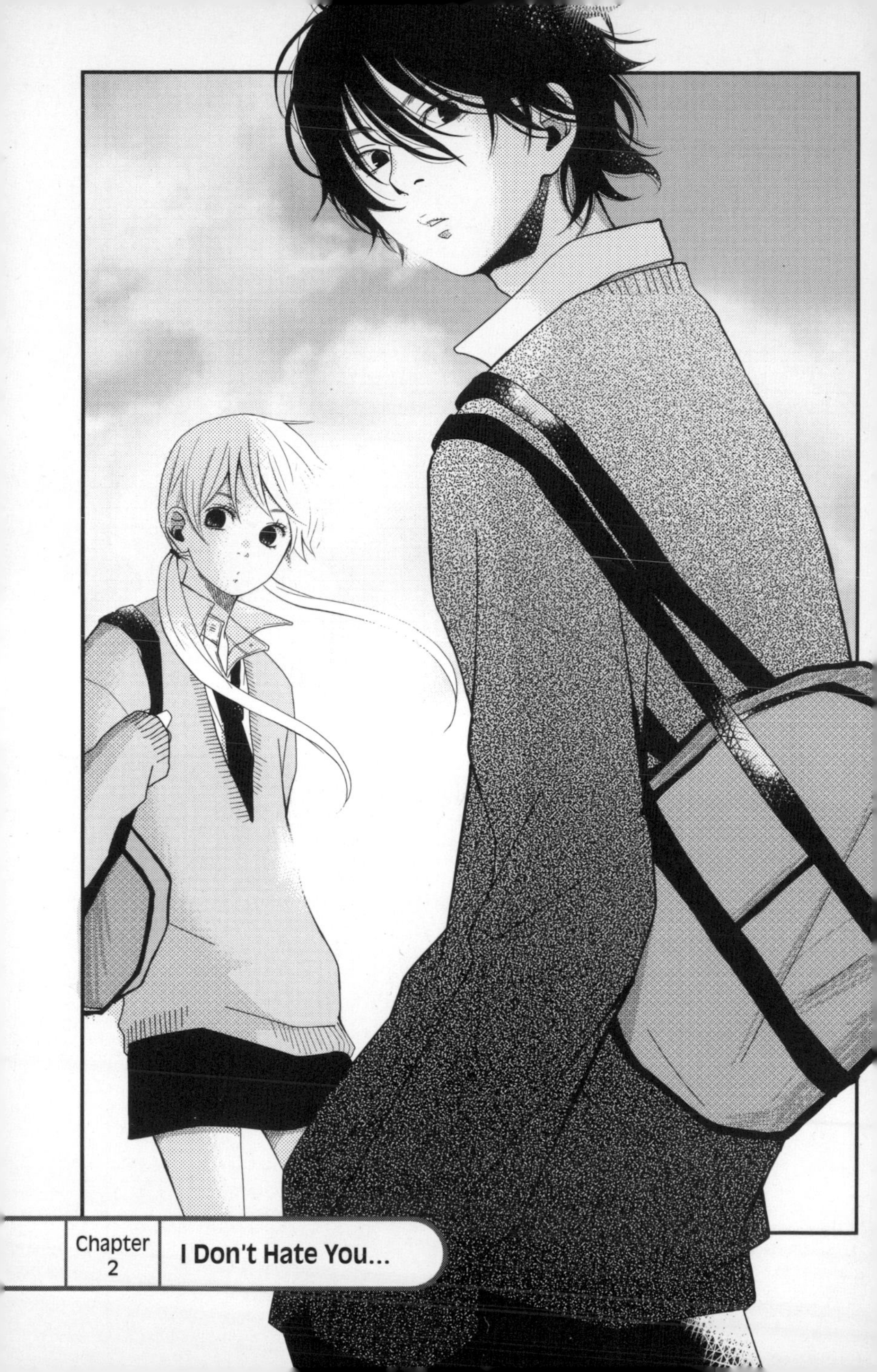
Chapter
2
I Don't Hate You...

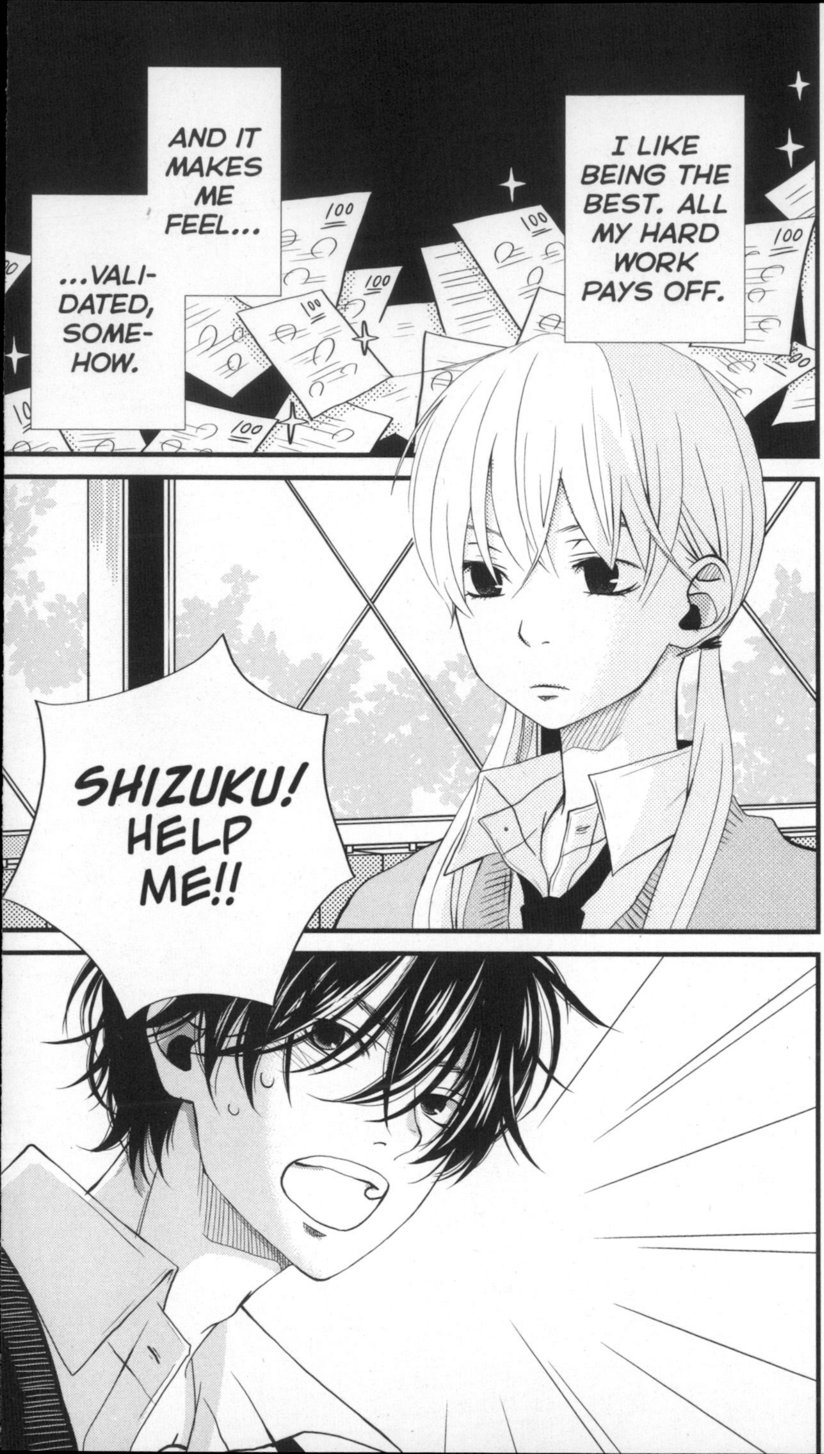
I LIKE BEING THE BEST. ALL MY HARD WORK PAYS OFF.
AND IT MAKES ME FEEL...
...VALIDATED, SOMEHOW.
SHIZUKU! HELP ME!!

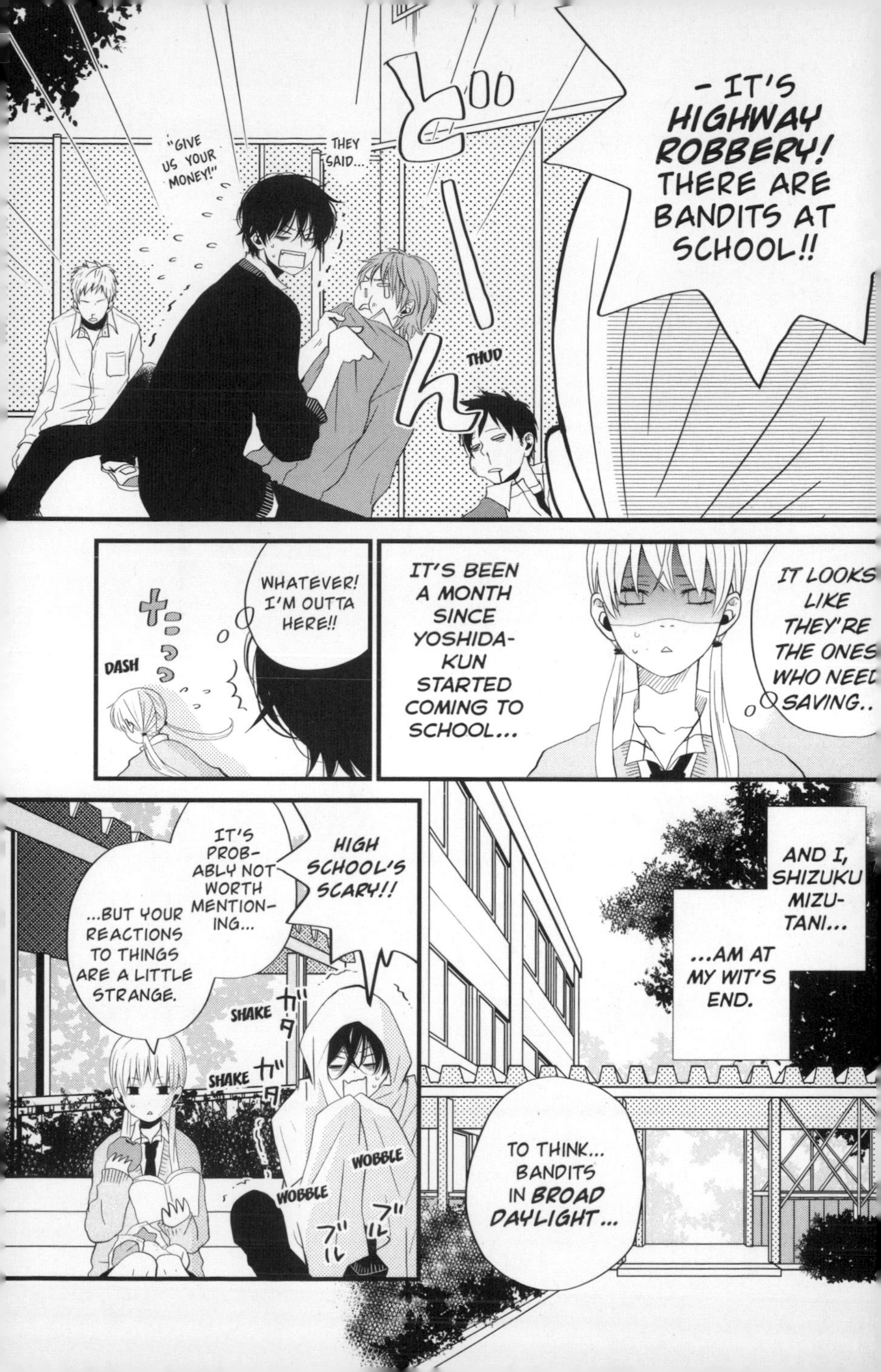
—IT'S HIGHWAY ROBBERY! THERE ARE BANDITS AT SCHOOL!!
THUD
THEY SAID...
"GIVE US YOUR MONEY!"
IT LOOKS LIKE THEY'RE THE ONES WHO NEED SAVING...
IT'S BEEN A MONTH SINCE YOSHIDA-KUN STARTED COMING TO SCHOOL...
WHATEVER! I'M OUTTA HERE!!
DASH
AND I, SHIZUKU MIZUTANI...
...AM AT MY WIT'S END.
TO THINK... BANDITS IN BROAD DAYLIGHT...
HIGH SCHOOL'S SCARY!!
IT'S PROBABLY NOT WORTH MENTIONING...
...BUT YOUR REACTIONS TO THINGS ARE A LITTLE STRANGE.
SHAKE
SHAKE
WOBBLE
WOBBLE

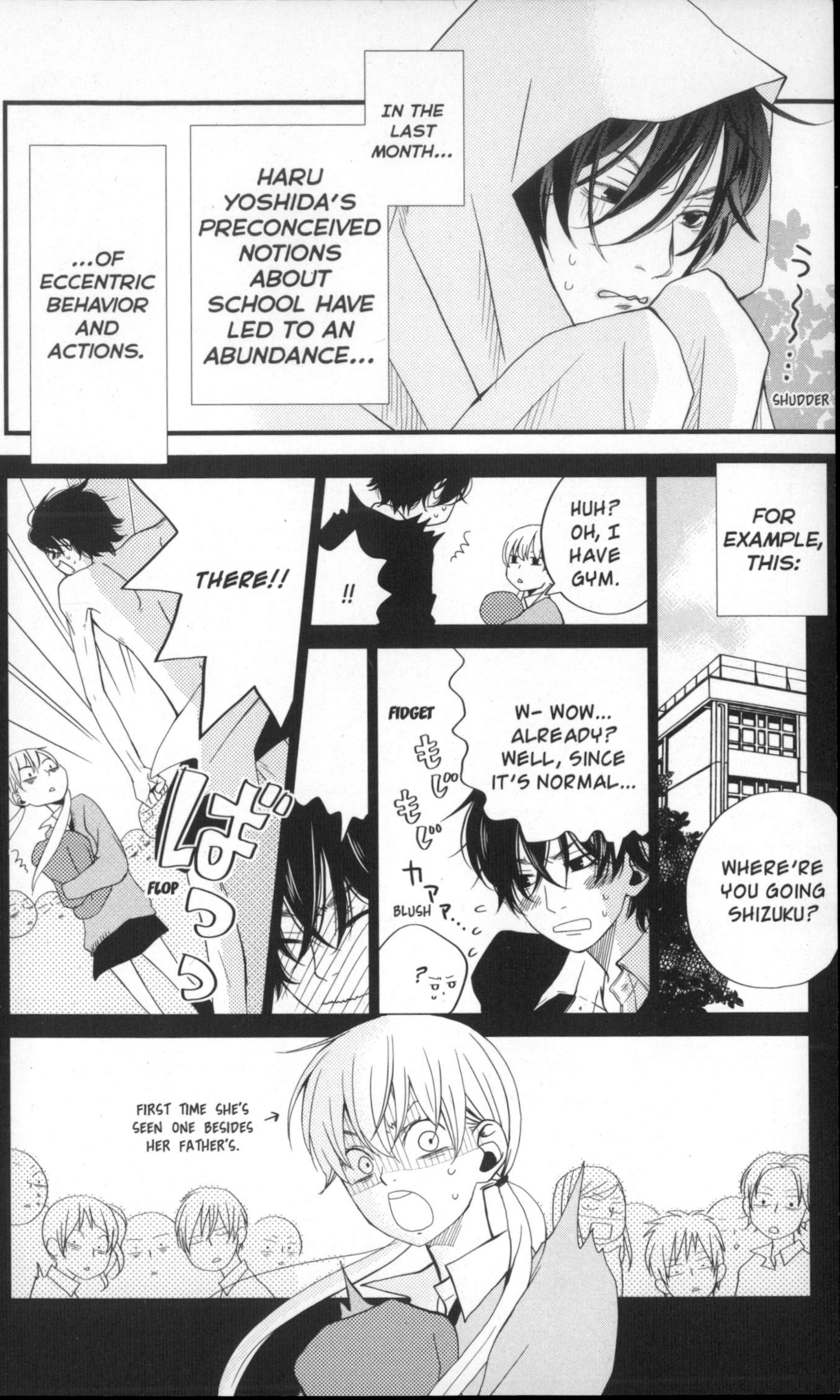
SHUDDER
IN THE LAST MONTH...
HARU YOSHIDA'S PRECONCEIVED NOTIONS ABOUT SCHOOL HAVE LED TO AN ABUNDANCE...
...OF ECCENTRIC BEHAVIOR AND ACTIONS.
FOR EXAMPLE, THIS:
WHERE'RE YOU GOING SHIZUKU?
HUH? OH, I HAVE GYM.
!!
W- WOW... ALREADY? WELL, SINCE IT'S NORMAL...
FIDGET
BLUSH
?
THERE!!
FLOP
FIRST TIME SHE'S SEEN ONE BESIDES HER FATHER'S.

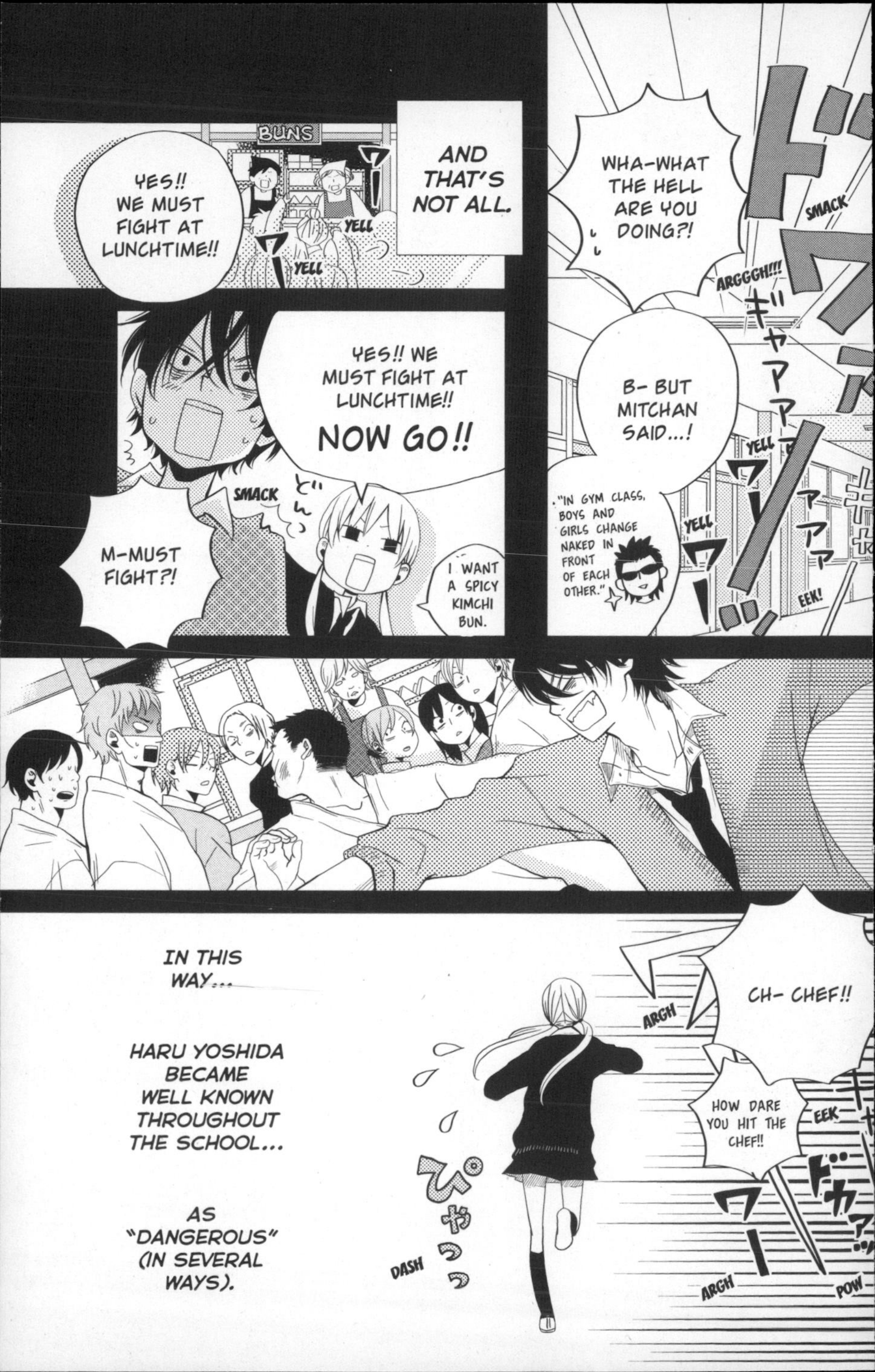
WHA-WHAT THE HELL ARE YOU DOING?!
SMACK
ARGGGH!!!
B- BUT MITCHAN SAID...!
YELL
YELL
"IN GYM CLASS, BOYS AND GIRLS CHANGE NAKED IN FRONT OF EACH OTHER."
EEK!
AND THAT'S NOT ALL.
BUNS
YELL
YES!! WE MUST FIGHT AT LUNCHTIME!!
YELL
YES!! WE MUST FIGHT AT LUNCHTIME!!
NOW GO!!
SMACK
I WANT A SPICY KIMCHI BUN.
M-MUST FIGHT?!
CH- CHEF!!
HOW DARE YOU HIT THE CHEF!!
EEK
ARGH
POW
ARGH
DASH
IN THIS WAY...
HARU YOSHIDA BECAME WELL KNOWN THROUGHOUT THE SCHOOL...
AS "DANGEROUS" (IN SEVERAL WAYS).

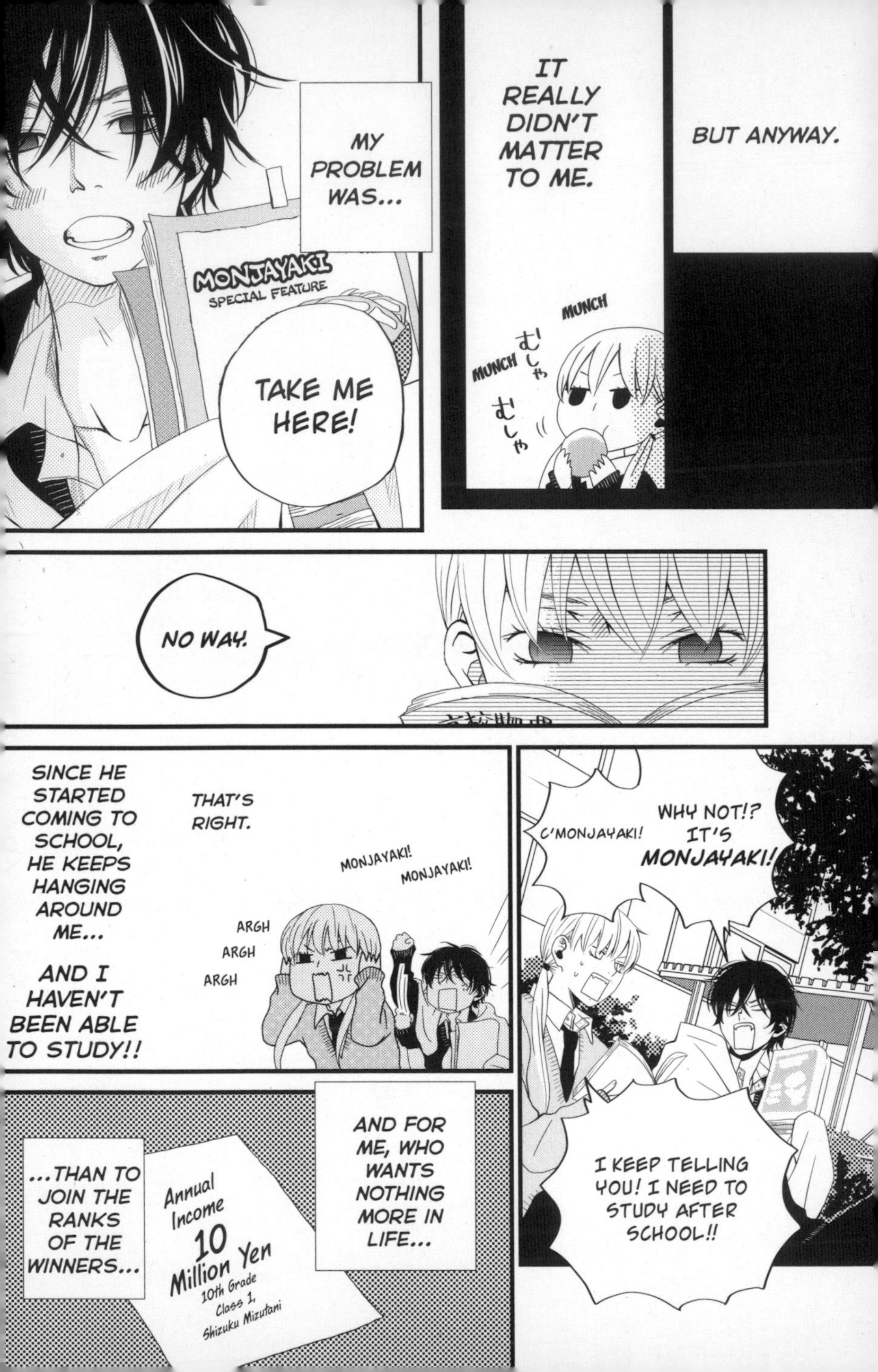
BUT ANYWAY.
IT REALLY DIDN'T MATTER TO ME.
MUNCH
むしゃ
MUNCH
むしゃ
MY PROBLEM WAS...
MONJAYAKI SPECIAL FEATURE
TAKE ME HERE!
NO WAY.
WHY NOT!? IT'S MONJAYAKI!
C'MONJAYAKI!
I KEEP TELLING YOU! I NEED TO STUDY AFTER SCHOOL!!
THAT'S RIGHT.
SINCE HE STARTED COMING TO SCHOOL, HE KEEPS HANGING AROUND ME...
MONJAYAKI!
MONJAYAKI!
ARGH
ARGH
ARGH
AND I HAVEN'T BEEN ABLE TO STUDY!!
AND FOR ME, WHO WANTS NOTHING MORE IN LIFE...
Annual Income 10 Million Yen 10th Grade Class 1, Shizuku Mizutani
...THAN TO JOIN THE RANKS OF THE WINNERS...

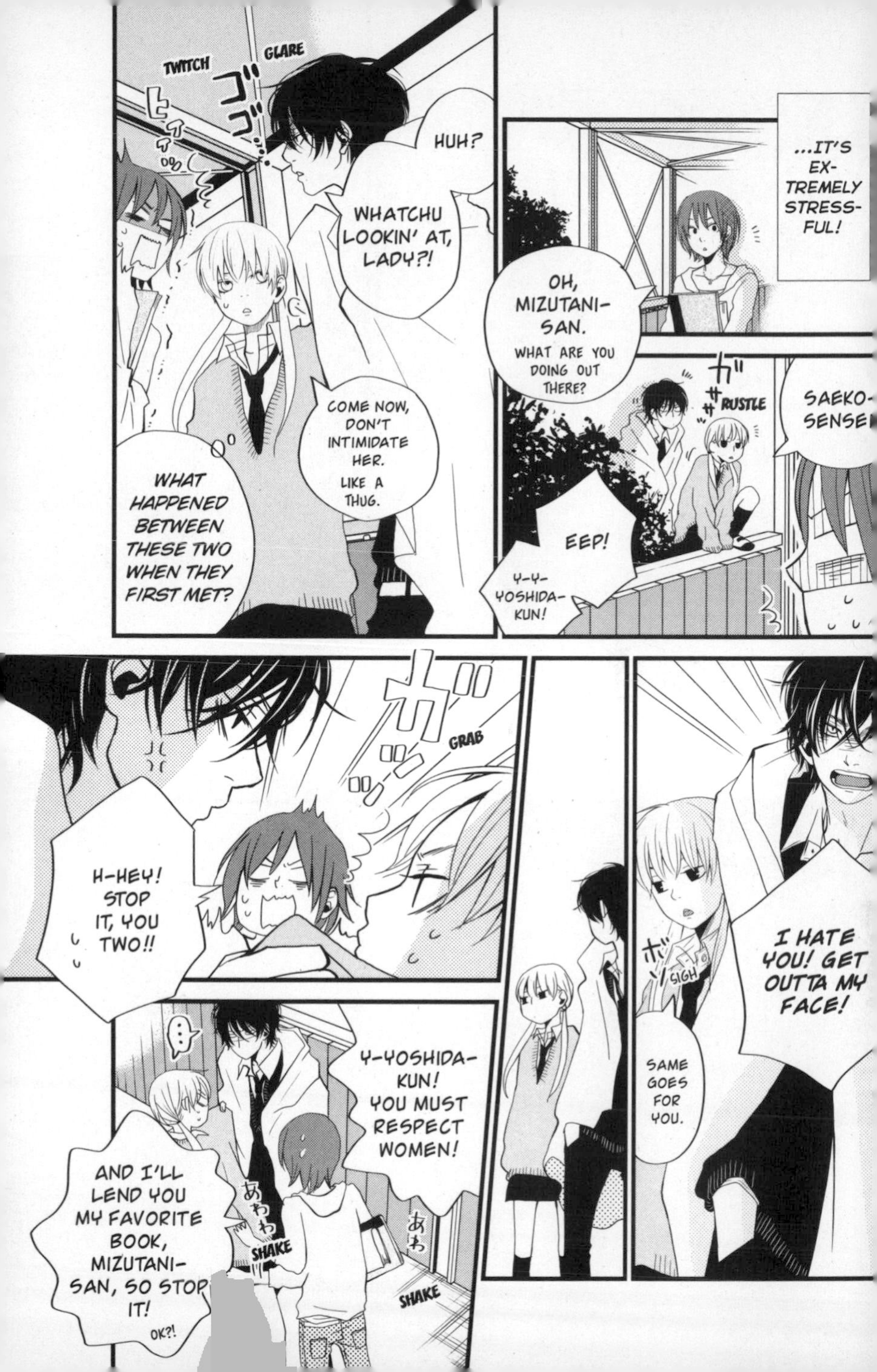
...IT'S EXTREMELY STRESSFUL!
OH, MIZUTANI-SAN.
WHAT ARE YOU DOING OUT THERE?
SAEKO-SENSE
RUSTLE
EEP!
Y-Y-YOSHIDA-KUN!
GLARE
TWITCH
HUH?
WHATCHU LOOKIN' AT, LADY?!
COME NOW, DON'T INTIMIDATE HER.
LIKE A THUG.
WHAT HAPPENED BETWEEN THESE TWO WHEN THEY FIRST MET?
I HATE YOU! GET OUTTA MY FACE!
SIGH
SAME GOES FOR YOU.
GRAB
H-HEY! STOP IT, YOU TWO!!
Y-YOSHIDA-KUN! YOU MUST RESPECT WOMEN!
SHAKE
SHAKE
AND I'LL LEND YOU MY FAVORITE BOOK, MIZUTANI-SAN, SO STOP IT!
OK?!

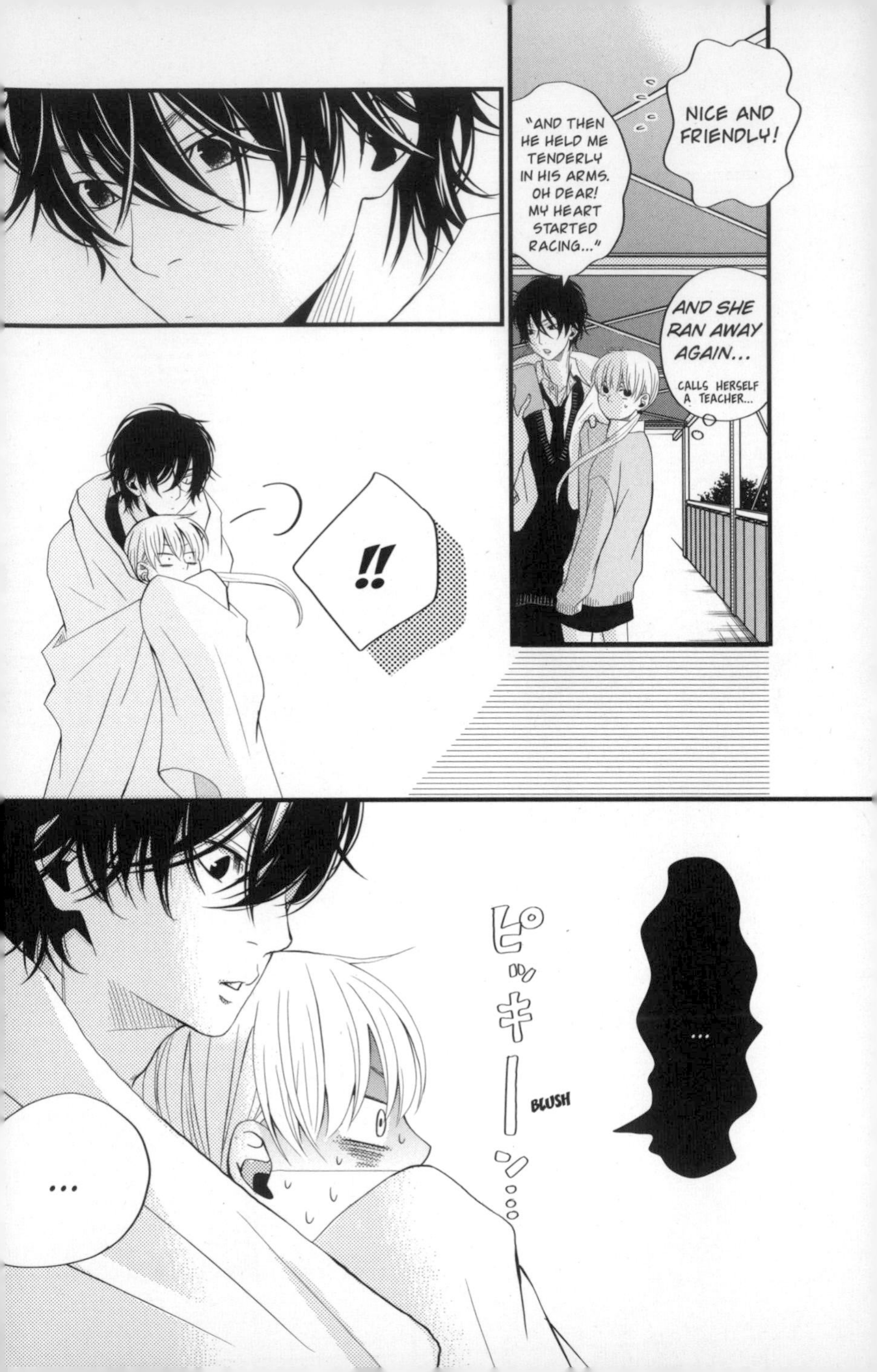
NICE AND FRIENDLY!
"AND THEN HE HELD ME TENDERLY IN HIS ARMS. OH DEAR! MY HEART STARTED RACING..."
AND SHE RAN AWAY AGAIN...
CALLS HERSELF A TEACHER...
!!
...
ピッキーッ
BLUSH
...

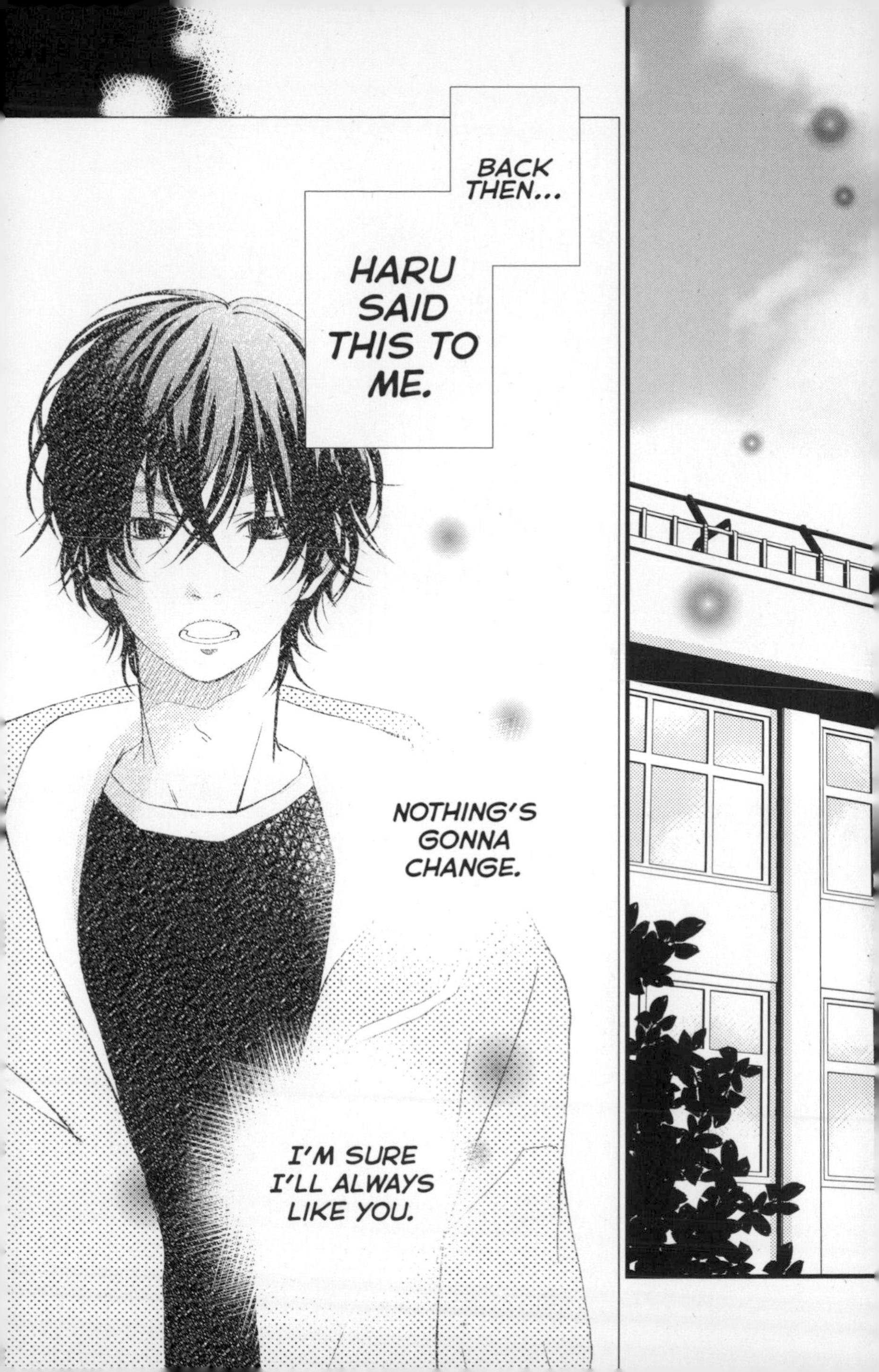
BACK THEN...
HARU SAID THIS TO ME.
NOTHING'S GONNA CHANGE.
I'M SURE I'LL ALWAYS LIKE YOU.

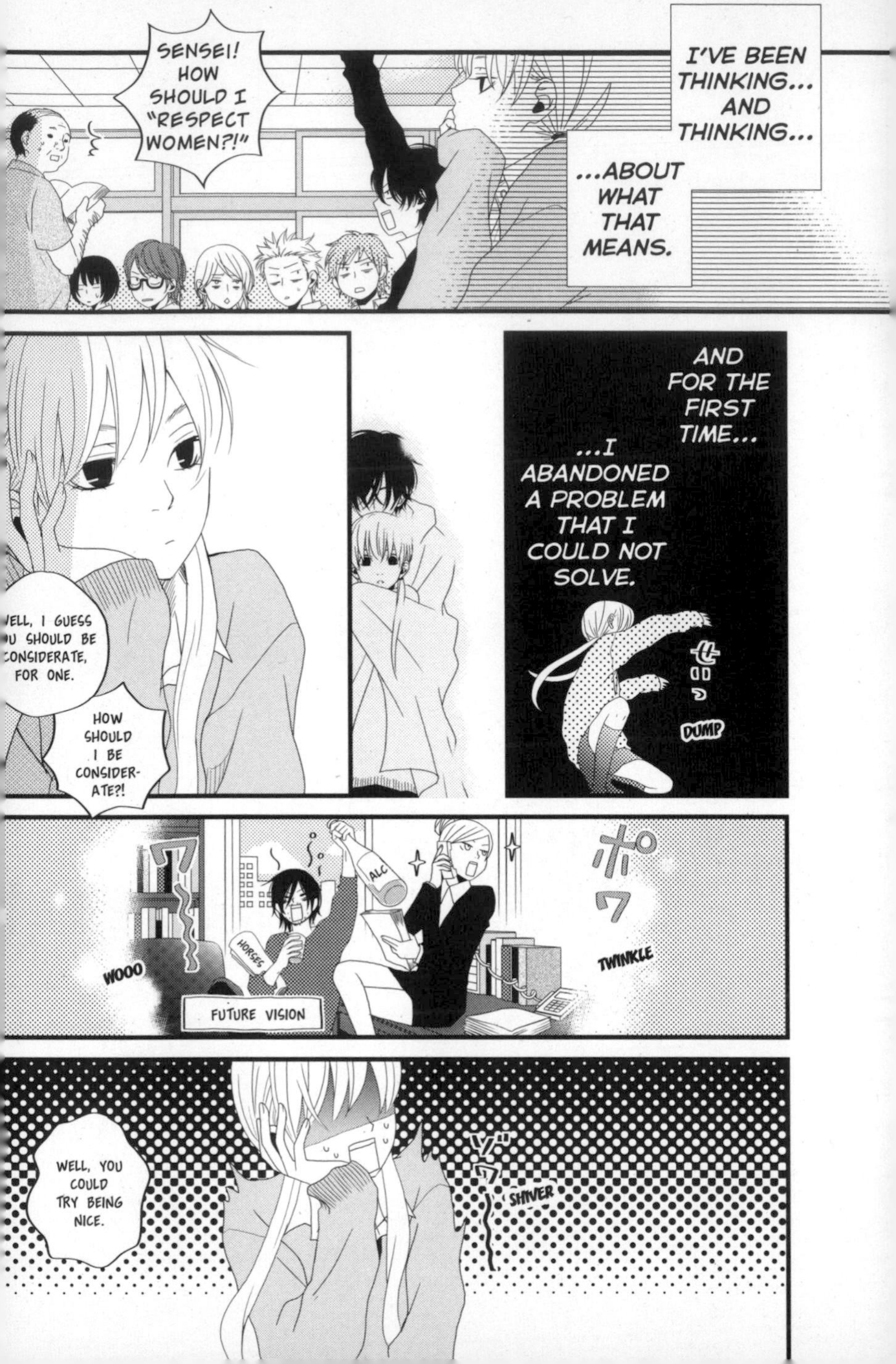
I'VE BEEN THINKING... AND THINKING...
...ABOUT WHAT THAT MEANS.
SENSEI! HOW SHOULD I "RESPECT WOMEN?!"
AND FOR THE FIRST TIME...
...I ABANDONED A PROBLEM THAT I COULD NOT SOLVE.
せっ
DUMP
ELL, I GUESS U SHOULD BE CONSIDERATE, FOR ONE.
HOW SHOULD I BE CONSIDER-ATE?!
ポワ
TWINKLE
ALC
HORSES
ワ～
WOOO
FUTURE VISION
ゾワ～
SHIVER
WELL, YOU COULD TRY BEING NICE.

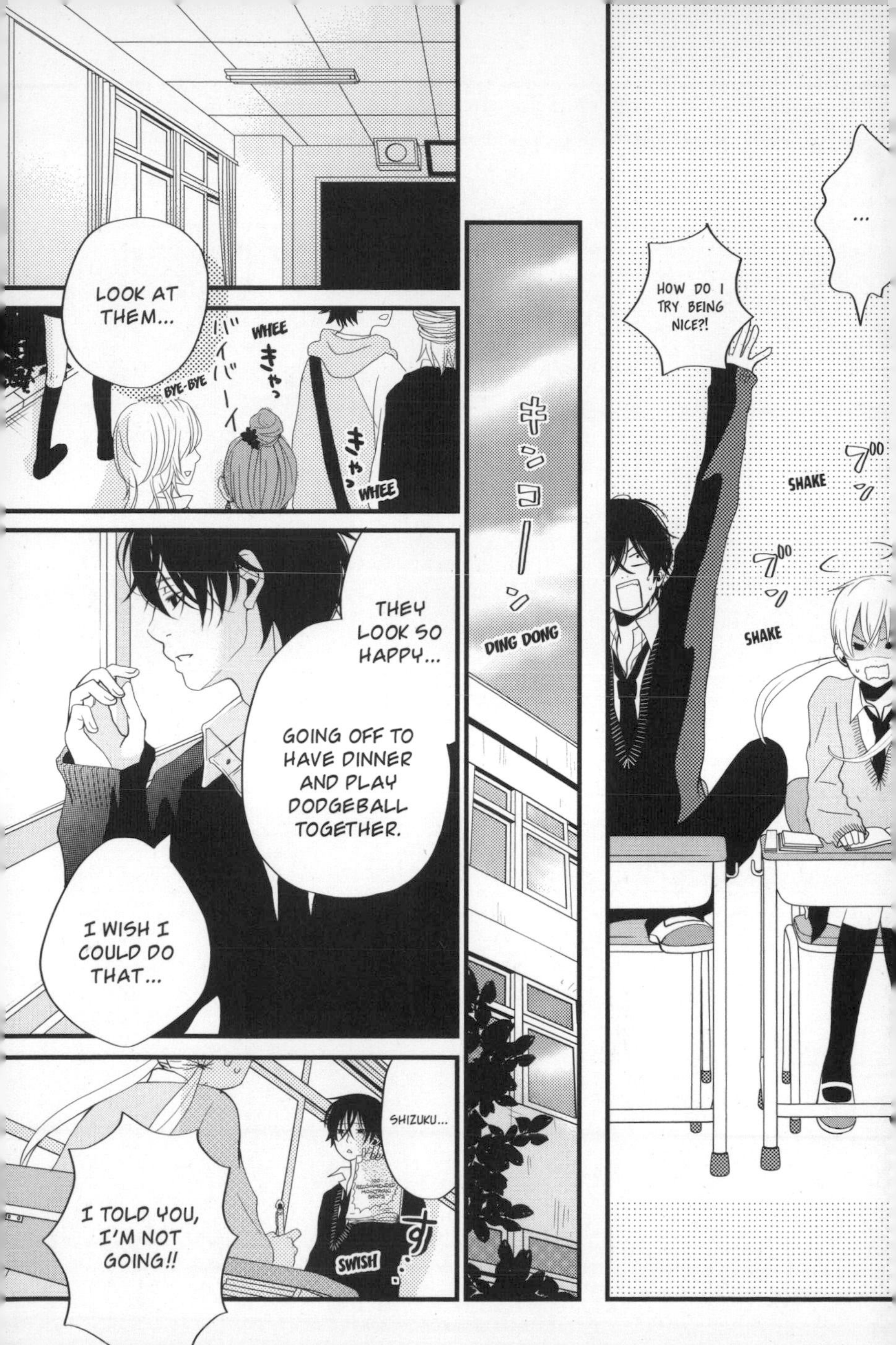
...
HOW DO I TRY BEING NICE?!
ブ SHAKE
ブ SHAKE
キンコーン
DING DONG
きゃっ WHEE
バイバーイ BYE-BYE
LOOK AT THEM...
きゃっ WHEE
THEY LOOK SO HAPPY...
GOING OFF TO HAVE DINNER AND PLAY DODGEBALL TOGETHER.
I WISH I COULD DO THAT...
SHIZUKU...
す... SWISH
I TOLD YOU, I'M NOT GOING!!

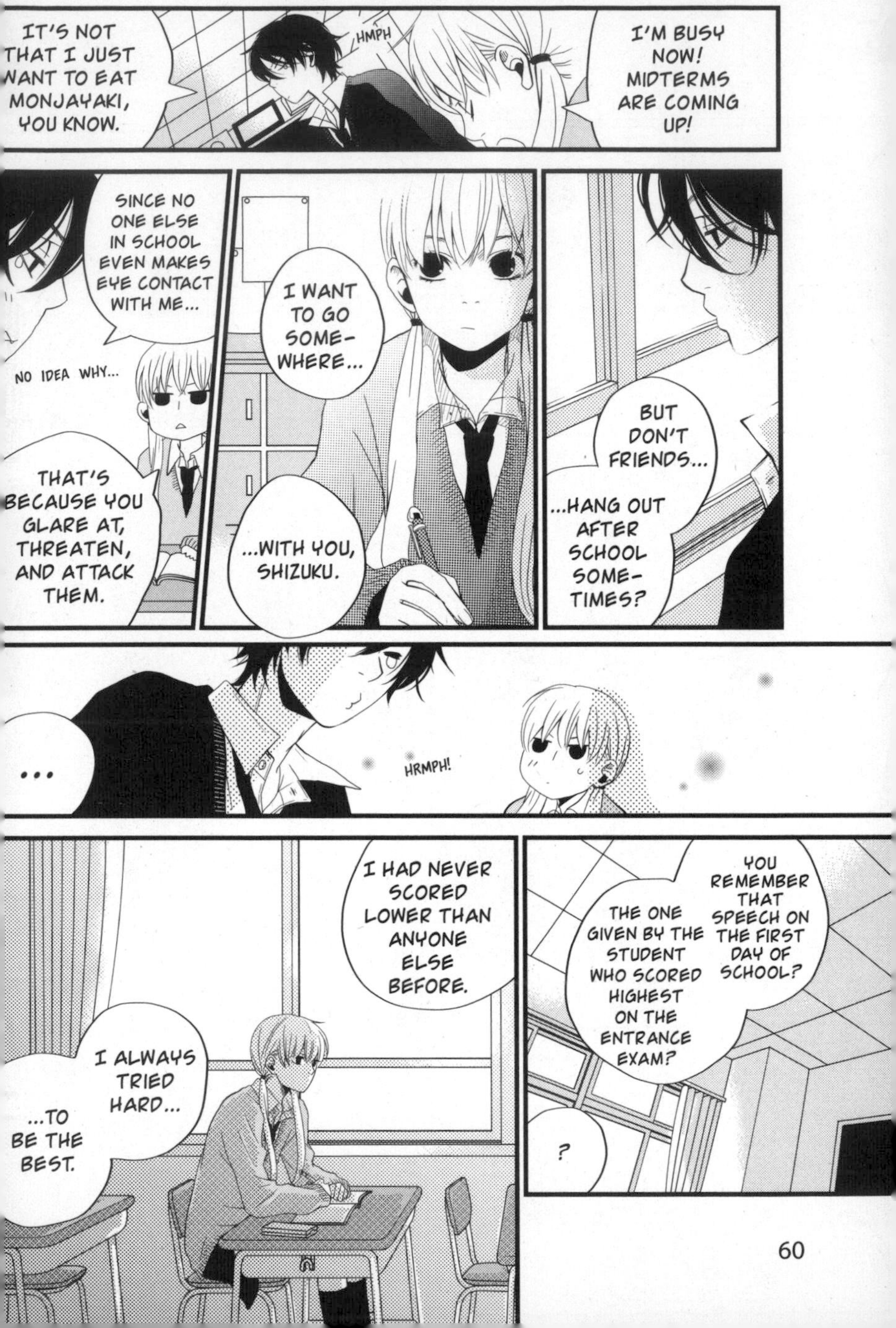
I'M BUSY NOW! MIDTERMS ARE COMING UP!
HMPH
IT'S NOT THAT I JUST WANT TO EAT MONJAYAKI, YOU KNOW.
BUT DON'T FRIENDS...
...HANG OUT AFTER SCHOOL SOMETIMES?
I WANT TO GO SOMEWHERE...
...WITH YOU, SHIZUKU.
SINCE NO ONE ELSE IN SCHOOL EVEN MAKES EYE CONTACT WITH ME...
NO IDEA WHY...
THAT'S BECAUSE YOU GLARE AT, THREATEN, AND ATTACK THEM.
HRMPH!
...
YOU REMEMBER THAT SPEECH ON THE FIRST DAY OF SCHOOL?
THE ONE GIVEN BY THE STUDENT WHO SCORED HIGHEST ON THE ENTRANCE EXAM?
?
I HAD NEVER SCORED LOWER THAN ANYONE ELSE BEFORE.
I ALWAYS TRIED HARD...
...TO BE THE BEST.

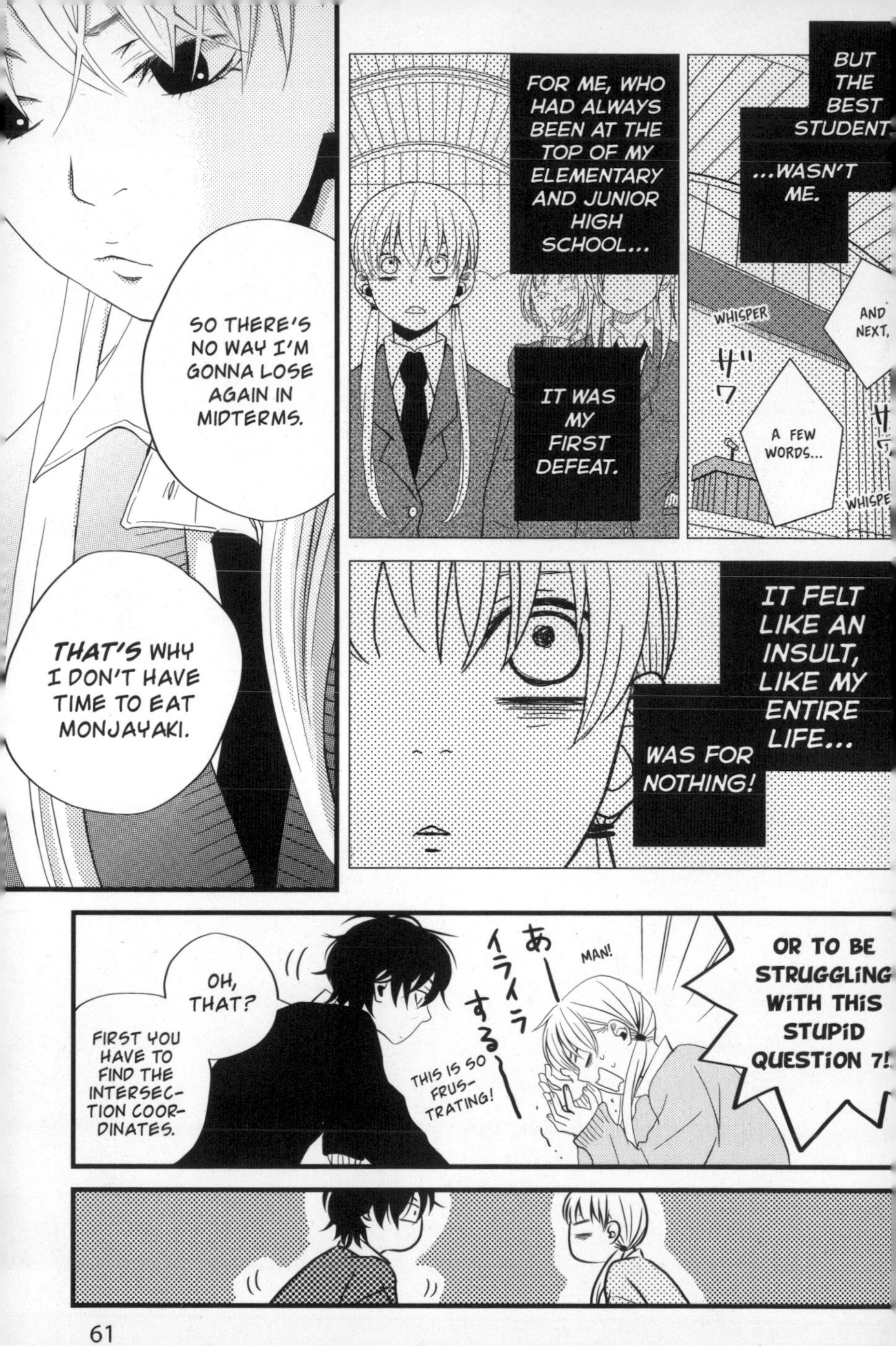
BUT THE BEST STUDENT
...WASN'T ME.
WHISPER
AND NEXT,
A FEW WORDS...
WHISPE
FOR ME, WHO HAD ALWAYS BEEN AT THE TOP OF MY ELEMENTARY AND JUNIOR HIGH SCHOOL...
IT WAS MY FIRST DEFEAT.
IT FELT LIKE AN INSULT, LIKE MY ENTIRE LIFE...
WAS FOR NOTHING!
SO THERE'S NO WAY I'M GONNA LOSE AGAIN IN MIDTERMS.
THAT'S WHY I DON'T HAVE TIME TO EAT MONJAYAKI.
OR TO BE STRUGGLING WITH THIS STUPID QUESTION 7!!
MAN!
THIS IS SO FRUS-TRATING!
OH, THAT?
FIRST YOU HAVE TO FIND THE INTERSEC-TION COOR-DINATES.

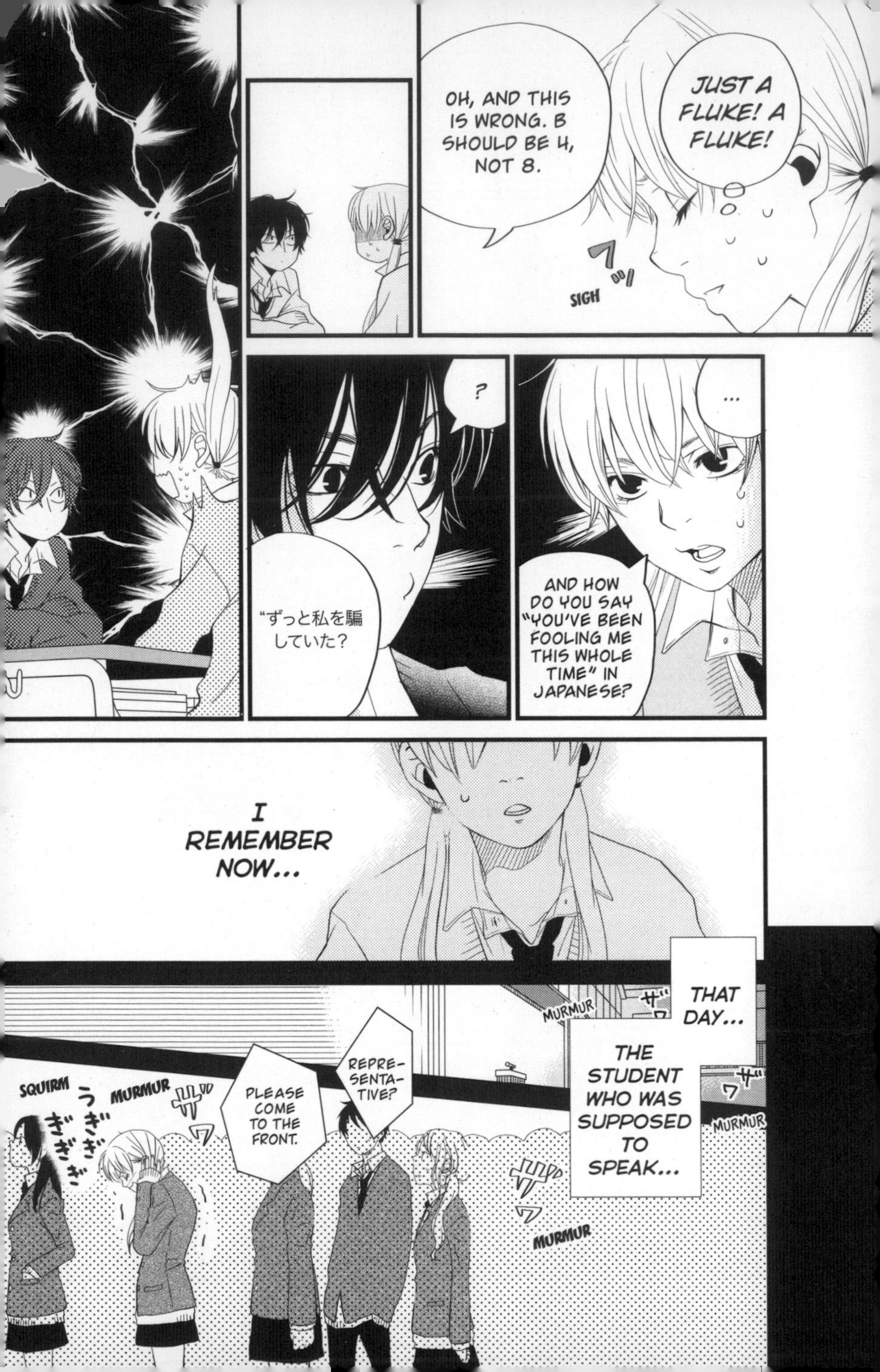
JUST A FLUKE! A FLUKE!
OH, AND THIS IS WRONG. B SHOULD BE 4, NOT 8.
SIGH
...
AND HOW DO YOU SAY "YOU'VE BEEN FOOLING ME THIS WHOLE TIME" IN JAPANESE?
?
“ずっと私を騙していた？
I REMEMBER NOW...
THAT DAY...
THE STUDENT WHO WAS SUPPOSED TO SPEAK...
ザワ
MURMUR
ザワ
MURMUR
MURMUR
ザワ
MURMUR
REPRESENTATIVE?
PLEASE COME TO THE FRONT.
ザワ
MURMUR
うぎぎぎぎぎ
SQUIRM

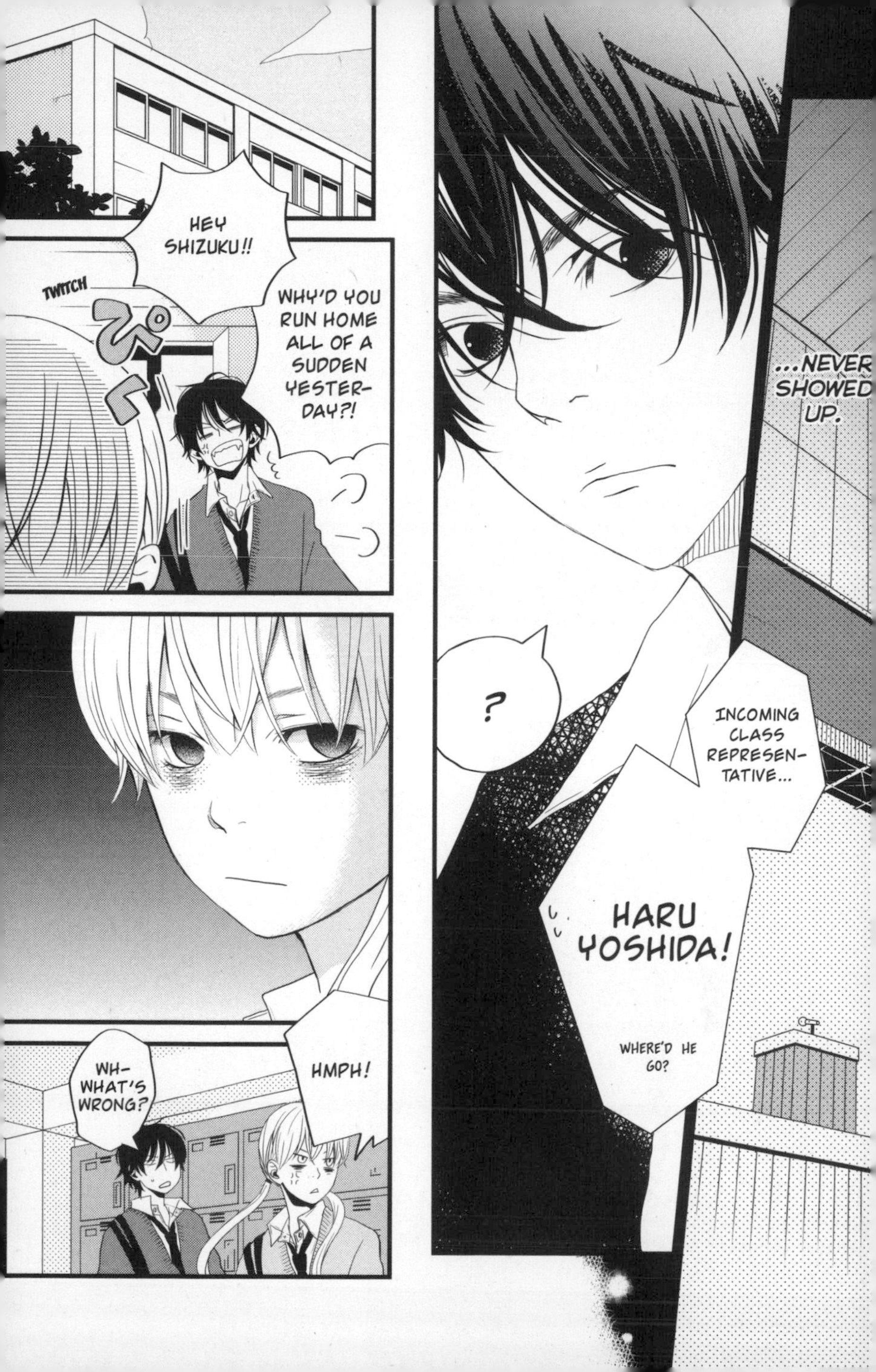
...NEVER SHOWED UP.
?
INCOMING CLASS REPRESEN-TATIVE...
HARU YOSHIDA!
WHERE'D HE GO?
HEY SHIZUKU!!
TWITCH
WHY'D YOU RUN HOME ALL OF A SUDDEN YESTER-DAY?!
HMPH!
WH-WHAT'S WRONG?

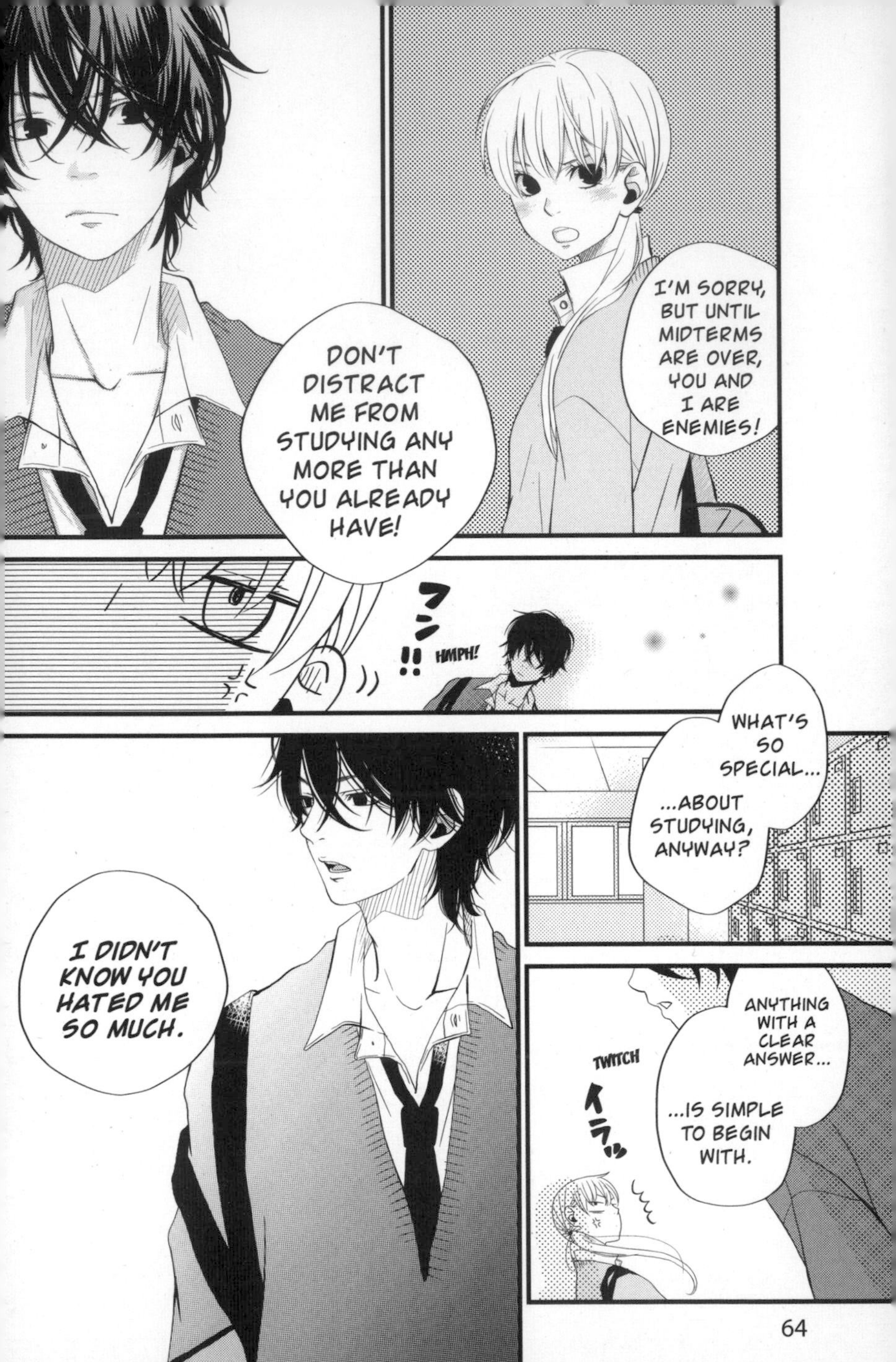
I'M SORRY, BUT UNTIL MIDTERMS ARE OVER, YOU AND I ARE ENEMIES!
DON'T DISTRACT ME FROM STUDYING ANY MORE THAN YOU ALREADY HAVE!
HMPH!
WHAT'S SO SPECIAL...
...ABOUT STUDYING, ANYWAY?
ANYTHING WITH A CLEAR ANSWER...
...IS SIMPLE TO BEGIN WITH.
TWITCH
I DIDN'T KNOW YOU HATED ME SO MUCH.

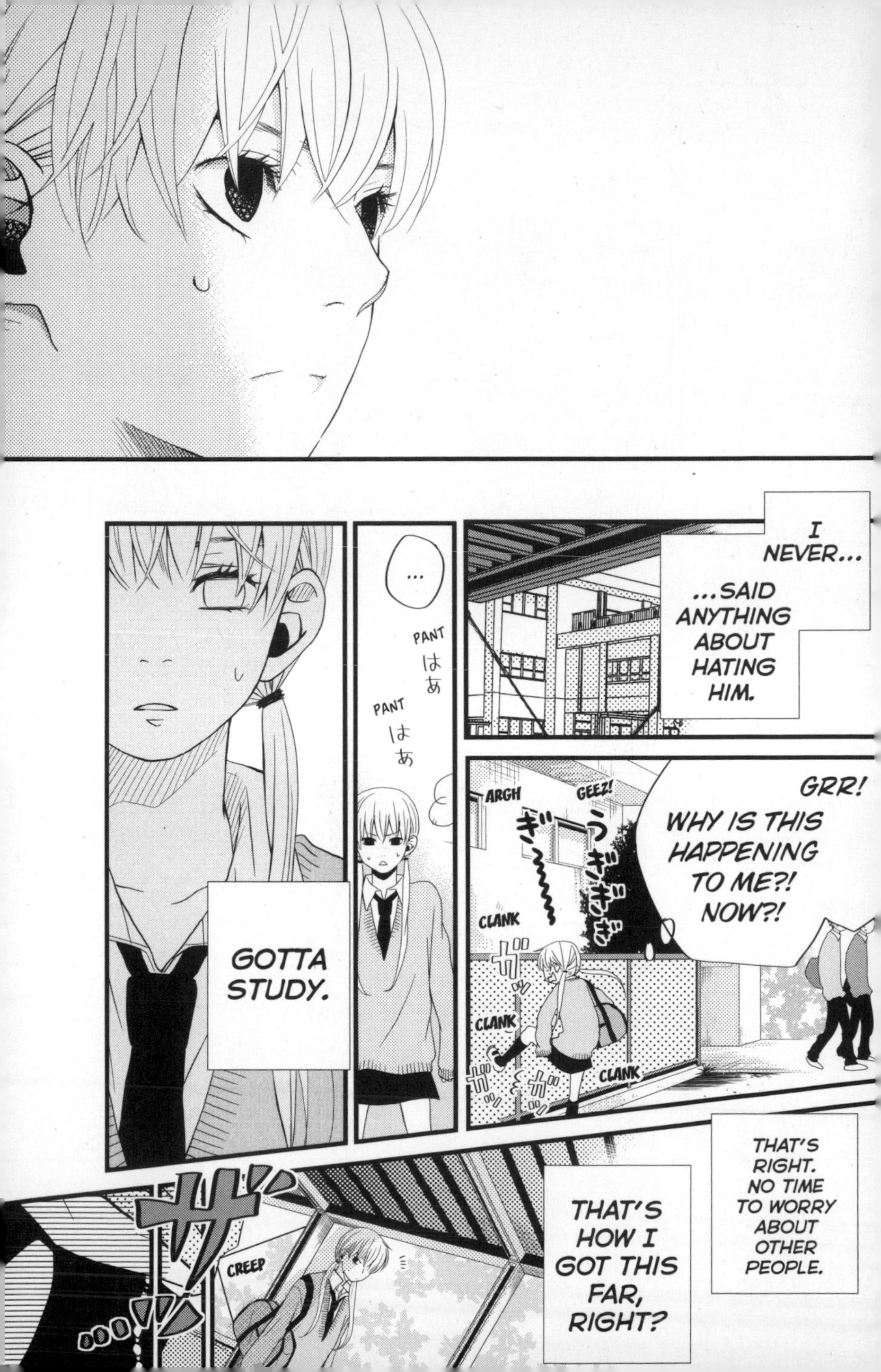
I NEVER...
...SAID ANYTHING ABOUT HATING HIM.
GRR! WHY IS THIS HAPPENING TO ME?! NOW?!
GEEZ!
うぎぎぎ
ARGH
ぎ~~~
CLANK
ガッ
CLANK
ガッ
CLANK
ガッ
ガッ
...
PANT
はあ
PANT
はあ
GOTTA STUDY.
THAT'S RIGHT. NO TIME TO WORRY ABOUT OTHER PEOPLE.
THAT'S HOW I GOT THIS FAR, RIGHT?
CREEP
ザ

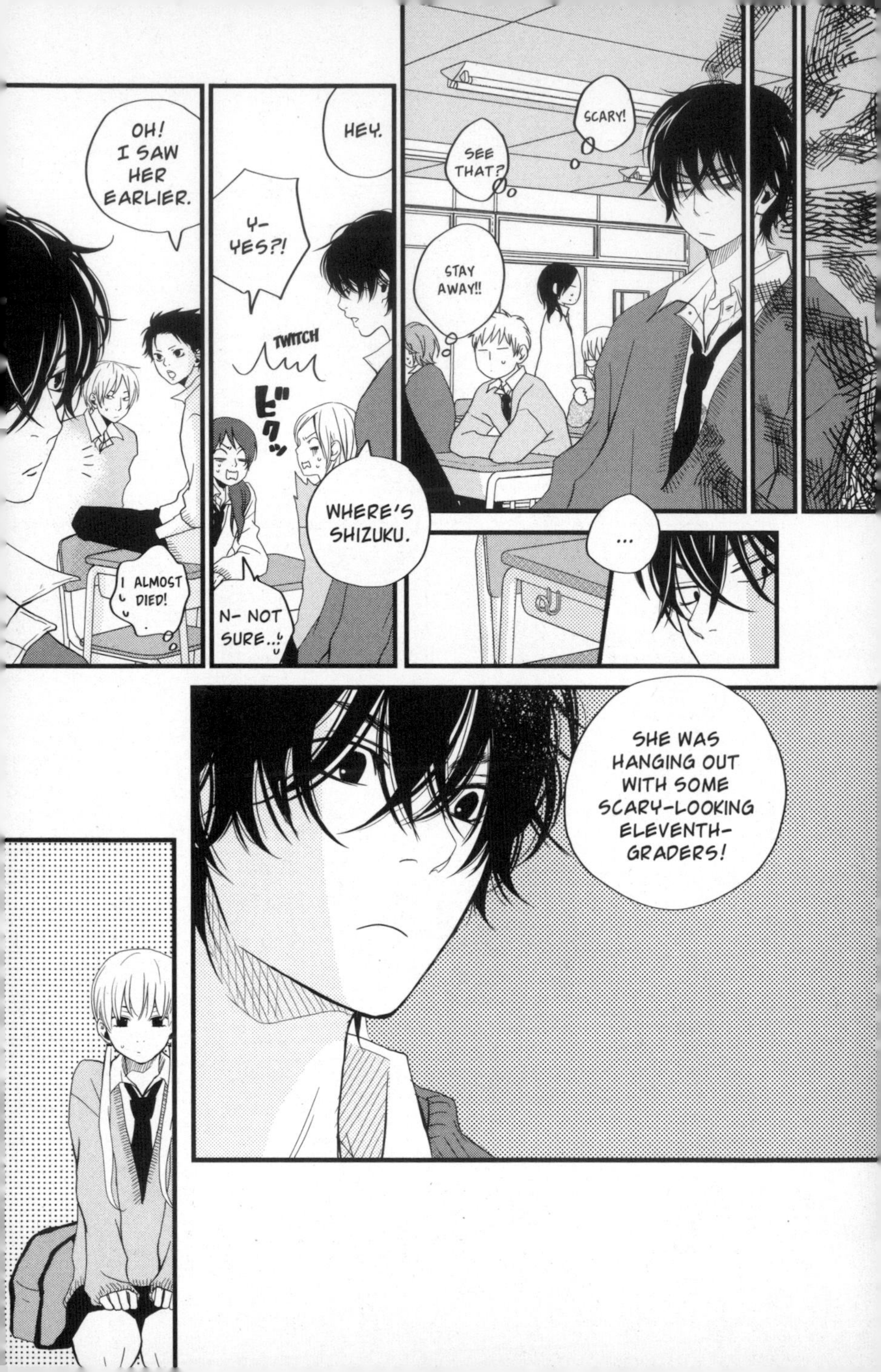
SCARY!
SEE THAT?
STAY AWAY!!
...
HEY.
Y- YES?!
TWITCH
ビクッ
WHERE'S SHIZUKU.
N- NOT SURE...
OH! I SAW HER EARLIER.
I ALMOST DIED!
SHE WAS HANGING OUT WITH SOME SCARY-LOOKING ELEVENTH-GRADERS!

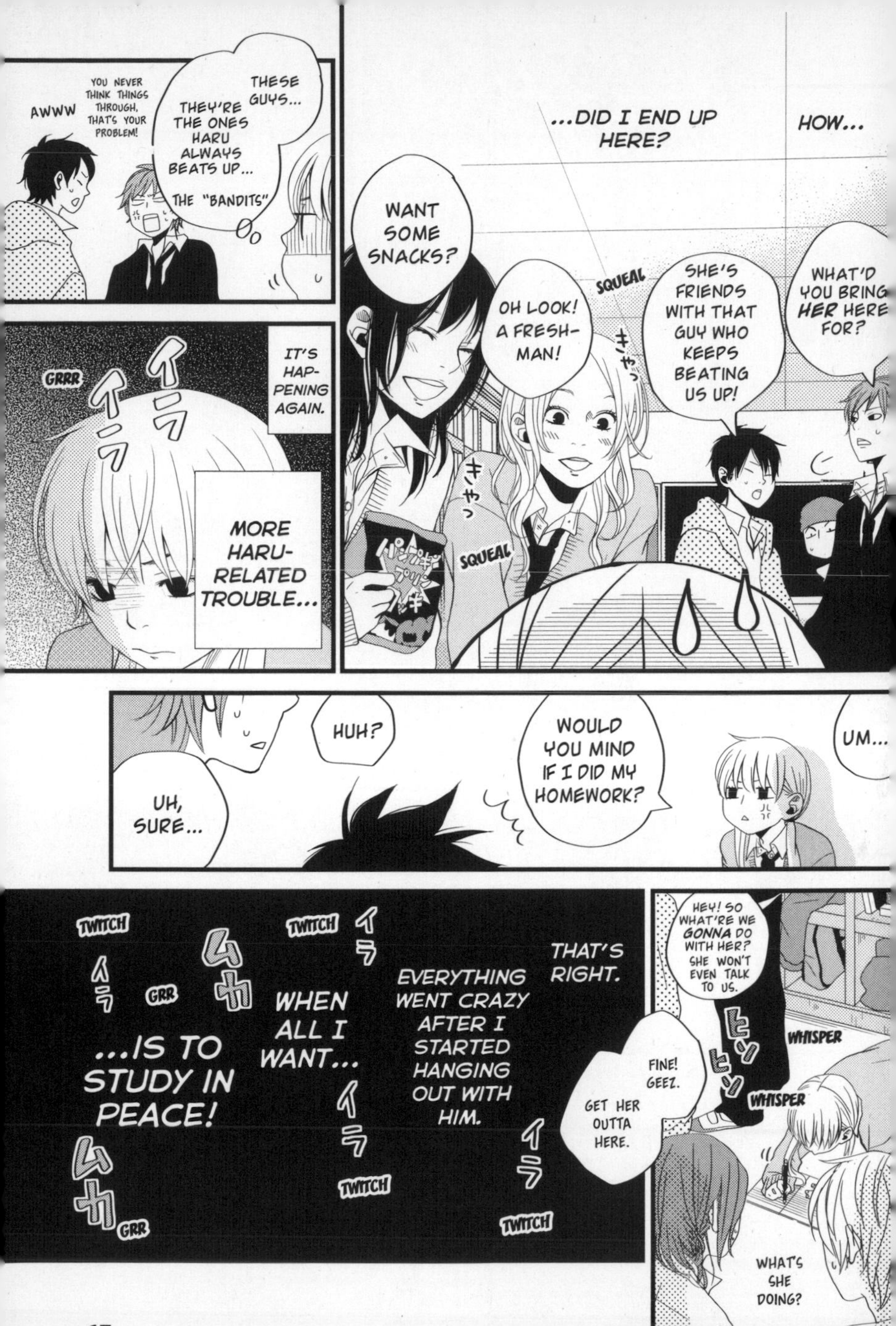
HOW...
...DID I END UP HERE?
WHAT'D YOU BRING HER HERE FOR?
SHE'S FRIENDS WITH THAT GUY WHO KEEPS BEATING US UP!
SQUEAL
キャっ
OH LOOK! A FRESH-MAN!
WANT SOME SNACKS?
キャっ
SQUEAL
THESE GUYS... THEY'RE THE ONES HARU ALWAYS BEATS UP... THE "BANDITS"
YOU NEVER THINK THINGS THROUGH, THAT'S YOUR PROBLEM!
AWWW
IT'S HAP-PENING AGAIN.
イラ
イラ
GRRR
MORE HARU-RELATED TROUBLE...
UM...
WOULD YOU MIND IF I DID MY HOMEWORK?
HUH?
UH, SURE...
HEY! SO WHAT'RE WE GONNA DO WITH HER? SHE WON'T EVEN TALK TO US.
WHISPER
ヒソ
ヒソ
WHISPER
FINE! GEEZ.
GET HER OUTTA HERE.
WHAT'S SHE DOING?
THAT'S RIGHT.
EVERYTHING WENT CRAZY AFTER I STARTED HANGING OUT WITH HIM.
イラ
TWITCH
TWITCH
イラ
WHEN ALL I WANT...
イラ
TWITCH
ムカ
GRR
TWITCH
イラ
...IS TO STUDY IN PEACE!
ムカ
GRR

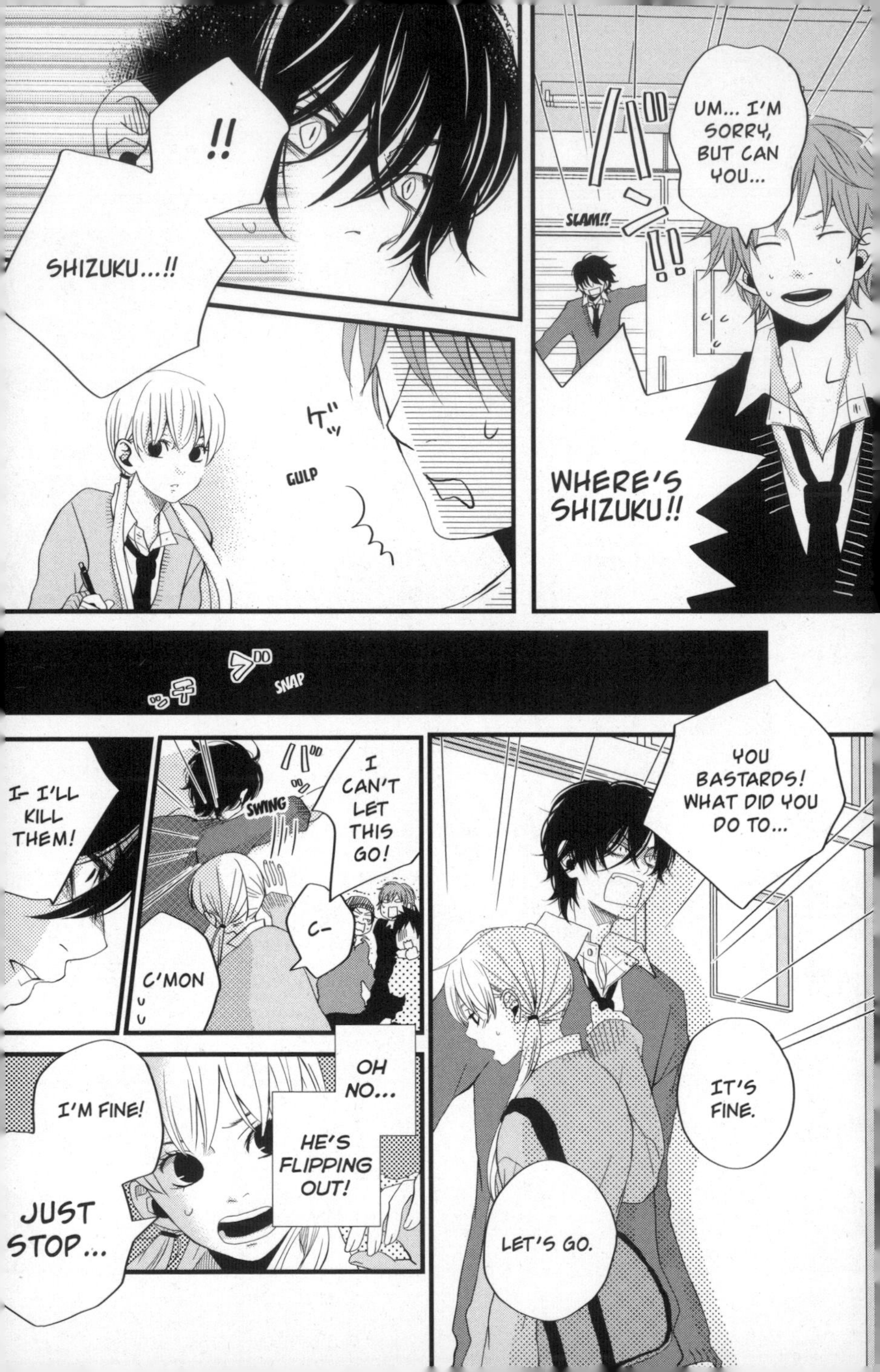
UM... I'M SORRY, BUT CAN YOU...
SLAM!!
WHERE'S SHIZUKU!!
!!
SHIZUKU...!!
GULP
SNAP
YOU BASTARDS! WHAT DID YOU DO TO...
IT'S FINE.
LET'S GO.
I CAN'T LET THIS GO!
SWING
C-
C'MON
I- I'LL KILL THEM!
OH NO...
HE'S FLIPPING OUT!
I'M FINE!
JUST STOP...

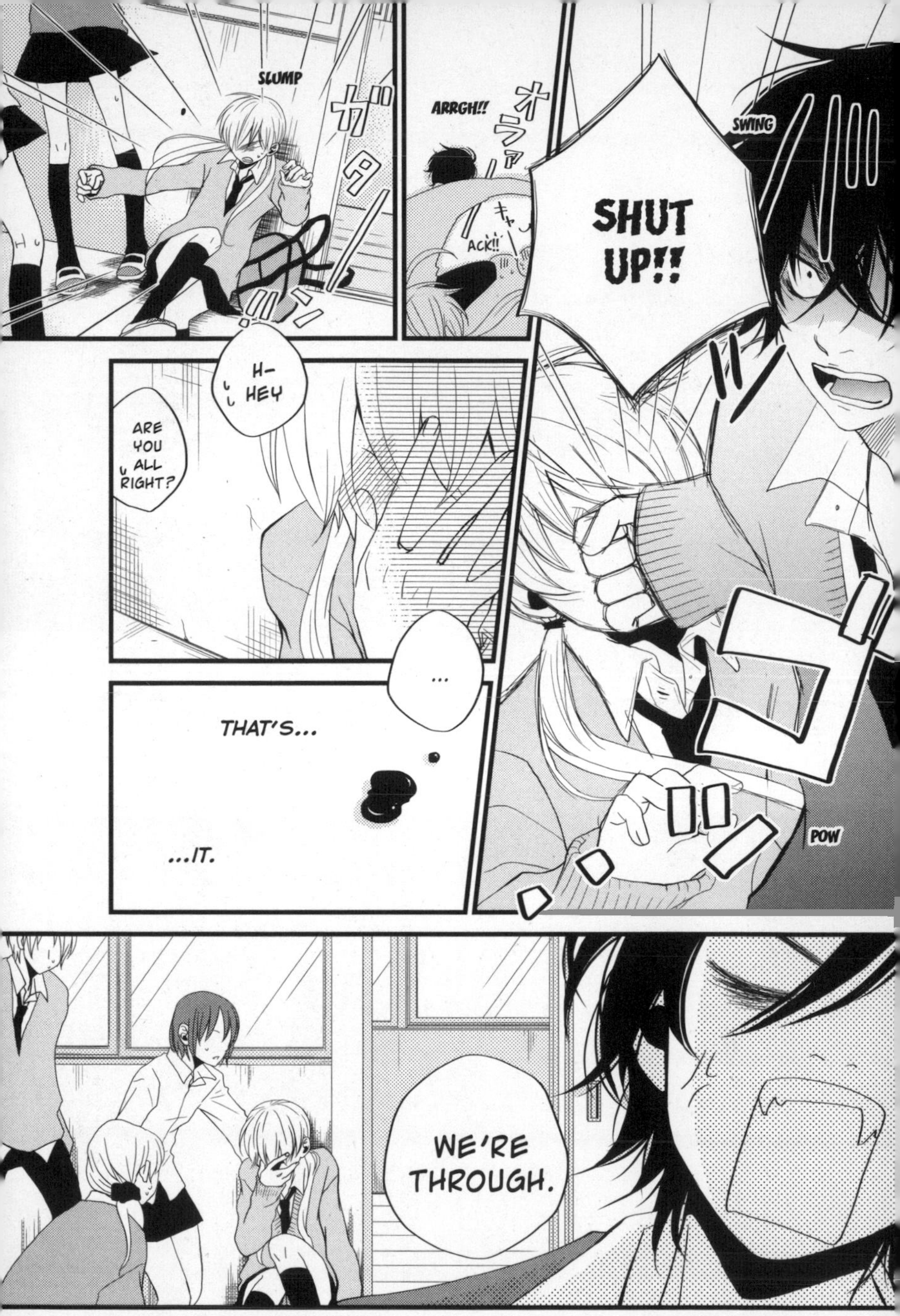
SWING
SHUT UP!!
POW
ARRGH!!
オラァ
ACK!!
SLUMP
ガタ
H-HEY
ARE YOU ALL RIGHT?
...
THAT'S...
...IT.
WE'RE THROUGH.

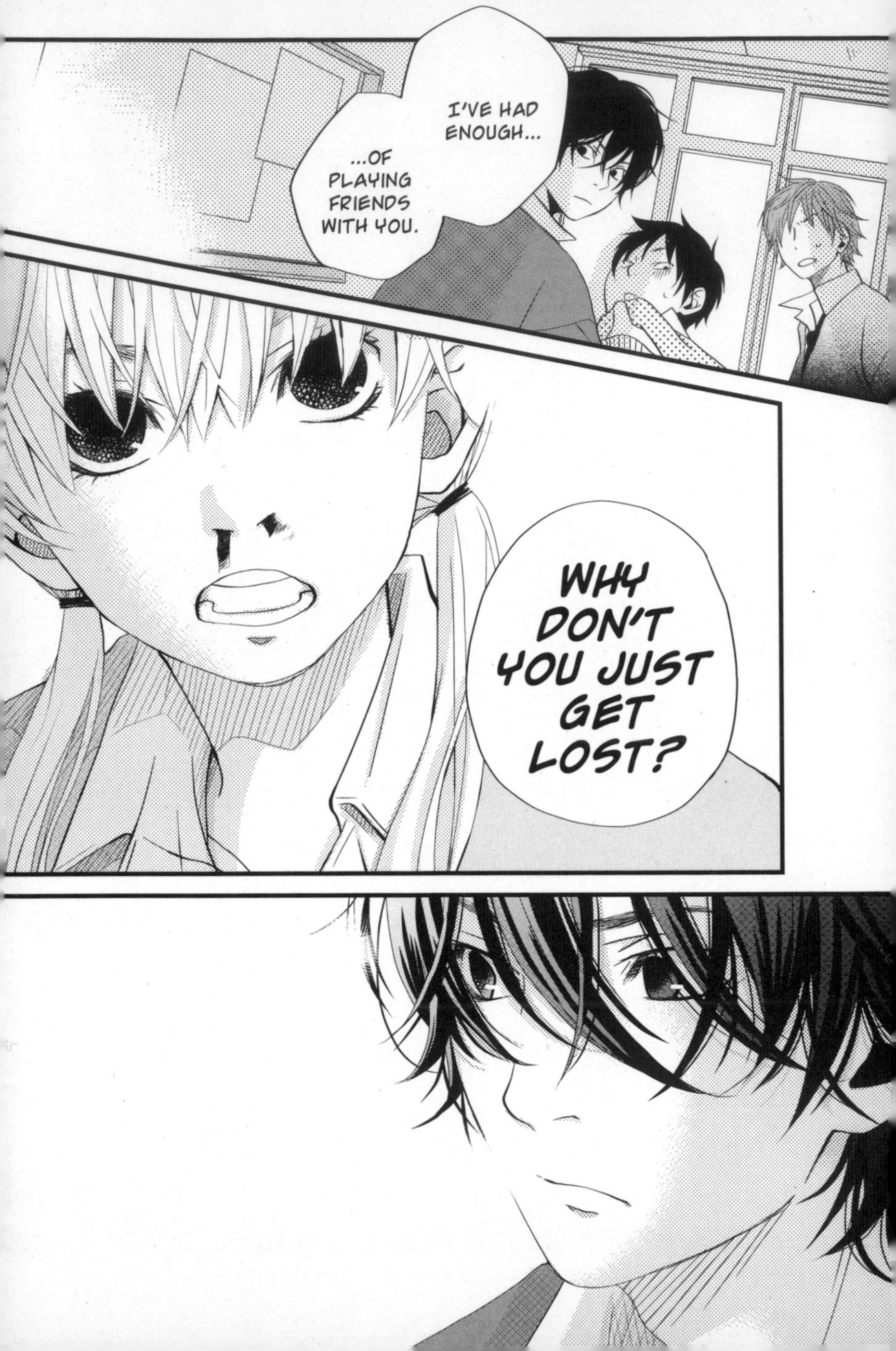
I'VE HAD ENOUGH...
...OF PLAYING FRIENDS WITH YOU.
WHY DON'T YOU JUST GET LOST?

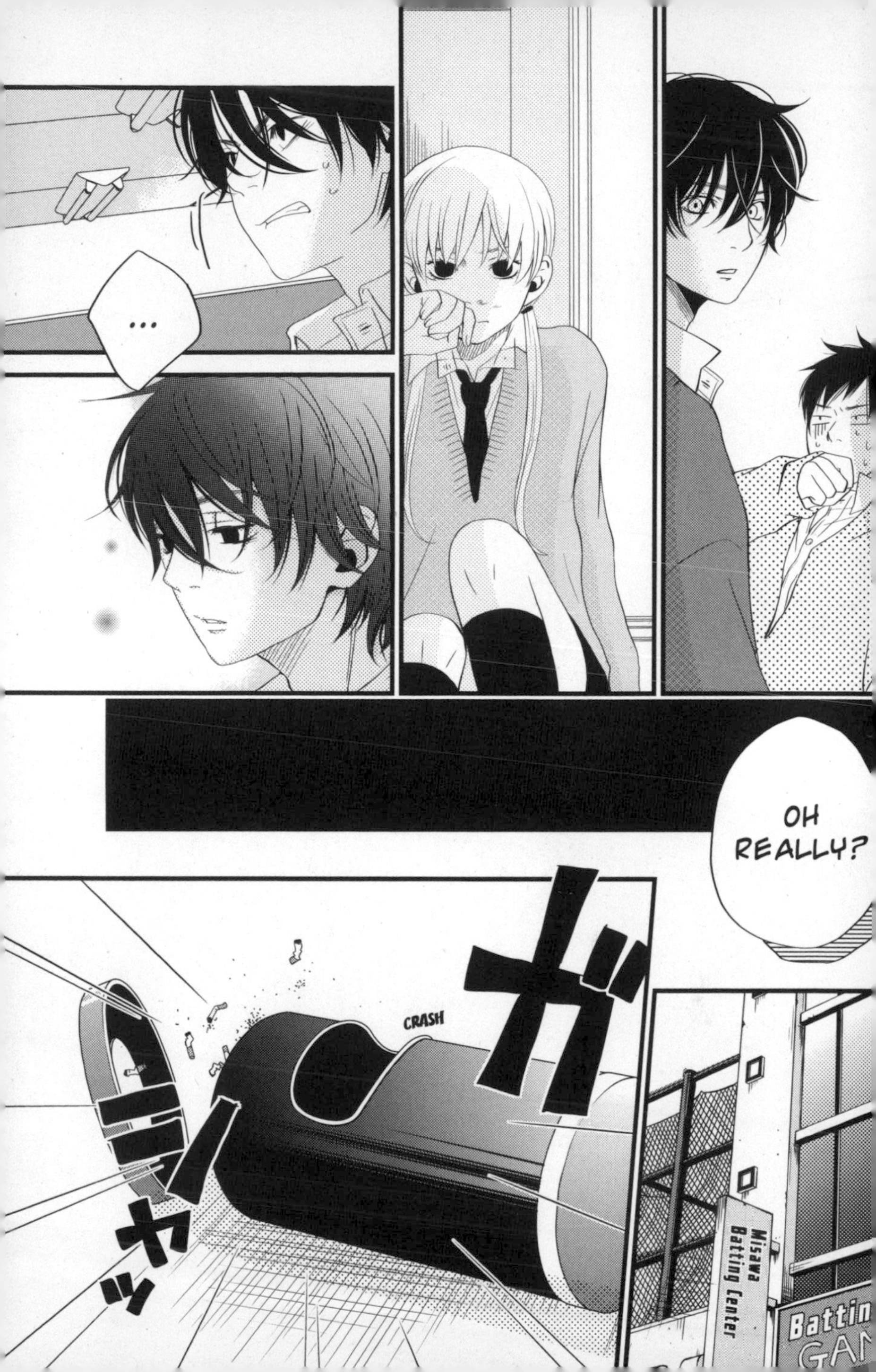
...
OH REALLY?
ガシャッ
CRASH
Misawa Batting Center

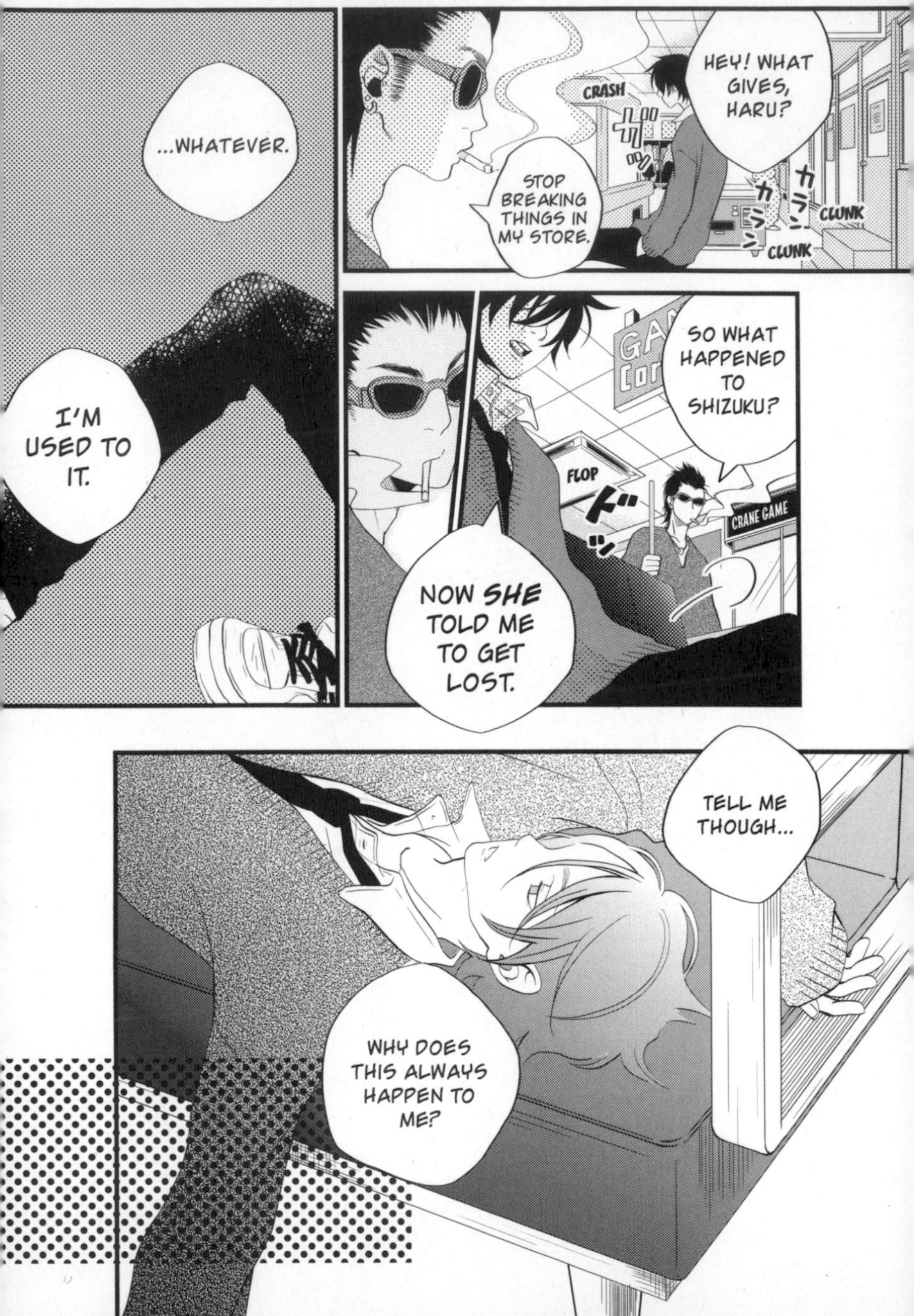
HEY! WHAT GIVES, HARU?
CRASH
STOP BREAKING THINGS IN MY STORE.
CLUNK
CLUNK
SO WHAT HAPPENED TO SHIZUKU?
CRANE GAME
FLOP
NOW *SHE* TOLD ME TO GET LOST.
...WHATEVER.
I'M USED TO IT.
TELL ME THOUGH...
WHY DOES THIS ALWAYS HAPPEN TO ME?

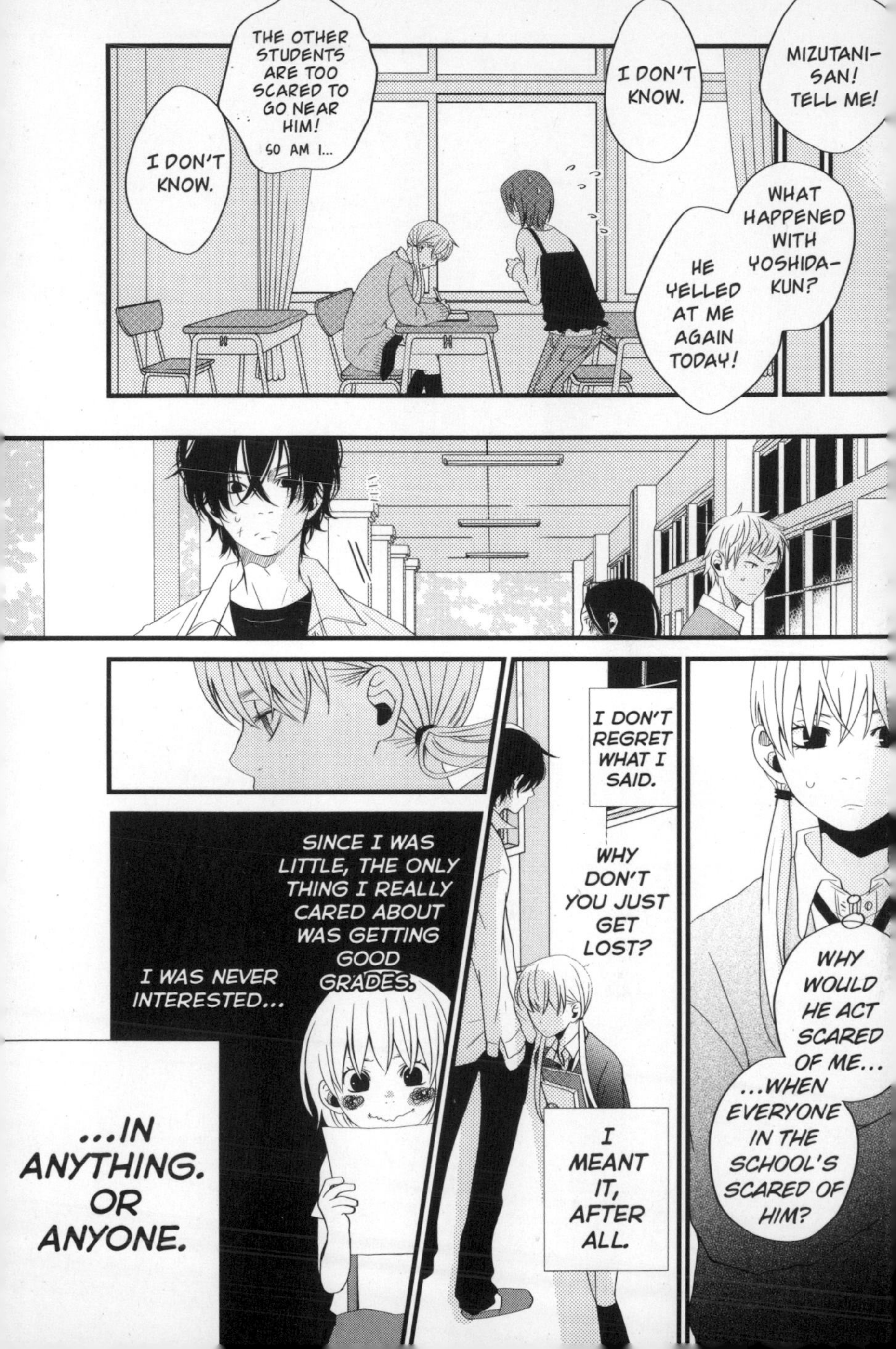
MIZUTANI-SAN! TELL ME!
WHAT HAPPENED WITH YOSHIDA-KUN?
HE YELLED AT ME AGAIN TODAY!
I DON'T KNOW.
THE OTHER STUDENTS ARE TOO SCARED TO GO NEAR HIM!
SO AM I...
I DON'T KNOW.
WHY WOULD HE ACT SCARED OF ME...
...WHEN EVERYONE IN THE SCHOOL'S SCARED OF HIM?
I DON'T REGRET WHAT I SAID.
WHY DON'T YOU JUST GET LOST?
I MEANT IT, AFTER ALL.
SINCE I WAS LITTLE, THE ONLY THING I REALLY CARED ABOUT WAS GETTING GOOD GRADES.
I WAS NEVER INTERESTED...
...IN ANYTHING. OR ANYONE.

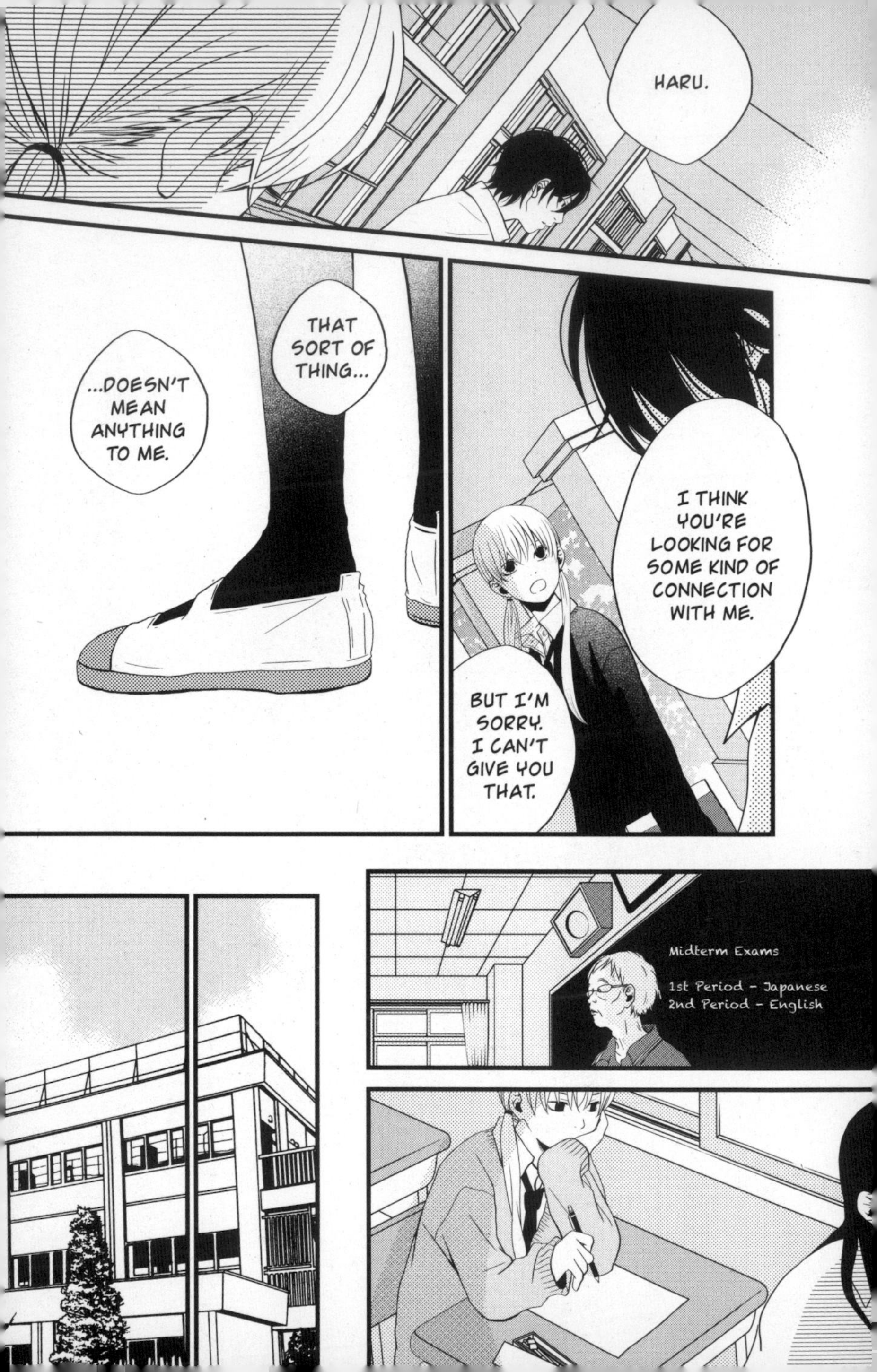
HARU.
I THINK YOU'RE LOOKING FOR SOME KIND OF CONNECTION WITH ME.
BUT I'M SORRY. I CAN'T GIVE YOU THAT.
THAT SORT OF THING...
...DOESN'T MEAN ANYTHING TO ME.
Midterm Exams
1st Period - Japanese
2nd Period - English

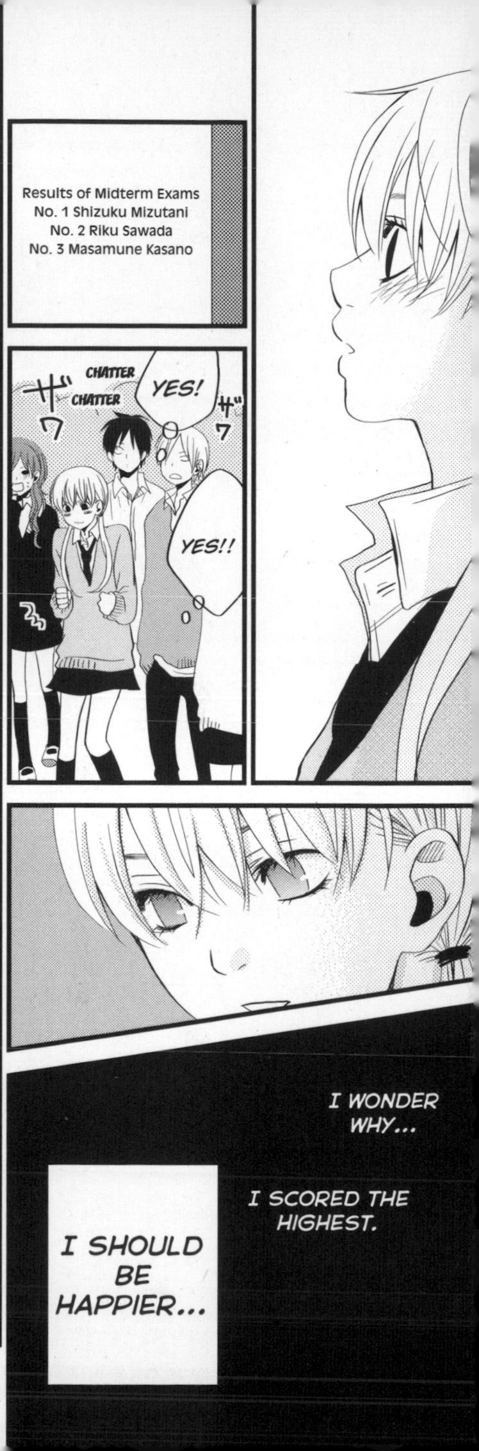
Results of Midterm Exams
No. 1 Shizuku Mizutani
No. 2 Riku Sawada
No. 3 Masamune Kasano
ザワ
YES!
CHATTER
CHATTER
ザワ
YES!!
I WONDER WHY...
I SCORED THE HIGHEST.
I SHOULD BE HAPPIER...
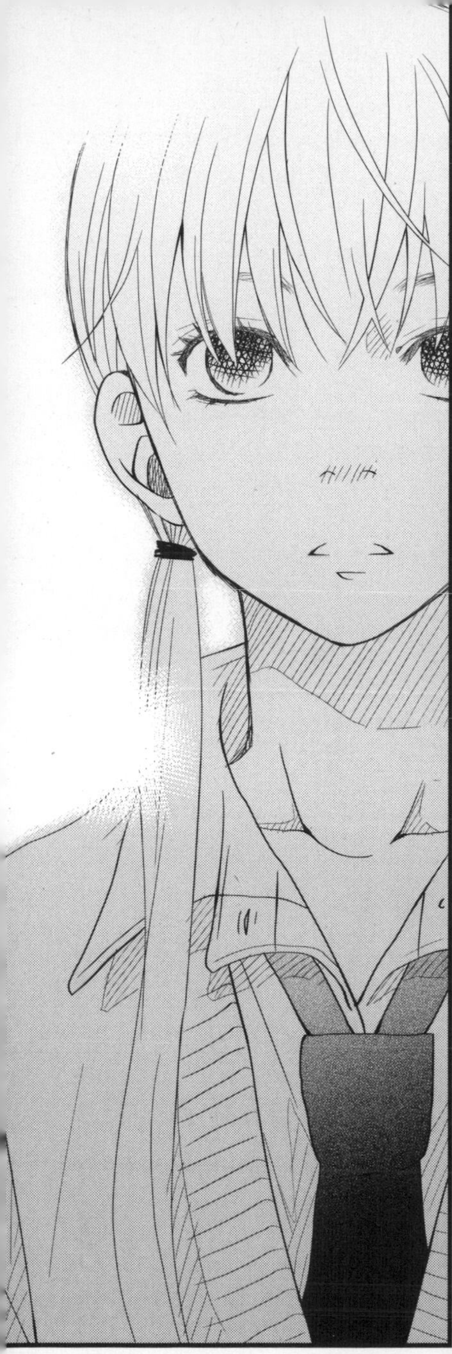

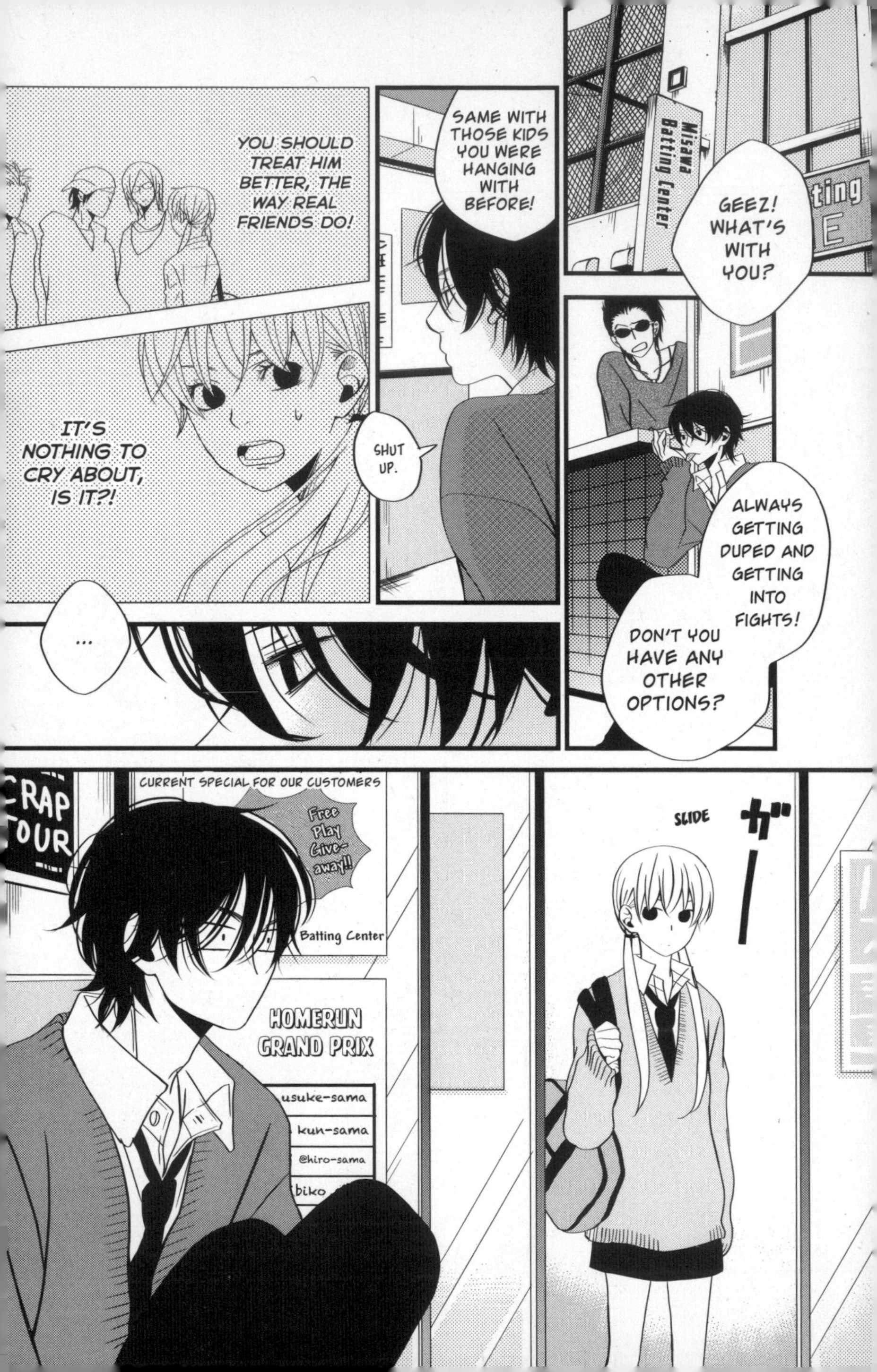
Misawa Batting Center
GEEZ! WHAT'S WITH YOU?
ALWAYS GETTING DUPED AND GETTING INTO FIGHTS!
DON'T YOU HAVE ANY OTHER OPTIONS?
SAME WITH THOSE KIDS YOU WERE HANGING WITH BEFORE!
SHUT UP.
YOU SHOULD TREAT HIM BETTER, THE WAY REAL FRIENDS DO!
IT'S NOTHING TO CRY ABOUT, IS IT?!
...
SLIDE
CURRENT SPECIAL FOR OUR CUSTOMERS
Free Play Give-away!!
Batting Center
HOMERUN GRAND PRIX
usuke-sama
kun-sama
@hiro-sama

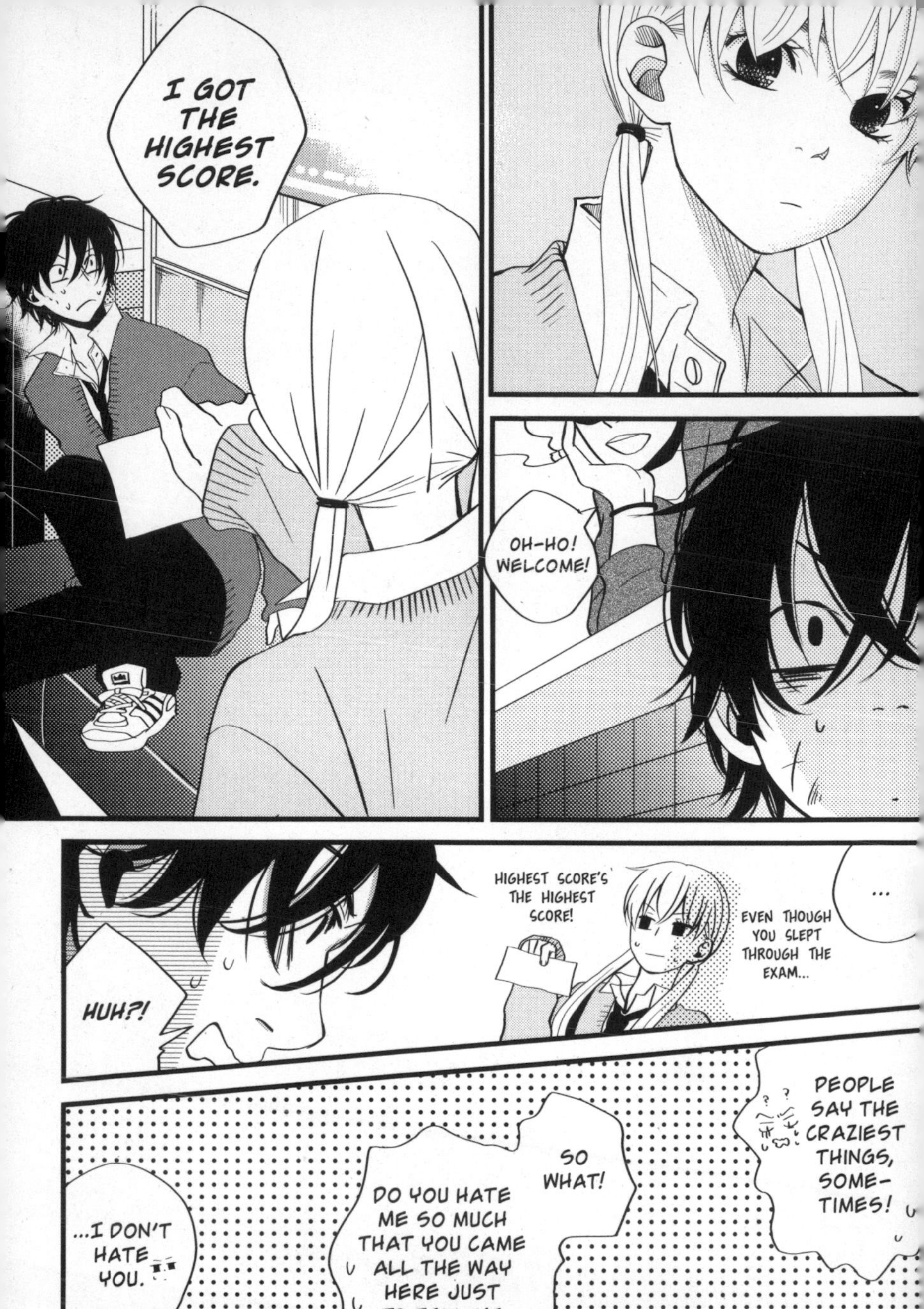
OH-HO! WELCOME!
I GOT THE HIGHEST SCORE.
...
EVEN THOUGH YOU SLEPT THROUGH THE EXAM...
HIGHEST SCORE'S THE HIGHEST SCORE!
HUH?!
PEOPLE SAY THE CRAZIEST THINGS, SOME-TIMES!
SO WHAT!
DO YOU HATE ME SO MUCH THAT YOU CAME ALL THE WAY HERE JUST TO TELL ME THAT!?
...I DON'T HATE YOU.

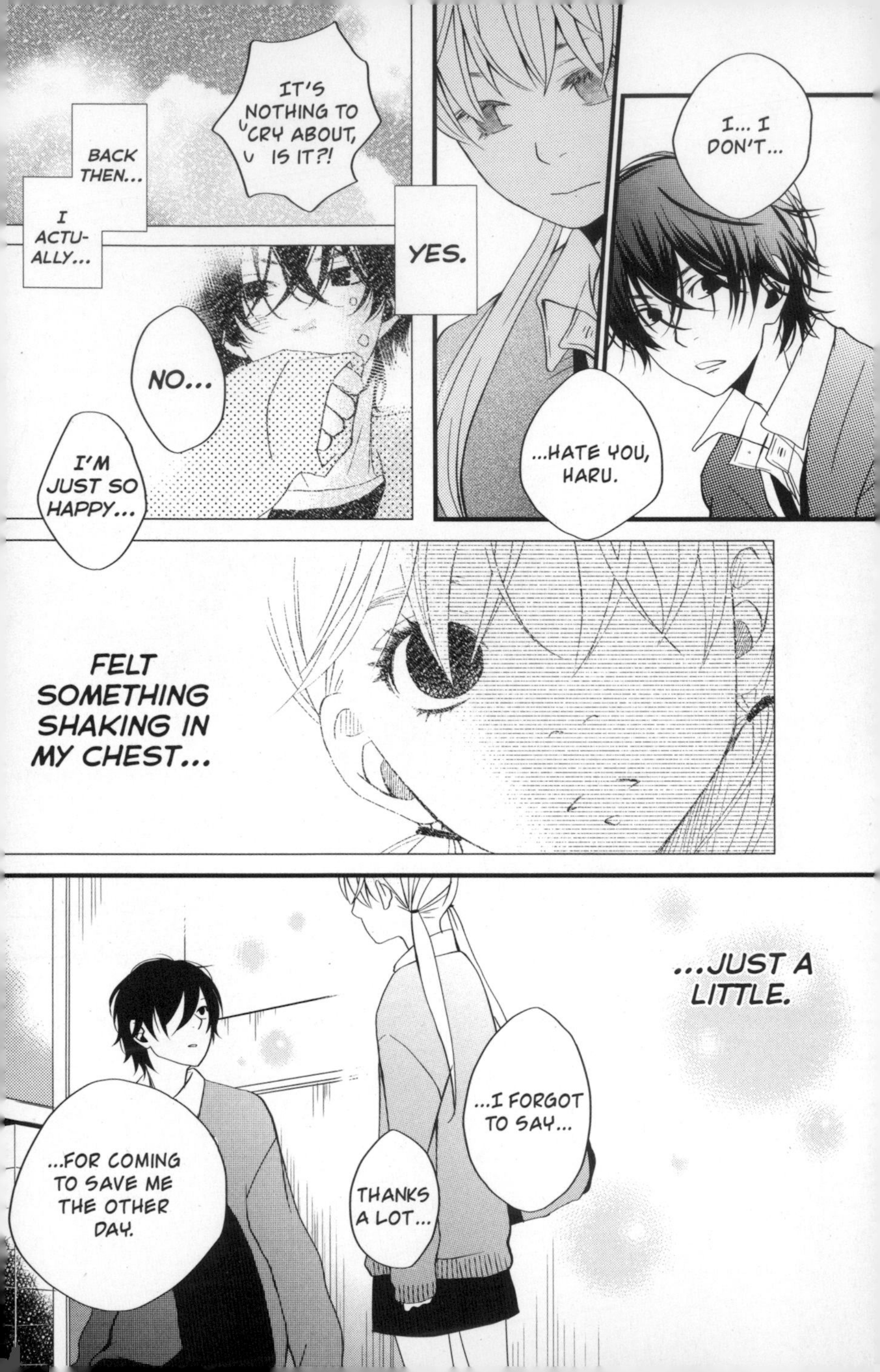
I... I DON'T...
...HATE YOU, HARU.
YES.
IT'S NOTHING TO CRY ABOUT, IS IT?!
BACK THEN...
I ACTUALLY...
NO...
I'M JUST SO HAPPY...
FELT SOMETHING SHAKING IN MY CHEST...
...JUST A LITTLE.
...I FORGOT TO SAY...
THANKS A LOT...
...FOR COMING TO SAVE ME THE OTHER DAY.

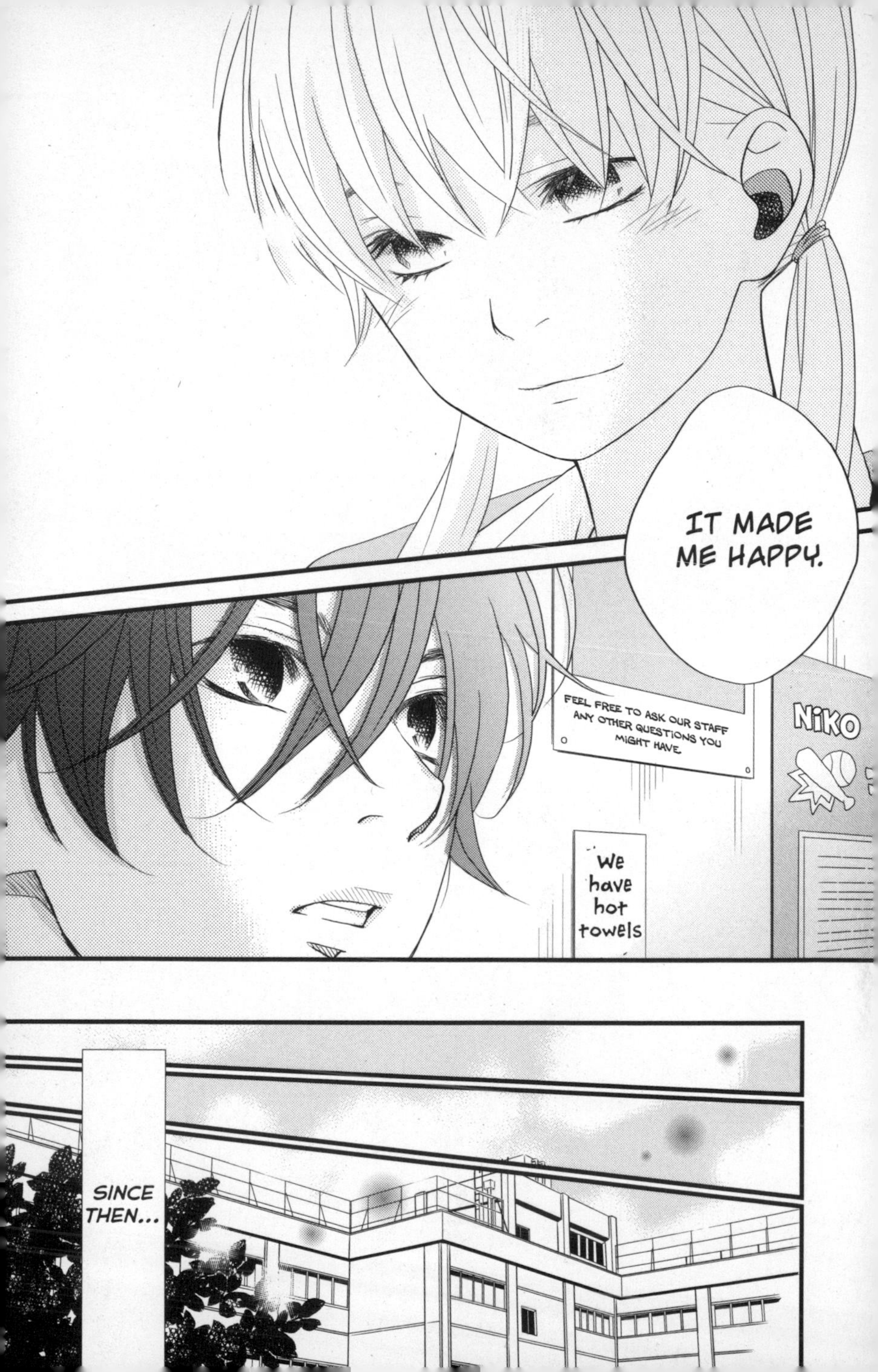
IT MADE ME HAPPY.
FEEL FREE TO ASK OUR STAFF ANY OTHER QUESTIONS YOU MIGHT HAVE.
NiKO
We have hot towels
SINCE THEN...

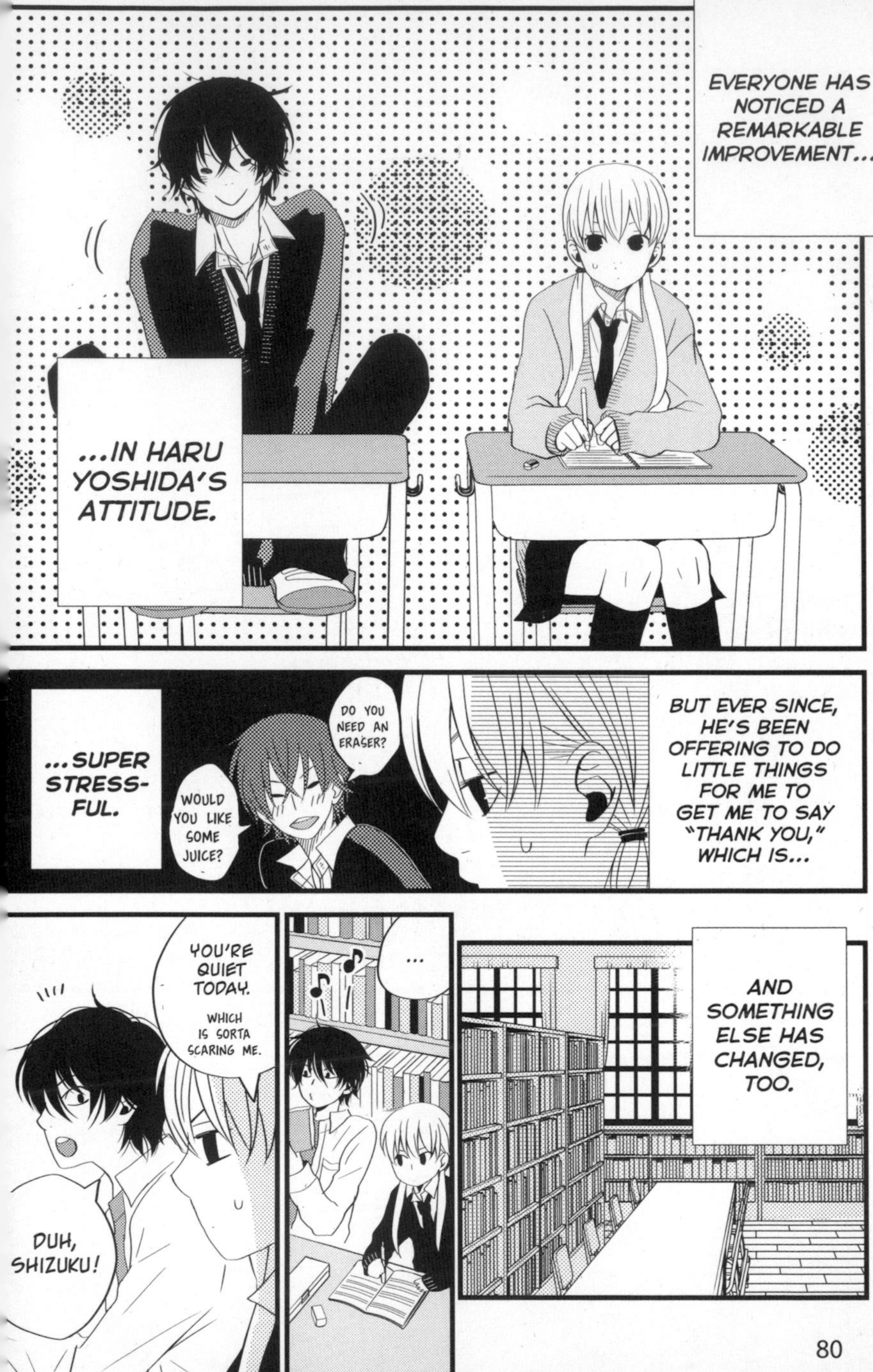
EVERYONE HAS NOTICED A REMARKABLE IMPROVEMENT...
...IN HARU YOSHIDA'S ATTITUDE.
BUT EVER SINCE, HE'S BEEN OFFERING TO DO LITTLE THINGS FOR ME TO GET ME TO SAY "THANK YOU," WHICH IS...
DO YOU NEED AN ERASER?
WOULD YOU LIKE SOME JUICE?
...SUPER STRESS-FUL.
AND SOMETHING ELSE HAS CHANGED, TOO.
...
YOU'RE QUIET TODAY.
WHICH IS SORTA SCARING ME.
DUH, SHIZUKU!

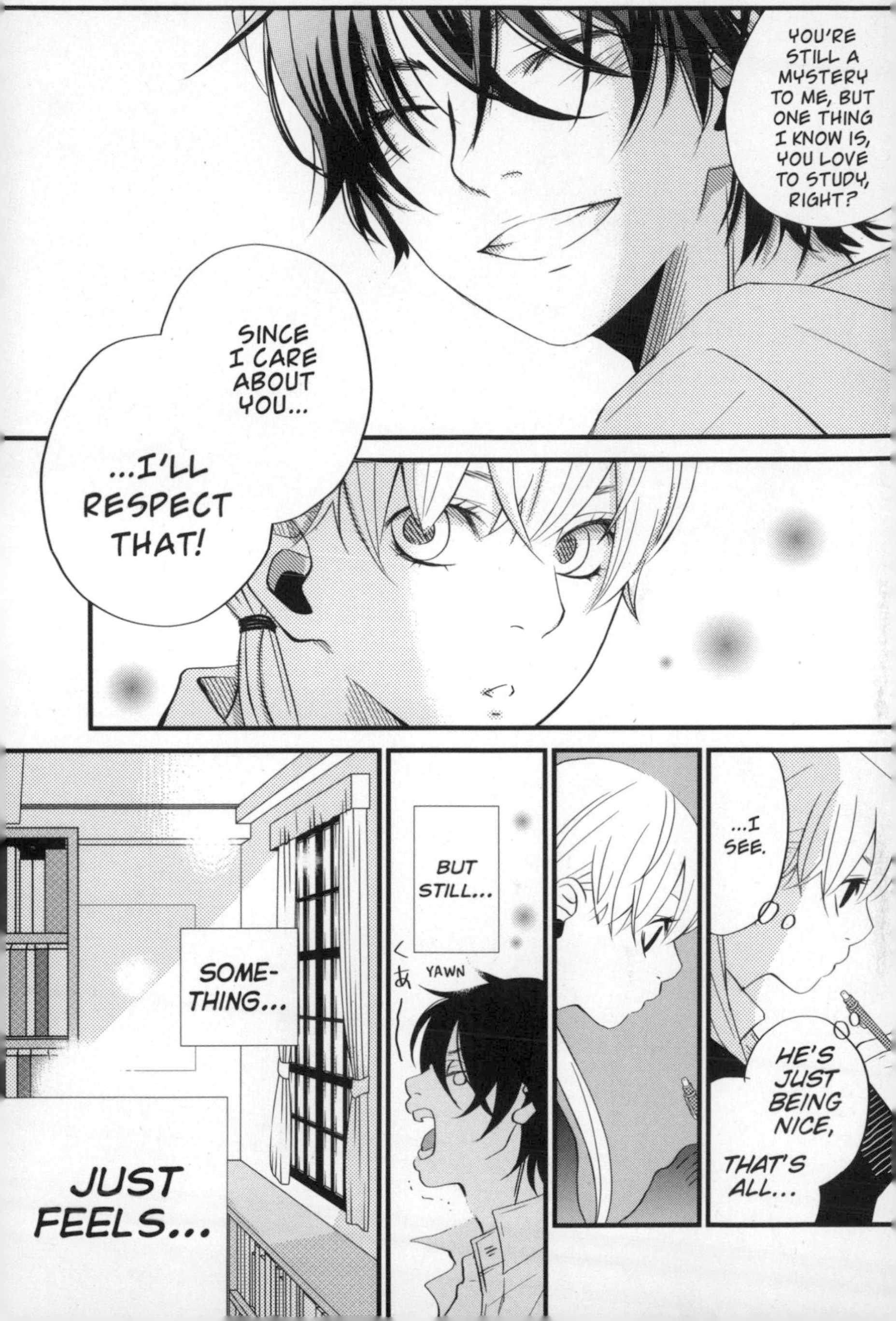
YOU'RE STILL A MYSTERY TO ME, BUT ONE THING I KNOW IS, YOU LOVE TO STUDY, RIGHT?
SINCE I CARE ABOUT YOU...
...I'LL RESPECT THAT!
...I SEE.
HE'S JUST BEING NICE,
THAT'S ALL...
BUT STILL...
くあ
YAWN
SOME-THING...
JUST FEELS...

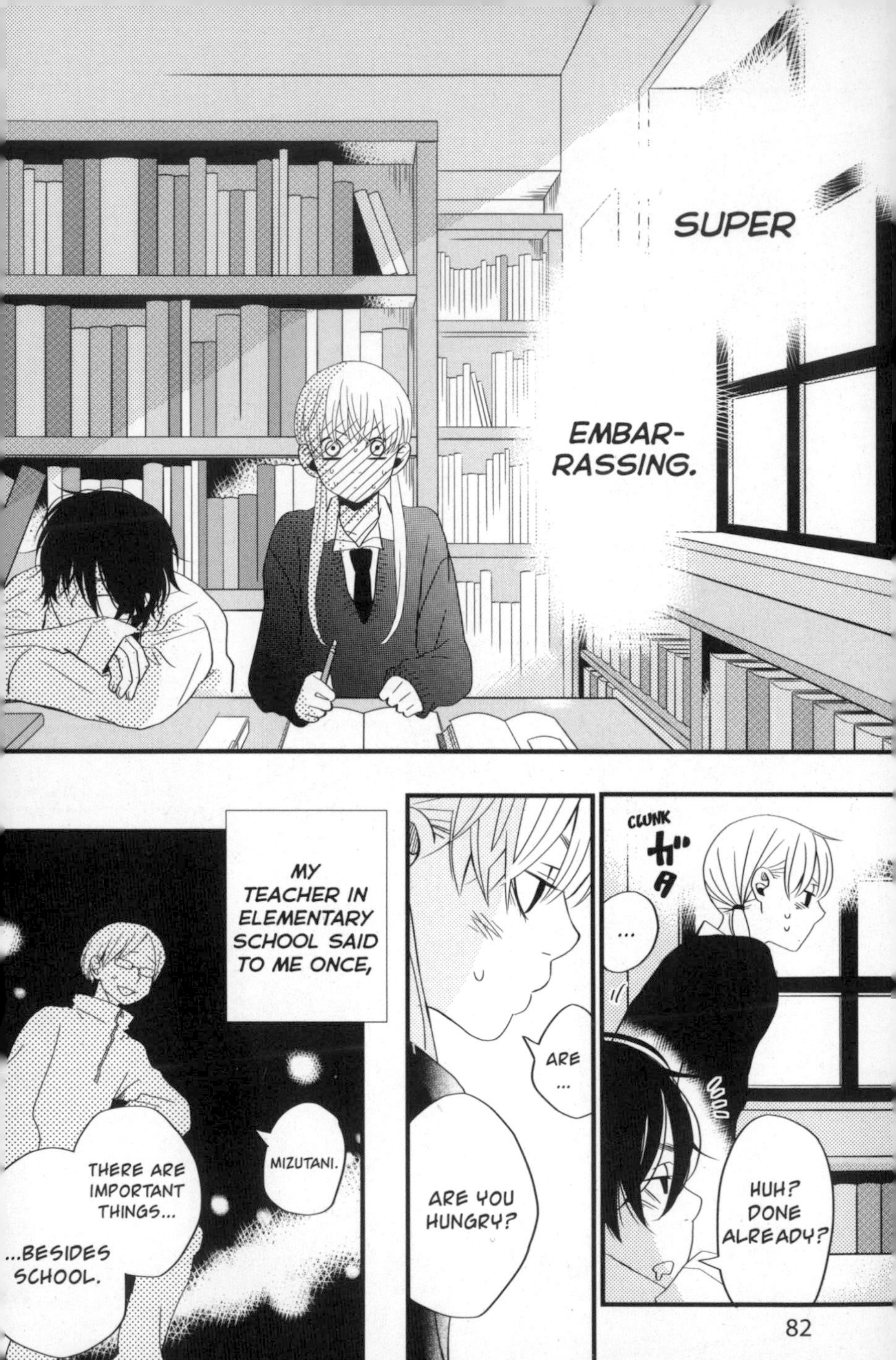
SUPER
EMBAR-RASSING.
CLUNK
ガタ
...
HUH? DONE ALREADY?
ARE ...
ARE YOU HUNGRY?
MY TEACHER IN ELEMENTARY SCHOOL SAID TO ME ONCE,
MIZUTANI.
THERE ARE IMPORTANT THINGS...
...BESIDES SCHOOL.

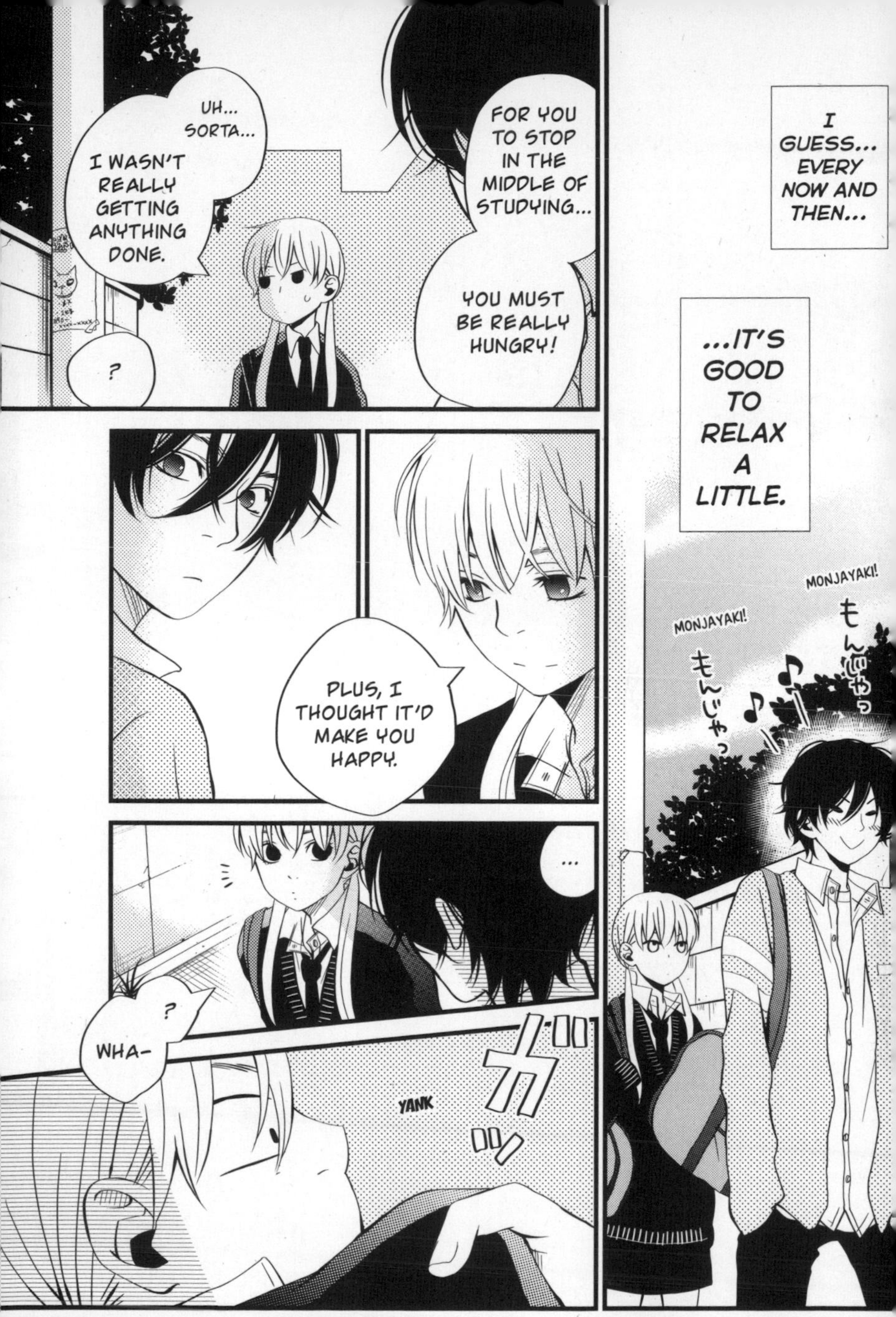
I GUESS... EVERY NOW AND THEN...
...IT'S GOOD TO RELAX A LITTLE.
MONJAYAKI!
MONJAYAKI!
FOR YOU TO STOP IN THE MIDDLE OF STUDYING...
YOU MUST BE REALLY HUNGRY!
UH... SORTA...
I WASN'T REALLY GETTING ANYTHING DONE.
?
PLUS, I THOUGHT IT'D MAKE YOU HAPPY.
...
?
WHA-
YANK

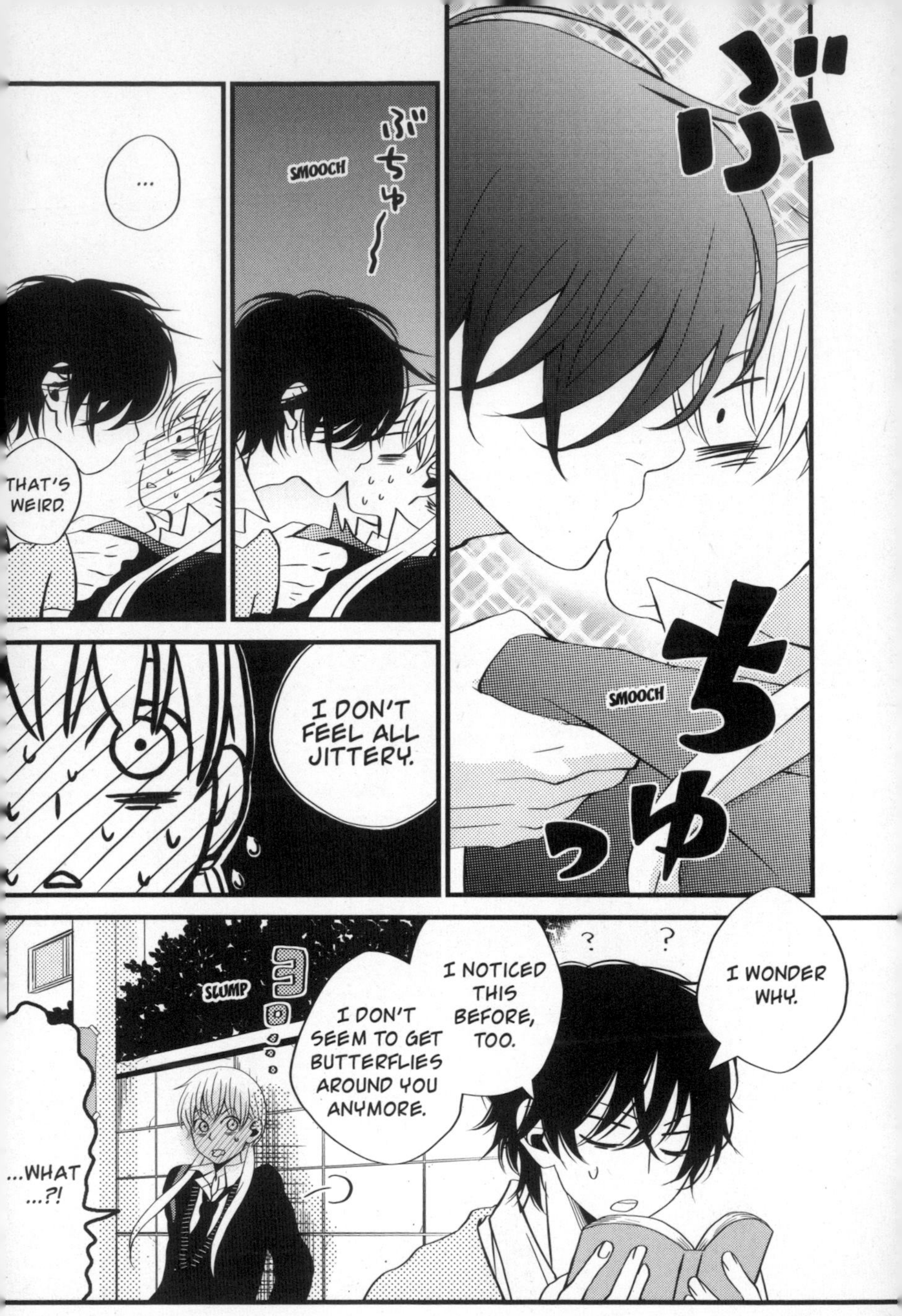
ちゅっ
SMOOCH
ぶちゅ〜〜
SMOOCH
...
THAT'S WEIRD.
I DON'T FEEL ALL JITTERY.
I WONDER WHY.
I NOTICED THIS BEFORE, TOO.
I DON'T SEEM TO GET BUTTERFLIES AROUND YOU ANYMORE.
SLUMP
...WHAT ...?!

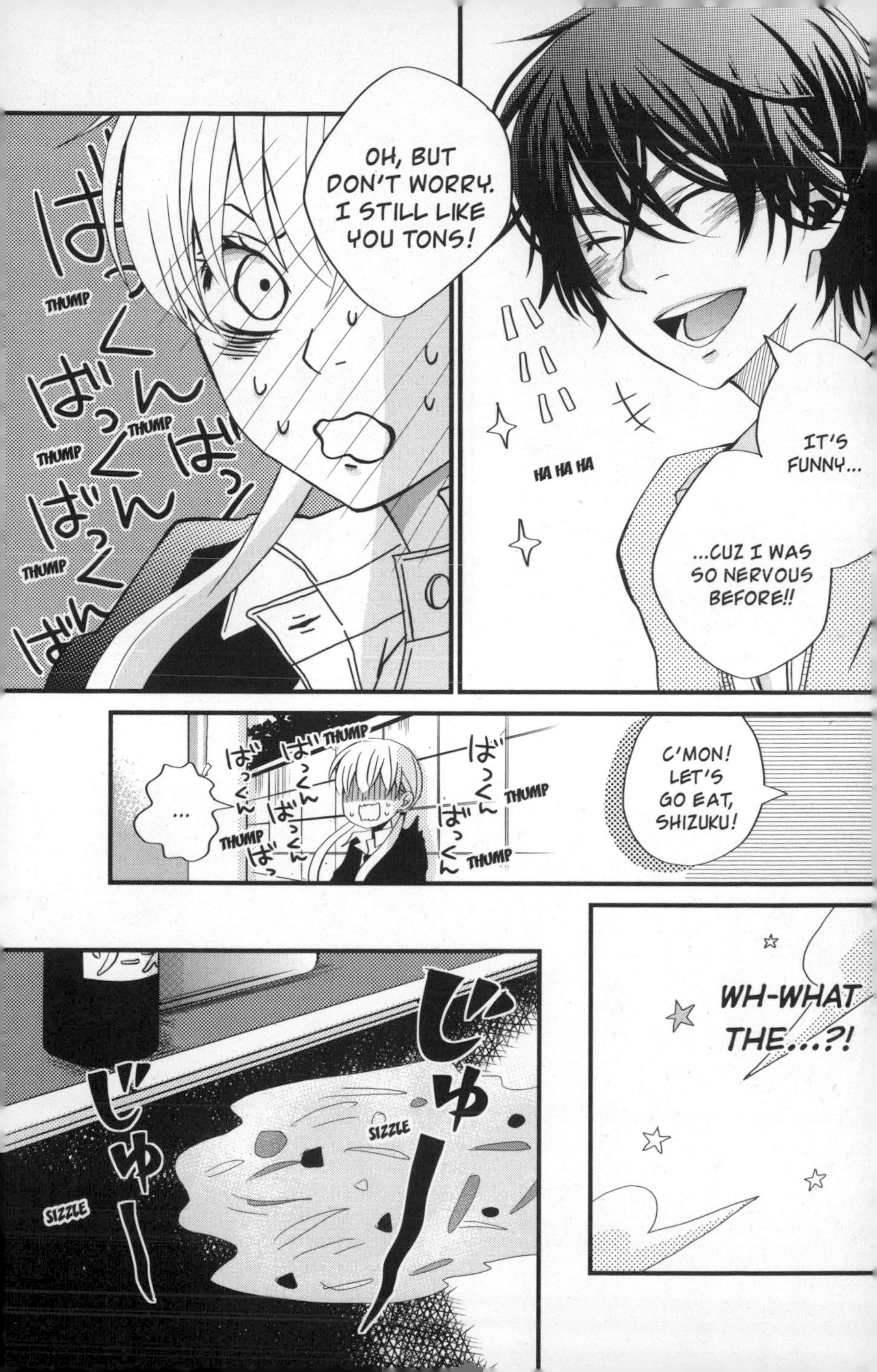
IT'S FUNNY...
...CUZ I WAS SO NERVOUS BEFORE!!
HA HA HA
OH, BUT DON'T WORRY. I STILL LIKE YOU TONS!
ばっくん ばっくん ばっくん ばっくん
THUMP
THUMP
THUMP
THUMP
C'MON! LET'S GO EAT, SHIZUKU!
...
ばっくん ばっくん ばっくん ばっくん ばっくん ばっ
THUMP
THUMP
THUMP
THUMP
WH-WHAT THE...?!
じゅー じゅー
SIZZLE
SIZZLE

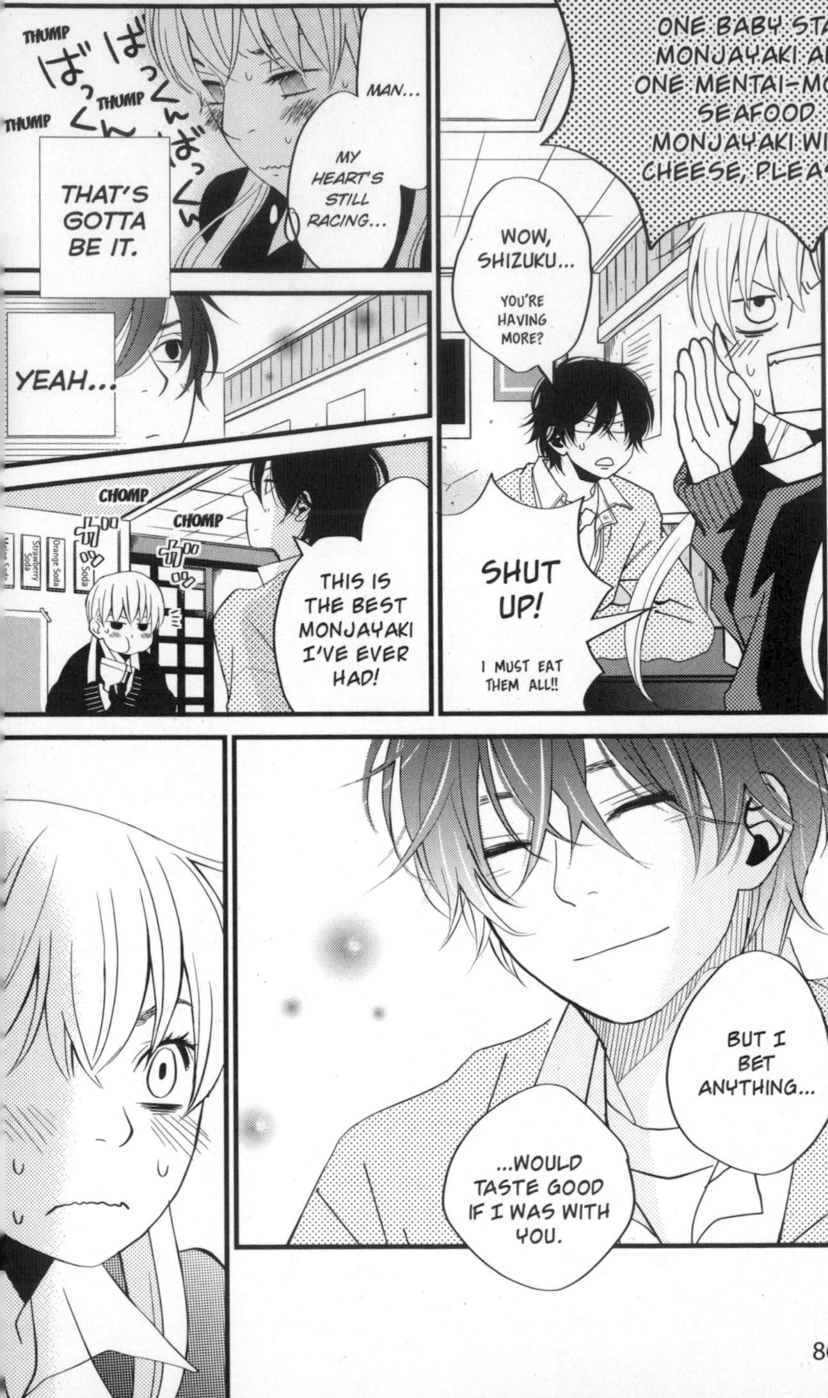
ONE BABY STAR MONJAYAKI AND ONE MENTAI-MOCHI SEAFOOD MONJAYAKI WITH CHEESE, PLEASE!!
WOW, SHIZUKU...
YOU'RE HAVING MORE?
SHUT UP!
I MUST EAT THEM ALL!!
THUMP
ばっくん
THUMP
ばっくん
THUMP
MAN...
MY HEART'S STILL RACING...
THAT'S GOTTA BE IT.
YEAH...
CHOMP
ガッ
CHOMP
ガッ
Strawberry Soda
Orange Soda
Soda
THIS IS THE BEST MONJAYAKI I'VE EVER HAD!
BUT I BET ANYTHING...
...WOULD TASTE GOOD IF I WAS WITH YOU.

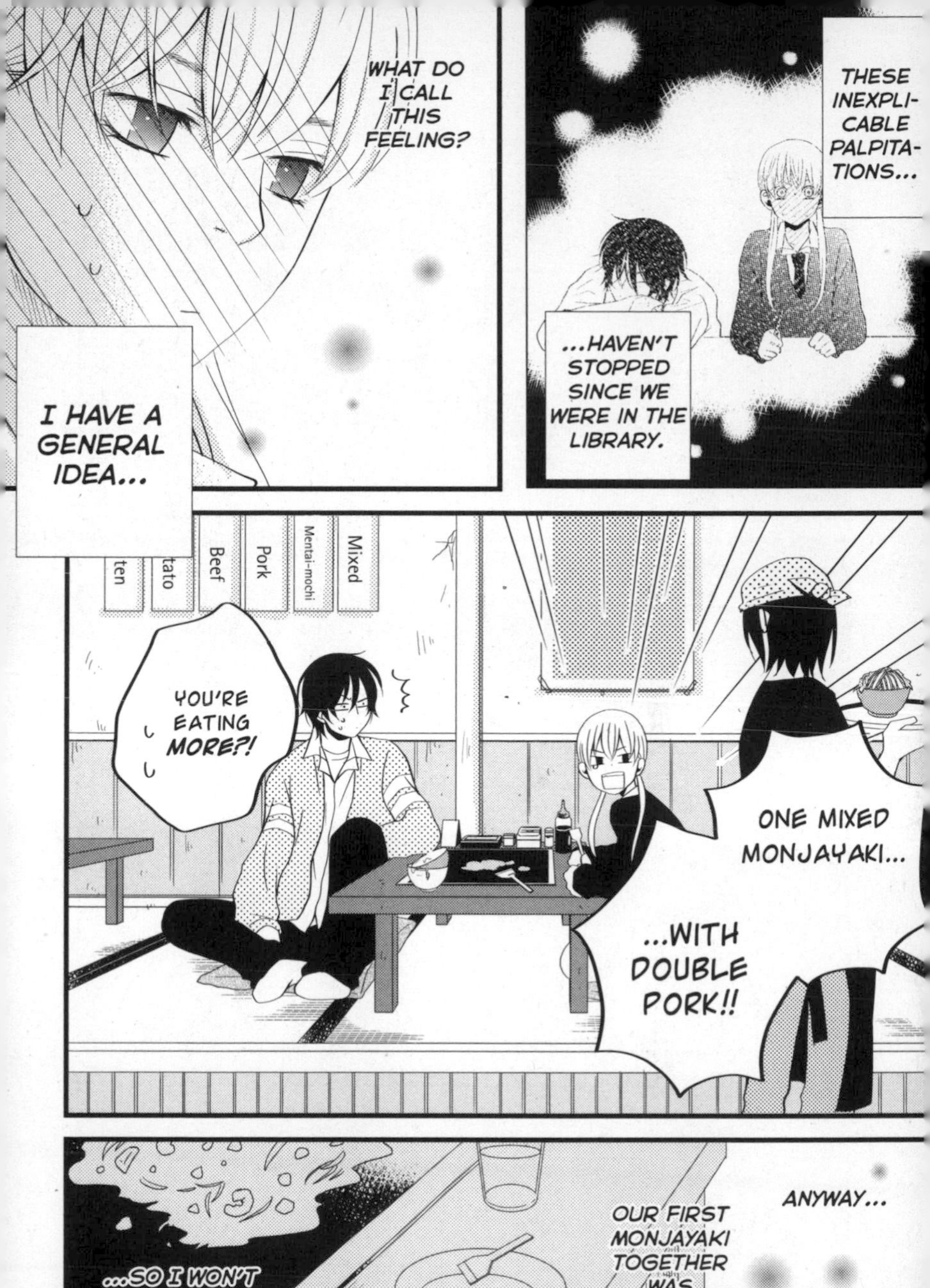
THESE INEXPLICABLE PALPITATIONS...
...HAVEN'T STOPPED SINCE WE WERE IN THE LIBRARY.
WHAT DO I CALL THIS FEELING?
I HAVE A GENERAL IDEA...
Mixed
Mentai-mochi
Pork
Beef
tato
ten
ONE MIXED MONJAYAKI...
...WITH DOUBLE PORK!!
YOU'RE EATING MORE?!
ANYWAY...
OUR FIRST MONJAYAKI TOGETHER WAS DELICIOUS...
...SO I WON'T WORRY ABOUT IT.

BECAUSE SHE'S A LADY

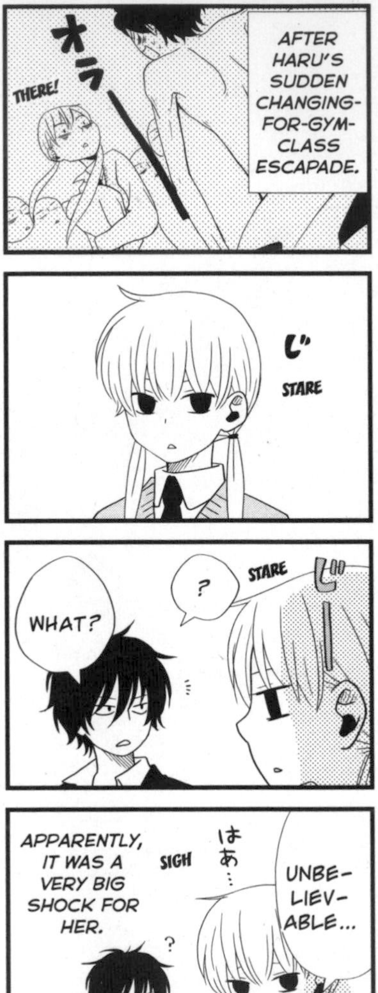
AFTER HARU'S SUDDEN CHANGING-FOR-GYM-CLASS ESCAPADE.
オラ
THERE!
じ
STARE
じー
STARE
?
WHAT?
UNBE-LIEV-ABLE...
はあ…
SIGH
APPARENTLY, IT WAS A VERY BIG SHOCK FOR HER.
?

IT'S HARD NOT TO SAY IT

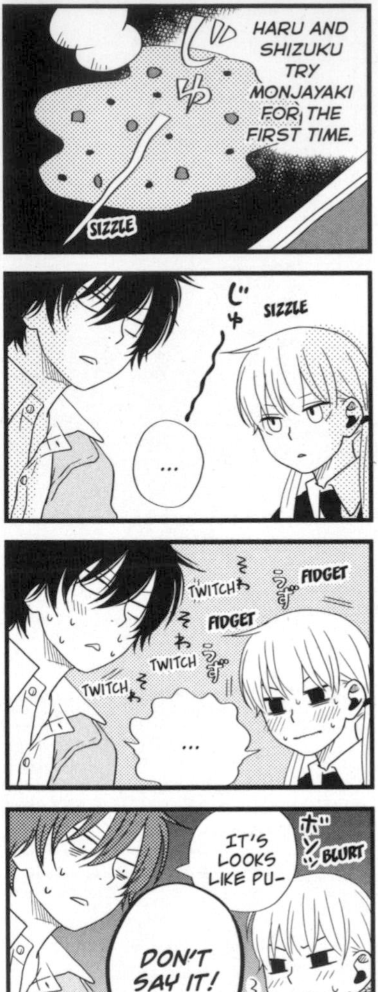
HARU AND SHIZUKU TRY MONJAYAKI FOR THE FIRST TIME.
じゅ
SIZZLE
じゅ
SIZZLE
...
うず
FIDGET
そわ
TWITCH
うず
FIDGET
そわ
TWITCH
そわ
TWITCH
...
ボソッ
BLURT
IT'S LOOKS LIKE PU-
DON'T SAY IT!

Chapter 3 Weird

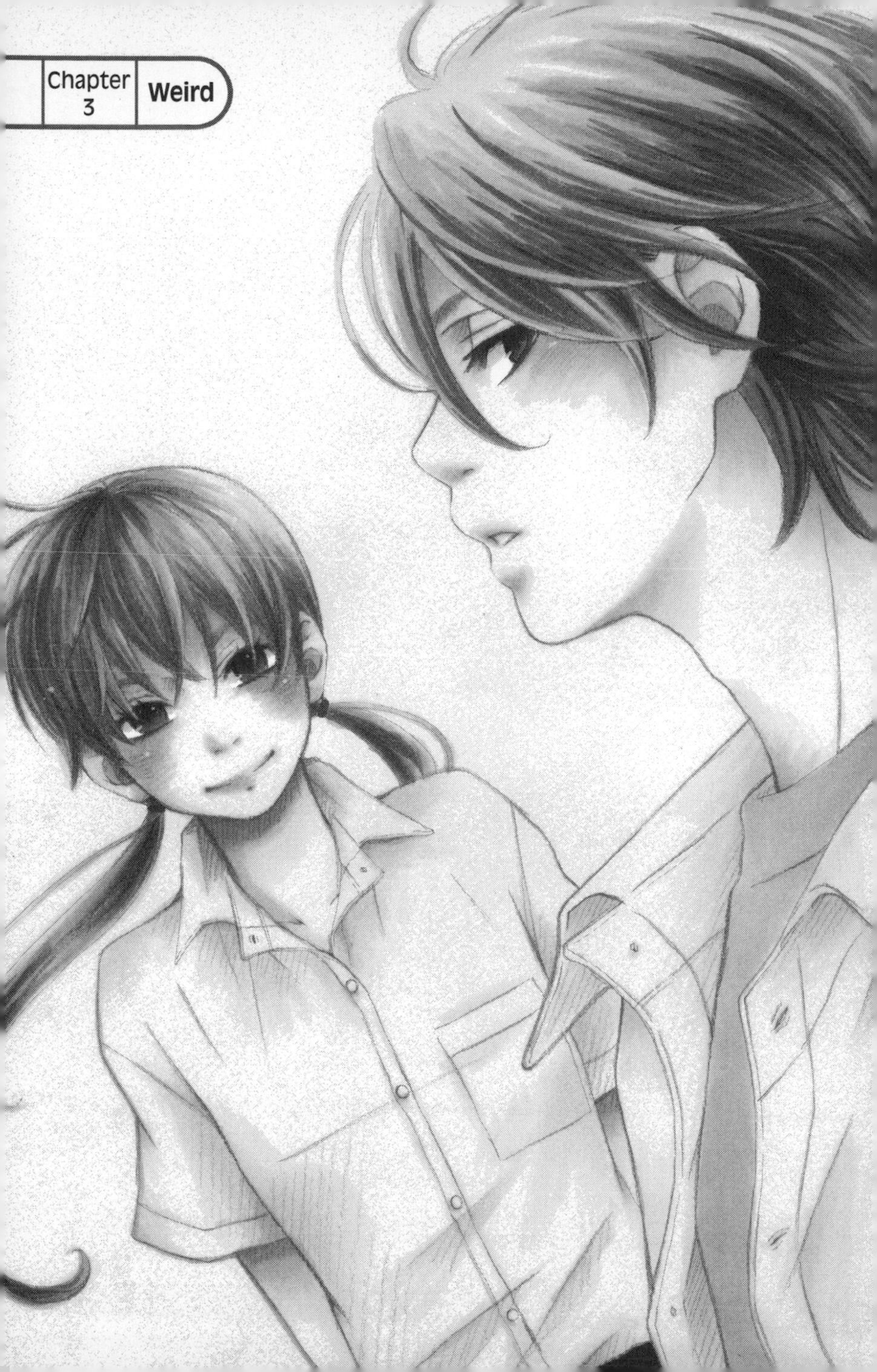

During the Midterms

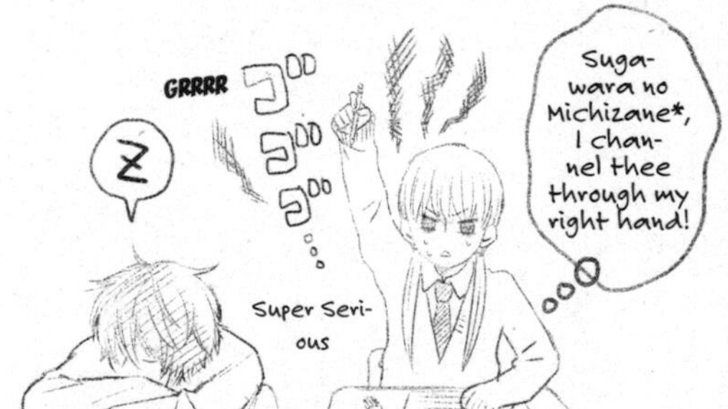
Suga-wara no Michizane*, I chan-nel thee through my right hand!
Super Seri-ous
GRRRR
Z

*Heian Period Scholar, Poet and Politician.

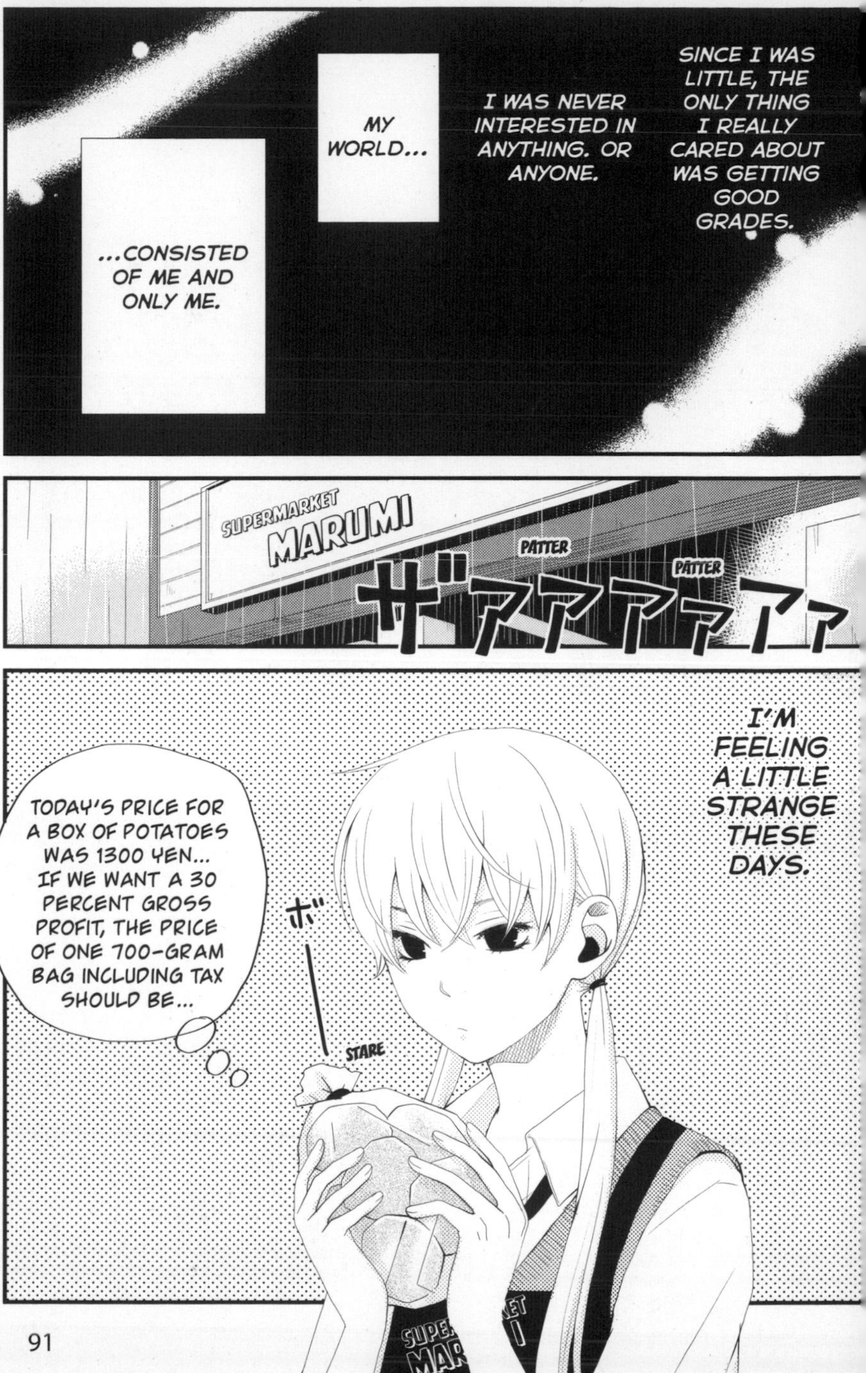
SINCE I WAS LITTLE, THE ONLY THING I REALLY CARED ABOUT WAS GETTING GOOD GRADES.
I WAS NEVER INTERESTED IN ANYTHING. OR ANYONE.
MY WORLD...
...CONSISTED OF ME AND ONLY ME.
SUPERMARKET MARUMI
PATTER
PATTER
ザアアァアァ
I'M FEELING A LITTLE STRANGE THESE DAYS.
TODAY'S PRICE FOR A BOX OF POTATOES WAS 1300 YEN... IF WE WANT A 30 PERCENT GROSS PROFIT, THE PRICE OF ONE 700-GRAM BAG INCLUDING TAX SHOULD BE...
ボ
STARE

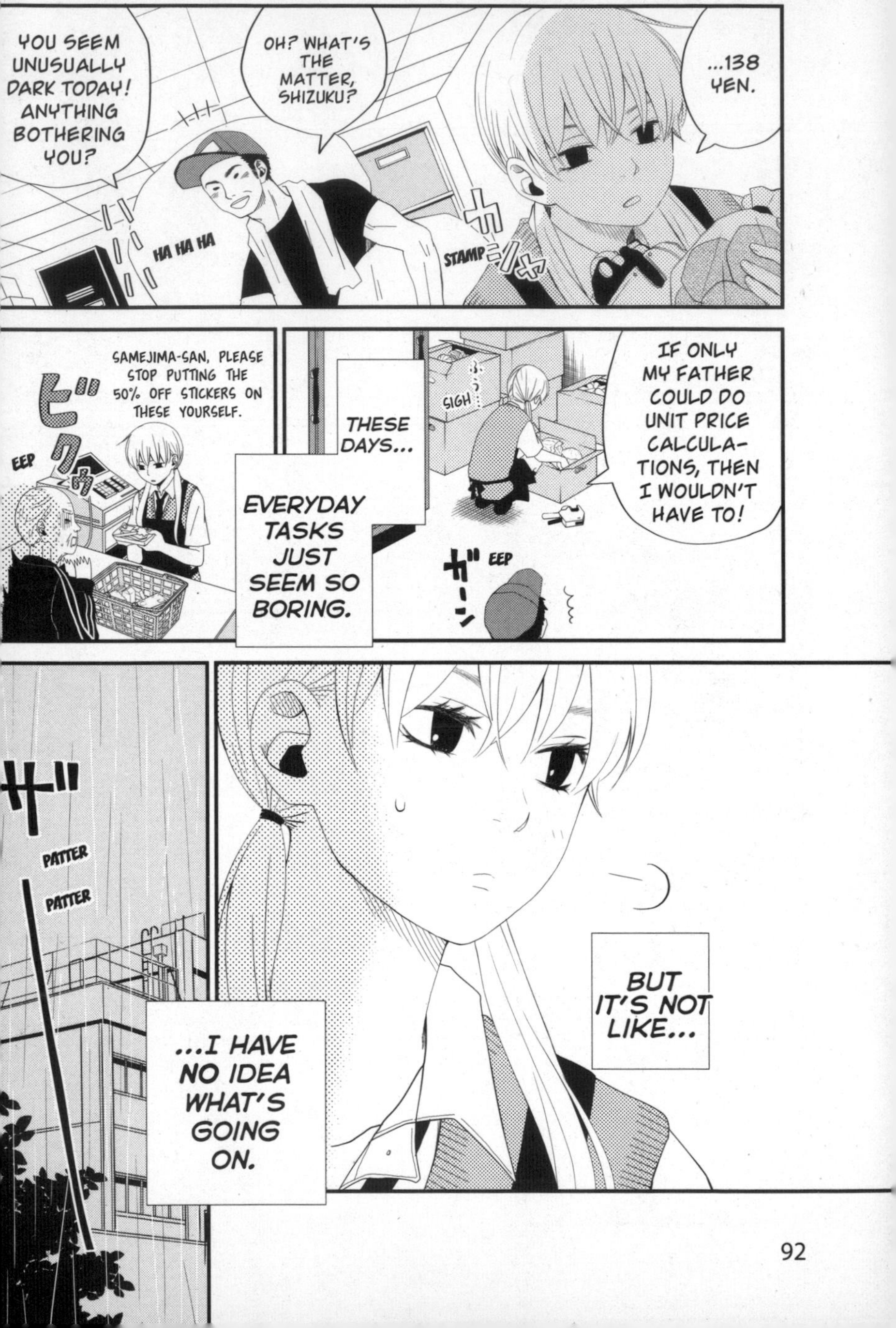

...138 YEN.
STAMP
OH? WHAT'S THE MATTER, SHIZUKU?
YOU SEEM UNUSUALLY DARK TODAY! ANYTHING BOTHERING YOU?
HA HA HA
IF ONLY MY FATHER COULD DO UNIT PRICE CALCULA-TIONS, THEN I WOULDN'T HAVE TO!
SIGH
THESE DAYS...
EEP
EVERYDAY TASKS JUST SEEM SO BORING.
SAMEJIMA-SAN, PLEASE STOP PUTTING THE 50% OFF STICKERS ON THESE YOURSELF.
EEP
BUT IT'S NOT LIKE...
...I HAVE NO IDEA WHAT'S GOING ON.
PATTER
PATTER

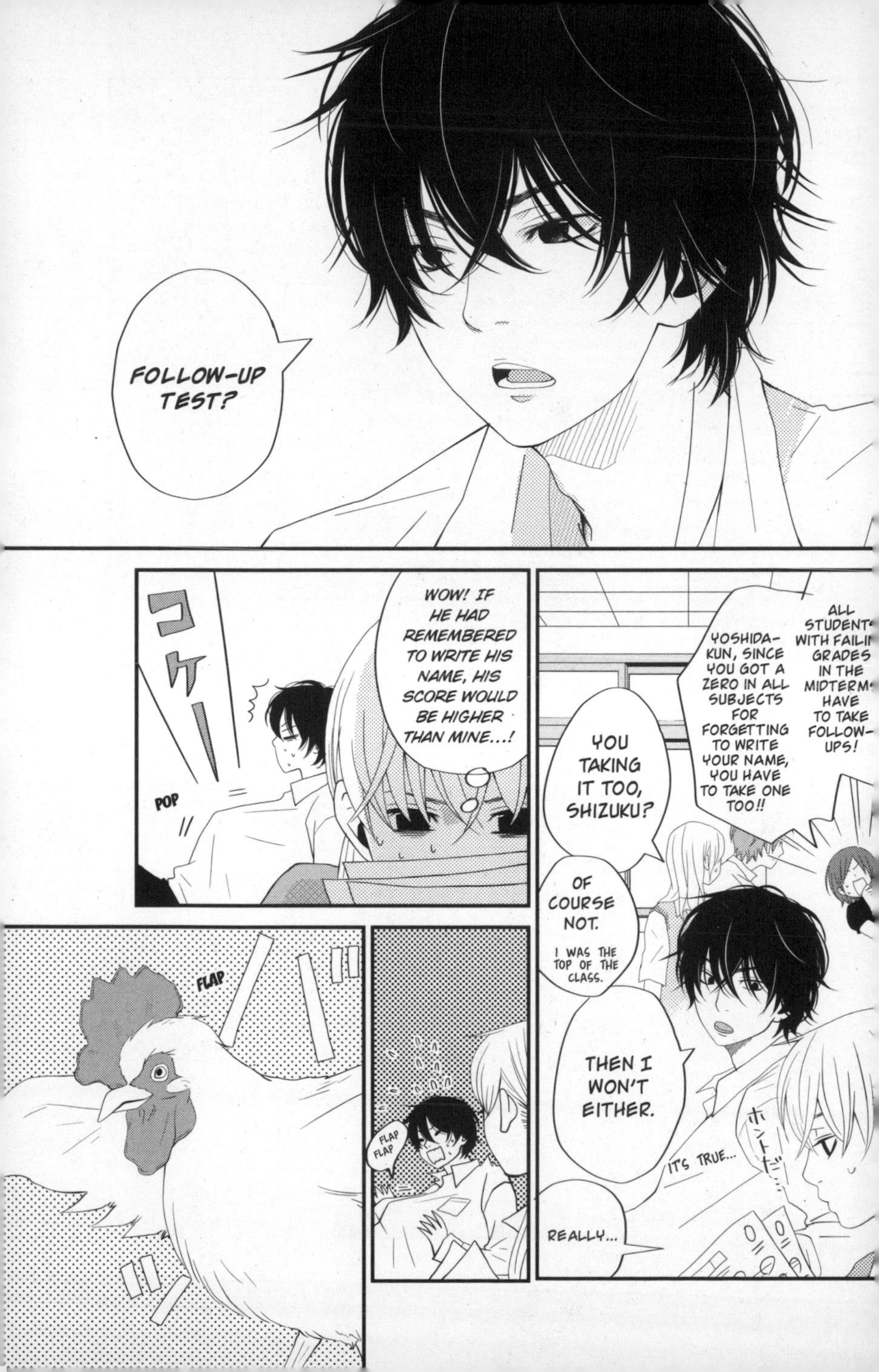
FOLLOW-UP TEST?
ALL STUDENT WITH FAILIN GRADES IN THE MIDTERM HAVE TO TAKE FOLLOW-UPS!
YOSHIDA-KUN, SINCE YOU GOT A ZERO IN ALL SUBJECTS FOR FORGETTING TO WRITE YOUR NAME, YOU HAVE TO TAKE ONE TOO!!
YOU TAKING IT TOO, SHIZUKU?
OF COURSE NOT.
I WAS THE TOP OF THE CLASS.
THEN I WON'T EITHER.
ホントだ…
IT'S TRUE...
REALLY...
WOW! IF HE HAD REMEMBERED TO WRITE HIS NAME, HIS SCORE WOULD BE HIGHER THAN MINE...!
コケー
POP
FLAP FLAP
FLAP

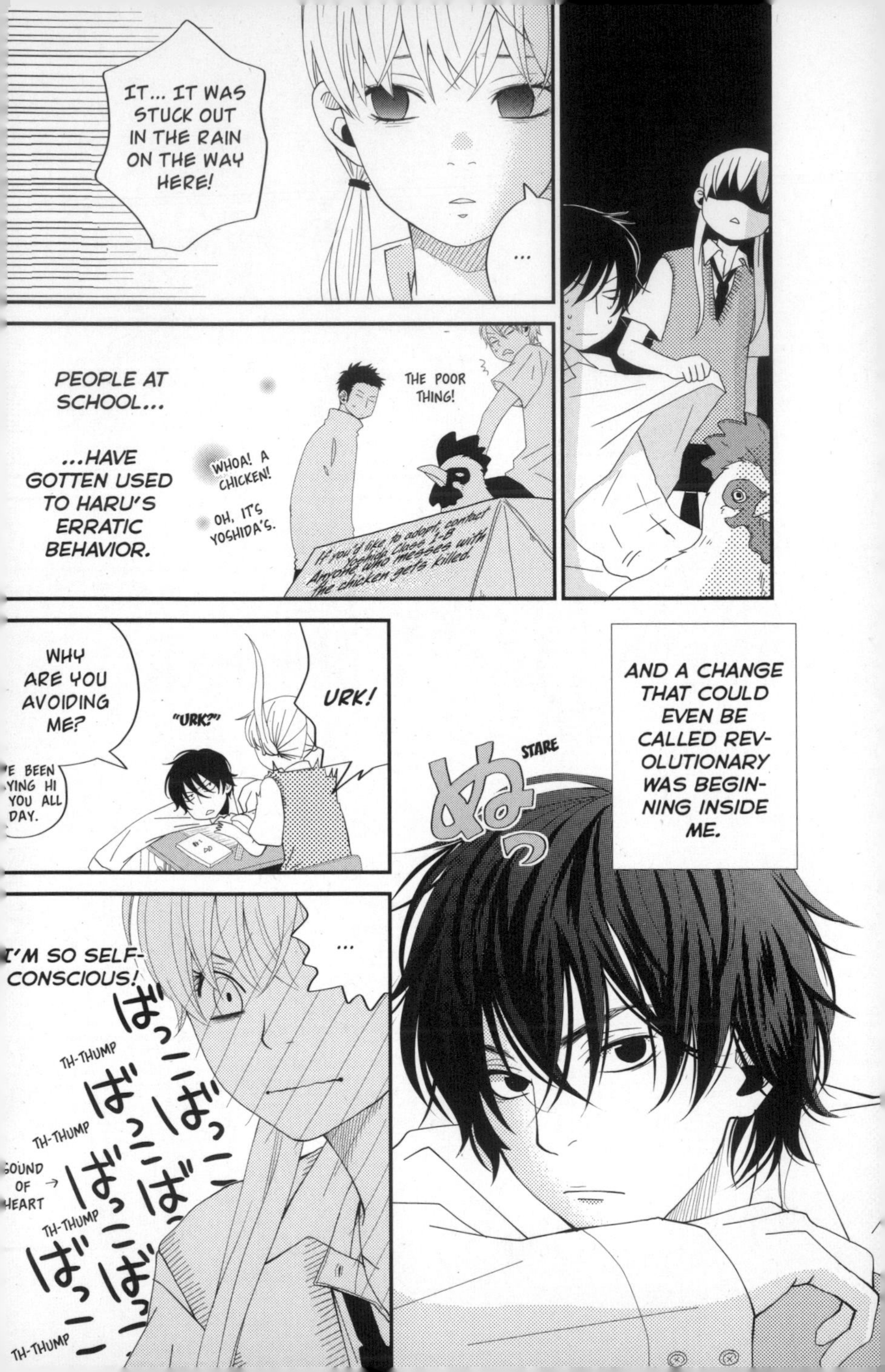
IT... IT WAS STUCK OUT IN THE RAIN ON THE WAY HERE!
...
PEOPLE AT SCHOOL...
...HAVE GOTTEN USED TO HARU'S ERRATIC BEHAVIOR.
THE POOR THING!
WHOA! A CHICKEN!
OH, IT'S YOSHIDA'S.
If you'd like to adopt, contact Yoshida Class 1-B
Anyone who messes with the chicken gets killed.
AND A CHANGE THAT COULD EVEN BE CALLED REV-OLUTIONARY WAS BEGIN-NING INSIDE ME.
ぬっ
STARE
WHY ARE YOU AVOIDING ME?
URK!
"URK?"
'E BEEN YING HI YOU ALL DAY.
...
I'M SO SELF-CONSCIOUS!
ばっこばっこばっこばっこばっこばっこ
TH-THUMP
TH-THUMP
SOUND OF → HEART
TH-THUMP
TH-THUMP

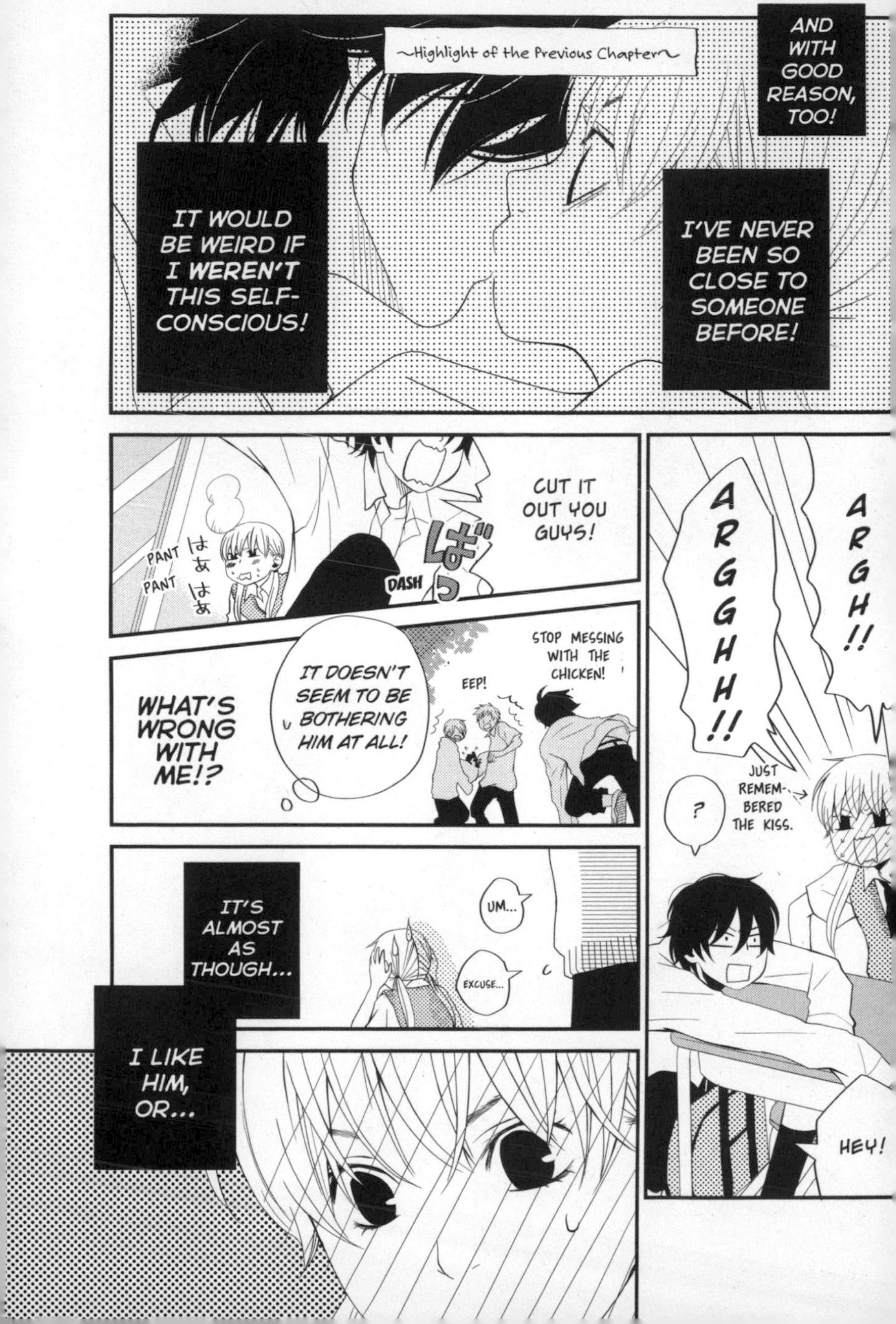
~Highlight of the Previous Chapter~
AND WITH GOOD REASON, TOO!
I'VE NEVER BEEN SO CLOSE TO SOMEONE BEFORE!
IT WOULD BE WEIRD IF I WEREN'T THIS SELF-CONSCIOUS!
ARGH!!
ARGGHH!!
JUST REMEMBERED THE KISS.
?
HEY!
CUT IT OUT YOU GUYS!
DASH
PANT PANT
STOP MESSING WITH THE CHICKEN!
EEP!
IT DOESN'T SEEM TO BE BOTHERING HIM AT ALL!
WHAT'S WRONG WITH ME!?
UM...
EXCUSE...
IT'S ALMOST AS THOUGH...
I LIKE HIM, OR...

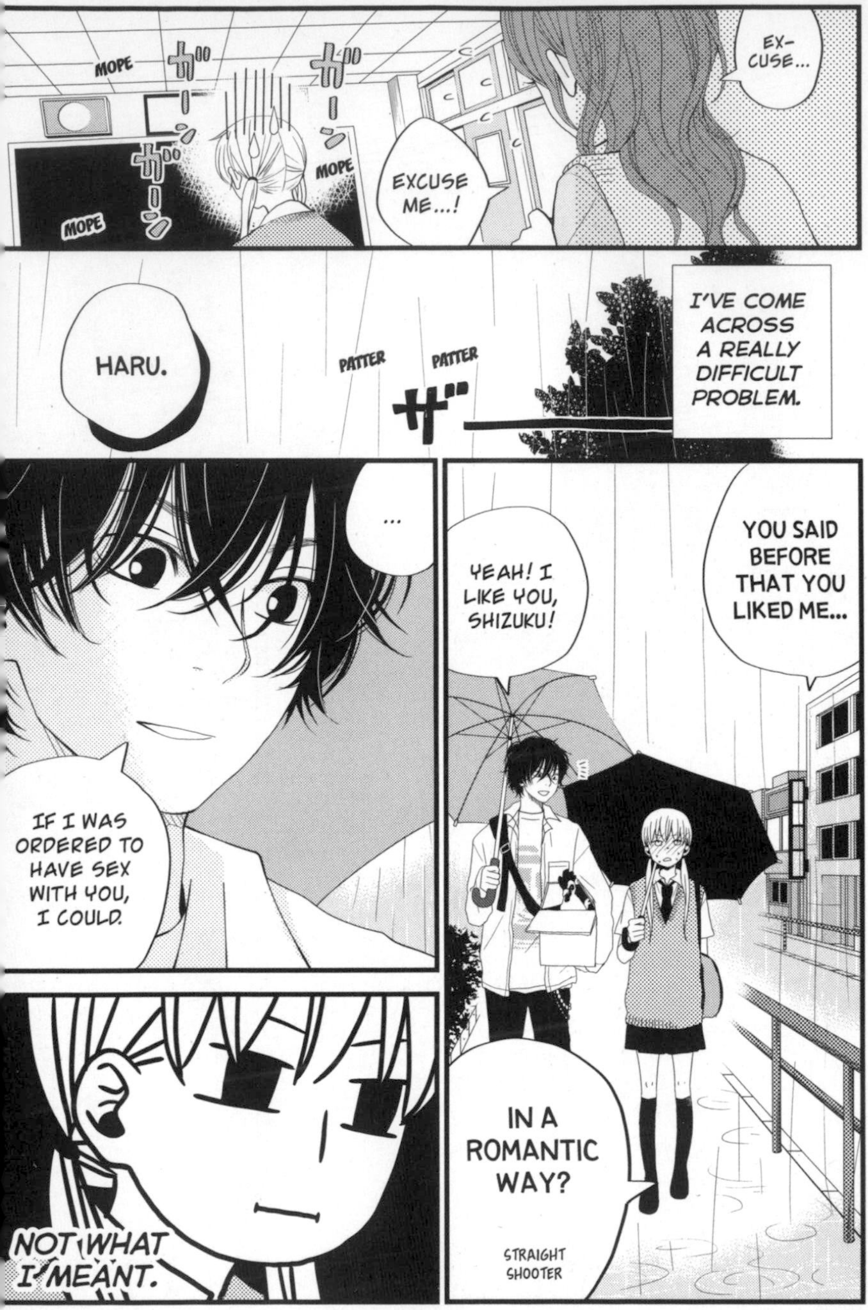
EX- CUSE...
EXCUSE ME...!
MOPE
MOPE
MOPE
I'VE COME ACROSS A REALLY DIFFICULT PROBLEM.
PATTER
PATTER
HARU.
YOU SAID BEFORE THAT YOU LIKED ME...
YEAH! I LIKE YOU, SHIZUKU!
IN A ROMANTIC WAY?
STRAIGHT SHOOTER
...
IF I WAS ORDERED TO HAVE SEX WITH YOU, I COULD.
NOT WHAT I MEANT.

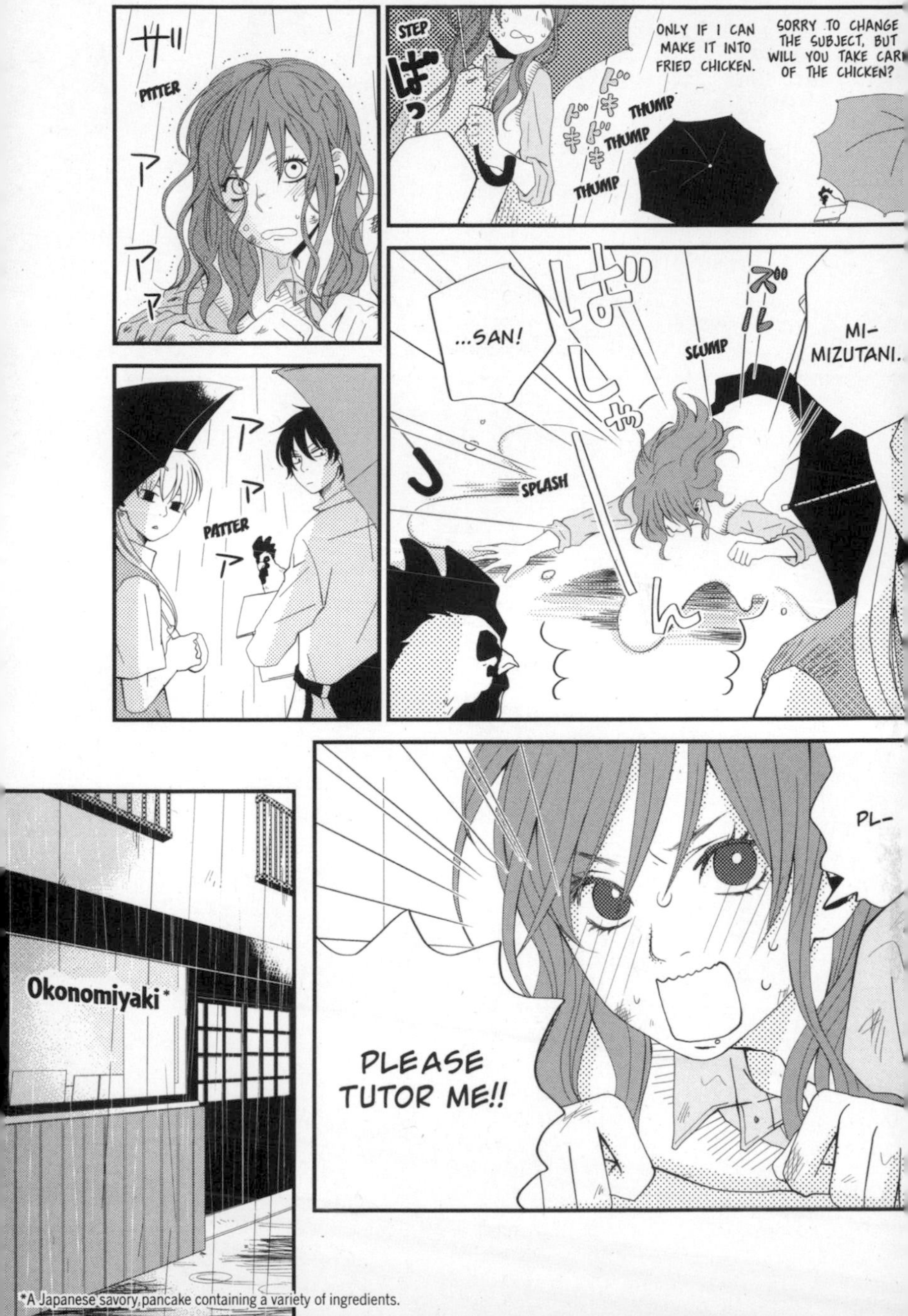
SORRY TO CHANGE THE SUBJECT, BUT WILL YOU TAKE CAR
OF THE CHICKEN?
ONLY IF I CAN MAKE IT INTO FRIED CHICKEN.
STEP
THUMP
THUMP
THUMP
PITTER
MI-MIZUTANI...
SLUMP
...SAN!
SPLASH
PATTER
PL-
PLEASE TUTOR ME!!
Okonomiyaki *

*A Japanese savory pancake containing a variety of ingredients.

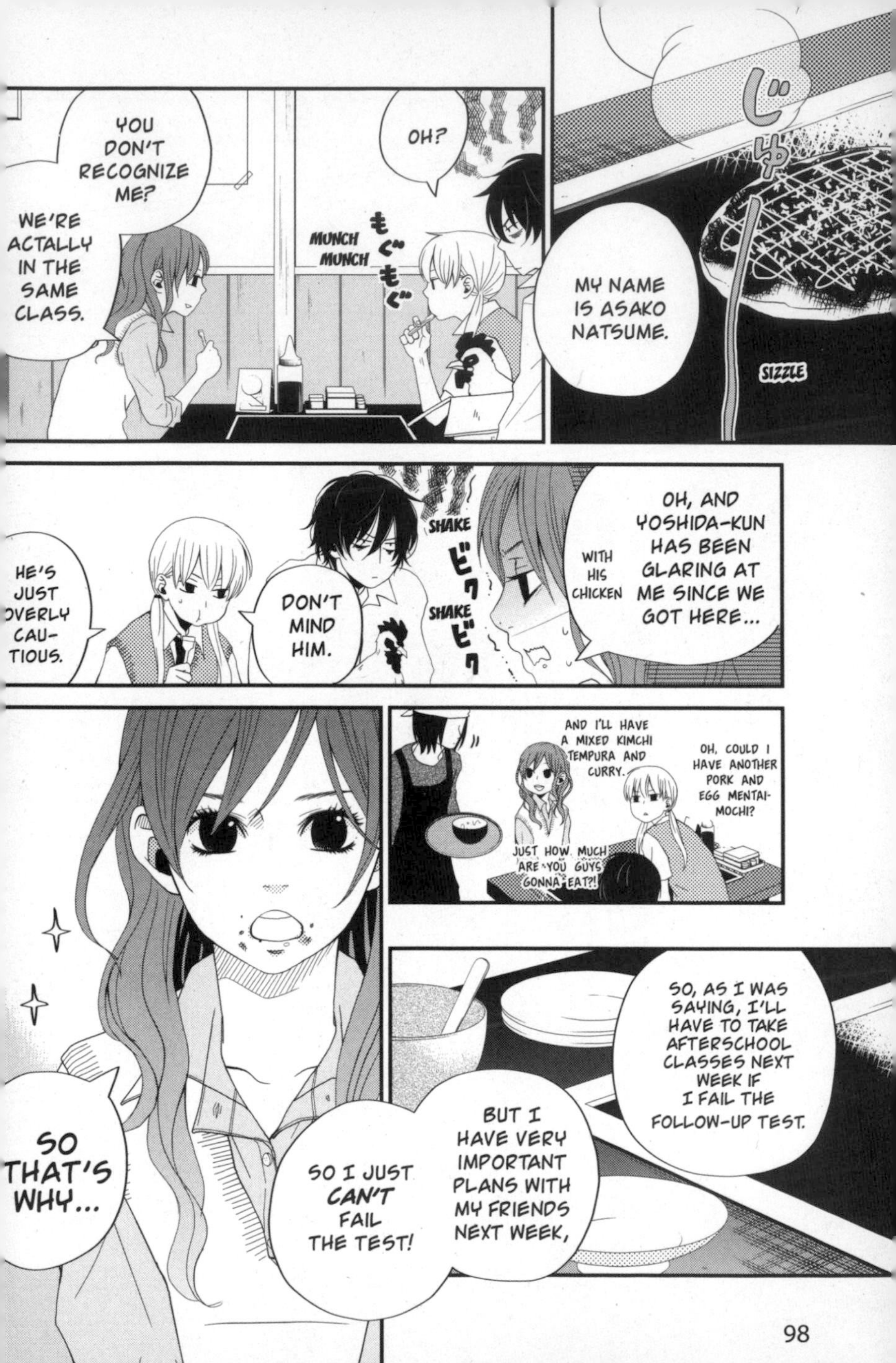
じゅ
MY NAME IS ASAKO NATSUME.
SIZZLE
OH?
MUNCH MUNCH
もぐもぐ
YOU DON'T RECOGNIZE ME?
WE'RE ACTALLY IN THE SAME CLASS.
OH, AND YOSHIDA-KUN HAS BEEN GLARING AT ME SINCE WE GOT HERE...
WITH HIS CHICKEN
SHAKE ビク SHAKE ビク
DON'T MIND HIM.
HE'S JUST OVERLY CAU-TIOUS.
OH, COULD I HAVE ANOTHER PORK AND EGG MENTAI-MOCHI?
AND I'LL HAVE A MIXED KIMCHI TEMPURA AND CURRY.
JUST HOW MUCH ARE YOU GUYS GONNA EAT?!
SO, AS I WAS SAYING, I'LL HAVE TO TAKE AFTERSCHOOL CLASSES NEXT WEEK IF I FAIL THE FOLLOW-UP TEST.
BUT I HAVE VERY IMPORTANT PLANS WITH MY FRIENDS NEXT WEEK,
SO I JUST *CAN'T* FAIL THE TEST!
SO THAT'S WHY...

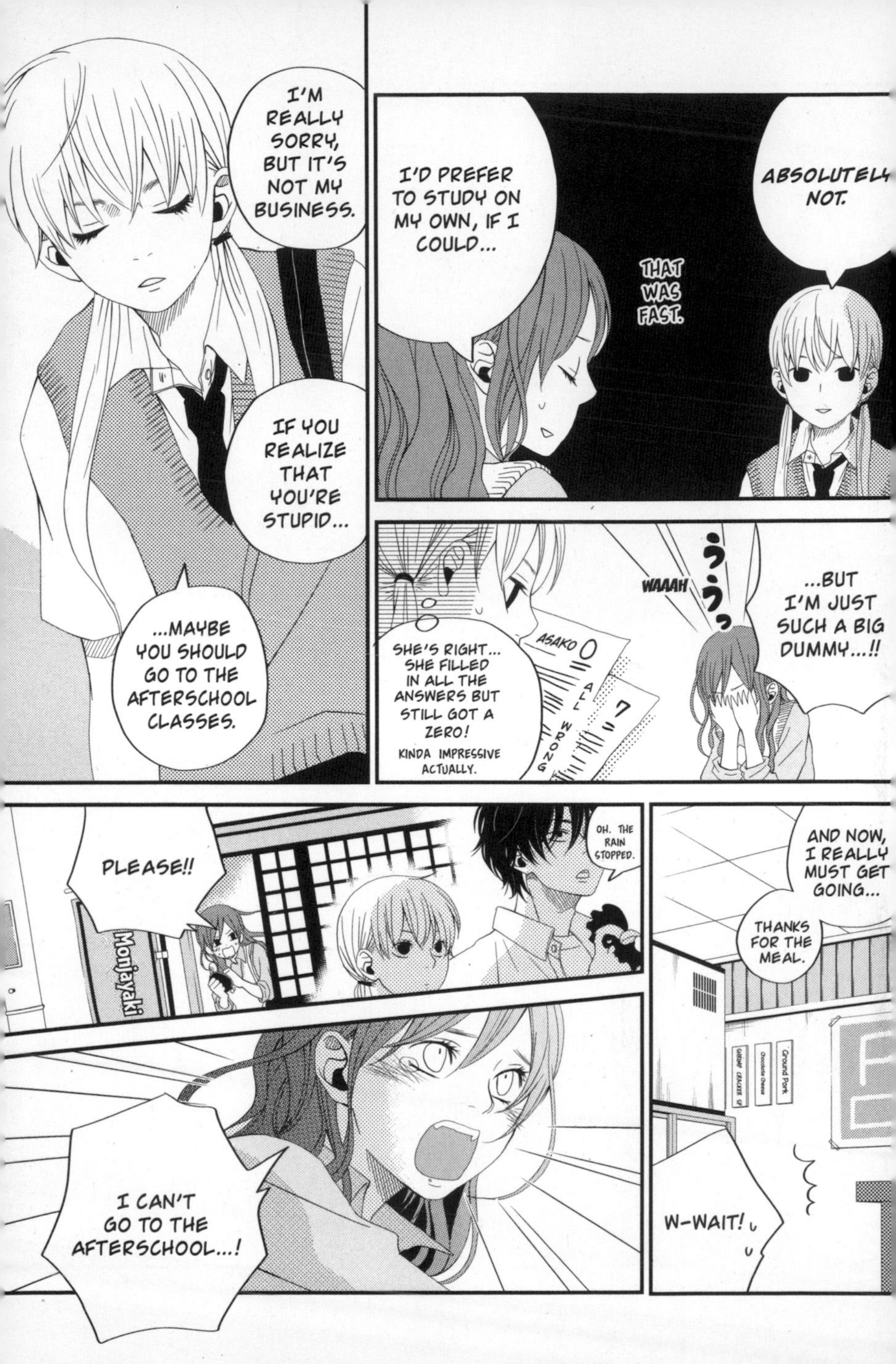
ABSOLUTELY NOT.
I'D PREFER TO STUDY ON MY OWN, IF I COULD...
THAT WAS FAST.
...BUT I'M JUST SUCH A BIG DUMMY...!!
うぅっ
WAAAH
SHE'S RIGHT... SHE FILLED IN ALL THE ANSWERS BUT STILL GOT A ZERO!
KINDA IMPRESSIVE ACTUALLY.
ASAKO 0
ALL WRONG
I'M REALLY SORRY, BUT IT'S NOT MY BUSINESS.
IF YOU REALIZE THAT YOU'RE STUPID...
...MAYBE YOU SHOULD GO TO THE AFTERSCHOOL CLASSES.
AND NOW, I REALLY MUST GET GOING...
THANKS FOR THE MEAL.
Ground Pork
Chocolate Cheese
W-WAIT!
OH. THE RAIN STOPPED.
PLEASE!!
Monjayaki
I CAN'T GO TO THE AFTERSCHOOL...!

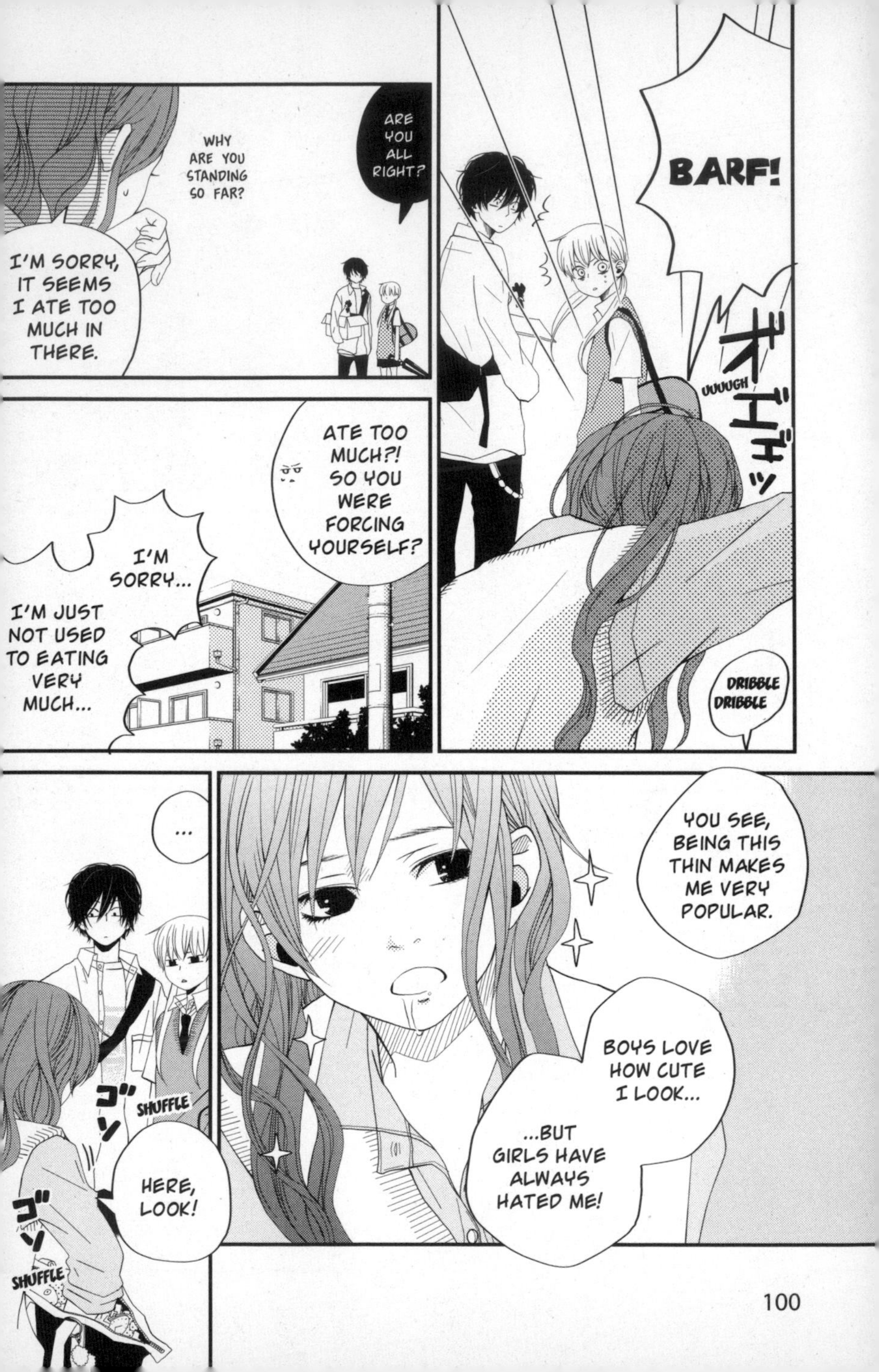
BARF!
オゲェッ
UUUUGH
DRIBBLE DRIBBLE
ARE YOU ALL RIGHT?
WHY ARE YOU STANDING SO FAR?
I'M SORRY, IT SEEMS I ATE TOO MUCH IN THERE.
ATE TOO MUCH?! SO YOU WERE FORCING YOURSELF?
I'M SORRY...
I'M JUST NOT USED TO EATING VERY MUCH...
YOU SEE, BEING THIS THIN MAKES ME VERY POPULAR.
BOYS LOVE HOW CUTE I LOOK...
...BUT GIRLS HAVE ALWAYS HATED ME!
...
ゴソ
SHUFFLE
HERE, LOOK!
ゴソ
SHUFFLE

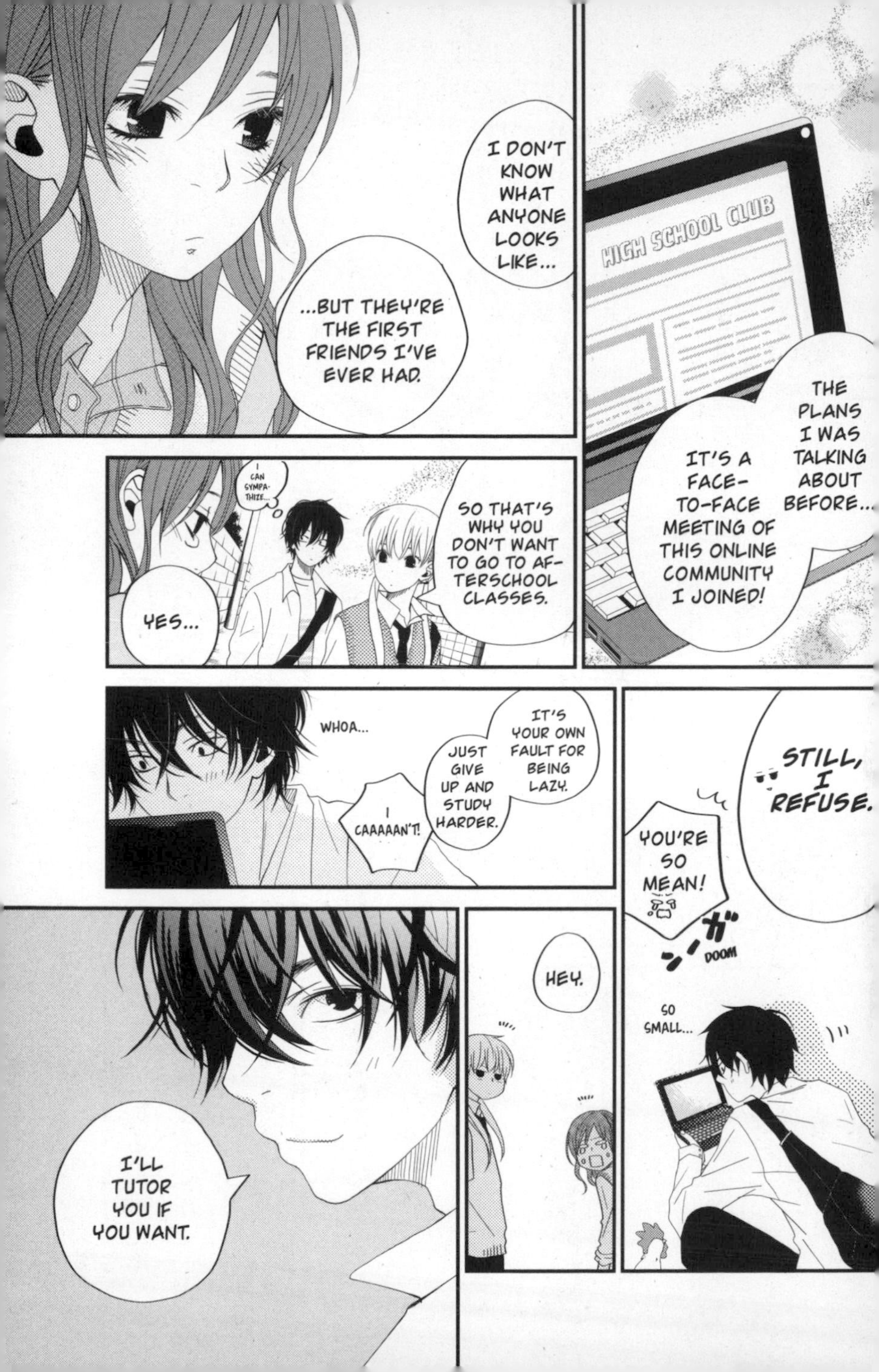

HIGH SCHOOL CLUB
THE PLANS I WAS TALKING ABOUT BEFORE...
IT'S A FACE-TO-FACE MEETING OF THIS ONLINE COMMUNITY I JOINED!
I DON'T KNOW WHAT ANYONE LOOKS LIKE...
...BUT THEY'RE THE FIRST FRIENDS I'VE EVER HAD.
SO THAT'S WHY YOU DON'T WANT TO GO TO AFTERSCHOOL CLASSES.
I CAN SYMPATHIZE...
YES...
STILL, I REFUSE.
YOU'RE SO MEAN!
DOOM
IT'S YOUR OWN FAULT FOR BEING LAZY.
JUST GIVE UP AND STUDY HARDER.
I CAAAAAAN'T!
WHOA...
SO SMALL...
HEY.
I'LL TUTOR YOU IF YOU WANT.

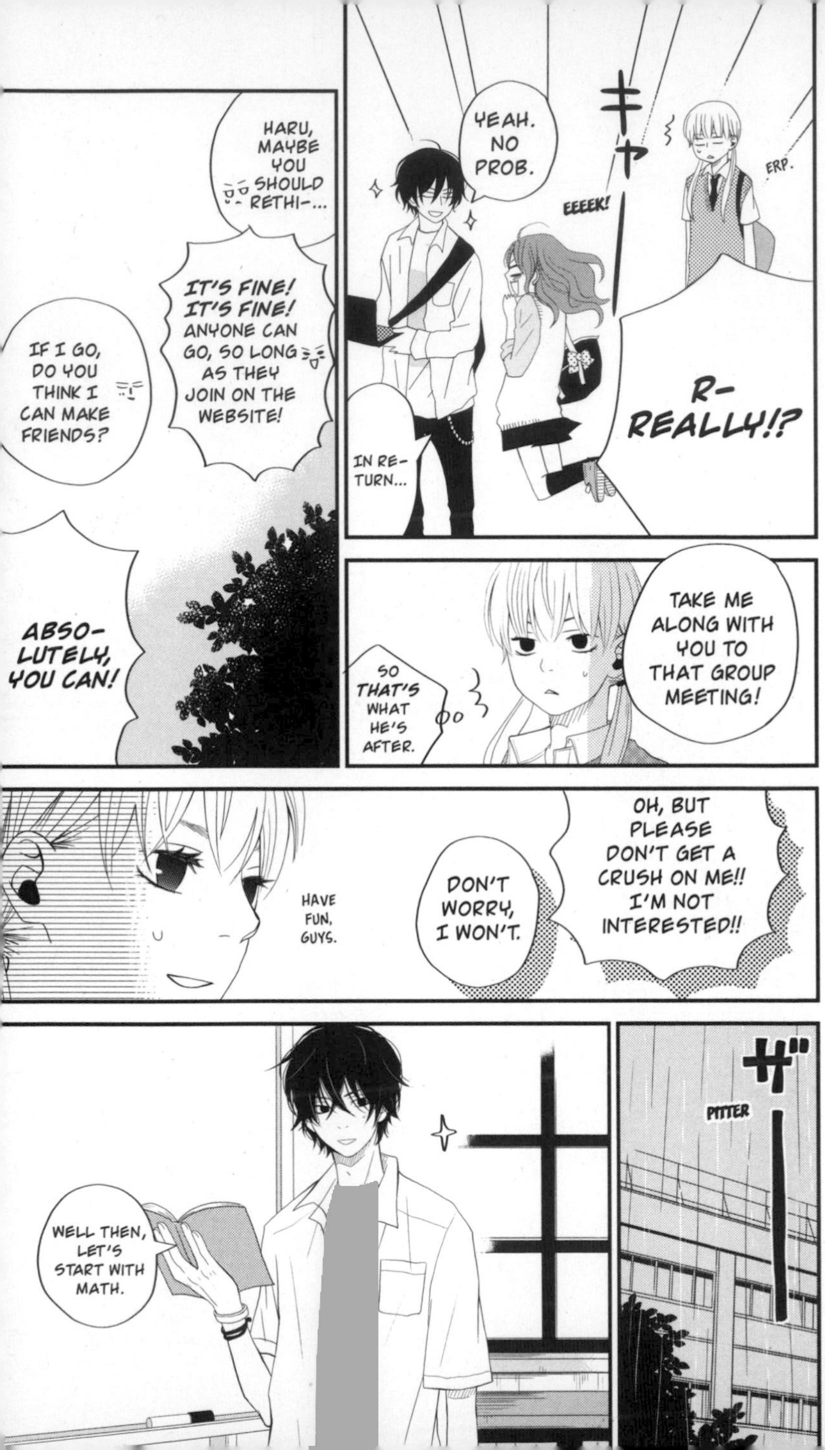
ERP.
キャー
EEEEK!
YEAH. NO PROB.
R-REALLY!?
IN RE-TURN...
TAKE ME ALONG WITH YOU TO THAT GROUP MEETING!
SO THAT'S WHAT HE'S AFTER.
HARU, MAYBE YOU SHOULD RETHI-...
IT'S FINE! IT'S FINE! ANYONE CAN GO, SO LONG AS THEY JOIN ON THE WEBSITE!
IF I GO, DO YOU THINK I CAN MAKE FRIENDS?
ABSO-LUTELY, YOU CAN!
OH, BUT PLEASE DON'T GET A CRUSH ON ME!! I'M NOT INTERESTED!!
DON'T WORRY, I WON'T.
HAVE FUN, GUYS.
ザー
PITTER
WELL THEN, LET'S START WITH MATH.

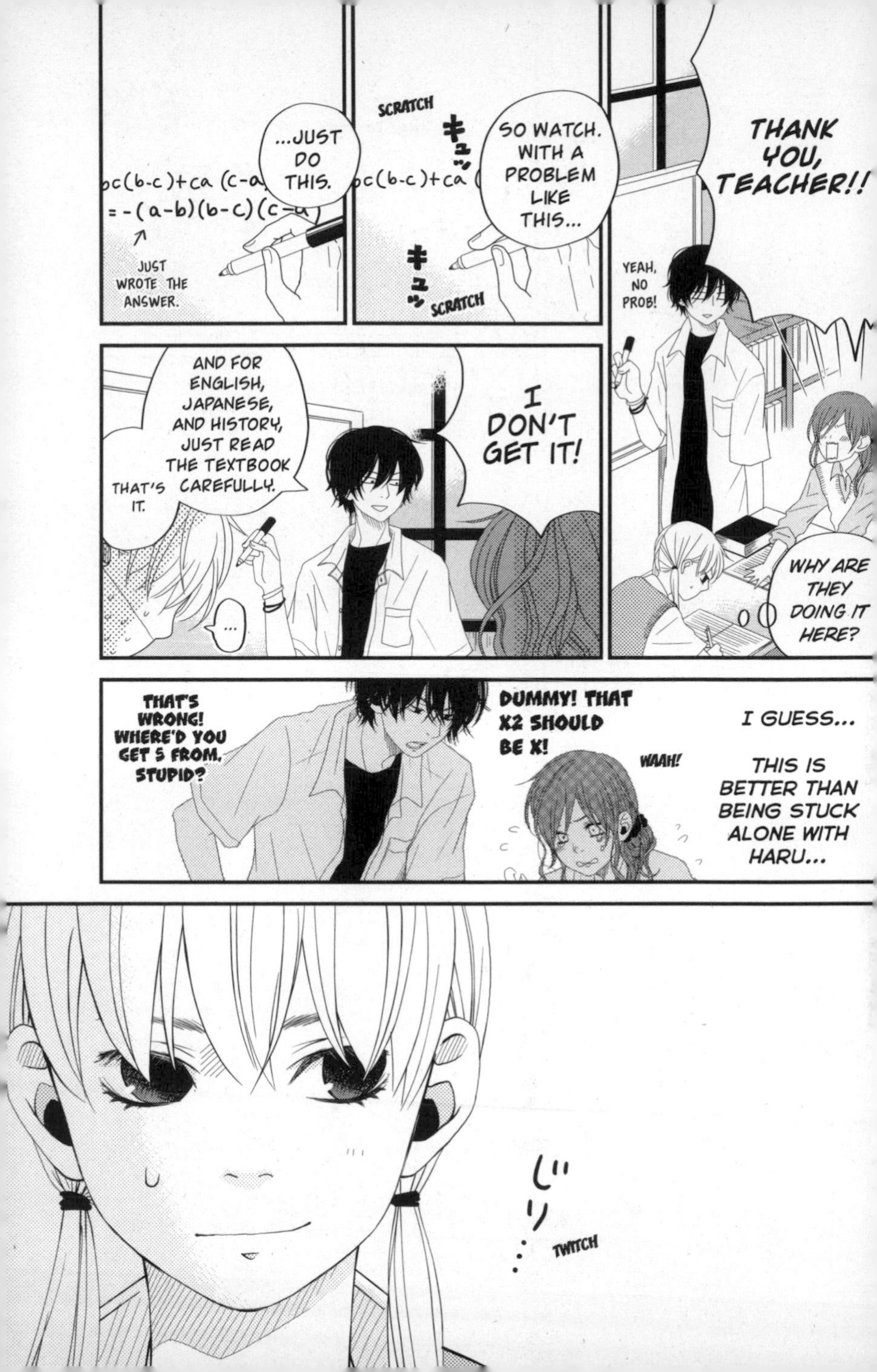
THANK YOU, TEACHER!!
YEAH, NO PROB!
WHY ARE THEY DOING IT HERE?
SCRATCH
キュッ
SO WATCH. WITH A PROBLEM LIKE THIS...
キュッ
SCRATCH
...JUST DO THIS.
= -(a-b)(b-c)(c-a)
JUST WROTE THE ANSWER.
I DON'T GET IT!
AND FOR ENGLISH, JAPANESE, AND HISTORY, JUST READ THE TEXTBOOK CAREFULLY.
THAT'S IT.
...
I GUESS...
THIS IS BETTER THAN BEING STUCK ALONE WITH HARU...
DUMMY! THAT X2 SHOULD BE X!
WAAH!
THAT'S WRONG! WHERE'D YOU GET 5 FROM, STUPID?
じりっ
TWITCH

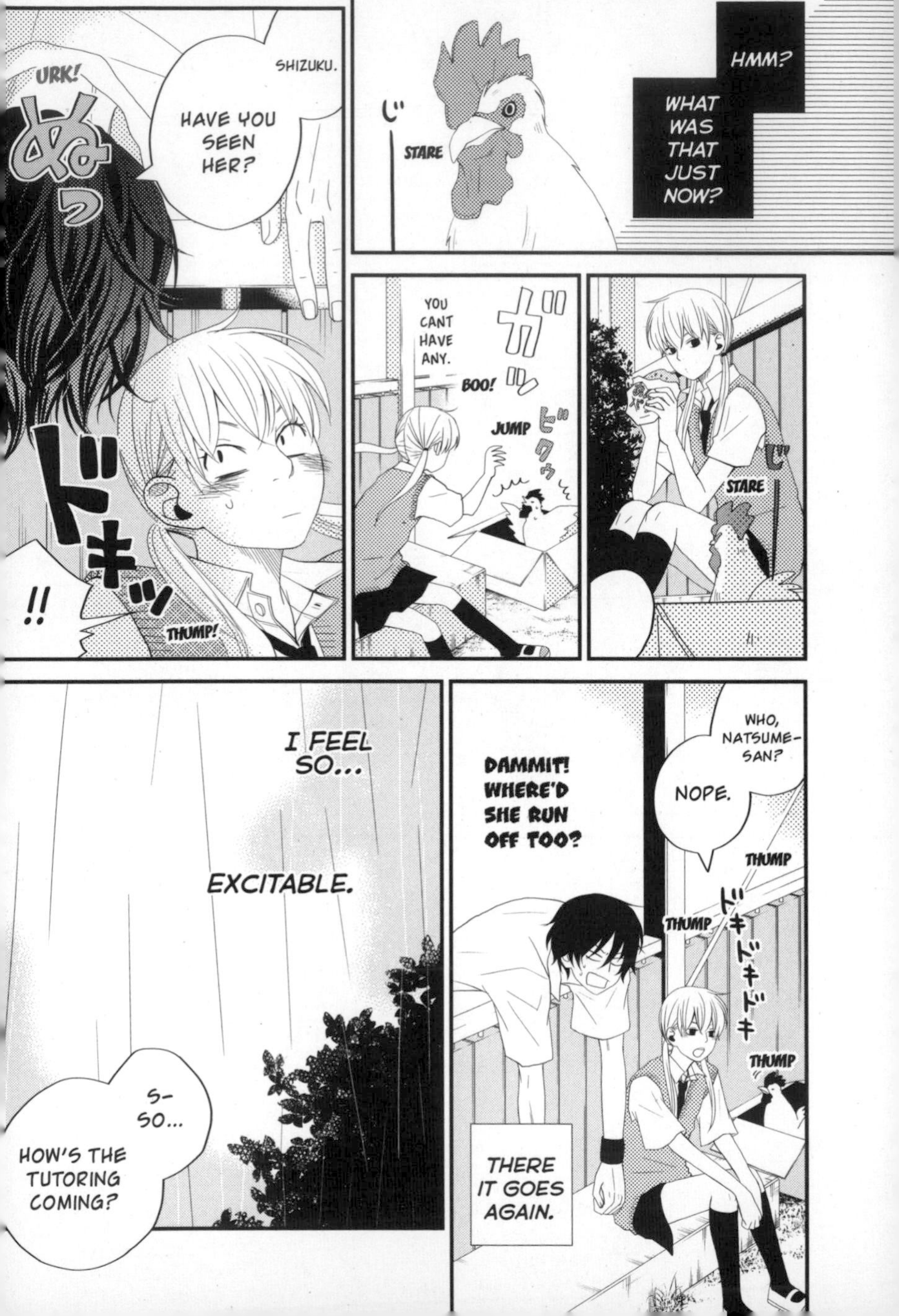

HMM?
WHAT WAS THAT JUST NOW?
じ
STARE
じ
STARE
YOU CANT HAVE ANY.
BOO!
JUMP
ビクゥ
URK!
ぬっ
SHIZUKU.
HAVE YOU SEEN HER?
ドキッ
!!
THUMP!
WHO, NATSUME-SAN?
NOPE.
DAMMIT! WHERE'D SHE RUN OFF TOO?
THUMP
THUMP
ドキドキドキ
THUMP
THERE IT GOES AGAIN.
I FEEL SO...
EXCITABLE.
S-SO...
HOW'S THE TUTORING COMING?

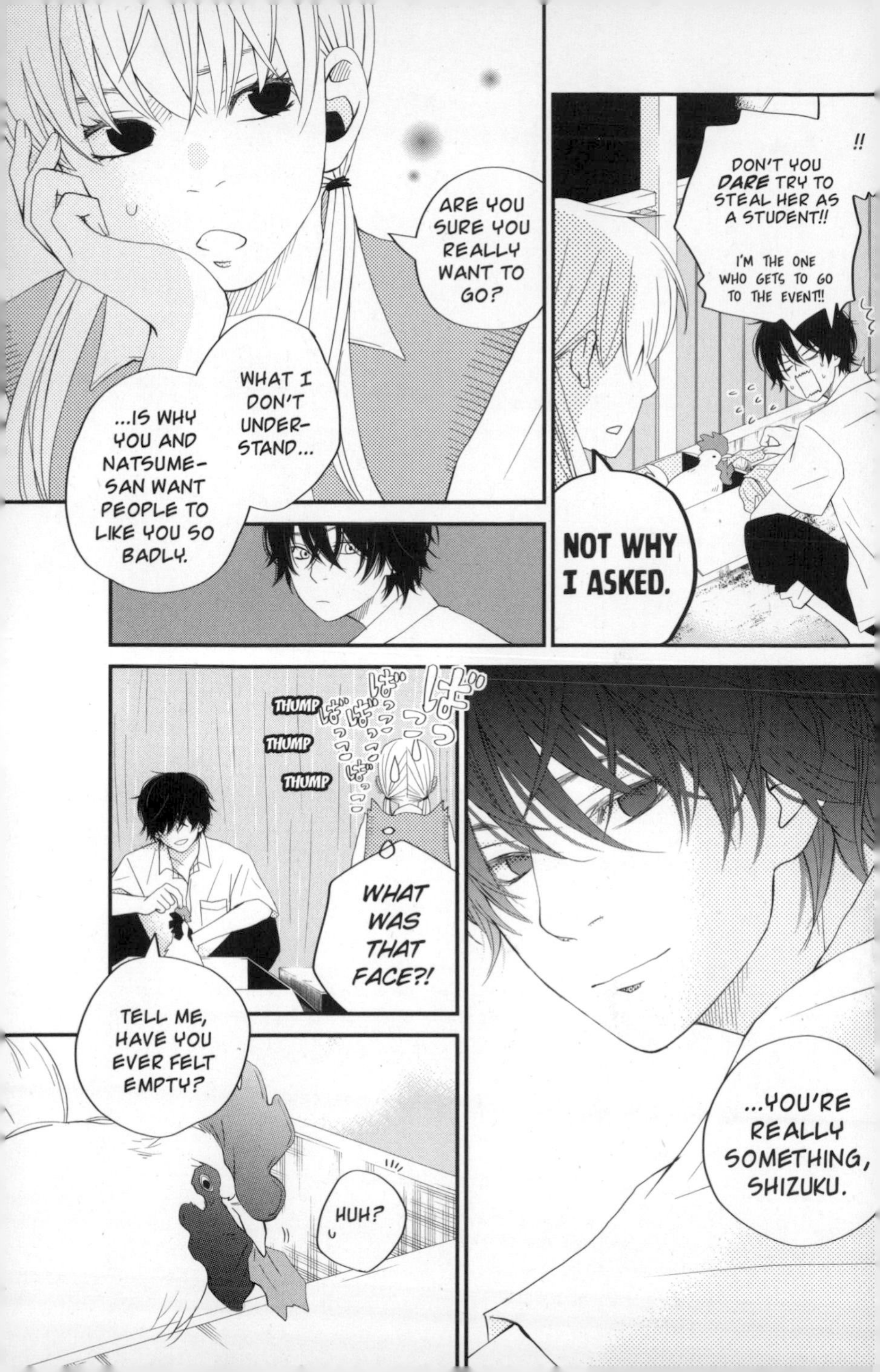
!!
DON'T YOU DARE TRY TO STEAL HER AS A STUDENT!!
I'M THE ONE WHO GETS TO GO TO THE EVENT!!
NOT WHY I ASKED.
ARE YOU SURE YOU REALLY WANT TO GO?
WHAT I DON'T UNDERSTAND...
...IS WHY YOU AND NATSUME-SAN WANT PEOPLE TO LIKE YOU SO BADLY.
...YOU'RE REALLY SOMETHING, SHIZUKU.
THUMP
THUMP
THUMP
ぼっ
WHAT WAS THAT FACE?!
TELL ME, HAVE YOU EVER FELT EMPTY?
HUH?

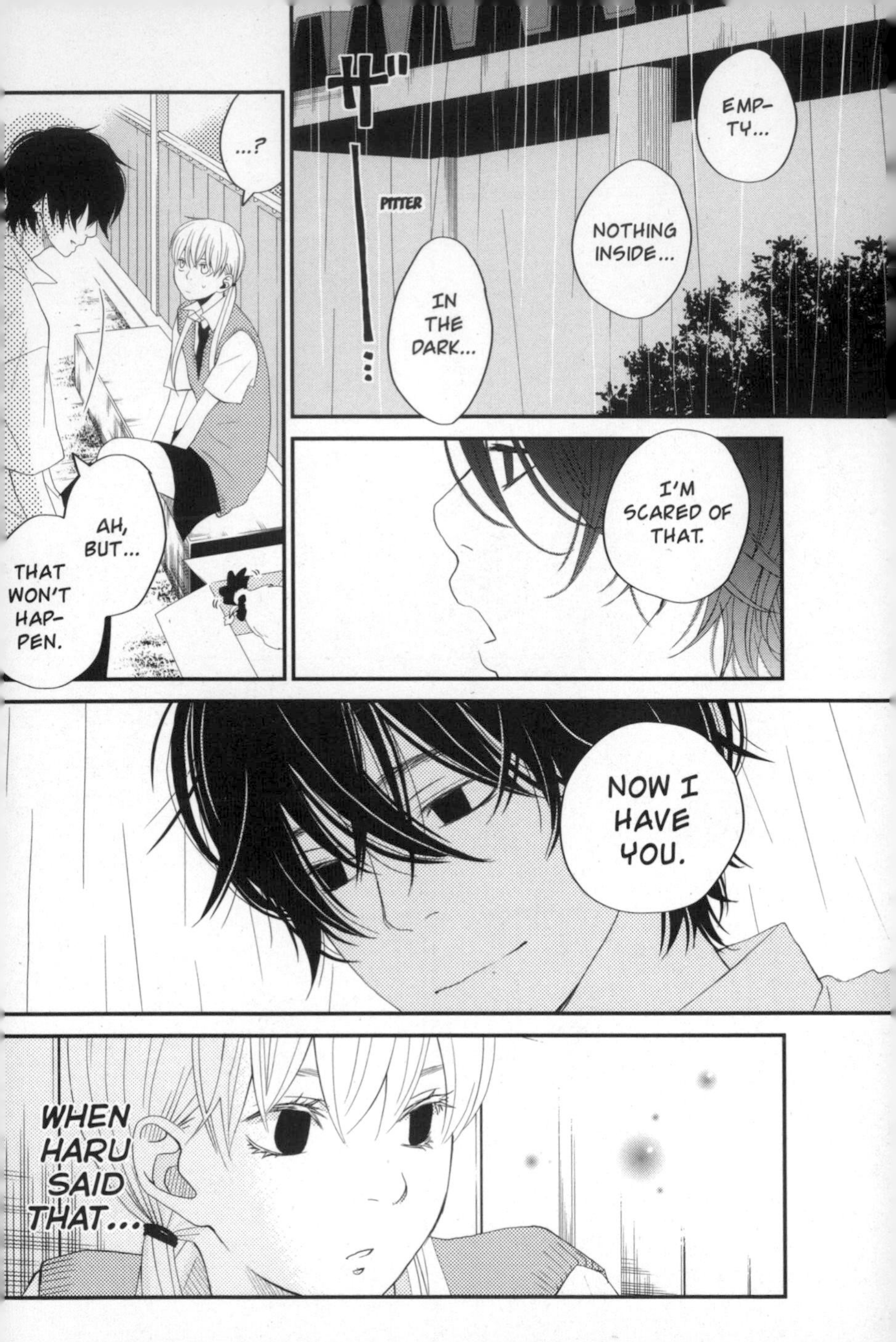
ザー
PITTER
EMP-TY...
NOTHING INSIDE...
IN THE DARK...
I'M SCARED OF THAT.
...?
AH, BUT...
THAT WON'T HAP-PEN.
NOW I HAVE YOU.
WHEN HARU SAID THAT...

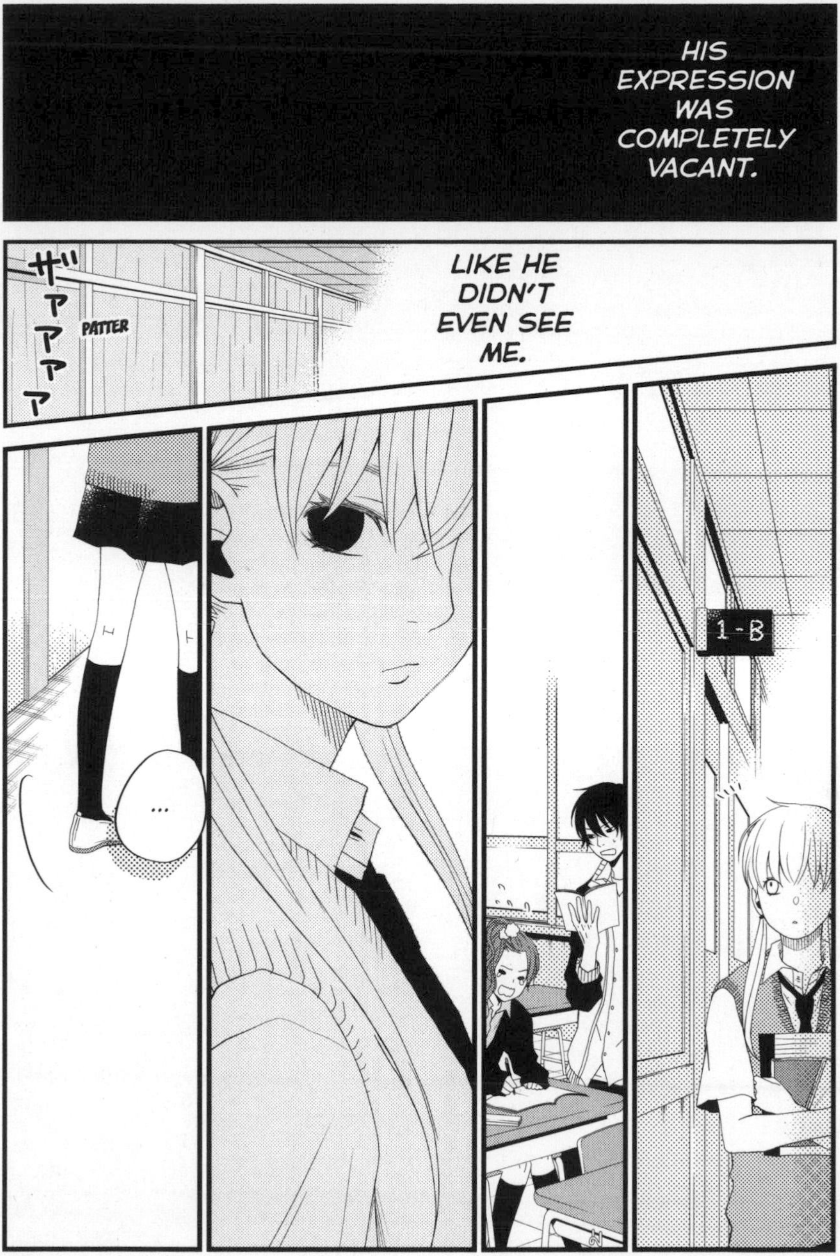
HIS EXPRESSION WAS COMPLETELY VACANT.
LIKE HE DIDN'T EVEN SEE ME.
ザァァァァ
PATTER
...

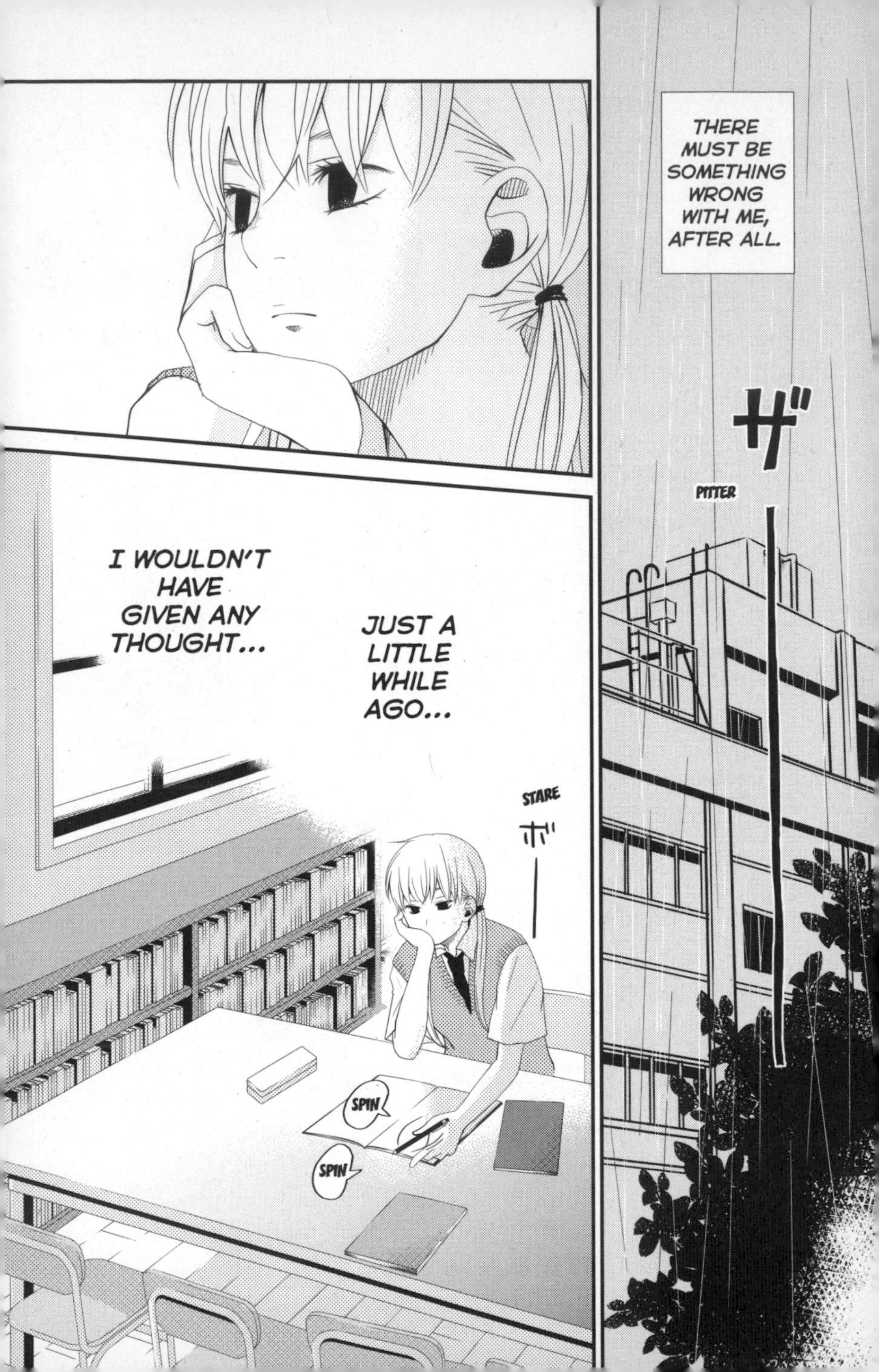
THERE MUST BE SOMETHING WRONG WITH ME, AFTER ALL.
ザ
PITTER
JUST A LITTLE WHILE AGO...
I WOULDN'T HAVE GIVEN ANY THOUGHT...
STARE
ボー
SPIN
SPIN

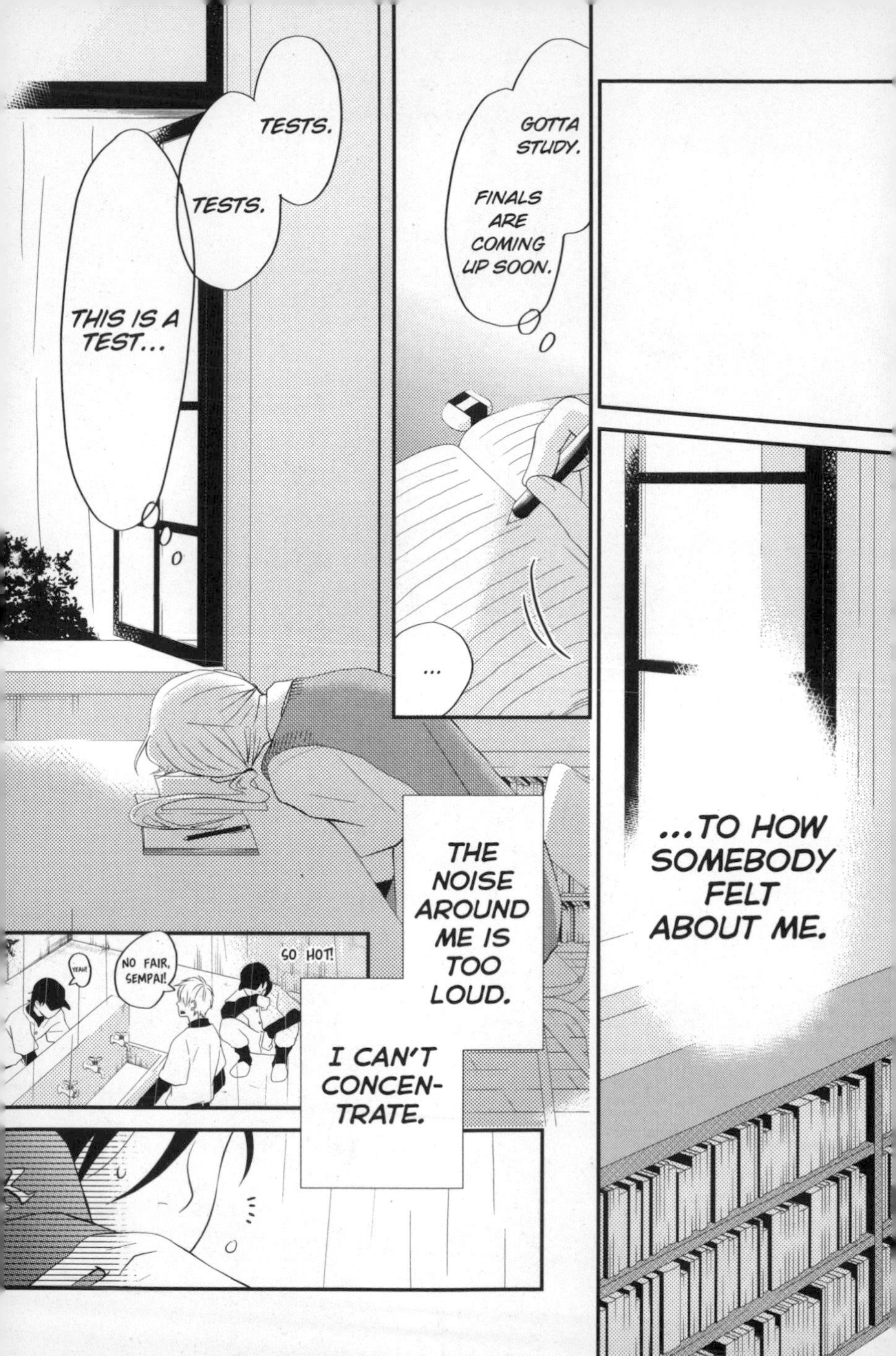
...TO HOW SOMEBODY FELT ABOUT ME.
GOTTA STUDY.
FINALS ARE COMING UP SOON.
...
TESTS.
TESTS.
THIS IS A TEST...
THE NOISE AROUND ME IS TOO LOUD.
SO HOT!
NO FAIR, SEMPAI!
YEAH!
I CAN'T CONCEN-TRATE.

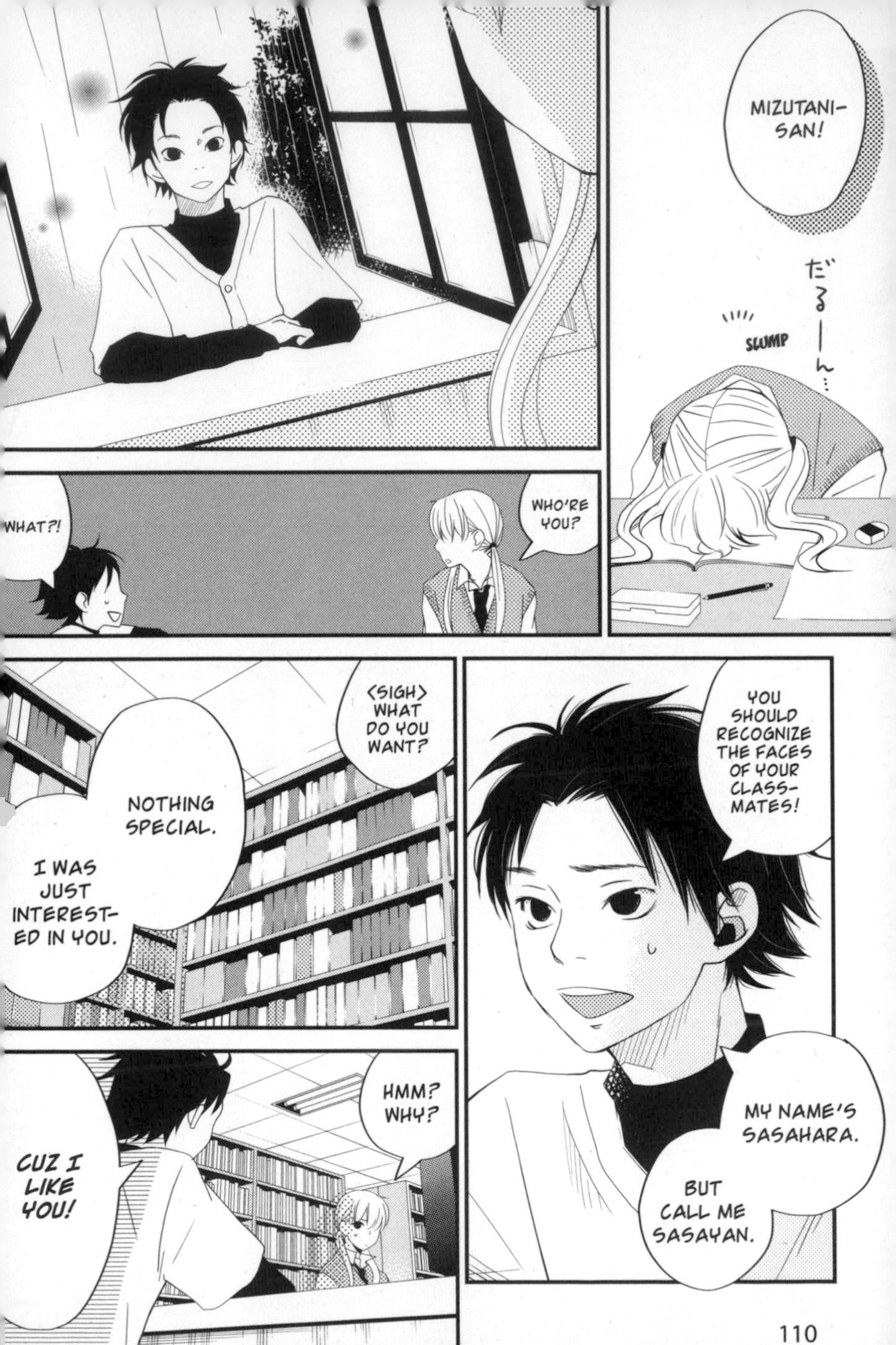
MIZUTANI-SAN!
だるーん…
SLUMP
WHO'RE YOU?
WHAT?!
YOU SHOULD RECOGNIZE THE FACES OF YOUR CLASS-MATES!
MY NAME'S SASAHARA.
BUT CALL ME SASAYAN.
<SIGH> WHAT DO YOU WANT?
NOTHING SPECIAL.
I WAS JUST INTEREST-ED IN YOU.
HMM? WHY?
CUZ I LIKE YOU!

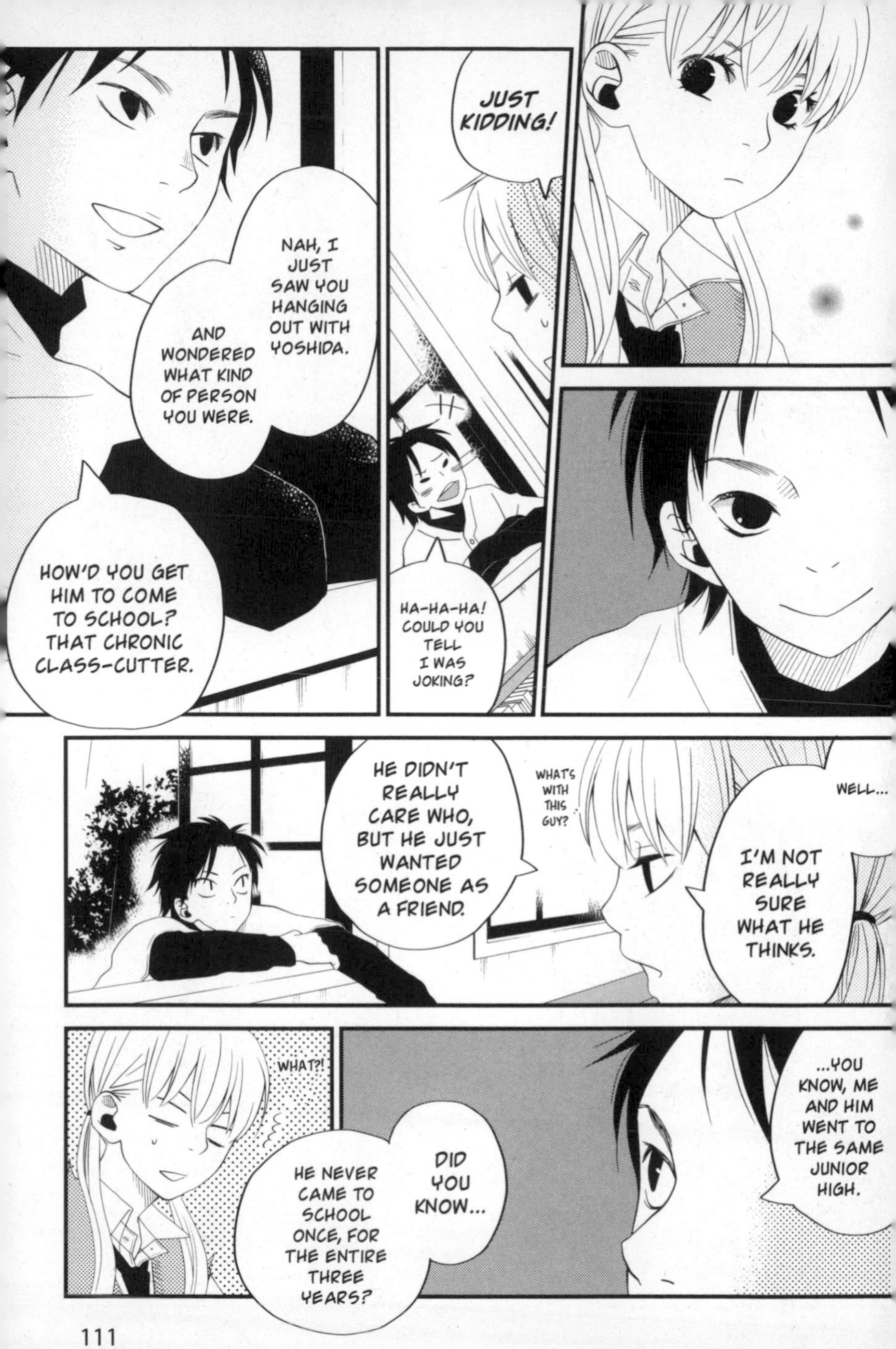
NAH, I JUST SAW YOU HANGING OUT WITH YOSHIDA.
AND WONDERED WHAT KIND OF PERSON YOU WERE.
HOW'D YOU GET HIM TO COME TO SCHOOL? THAT CHRONIC CLASS-CUTTER.
JUST KIDDING!
HA-HA-HA! COULD YOU TELL I WAS JOKING?
WELL...
I'M NOT REALLY SURE WHAT HE THINKS.
WHAT'S WITH THIS GUY?
HE DIDN'T REALLY CARE WHO, BUT HE JUST WANTED SOMEONE AS A FRIEND.
...YOU KNOW, ME AND HIM WENT TO THE SAME JUNIOR HIGH.
DID YOU KNOW...
HE NEVER CAME TO SCHOOL ONCE, FOR THE ENTIRE THREE YEARS?
WHAT?!

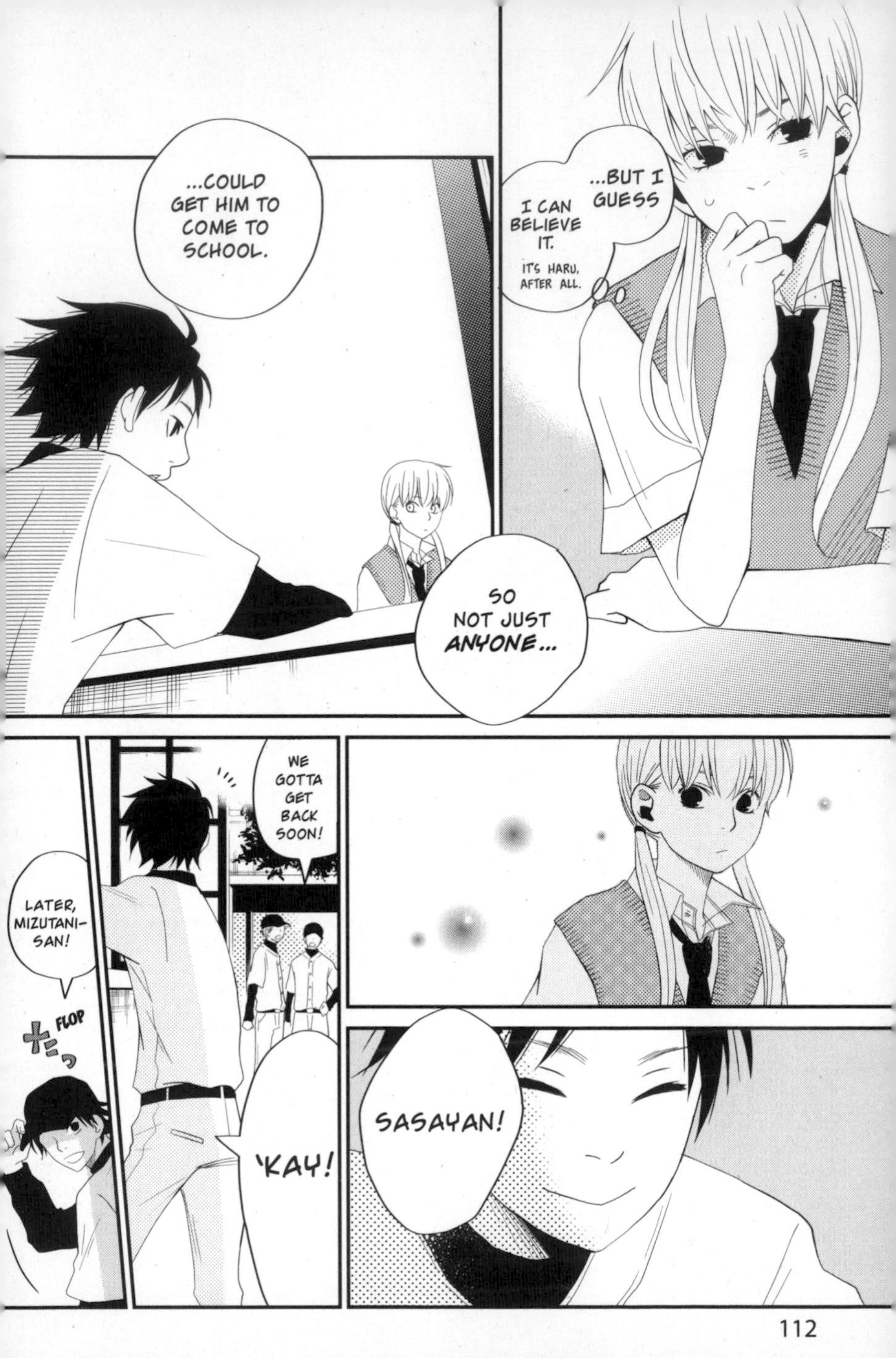
...BUT I GUESS I CAN BELIEVE IT.
IT'S HARU, AFTER ALL.
...COULD GET HIM TO COME TO SCHOOL.
SO NOT JUST ANYONE...
SASAYAN!
WE GOTTA GET BACK SOON!
'KAY!
LATER, MIZUTANI-SAN!
FLOP

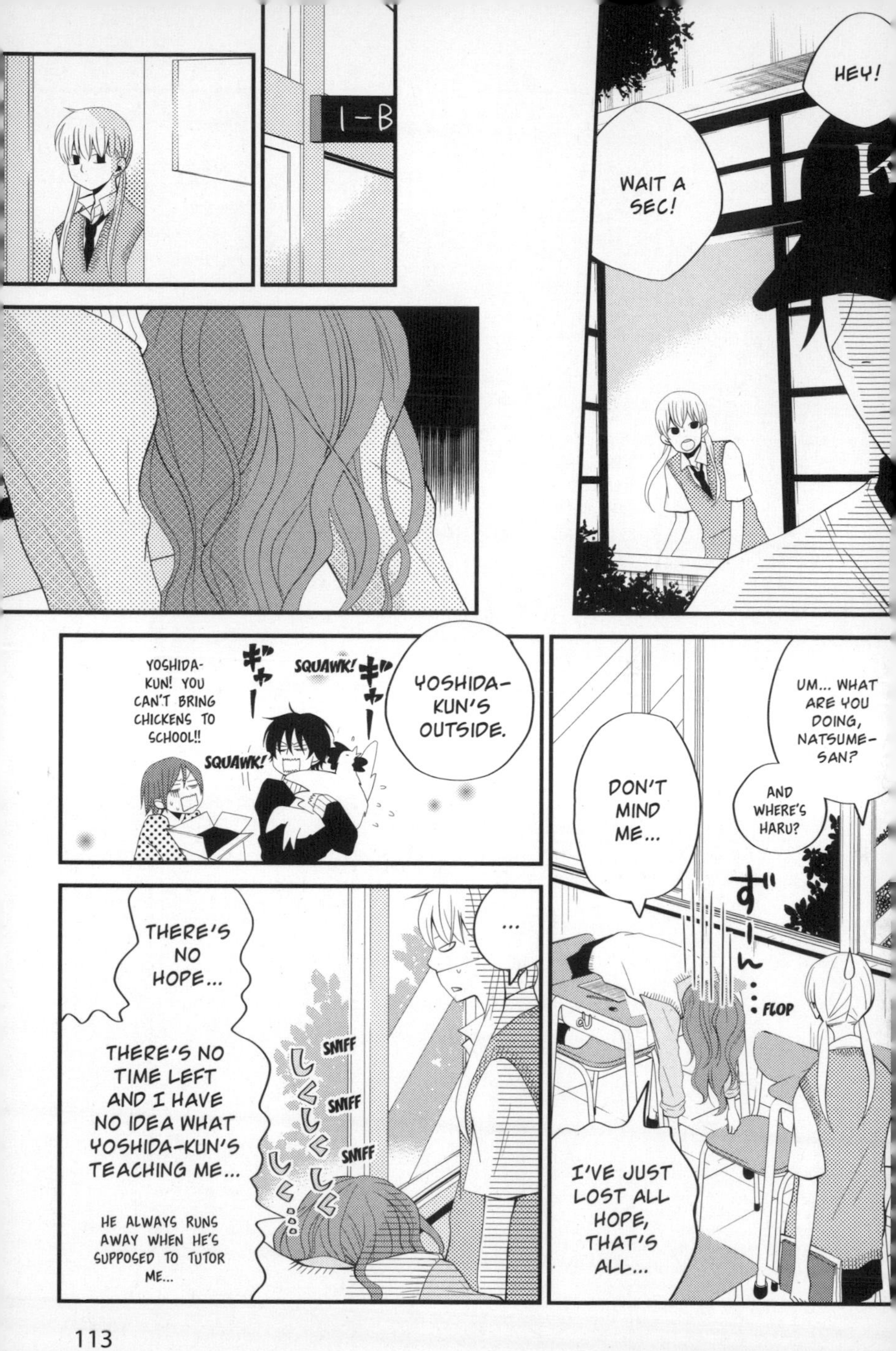
HEY!
WAIT A SEC!
1-B
UM... WHAT ARE YOU DOING, NATSUME-SAN?
AND WHERE'S HARU?
DON'T MIND ME...
ずーん
FLOP
I'VE JUST LOST ALL HOPE, THAT'S ALL...
YOSHIDA-KUN'S OUTSIDE.
ギャー
SQUAWK!
ギャー
YOSHIDA-KUN! YOU CAN'T BRING CHICKENS TO SCHOOL!!
SQUAWK!
...
THERE'S NO HOPE...
THERE'S NO TIME LEFT AND I HAVE NO IDEA WHAT YOSHIDA-KUN'S TEACHING ME...
HE ALWAYS RUNS AWAY WHEN HE'S SUPPOSED TO TUTOR ME...
SNIFF
SNIFF
SNIFF

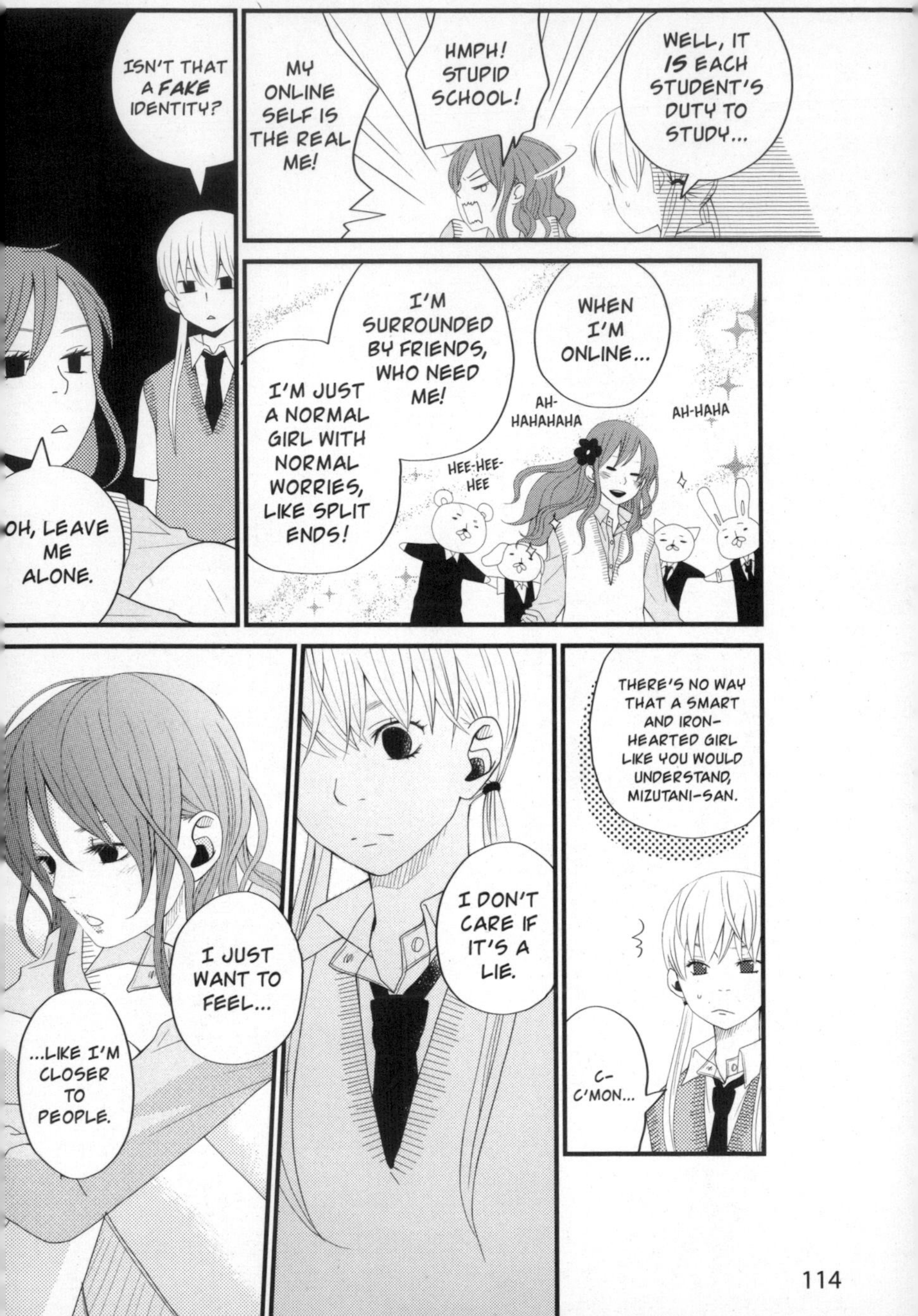
WELL, IT IS EACH STUDENT'S DUTY TO STUDY...
HMPH! STUPID SCHOOL!
MY ONLINE SELF IS THE REAL ME!
WHEN I'M ONLINE...
I'M SURROUNDED BY FRIENDS, WHO NEED ME!
AH-HAHA
AH-HAHAHAHA
HEE-HEE-HEE
I'M JUST A NORMAL GIRL WITH NORMAL WORRIES, LIKE SPLIT ENDS!
ISN'T THAT A FAKE IDENTITY?
OH, LEAVE ME ALONE.
THERE'S NO WAY THAT A SMART AND IRON-HEARTED GIRL LIKE YOU WOULD UNDERSTAND, MIZUTANI-SAN.
C-C'MON...
I DON'T CARE IF IT'S A LIE.
I JUST WANT TO FEEL...
...LIKE I'M CLOSER TO PEOPLE.

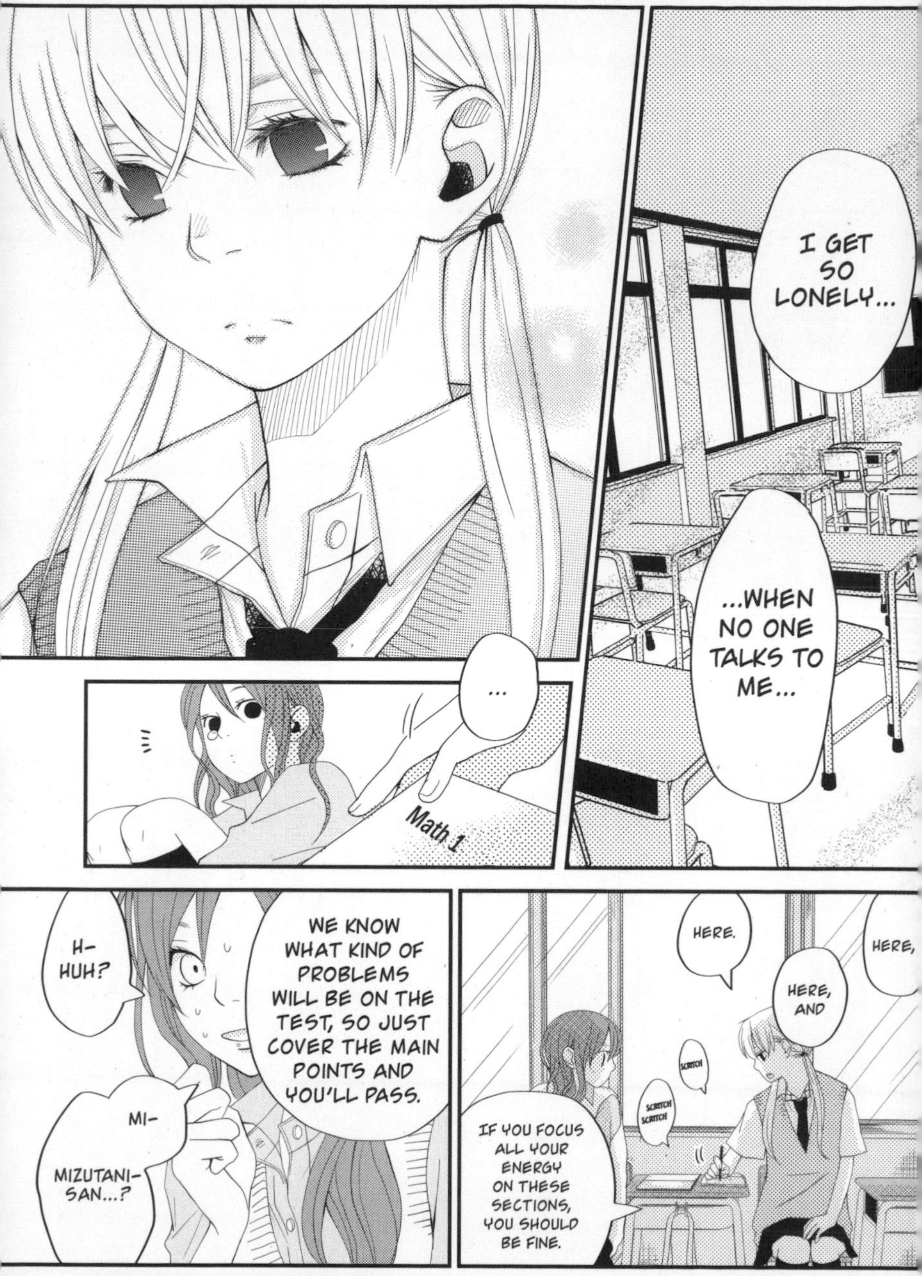
I GET SO LONELY...
...WHEN NO ONE TALKS TO ME...
...
Math 1
HERE,
HERE, AND
HERE.
SCRITCH
SCRITCH SCRITCH
IF YOU FOCUS ALL YOUR ENERGY ON THESE SECTIONS, YOU SHOULD BE FINE.
WE KNOW WHAT KIND OF PROBLEMS WILL BE ON THE TEST, SO JUST COVER THE MAIN POINTS AND YOU'LL PASS.
H-HUH?
MI-
MIZUTANI-SAN...?

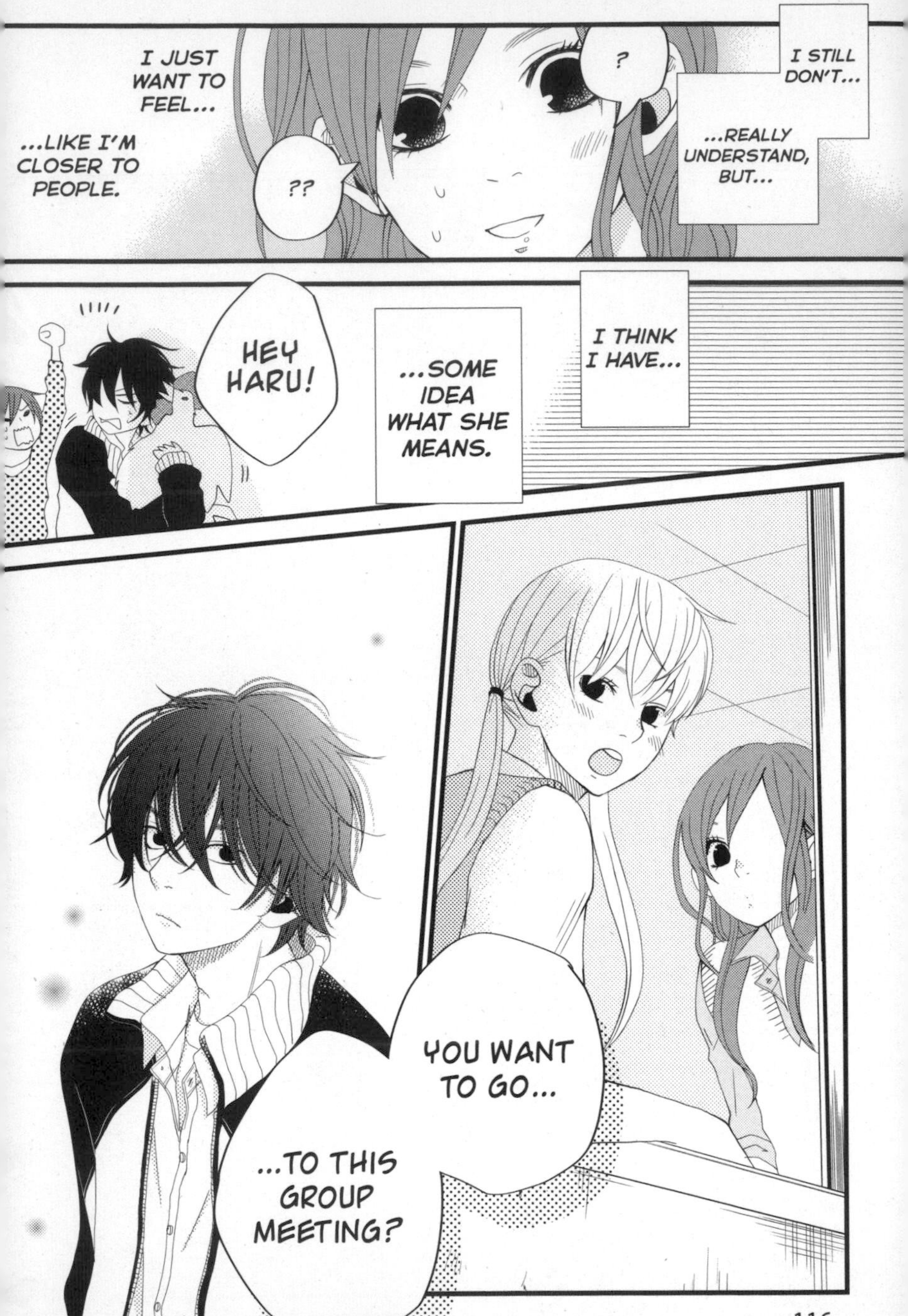
I STILL DON'T...
...REALLY UNDERSTAND, BUT...
?
??
I JUST WANT TO FEEL...
...LIKE I'M CLOSER TO PEOPLE.
I THINK I HAVE...
...SOME IDEA WHAT SHE MEANS.
HEY HARU!
YOU WANT TO GO...
...TO THIS GROUP MEETING?

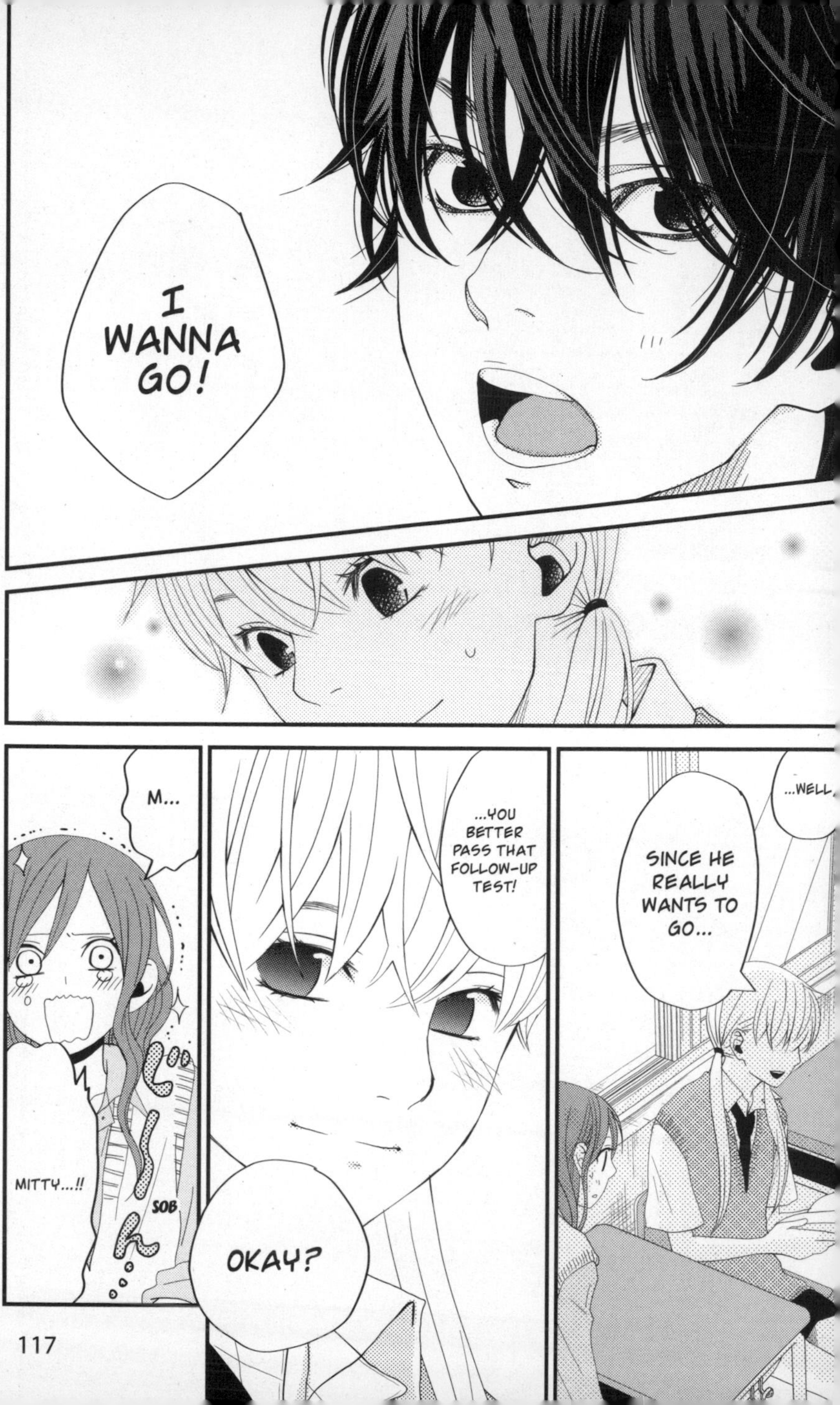
I WANNA GO!
...WELL,
SINCE HE REALLY WANTS TO GO...
...YOU BETTER PASS THAT FOLLOW-UP TEST!
OKAY?
M...
MITTY...!!
SOB

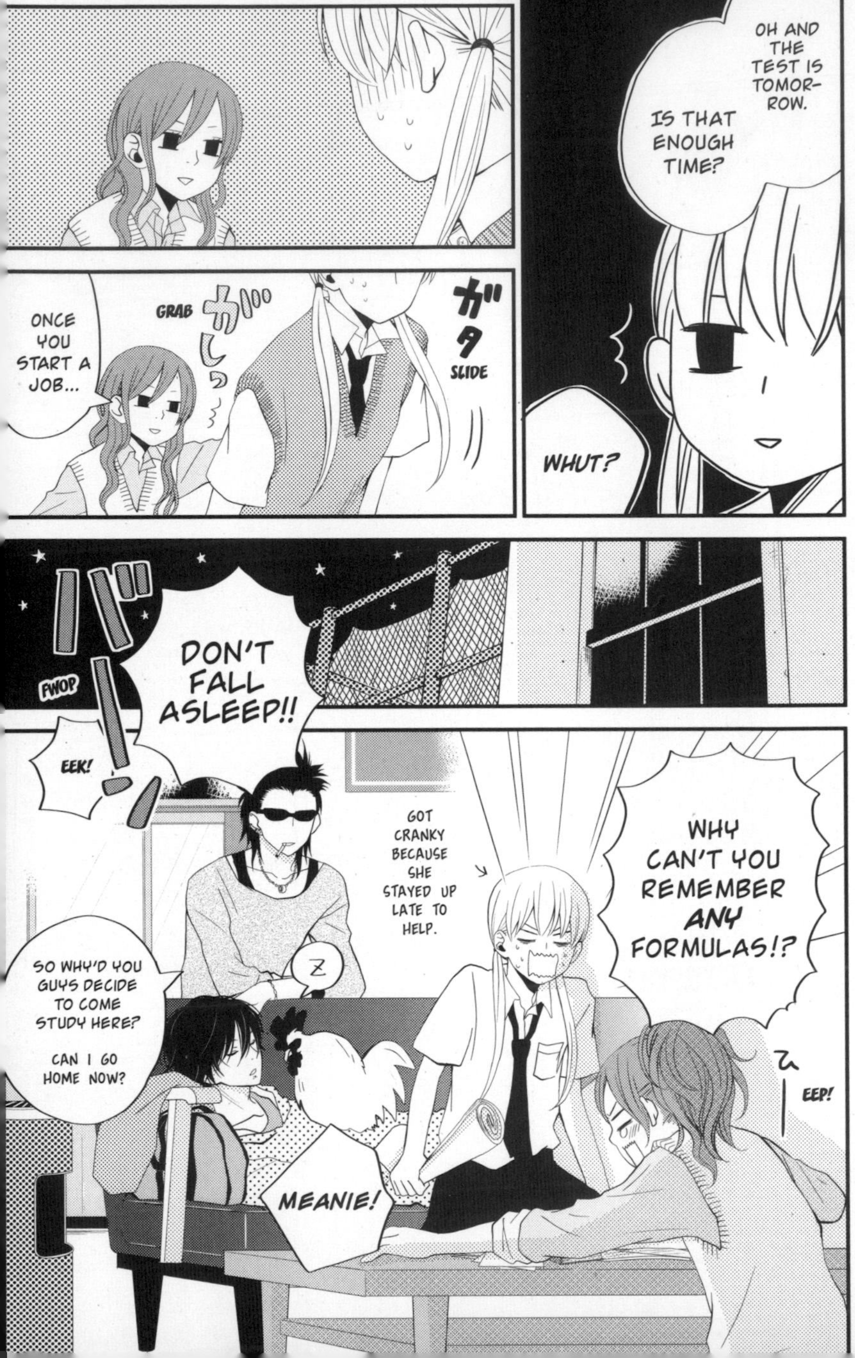
OH AND THE TEST IS TOMORROW.
IS THAT ENOUGH TIME?
WHUT?
ガタ
SLIDE
GRAB
がしっ
ONCE YOU START A JOB...
バ
FWOP
DON'T FALL ASLEEP!!
EEK!
WHY CAN'T YOU REMEMBER ANY FORMULAS!?
ひー
EEP!
GOT CRANKY BECAUSE SHE STAYED UP LATE TO HELP.
Z
MEANIE!
SO WHY'D YOU GUYS DECIDE TO COME STUDY HERE?
CAN I GO HOME NOW?

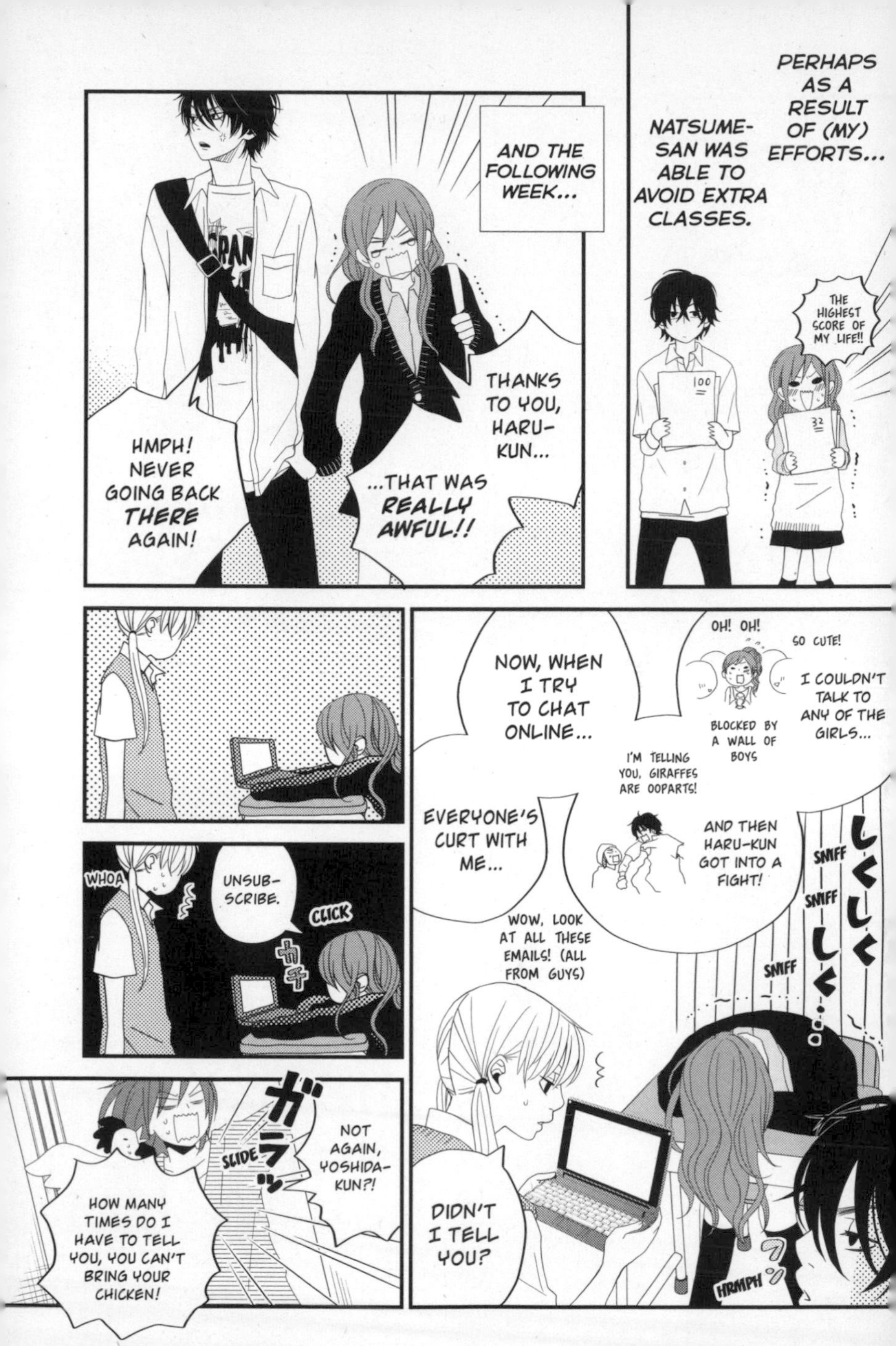
PERHAPS AS A RESULT OF (MY) EFFORTS...
NATSUME-SAN WAS ABLE TO AVOID EXTRA CLASSES.
THE HIGHEST SCORE OF MY LIFE!!
AND THE FOLLOWING WEEK...
THANKS TO YOU, HARU-KUN...
...THAT WAS REALLY AWFUL!!
HMPH! NEVER GOING BACK THERE AGAIN!
NOW, WHEN I TRY TO CHAT ONLINE...
OH! OH!
SO CUTE!
I COULDN'T TALK TO ANY OF THE GIRLS...
BLOCKED BY A WALL OF BOYS
I'M TELLING YOU, GIRAFFES ARE OOPARTS!
AND THEN HARU-KUN GOT INTO A FIGHT!
EVERYONE'S CURT WITH ME...
SNIFF
SNIFF
SNIFF
WOW, LOOK AT ALL THESE EMAILS! (ALL FROM GUYS)
DIDN'T I TELL YOU?
HRMPH
WHOA
UNSUB-SCRIBE.
CLICK
NOT AGAIN, YOSHIDA-KUN?!
SLIDE
HOW MANY TIMES DO I HAVE TO TELL YOU, YOU CAN'T BRING YOUR CHICKEN!

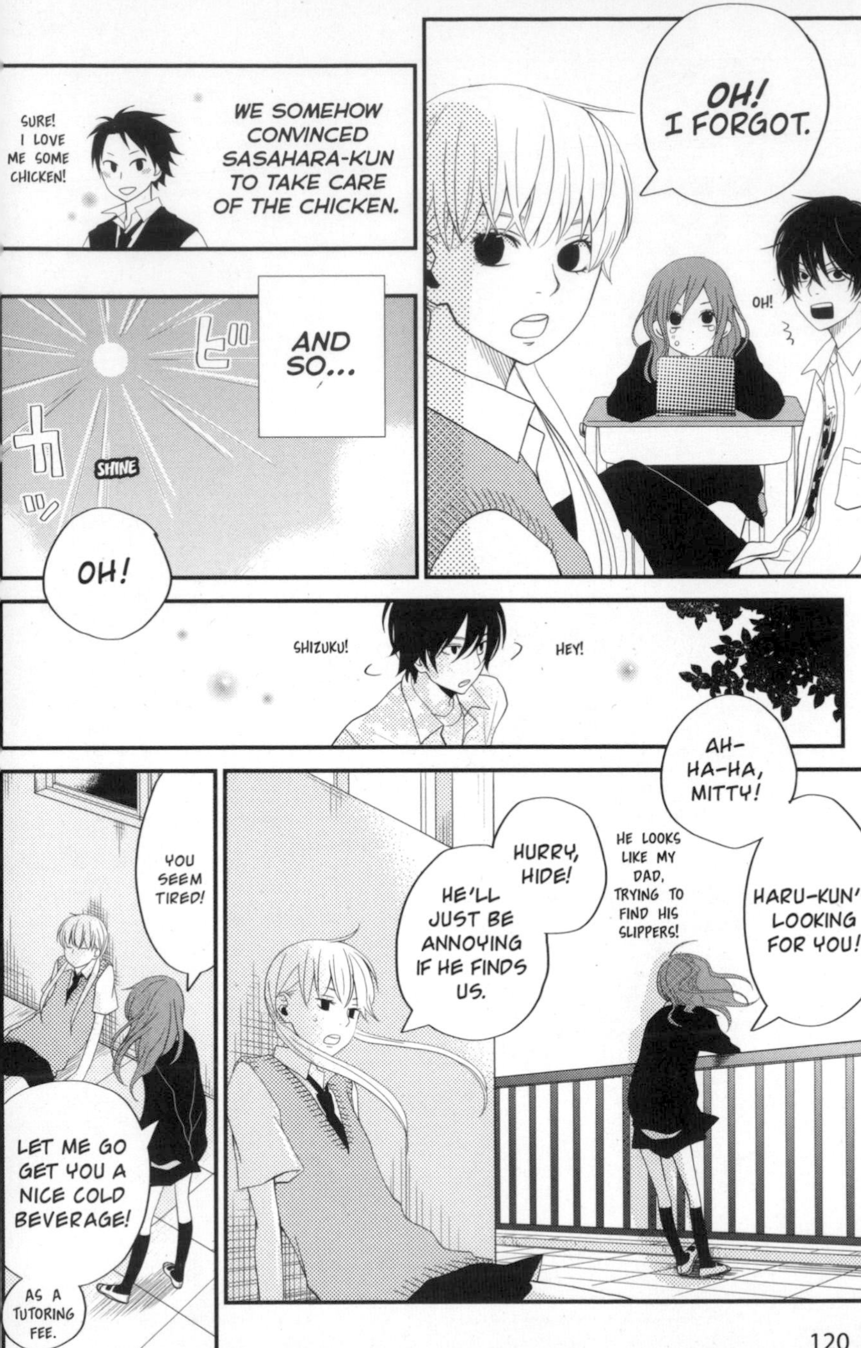
OH! I FORGOT.
OH!
WE SOMEHOW CONVINCED SASAHARA-KUN TO TAKE CARE OF THE CHICKEN.
SURE! I LOVE ME SOME CHICKEN!
AND SO...
SHINE
OH!
HEY!
SHIZUKU!
AH-HA-HA, MITTY!
HARU-KUN'S LOOKING FOR YOU!
HE LOOKS LIKE MY DAD, TRYING TO FIND HIS SLIPPERS!
HURRY, HIDE!
HE'LL JUST BE ANNOYING IF HE FINDS US.
YOU SEEM TIRED!
LET ME GO GET YOU A NICE COLD BEVERAGE!
AS A TUTORING FEE.

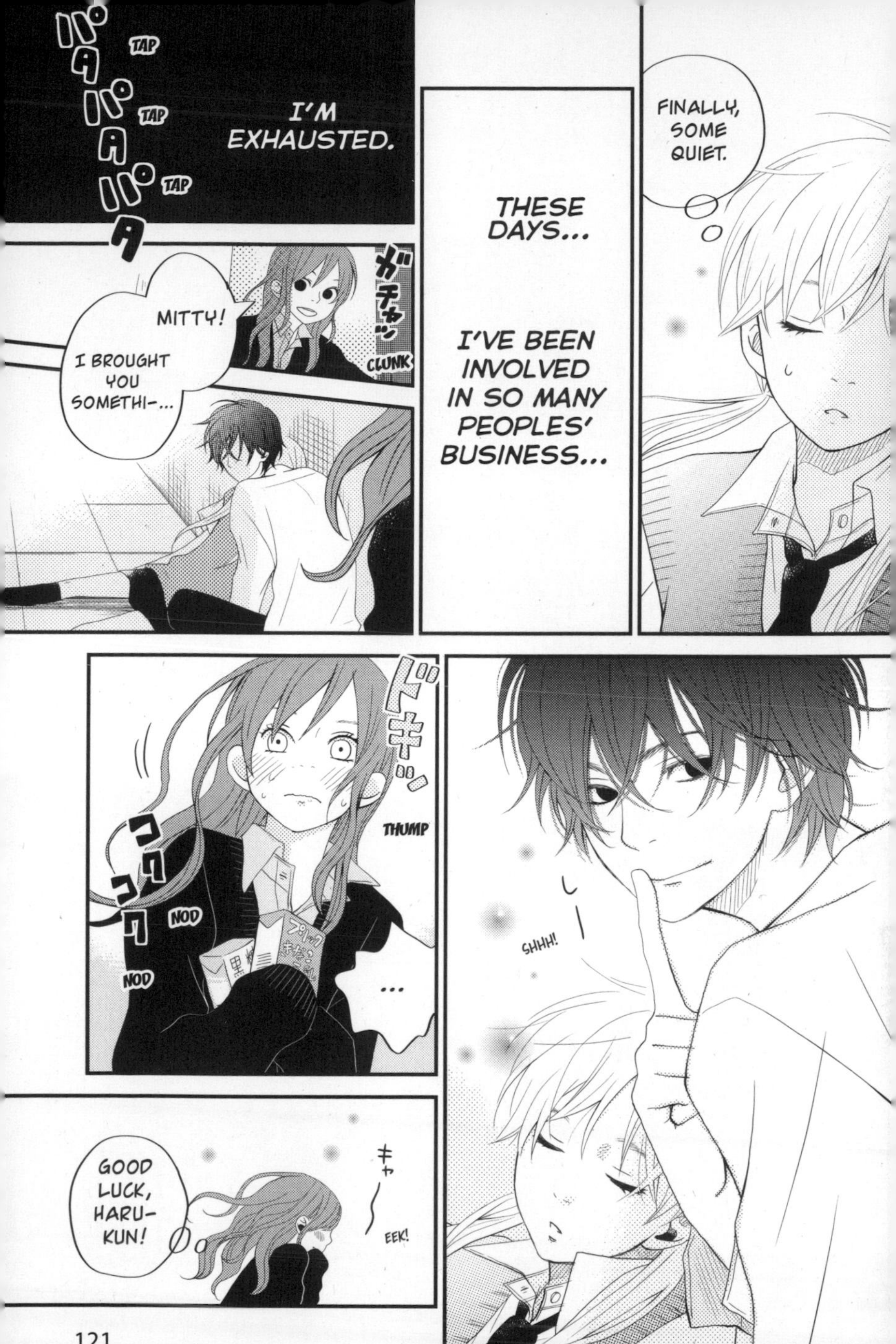
FINALLY, SOME QUIET.
THESE DAYS...
I'VE BEEN INVOLVED IN SO MANY PEOPLES' BUSINESS...
I'M EXHAUSTED.
TAP
TAP
TAP
MITTY!
I BROUGHT YOU SOMETHI-...
CLUNK
SHHH!
THUMP
NOD
NOD
...
GOOD LUCK, HARU-KUN!
EEK!

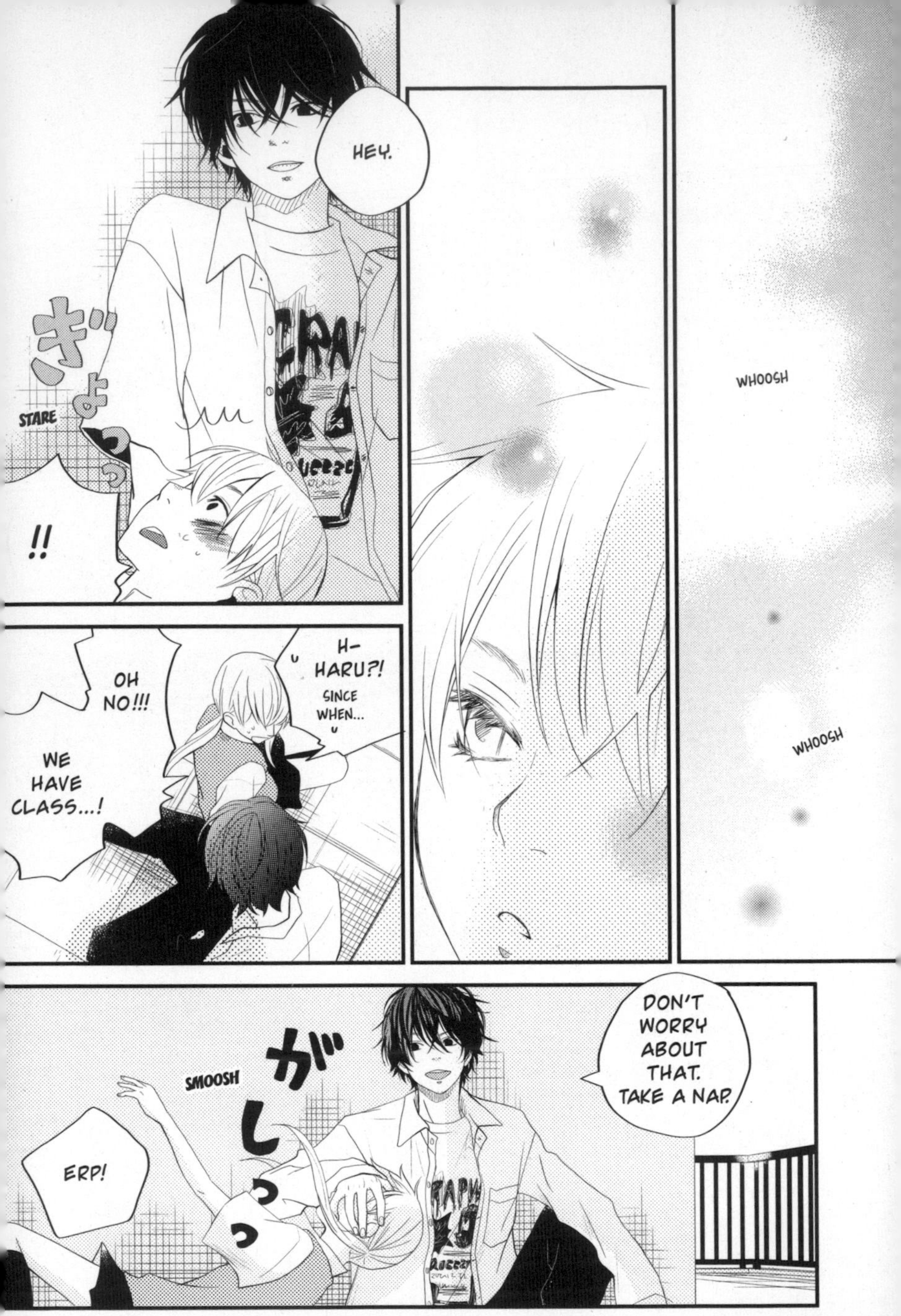
WHOOSH
WHOOSH
HEY.
ぎょっ
STARE
!!
H-HARU?!
SINCE WHEN...
OH NO!!!
WE HAVE CLASS...!
DON'T WORRY ABOUT THAT. TAKE A NAP.
がしっ
SMOOSH
ERP!

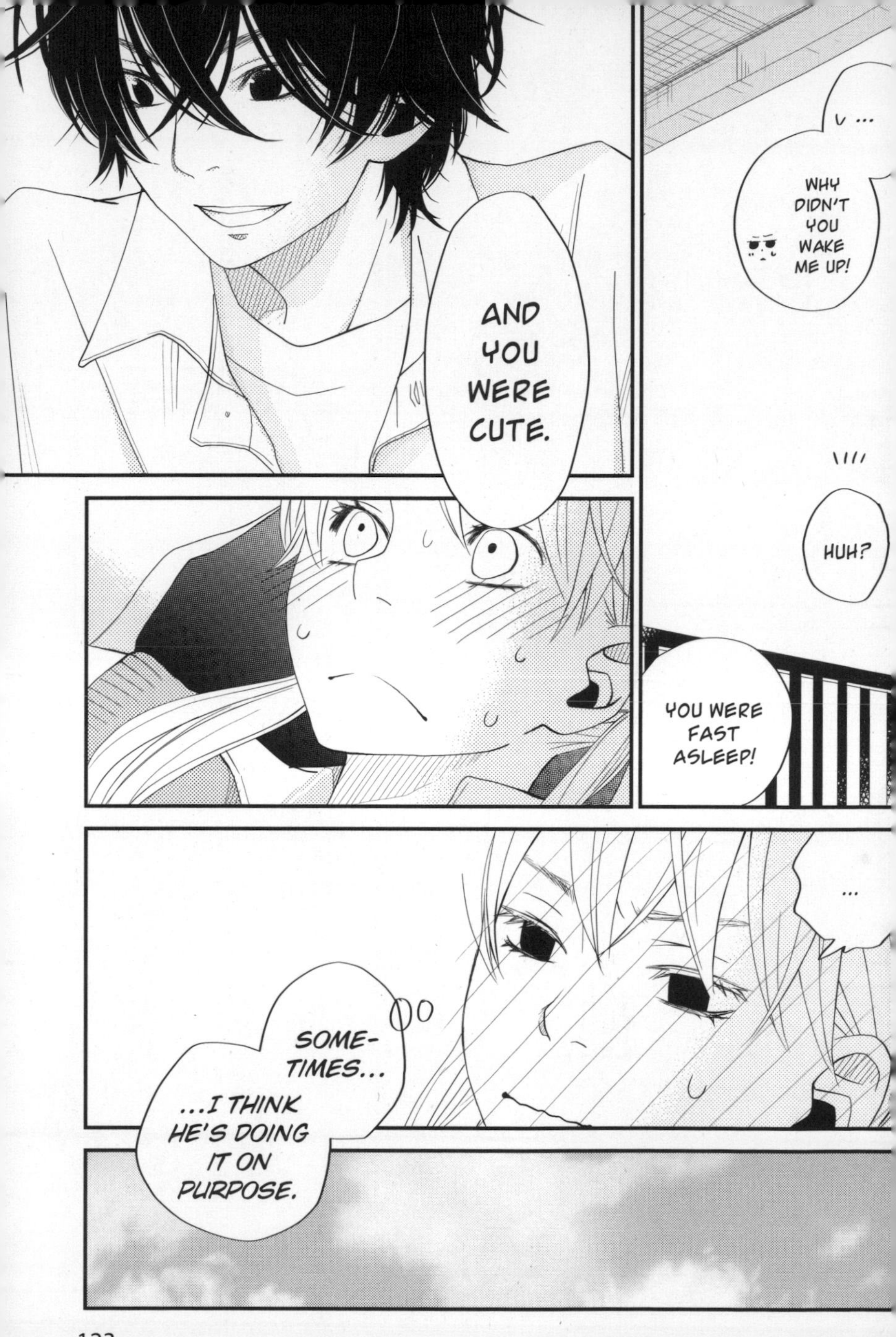
V...
WHY DIDN'T YOU WAKE ME UP!
HUH?
YOU WERE FAST ASLEEP!
AND YOU WERE CUTE.
...
SOME-TIMES...
...I THINK HE'S DOING IT ON PURPOSE.

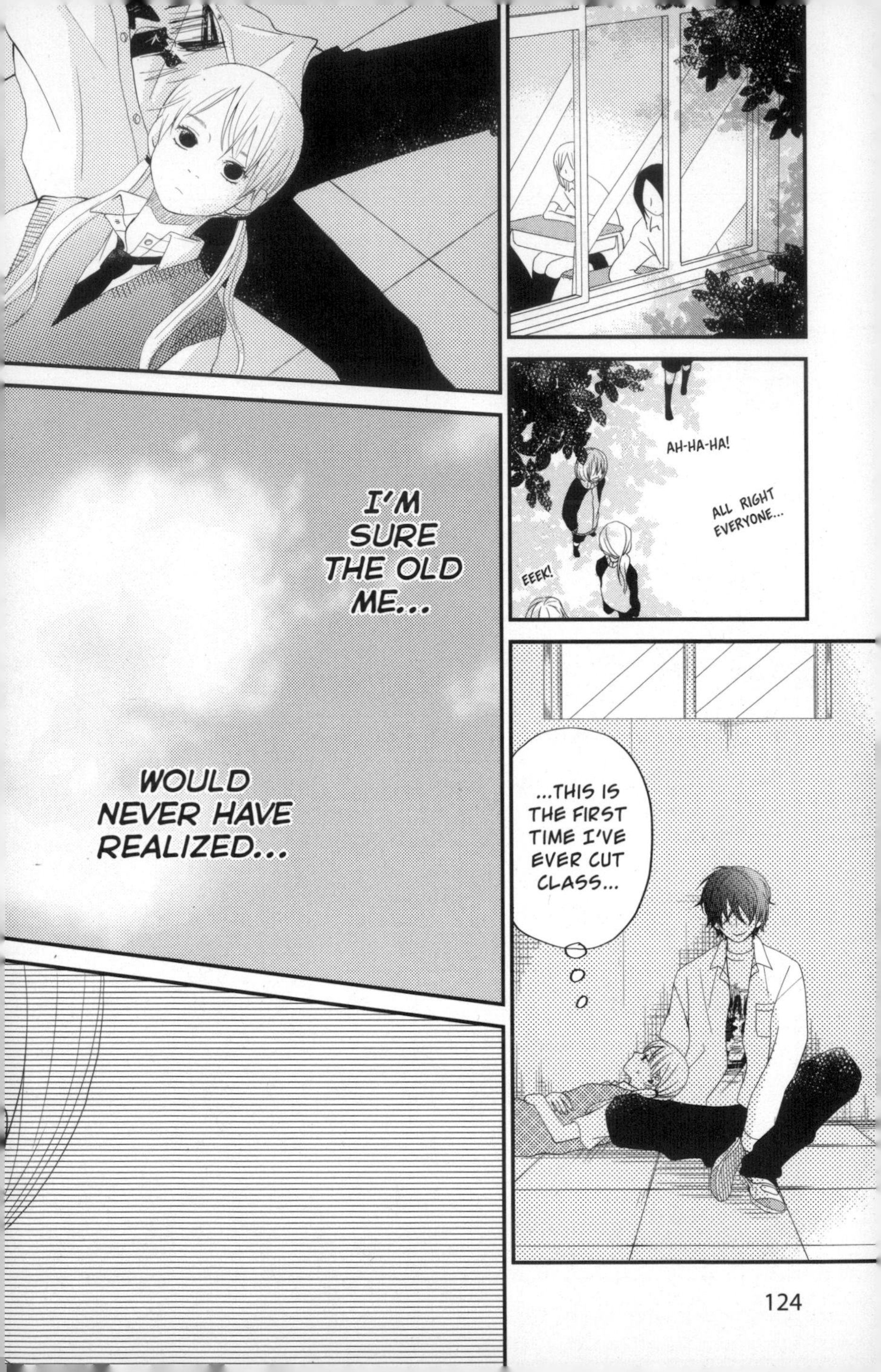
AH-HA-HA!
ALL RIGHT EVERYONE...
EEEK!
I'M SURE THE OLD ME...
WOULD NEVER HAVE REALIZED...
...THIS IS THE FIRST TIME I'VE EVER CUT CLASS...

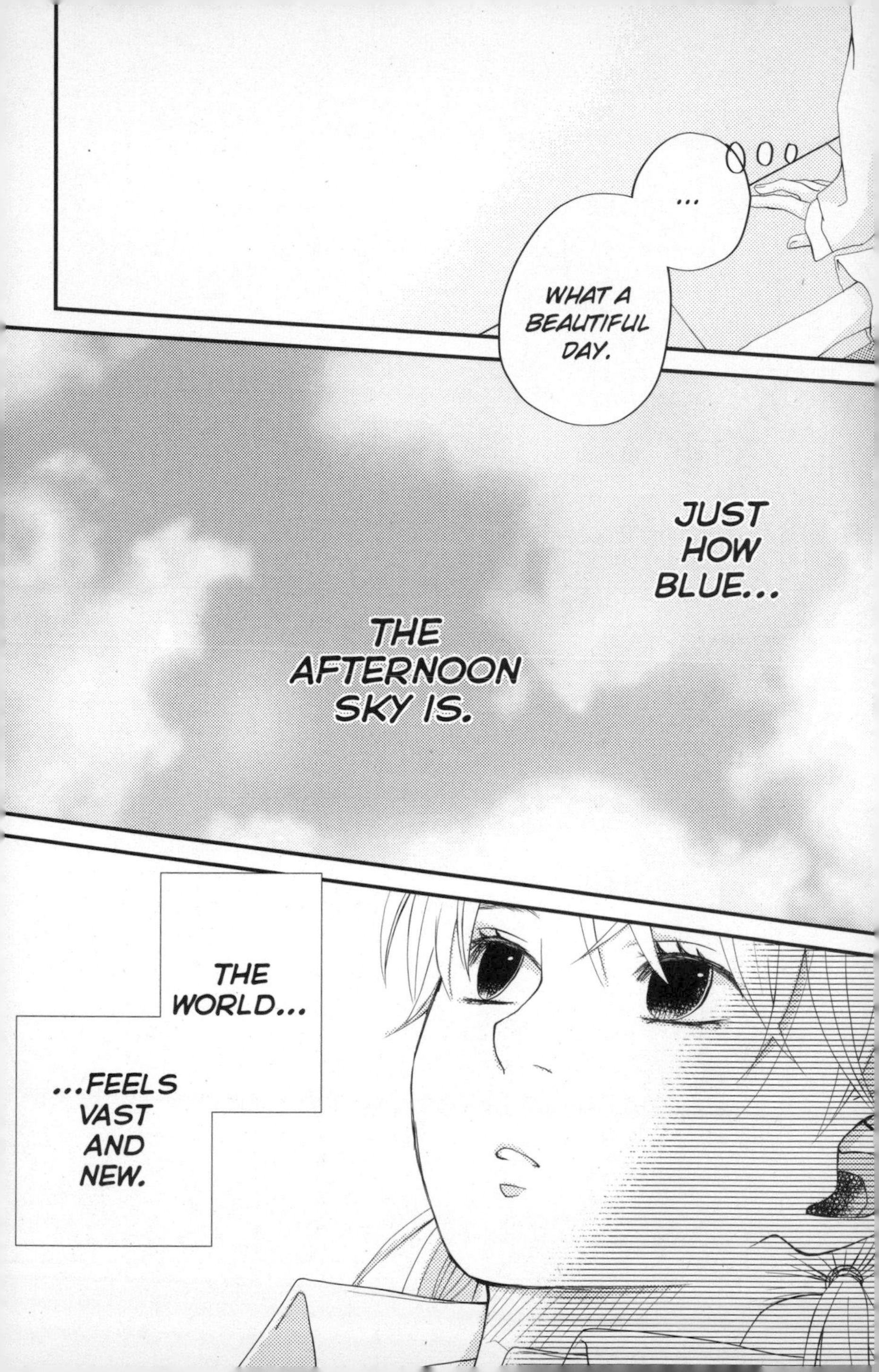
...
WHAT A BEAUTIFUL DAY.
JUST HOW BLUE...
THE AFTERNOON SKY IS.
THE WORLD...
...FEELS VAST AND NEW.

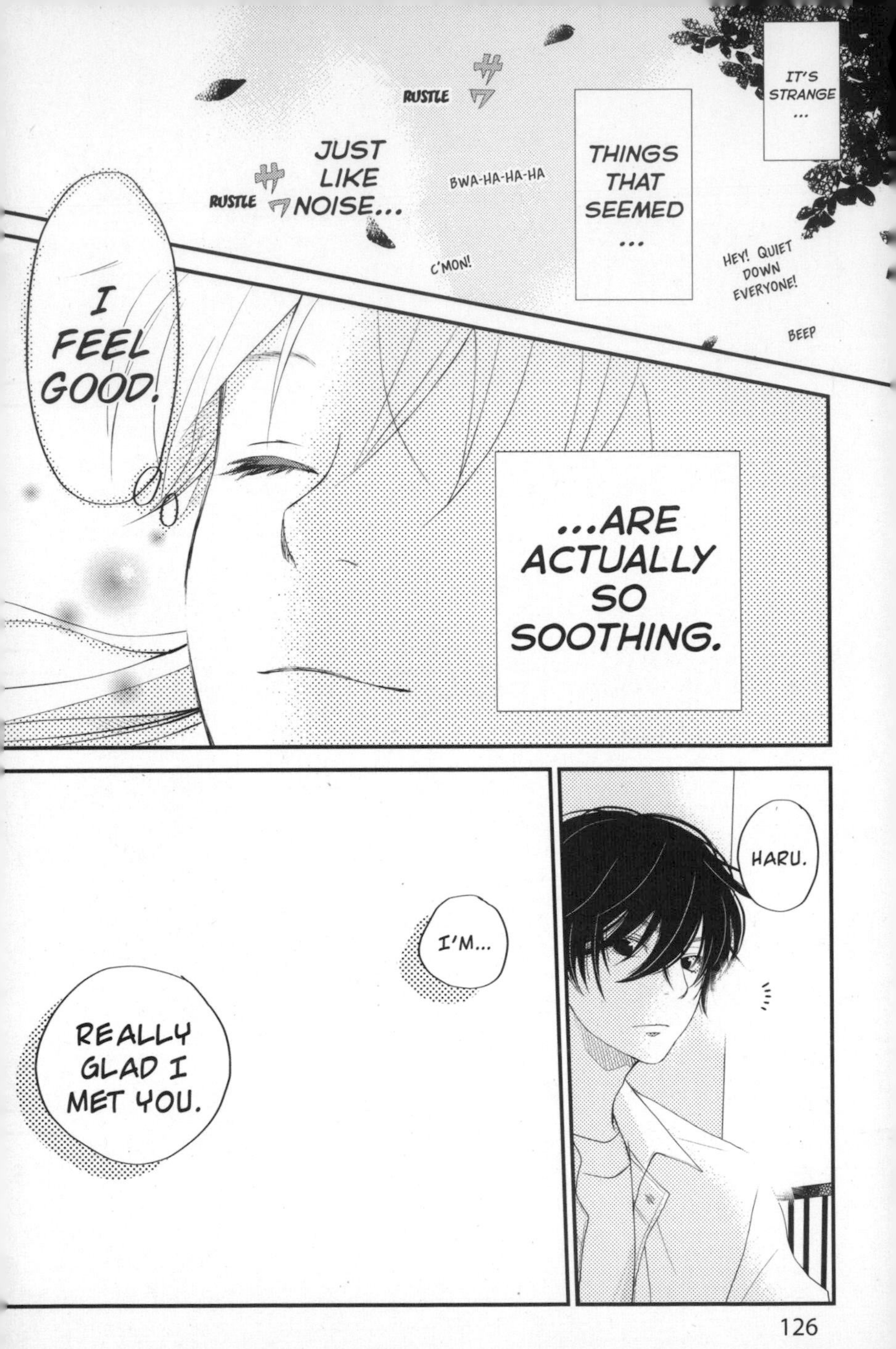
IT'S STRANGE...
THINGS THAT SEEMED...
HEY! QUIET DOWN EVERYONE!
BEEP
RUSTLE
BWA-HA-HA-HA
C'MON!
JUST LIKE NOISE...
RUSTLE
...ARE ACTUALLY SO SOOTHING.
I FEEL GOOD.
HARU.
I'M...
REALLY GLAD I MET YOU.

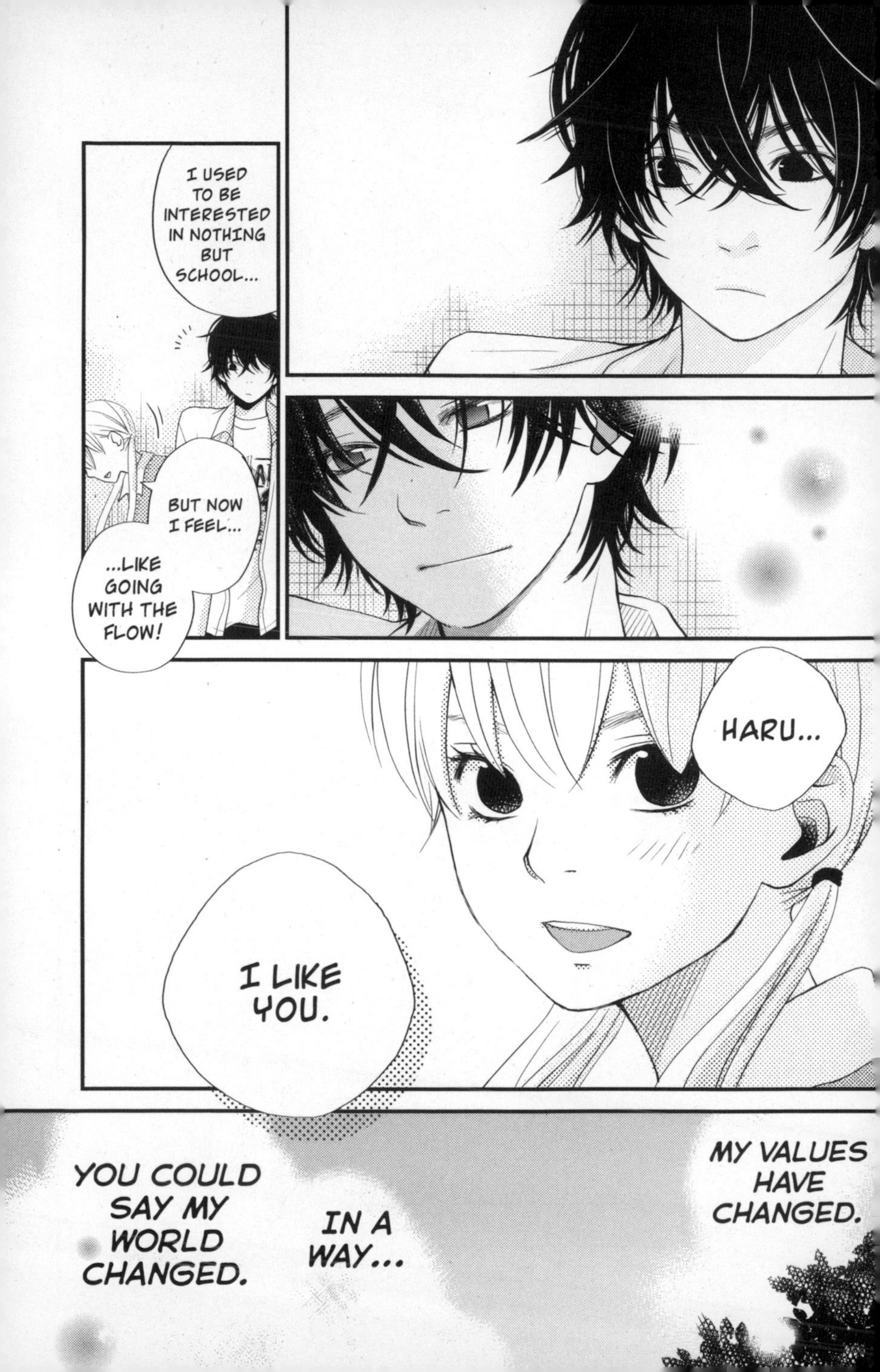
I USED TO BE INTERESTED IN NOTHING BUT SCHOOL...
BUT NOW I FEEL...
...LIKE GOING WITH THE FLOW!
HARU...
I LIKE YOU.
MY VALUES HAVE CHANGED.
IN A WAY...
YOU COULD SAY MY WORLD CHANGED.

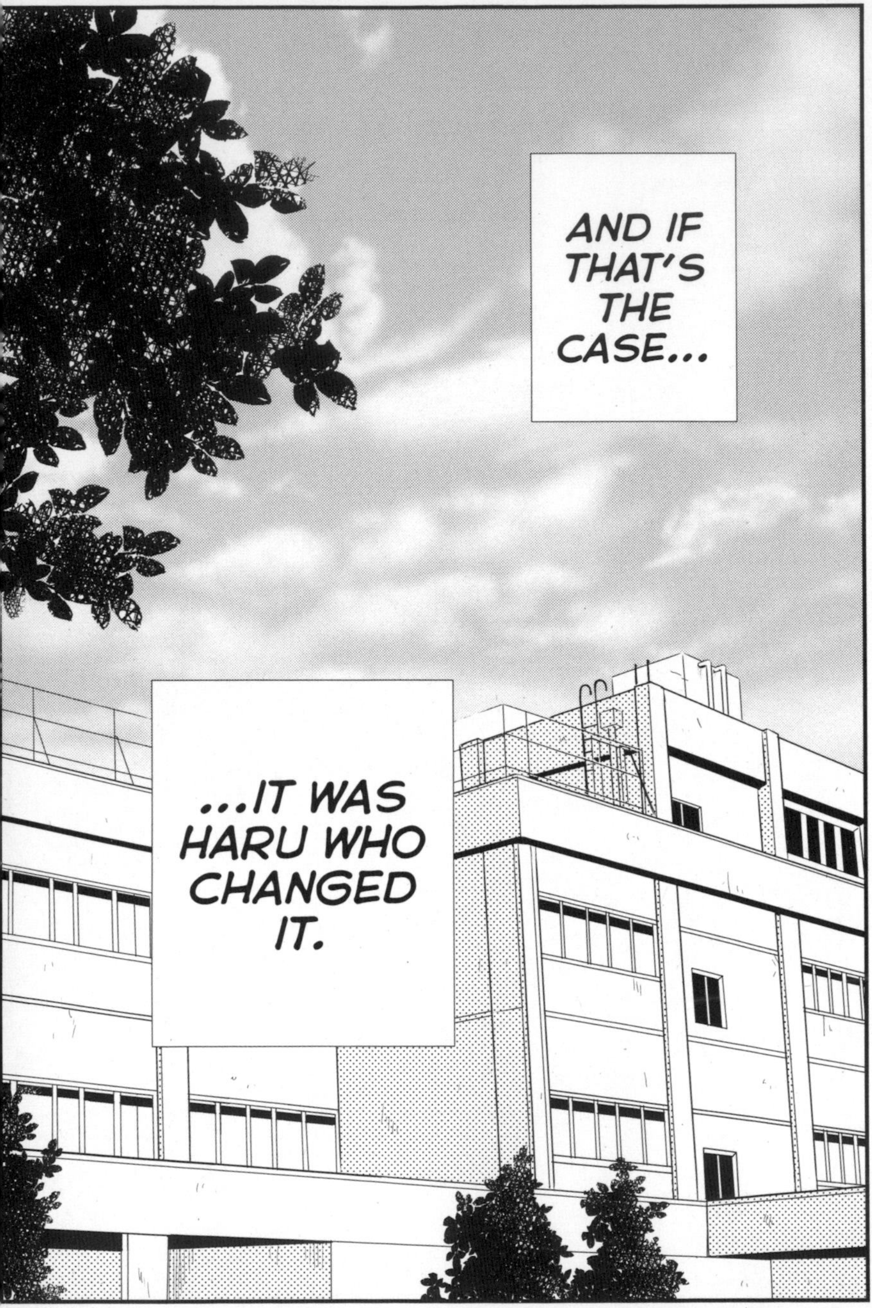
AND IF THAT'S THE CASE...
...IT WAS HARU WHO CHANGED IT.

NATSUME AND HARU 1

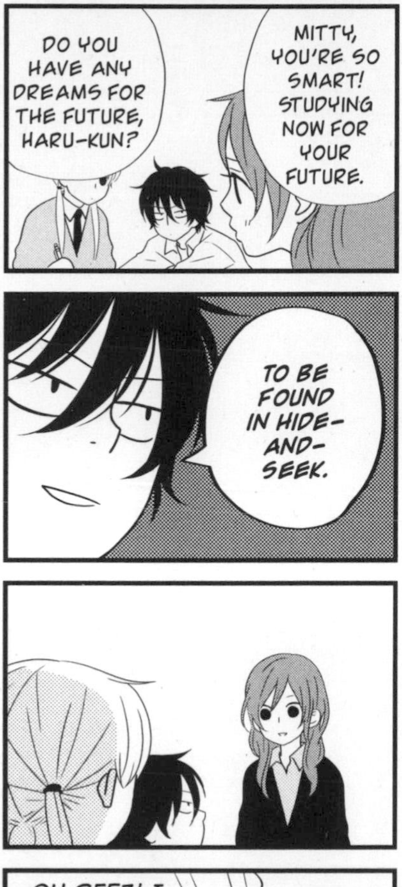
MITTY, YOU'RE SO SMART! STUDYING NOW FOR YOUR FUTURE.
DO YOU HAVE ANY DREAMS FOR THE FUTURE, HARU-KUN?
TO BE FOUND IN HIDE-AND-SEEK.
I-I KNOW WHAT YOU MEAN!
OH GEEZ! I HAVE NO IDEA WHAT THEY MEAN!

NATSUME AND HARU 2

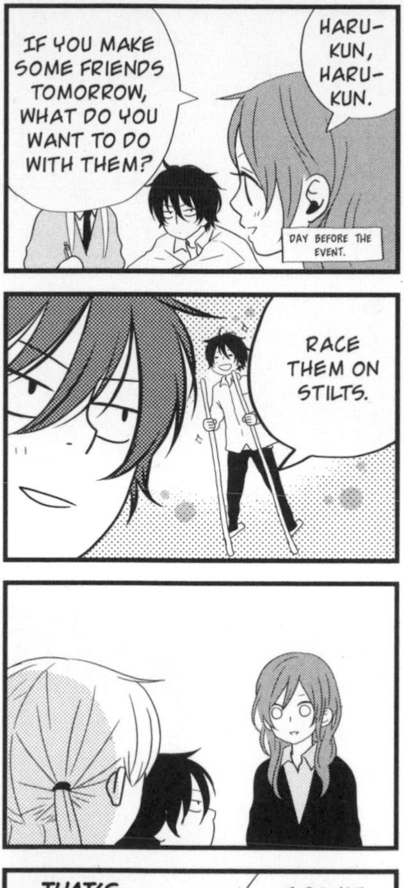
HARU-KUN, HARU-KUN.
IF YOU MAKE SOME FRIENDS TOMORROW, WHAT DO YOU WANT TO DO WITH THEM?
DAY BEFORE THE EVENT.
RACE THEM ON STILTS.
I DON'T THINK THERE'LL BE ENOUGH SPACE...
IT'S IN A STORE...
THAT'S THE ONLY PROBLEM SHE SEES!?

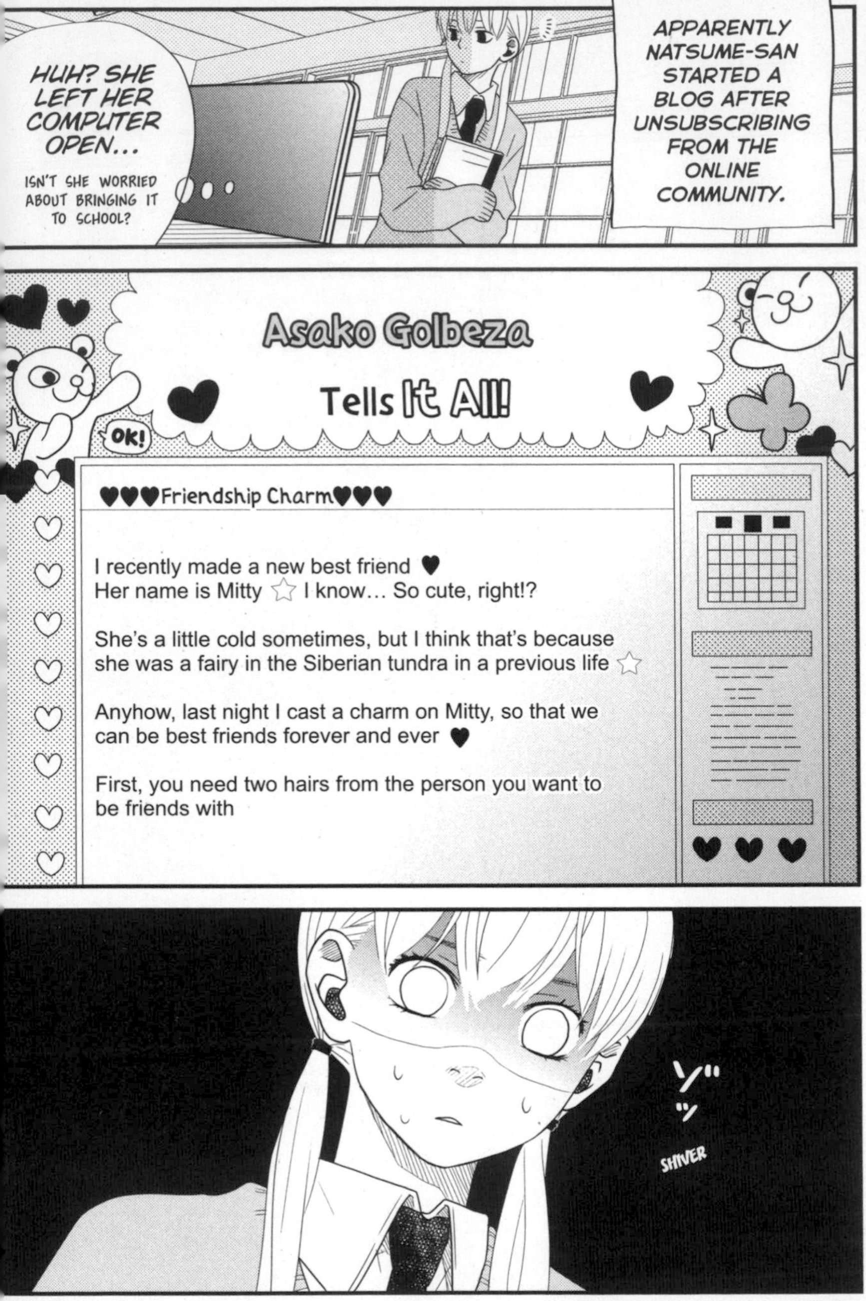
APPARENTLY NATSUME-SAN STARTED A BLOG AFTER UNSUBSCRIBING FROM THE ONLINE COMMUNITY.
HUH? SHE LEFT HER COMPUTER OPEN...
ISN'T SHE WORRIED ABOUT BRINGING IT TO SCHOOL?
Asako Golbeza
Tells It All!
OK!
♥♥♥Friendship Charm♥♥♥
I recently made a new best friend ♥
Her name is Mitty ☆ I know... So cute, right!?
She's a little cold sometimes, but I think that's because she was a fairy in the Siberian tundra in a previous life ☆
Anyhow, last night I cast a charm on Mitty, so that we can be best friends forever and ever ♥
First, you need two hairs from the person you want to be friends with
ゾッ
SHIVER

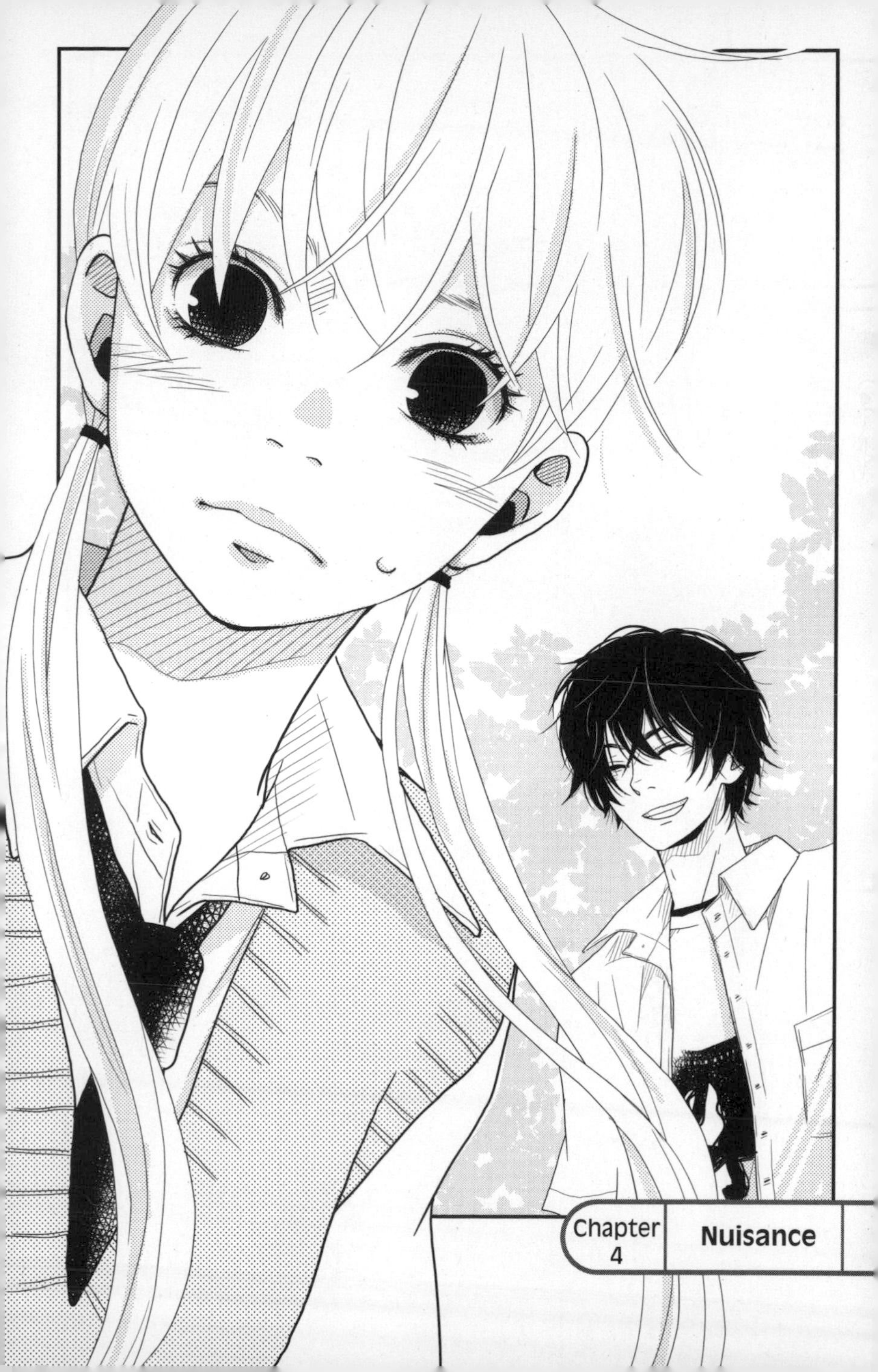
Chapter 4
Nuisance

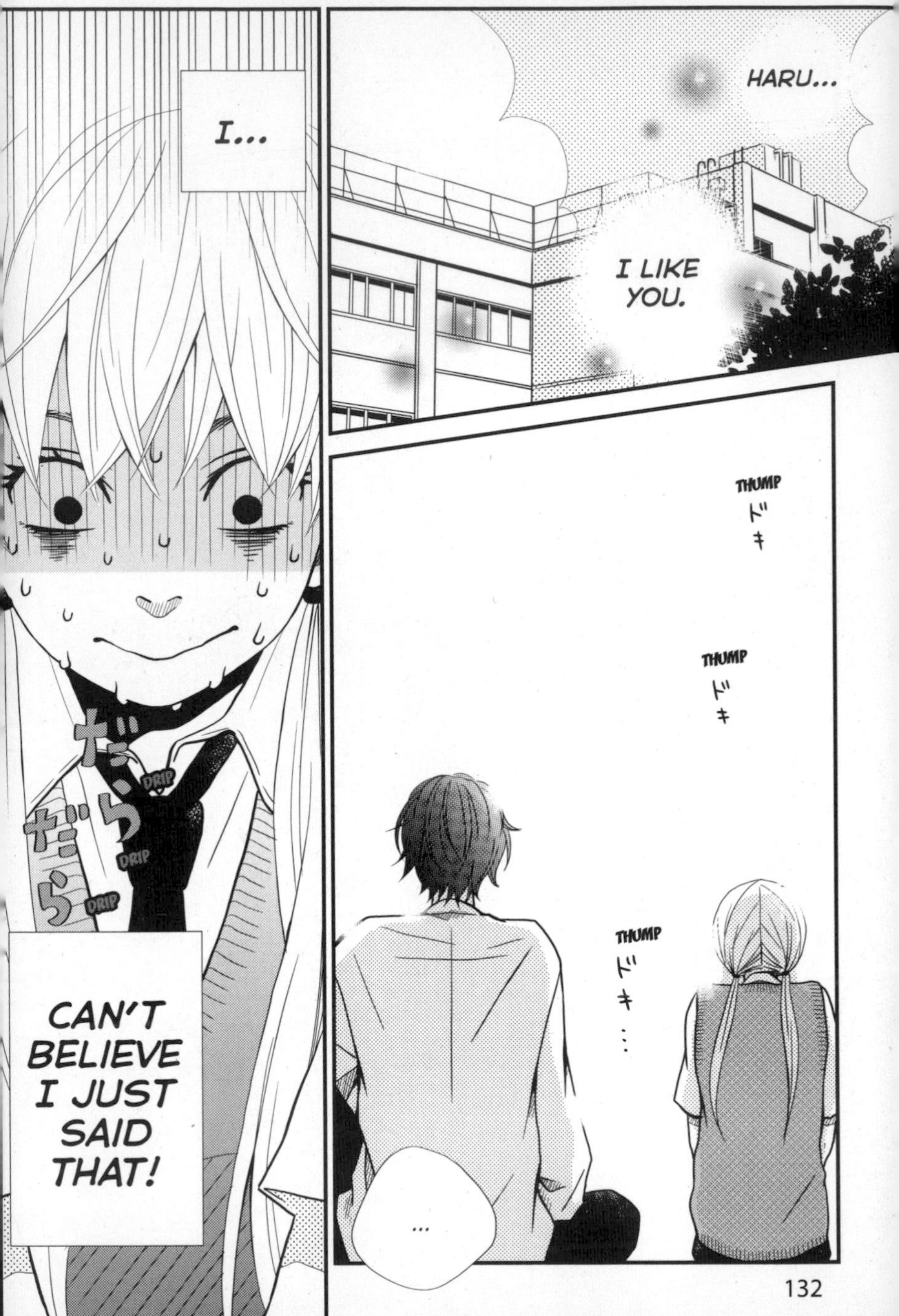
HARU...
I LIKE YOU.
THUMP
ドキ
THUMP
ドキ
THUMP
ドキ…
...
I...
だら DRIP
だら DRIP
DRIP
CAN'T BELIEVE I JUST SAID THAT!

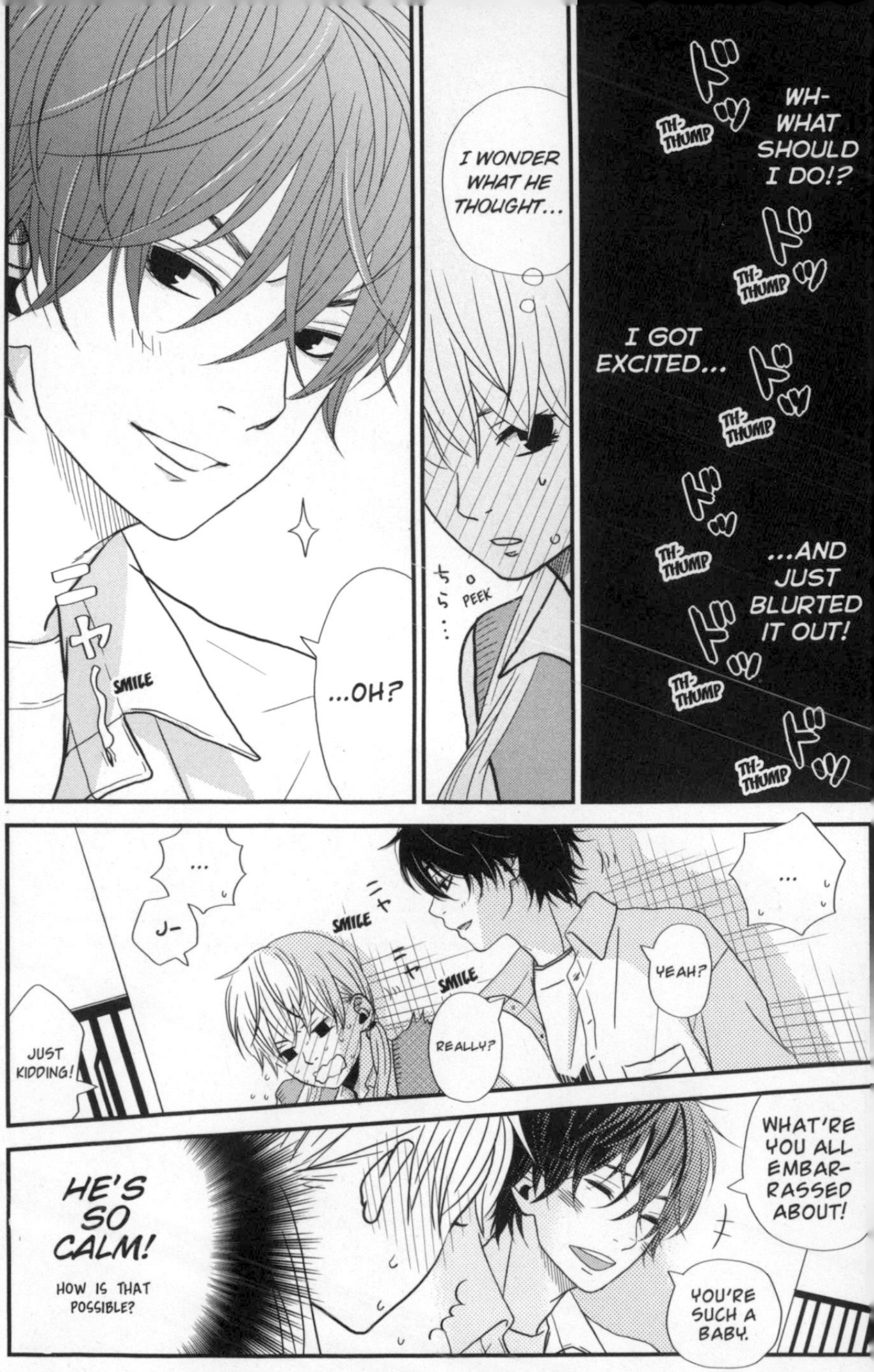
WH- WHAT SHOULD I DO!?
TH-THUMP
TH-THUMP
I GOT EXCITED...
TH-THUMP
TH-THUMP
...AND JUST BLURTED IT OUT!
TH-THUMP
TH-THUMP
I WONDER WHAT HE THOUGHT...
PEEK
...OH?
SMILE
...
YEAH?
SMILE
SMILE
REALLY?
...
J-
JUST KIDDING!
WHAT'RE YOU ALL EMBARRASSED ABOUT!
YOU'RE SUCH A BABY.
HE'S SO CALM!
HOW IS THAT POSSIBLE?

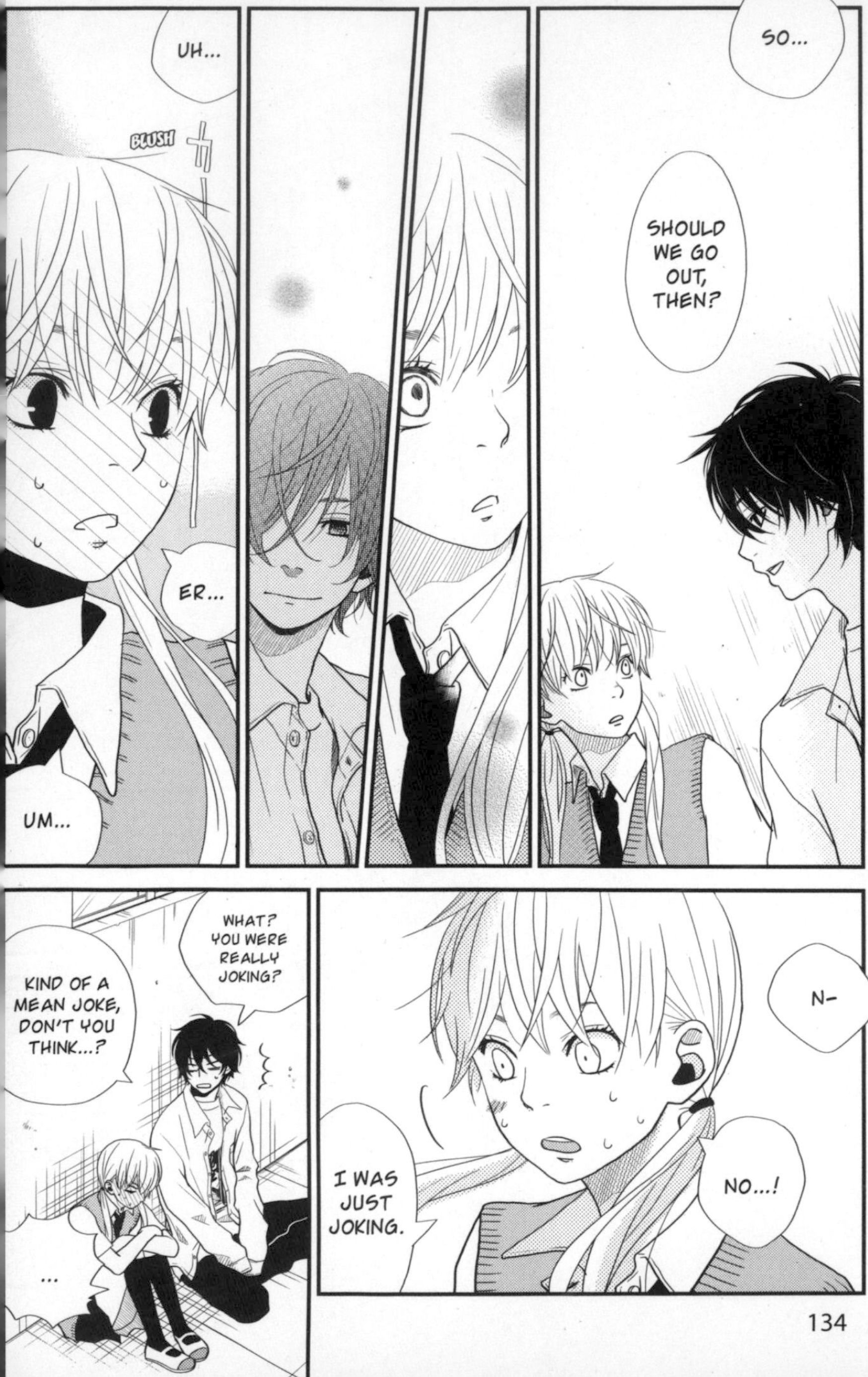
SO...
SHOULD WE GO OUT, THEN?
UH...
BLUSH
ER...
UM...
N-
NO...!
I WAS JUST JOKING.
WHAT? YOU WERE REALLY JOKING?
KIND OF A MEAN JOKE, DON'T YOU THINK...?
...

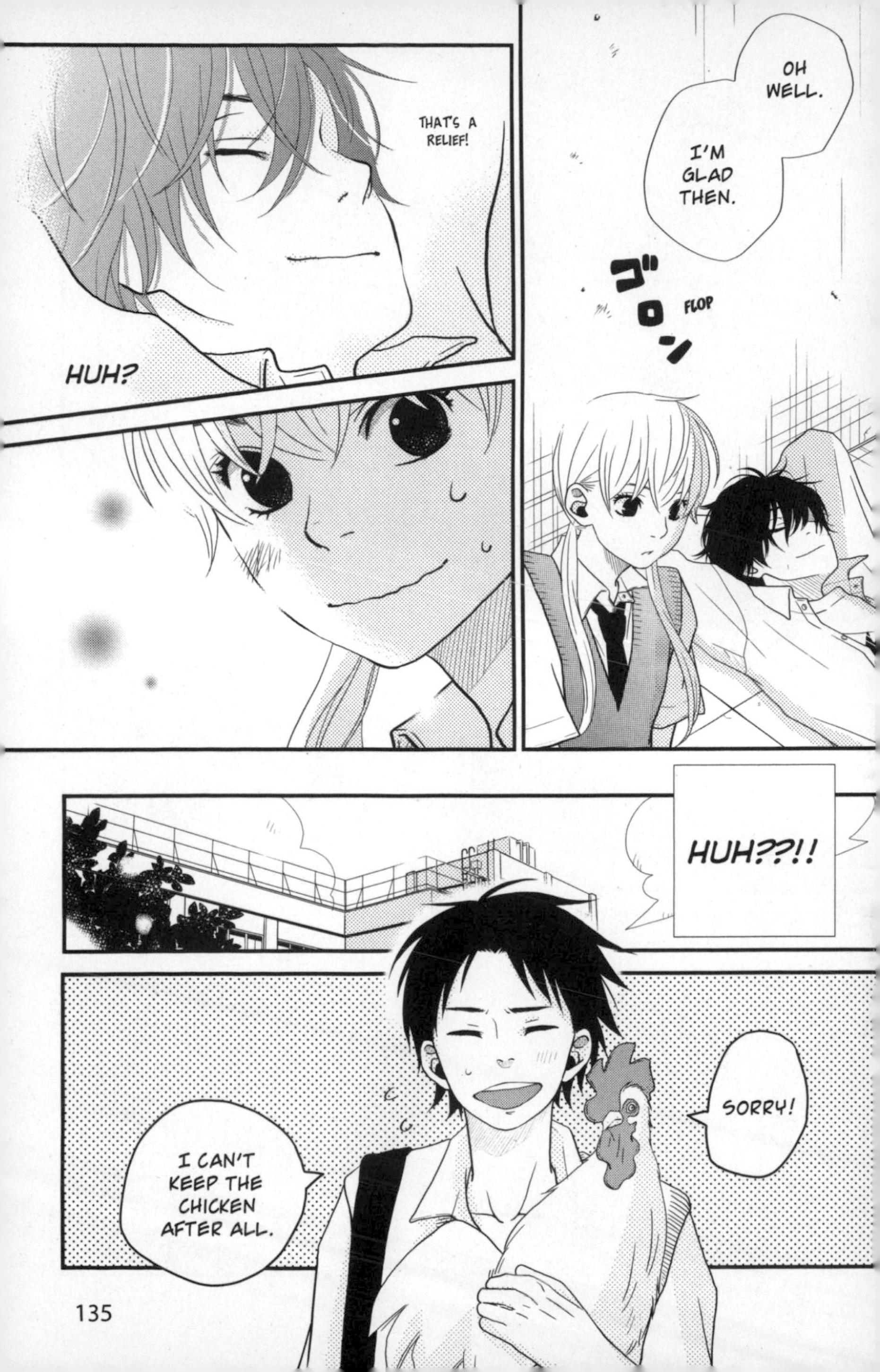
OH WELL.
I'M GLAD THEN.
ゴロン
FLOP
THAT'S A RELIEF!
HUH?
HUH??!!
SORRY!
I CAN'T KEEP THE CHICKEN AFTER ALL.

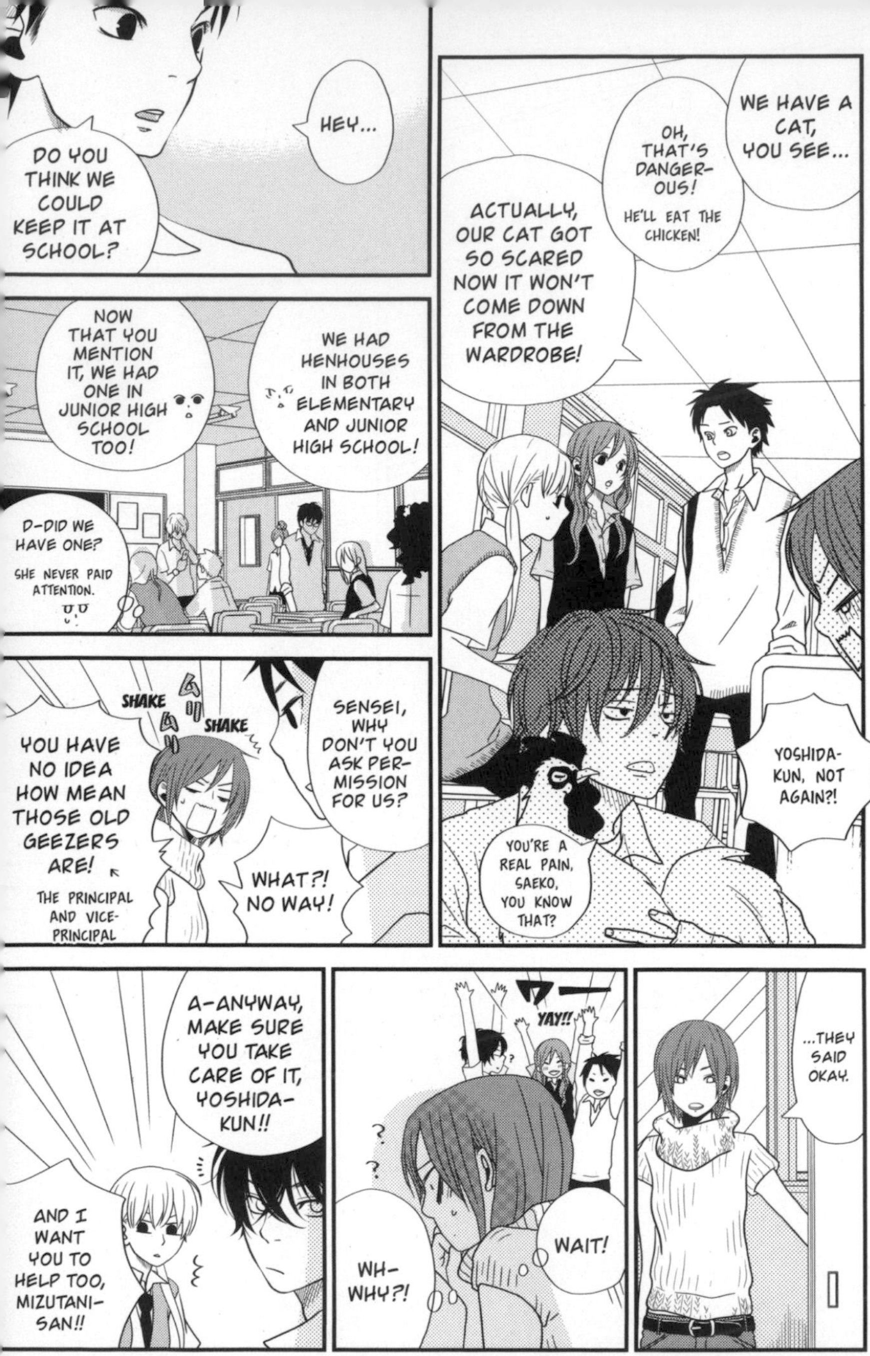
WE HAVE A CAT, YOU SEE...
OH, THAT'S DANGER-OUS!
HE'LL EAT THE CHICKEN!
ACTUALLY, OUR CAT GOT SO SCARED NOW IT WON'T COME DOWN FROM THE WARDROBE!
YOSHIDA-KUN, NOT AGAIN?!
YOU'RE A REAL PAIN, SAEKO, YOU KNOW THAT?
HEY...
DO YOU THINK WE COULD KEEP IT AT SCHOOL?
WE HAD HENHOUSES IN BOTH ELEMENTARY AND JUNIOR HIGH SCHOOL!
NOW THAT YOU MENTION IT, WE HAD ONE IN JUNIOR HIGH SCHOOL TOO!
D-DID WE HAVE ONE?
SHE NEVER PAID ATTENTION.
SENSEI, WHY DON'T YOU ASK PER-MISSION FOR US?
SHAKE
SHAKE
YOU HAVE NO IDEA HOW MEAN THOSE OLD GEEZERS ARE!
THE PRINCIPAL AND VICE-PRINCIPAL
WHAT?! NO WAY!
...THEY SAID OKAY.
YAY!!
WAIT!
WH-WHY?!
A-ANYWAY, MAKE SURE YOU TAKE CARE OF IT, YOSHIDA-KUN!!
AND I WANT YOU TO HELP TOO, MIZUTANI-SAN!!

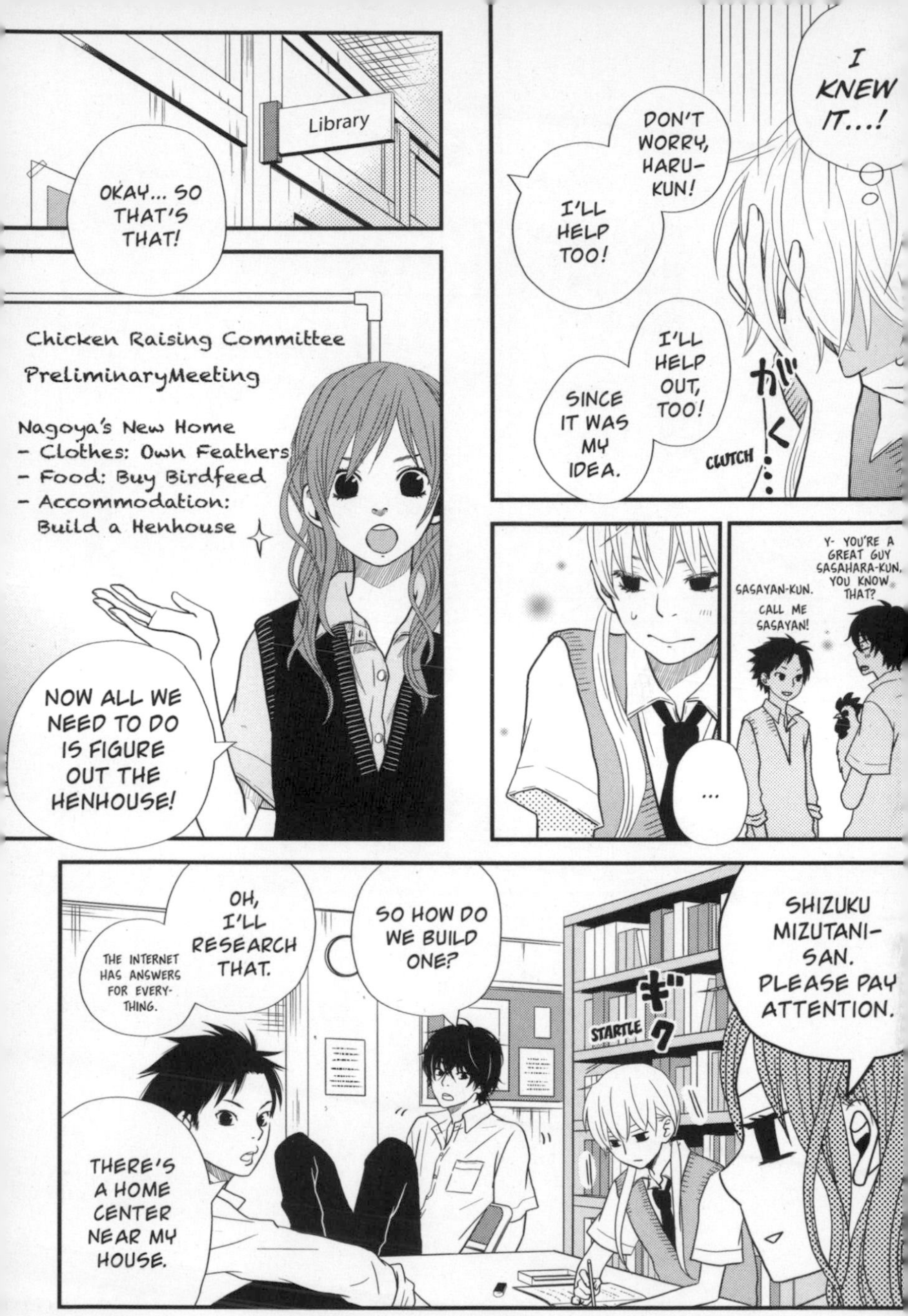
I KNEW IT...!
DON'T WORRY, HARU-KUN! I'LL HELP TOO!
I'LL HELP OUT, TOO! SINCE IT WAS MY IDEA.
CLUTCH
Library
OKAY... SO THAT'S THAT!
Chicken Raising Committee
PreliminaryMeeting
Nagoya's New Home
- Clothes: Own Feathers
- Food: Buy Birdfeed
- Accommodation: Build a Henhouse
NOW ALL WE NEED TO DO IS FIGURE OUT THE HENHOUSE!
Y- YOU'RE A GREAT GUY SASAHARA-KUN, YOU KNOW THAT?
SASAYAN-KUN. CALL ME SASAYAN!
...
SHIZUKU MIZUTANI-SAN. PLEASE PAY ATTENTION.
STARTLE
SO HOW DO WE BUILD ONE?
OH, I'LL RESEARCH THAT.
THE INTERNET HAS ANSWERS FOR EVERYTHING.
THERE'S A HOME CENTER NEAR MY HOUSE.

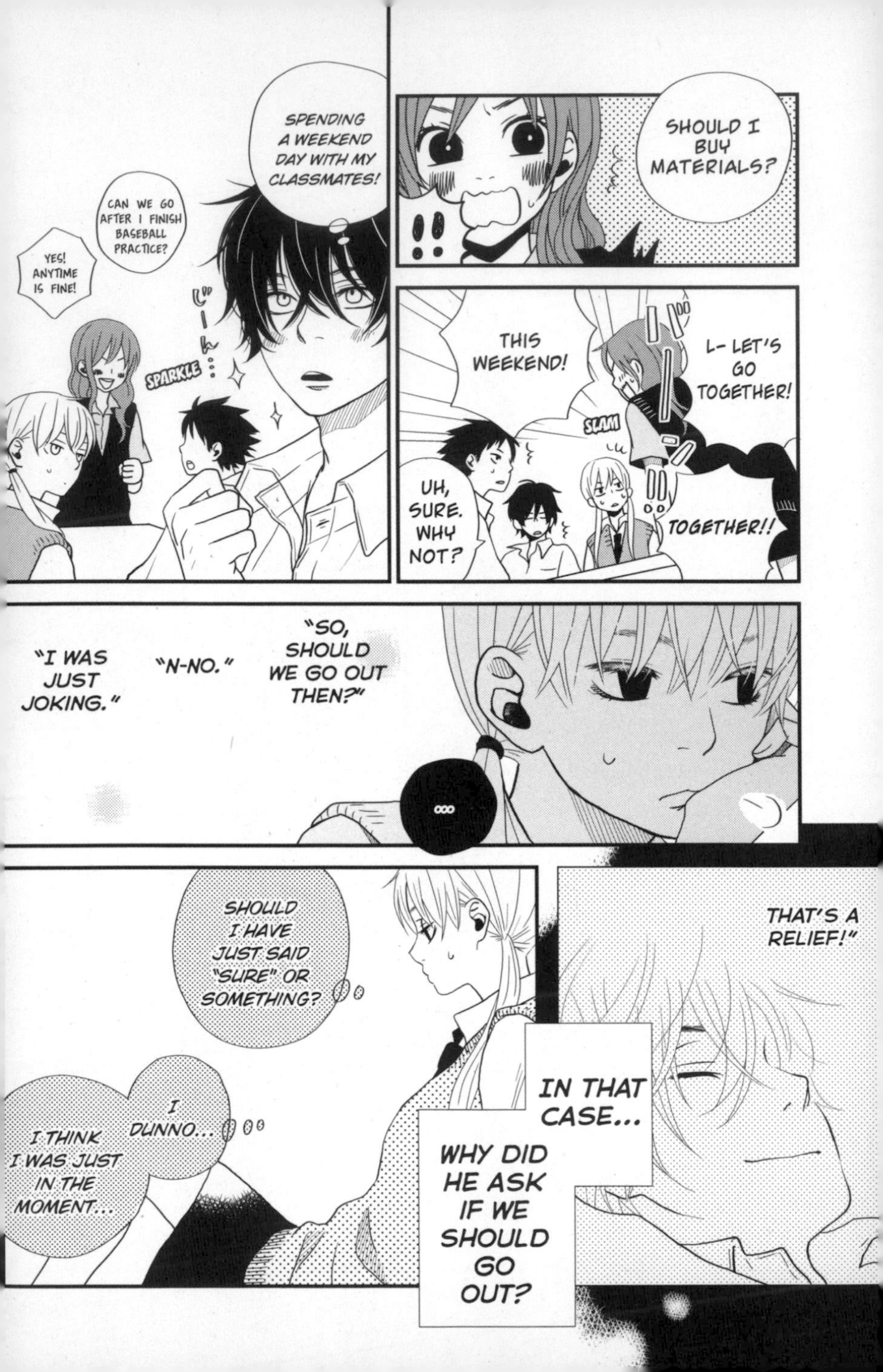
SHOULD I BUY MATERIALS?
L- LET'S GO TOGETHER!
THIS WEEKEND!
SLAM
TOGETHER!!
UH, SURE. WHY NOT?
SPENDING A WEEKEND DAY WITH MY CLASSMATES!
CAN WE GO AFTER I FINISH BASEBALL PRACTICE?
YES! ANYTIME IS FINE!
SPARKLE
"SO, SHOULD WE GO OUT THEN?"
"N-NO."
"I WAS JUST JOKING."
THAT'S A RELIEF!"
IN THAT CASE...
WHY DID HE ASK IF WE SHOULD GO OUT?
SHOULD I HAVE JUST SAID "SURE" OR SOMETHING?
I DUNNO...
I THINK I WAS JUST IN THE MOMENT...

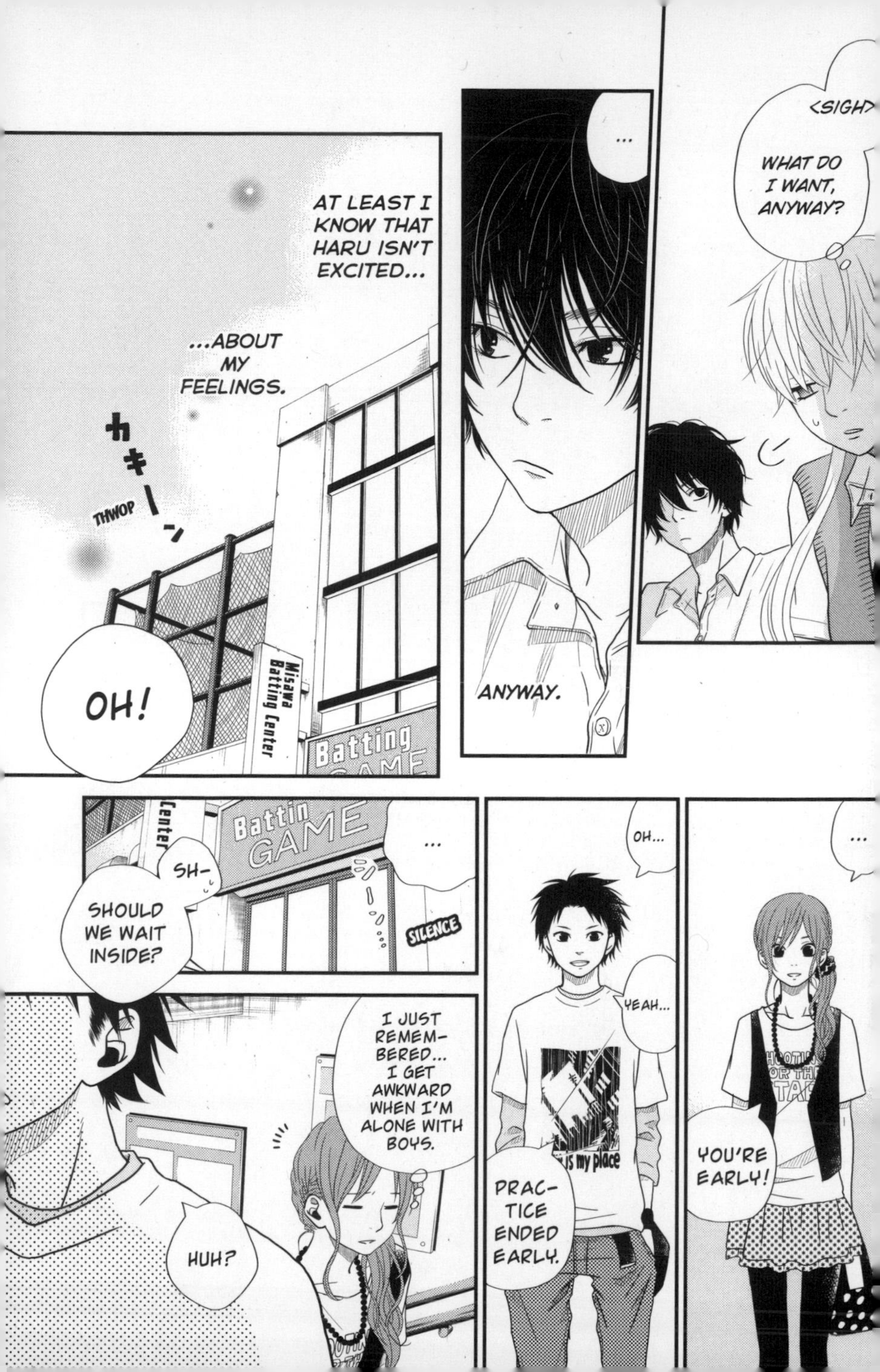
<SIGH>
WHAT DO I WANT, ANYWAY?
...
ANYWAY.
AT LEAST I KNOW THAT HARU ISN'T EXCITED...
...ABOUT MY FEELINGS.
カキーン
THWOP
Misawa Batting Center
Batting GAME
OH!
...
YOU'RE EARLY!
OH...
YEAH...
PRAC-TICE ENDED EARLY.
Battin GAME
...
SILENCE
SH-
SHOULD WE WAIT INSIDE?
I JUST REMEM-BERED... I GET AWKWARD WHEN I'M ALONE WITH BOYS.
HUH?

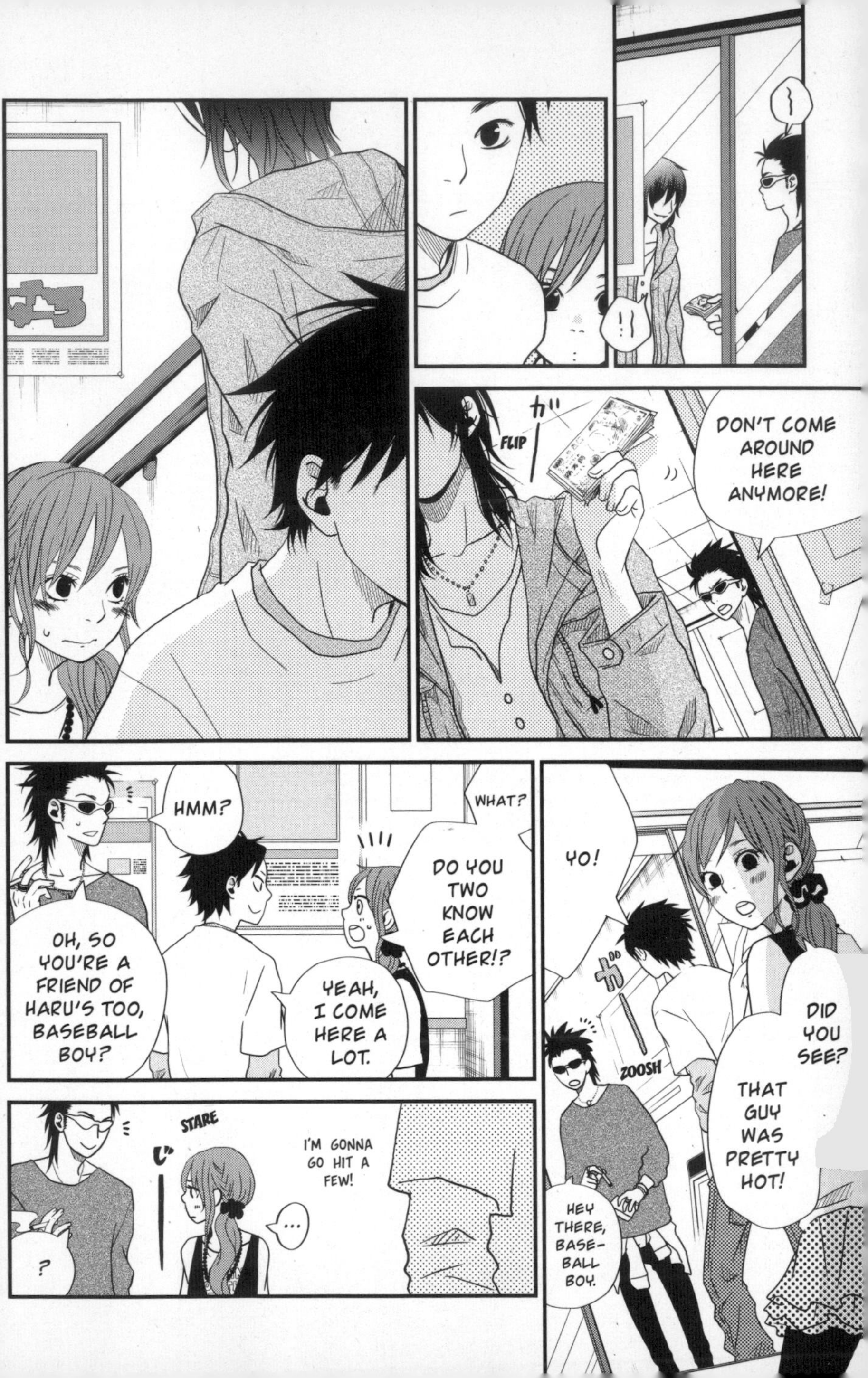
!
!!
FLIP
DON'T COME AROUND HERE ANYMORE!
YO!
DID YOU SEE?
THAT GUY WAS PRETTY HOT!
ZOOSH
HEY THERE, BASE-BALL BOY.
WHAT?
DO YOU TWO KNOW EACH OTHER!?
HMM?
OH, SO YOU'RE A FRIEND OF HARU'S TOO, BASEBALL BOY?
YEAH, I COME HERE A LOT.
I'M GONNA GO HIT A FEW!
STARE
...
?

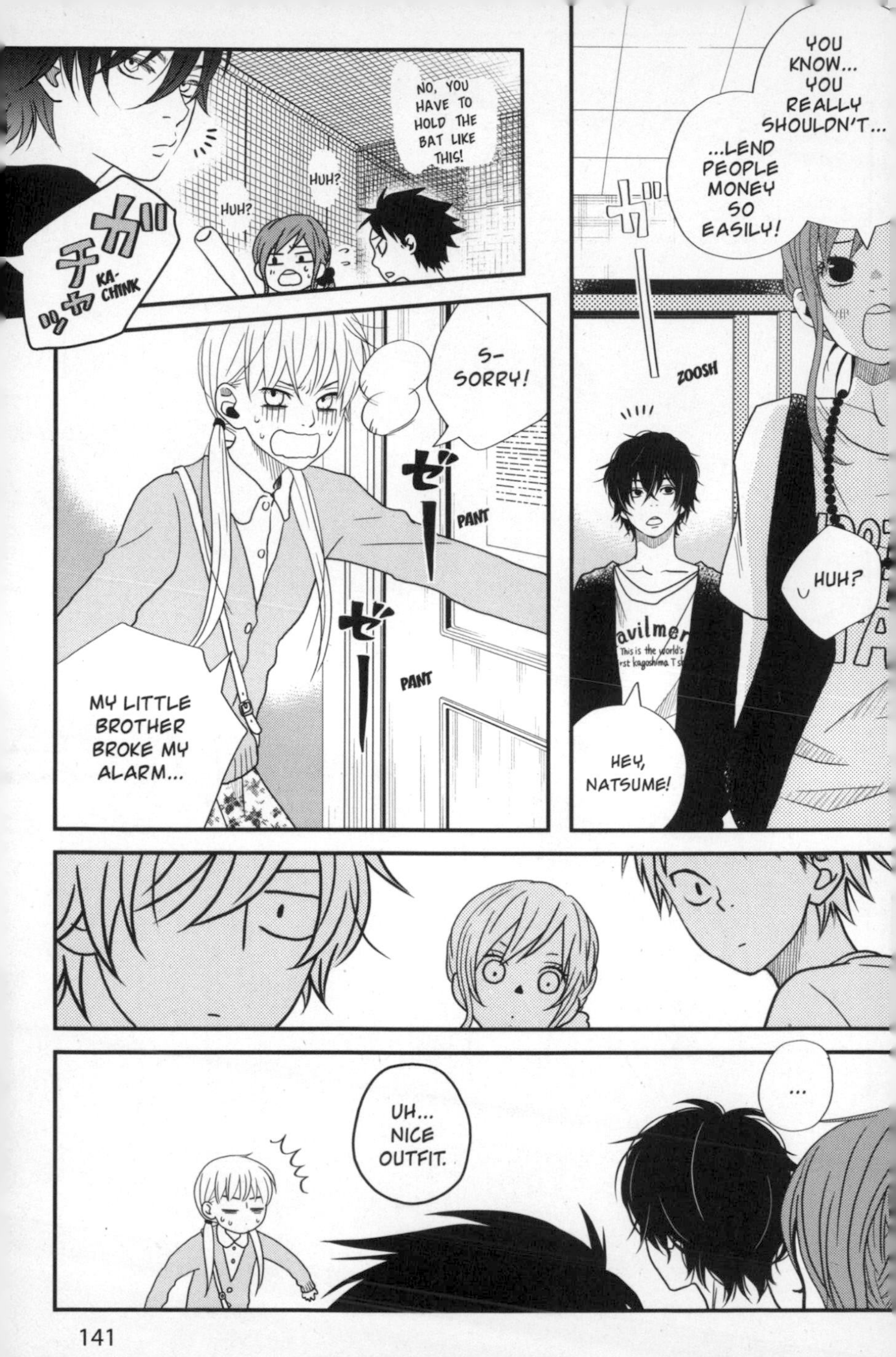
YOU KNOW... YOU REALLY SHOULDN'T...
...LEND PEOPLE MONEY SO EASILY!
ZOOSH
HUH?
HEY, NATSUME!
NO, YOU HAVE TO HOLD THE BAT LIKE THIS!
HUH?
HUH?
KA-CHINK
S-SORRY!
PANT
PANT
MY LITTLE BROTHER BROKE MY ALARM...
...
UH... NICE OUTFIT.

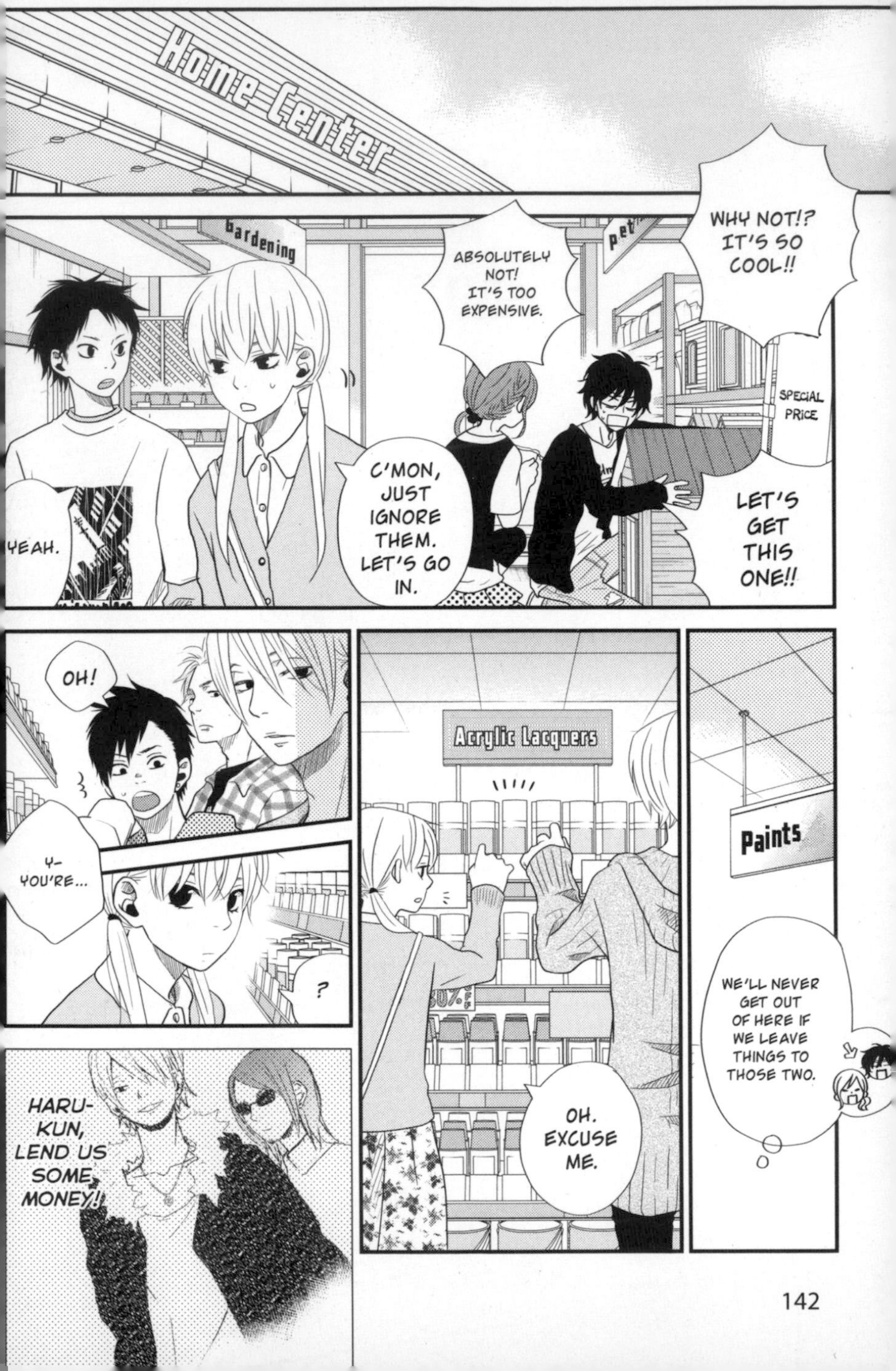
Home Center
Gardening
pet
WHY NOT!? IT'S SO COOL!!
ABSOLUTELY NOT! IT'S TOO EXPENSIVE.
SPECIAL PRICE
LET'S GET THIS ONE!!
C'MON, JUST IGNORE THEM. LET'S GO IN.
YEAH.
Paints
WE'LL NEVER GET OUT OF HERE IF WE LEAVE THINGS TO THOSE TWO.
Acrylic Lacquers
OH. EXCUSE ME.
OH!
Y-YOU'RE...
?
HARU-KUN, LEND US SOME MONEY!!

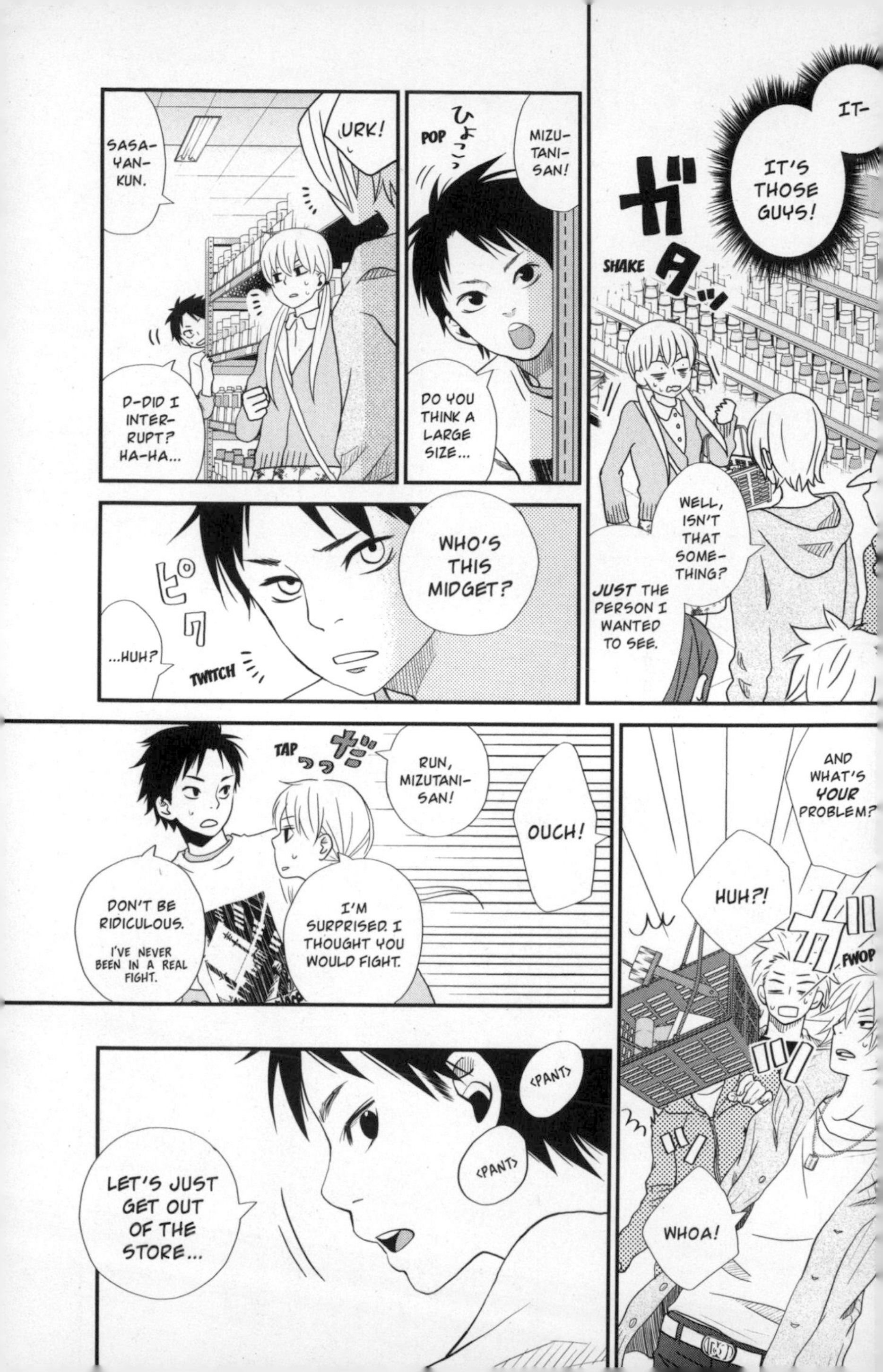
IT-
IT'S THOSE GUYS!
ガタッ
SHAKE
WELL, ISN'T THAT SOME-THING?
JUST THE PERSON I WANTED TO SEE.
ひよこっ
POP
MIZU-TANI-SAN!
DO YOU THINK A LARGE SIZE...
URK!
SASA-YAN-KUN.
D-DID I INTER-RUPT? HA-HA...
WHO'S THIS MIDGET?
ピク
TWITCH
...HUH?
AND WHAT'S YOUR PROBLEM?
HUH?!
ガッ
FWOP
WHOA!
TAP
RUN, MIZUTANI-SAN!
OUCH!
I'M SURPRISED. I THOUGHT YOU WOULD FIGHT.
DON'T BE RIDICULOUS.
I'VE NEVER BEEN IN A REAL FIGHT.
<PANT>
<PANT>
LET'S JUST GET OUT OF THE STORE...

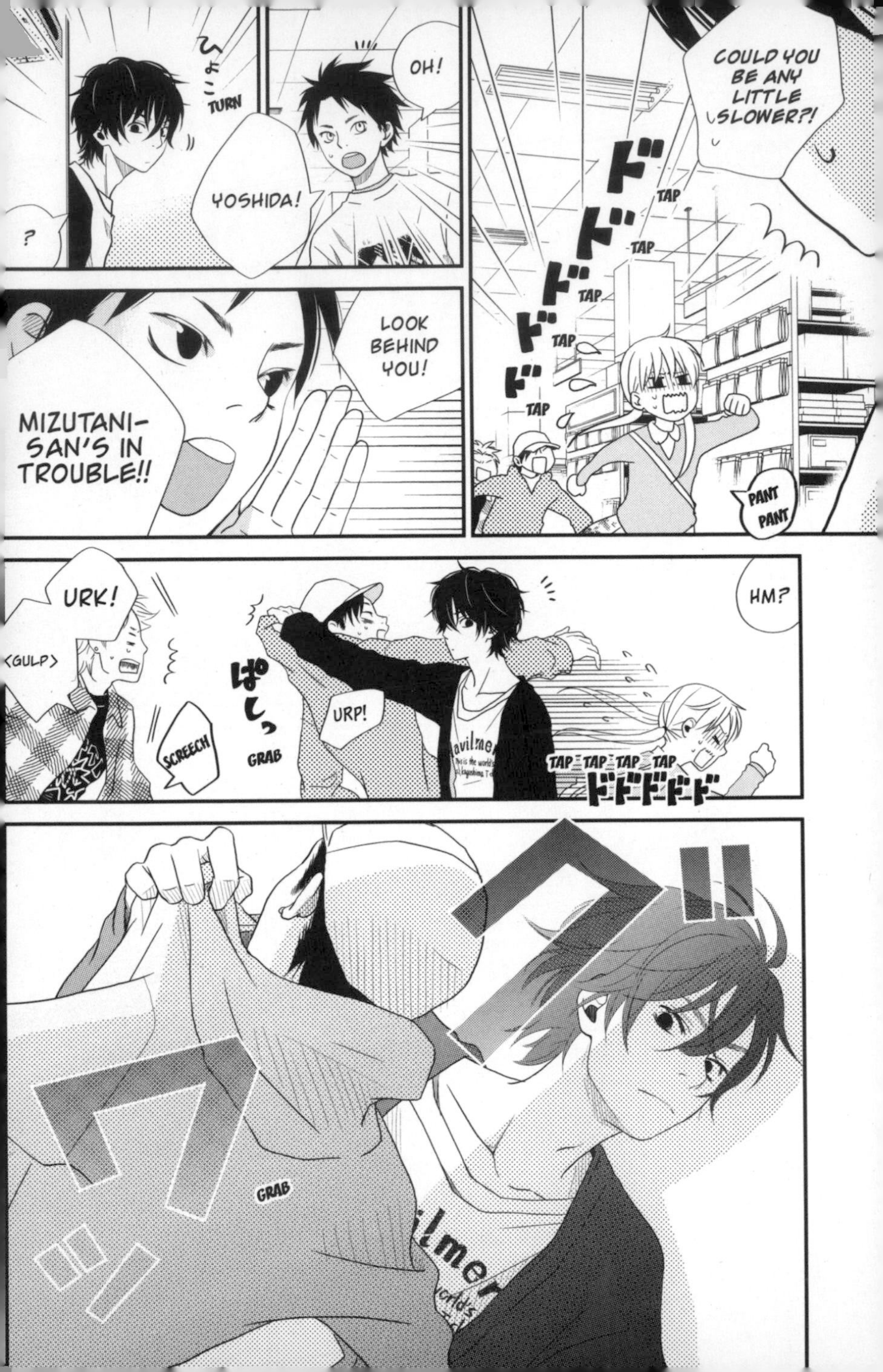

COULD YOU BE ANY LITTLE SLOWER?!
ドドドドド
TAP TAP TAP TAP TAP
PANT PANT
OH!
YOSHIDA!
ひょこ
TURN
?
LOOK BEHIND YOU!
MIZUTANI-SAN'S IN TROUBLE!!
HM?
TAP TAP TAP TAP
ドドドドド
URP!
ぱしっ
GRAB
SCREECH
URK!
<GULP>
GRAB

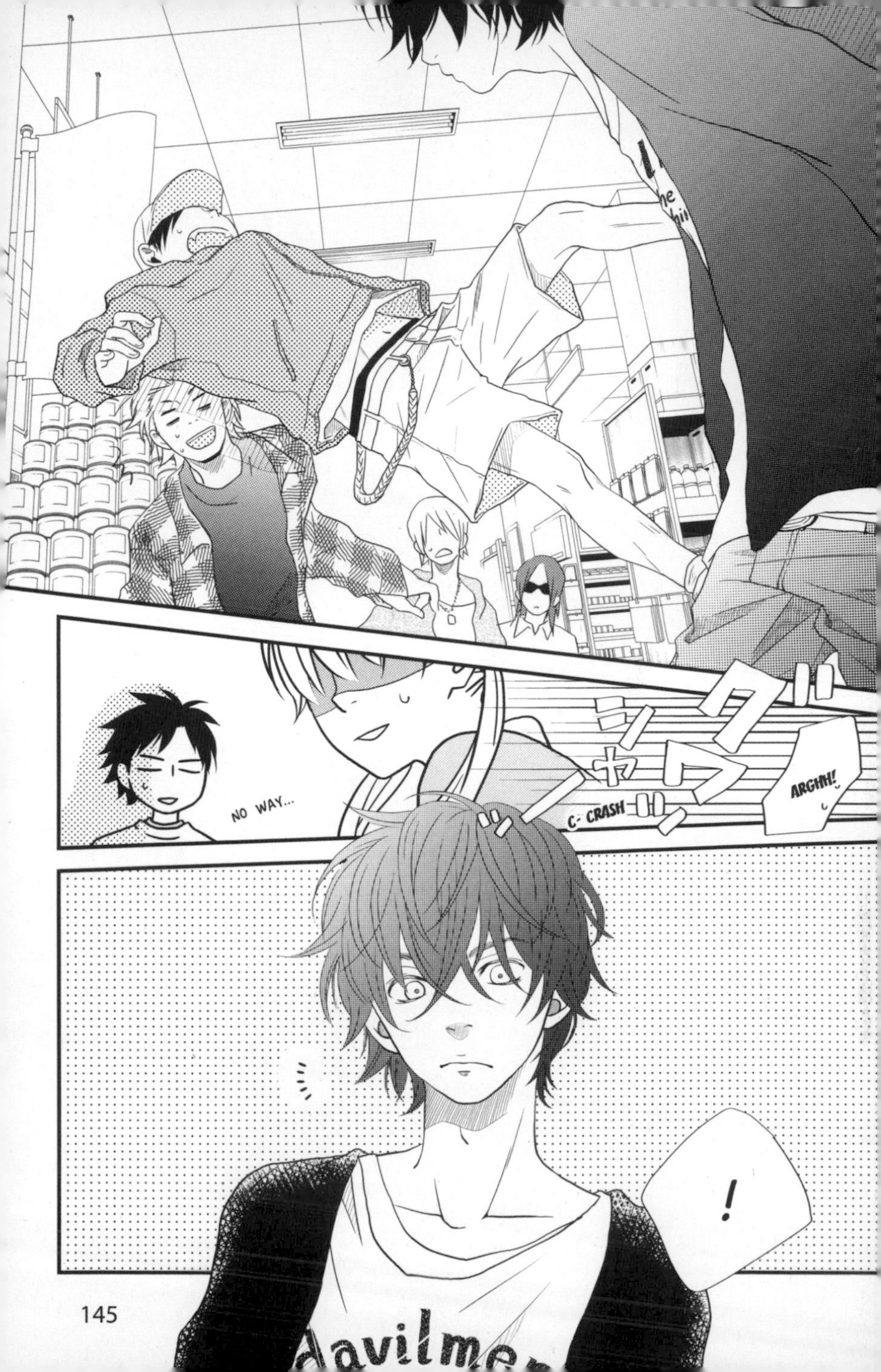
ARGHH!
C- CRASH
NO WAY...
!

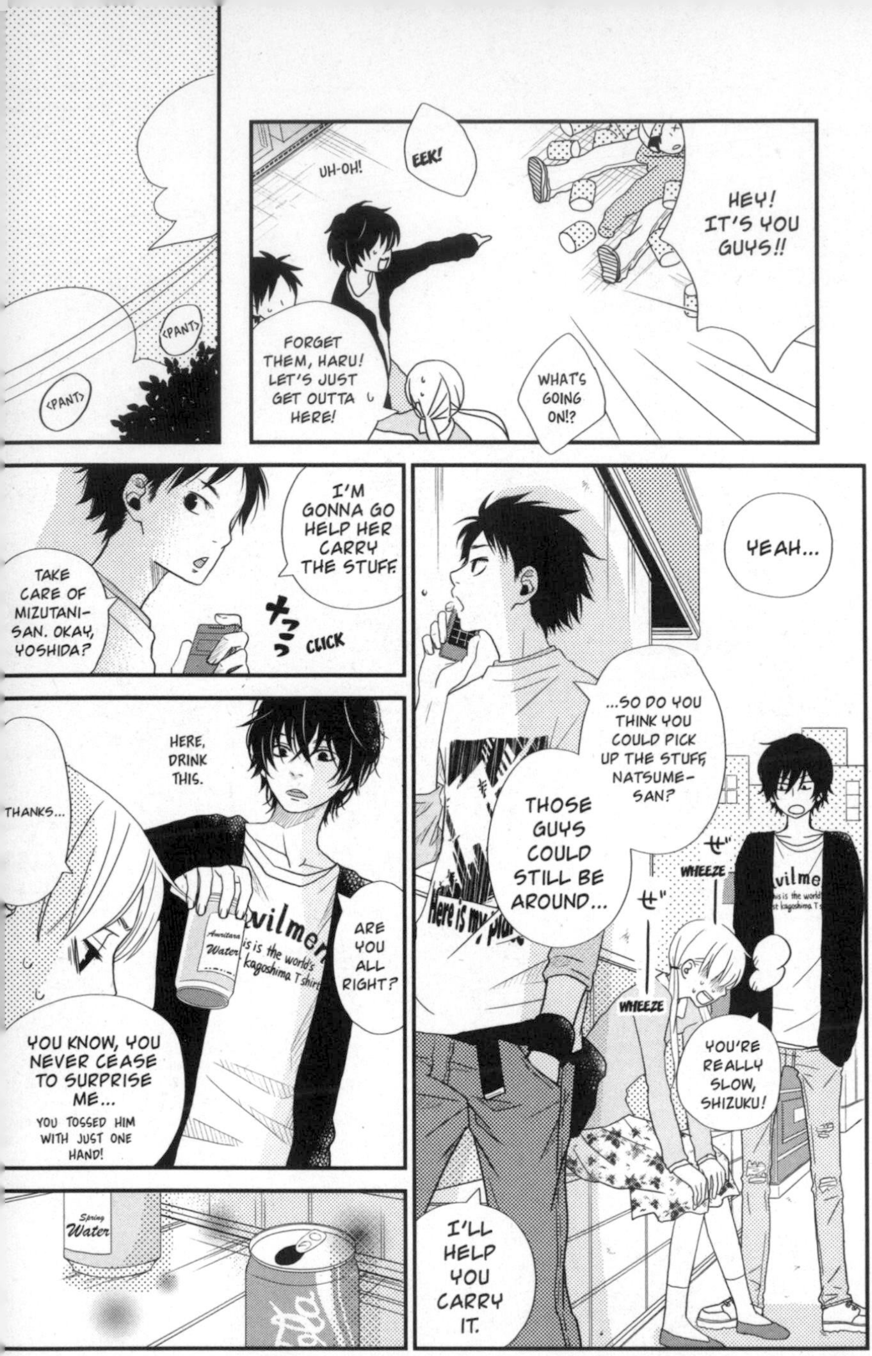
HEY! IT'S YOU GUYS!!
EEK!
UH-OH!
WHAT'S GOING ON!?
FORGET THEM, HARU! LET'S JUST GET OUTTA HERE!
<PANT>
<PANT>
YEAH...
...SO DO YOU THINK YOU COULD PICK UP THE STUFF, NATSUME-SAN?
THOSE GUYS COULD STILL BE AROUND...
WHEEZE
WHEEZE
YOU'RE REALLY SLOW, SHIZUKU!
I'LL HELP YOU CARRY IT.
I'M GONNA GO HELP HER CARRY THE STUFF.
TAKE CARE OF MIZUTANI-SAN. OKAY, YOSHIDA?
CLICK
HERE, DRINK THIS.
ARE YOU ALL RIGHT?
THANKS...
YOU KNOW, YOU NEVER CEASE TO SURPRISE ME...
YOU TOSSED HIM WITH JUST ONE HAND!
Spring Water

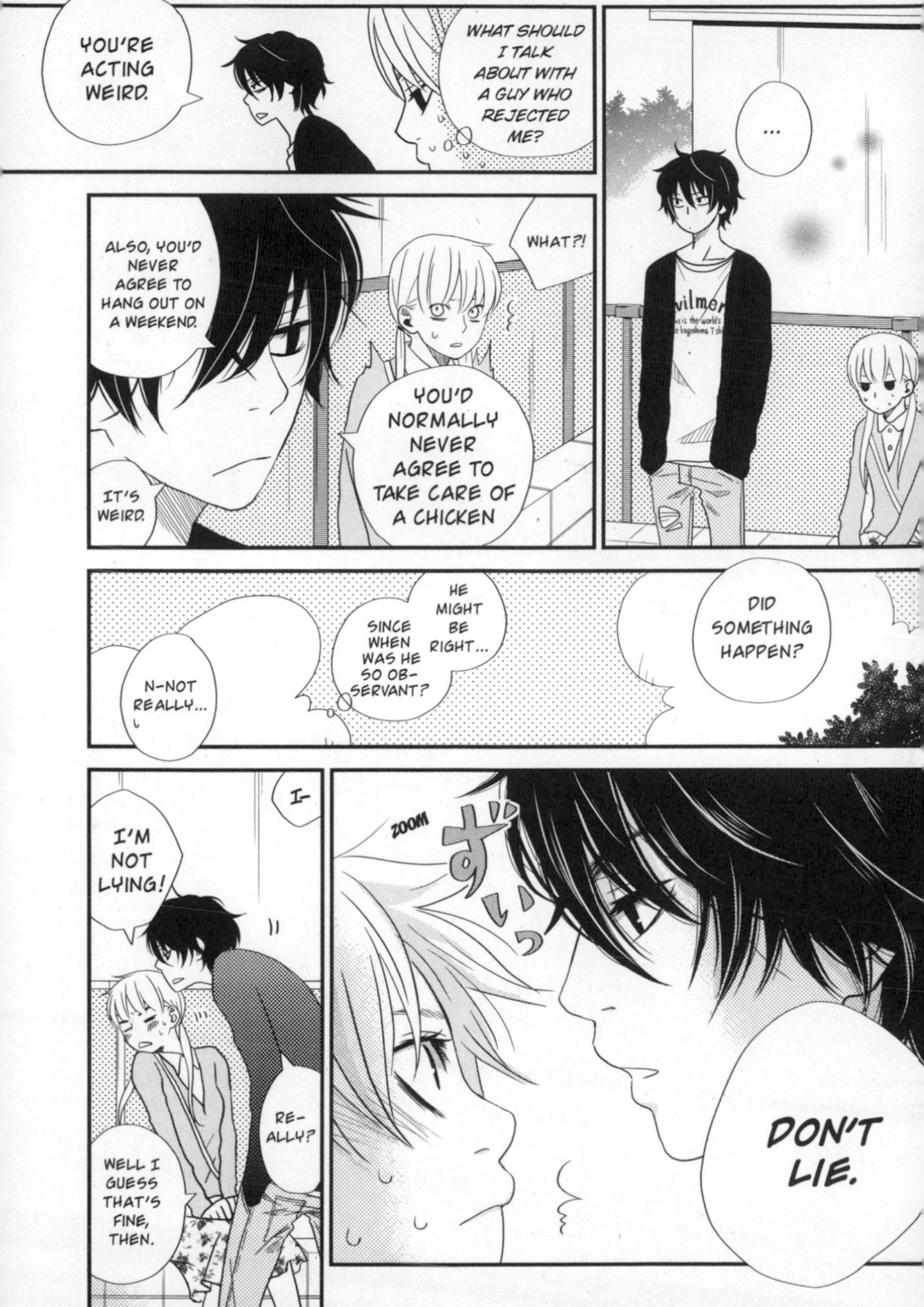
...
WHAT SHOULD I TALK ABOUT WITH A GUY WHO REJECTED ME?
YOU'RE ACTING WEIRD.
WHAT?!
ALSO, YOU'D NEVER AGREE TO HANG OUT ON A WEEKEND.
YOU'D NORMALLY NEVER AGREE TO TAKE CARE OF A CHICKEN
IT'S WEIRD.
DID SOMETHING HAPPEN?
HE MIGHT BE RIGHT...
SINCE WHEN WAS HE SO OB-SERVANT?
N-NOT REALLY...
ZOOM
DON'T LIE.
I-
I'M NOT LYING!
RE-ALLY?
WELL I GUESS THAT'S FINE, THEN.

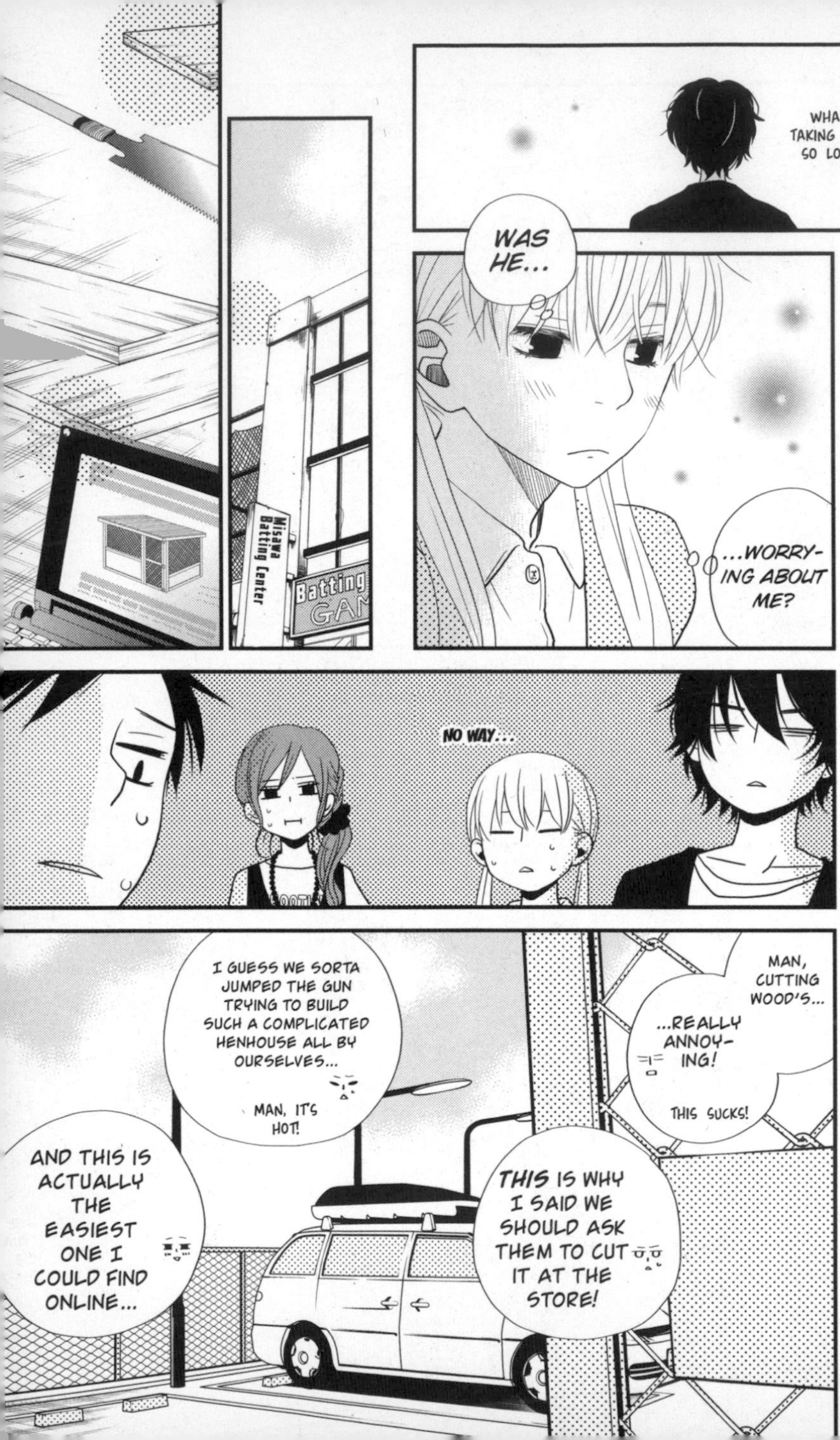
WHAT'S TAKING THEM SO LONG?
WAS HE...
...WORRYING ABOUT ME?
Misawa Batting Center
NO WAY...
MAN, CUTTING WOOD'S...
...REALLY ANNOYING!
THIS SUCKS!
I GUESS WE SORTA JUMPED THE GUN TRYING TO BUILD SUCH A COMPLICATED HENHOUSE ALL BY OURSELVES...
MAN, IT'S HOT!
THIS IS WHY I SAID WE SHOULD ASK THEM TO CUT IT AT THE STORE!
AND THIS IS ACTUALLY THE EASIEST ONE I COULD FIND ONLINE...

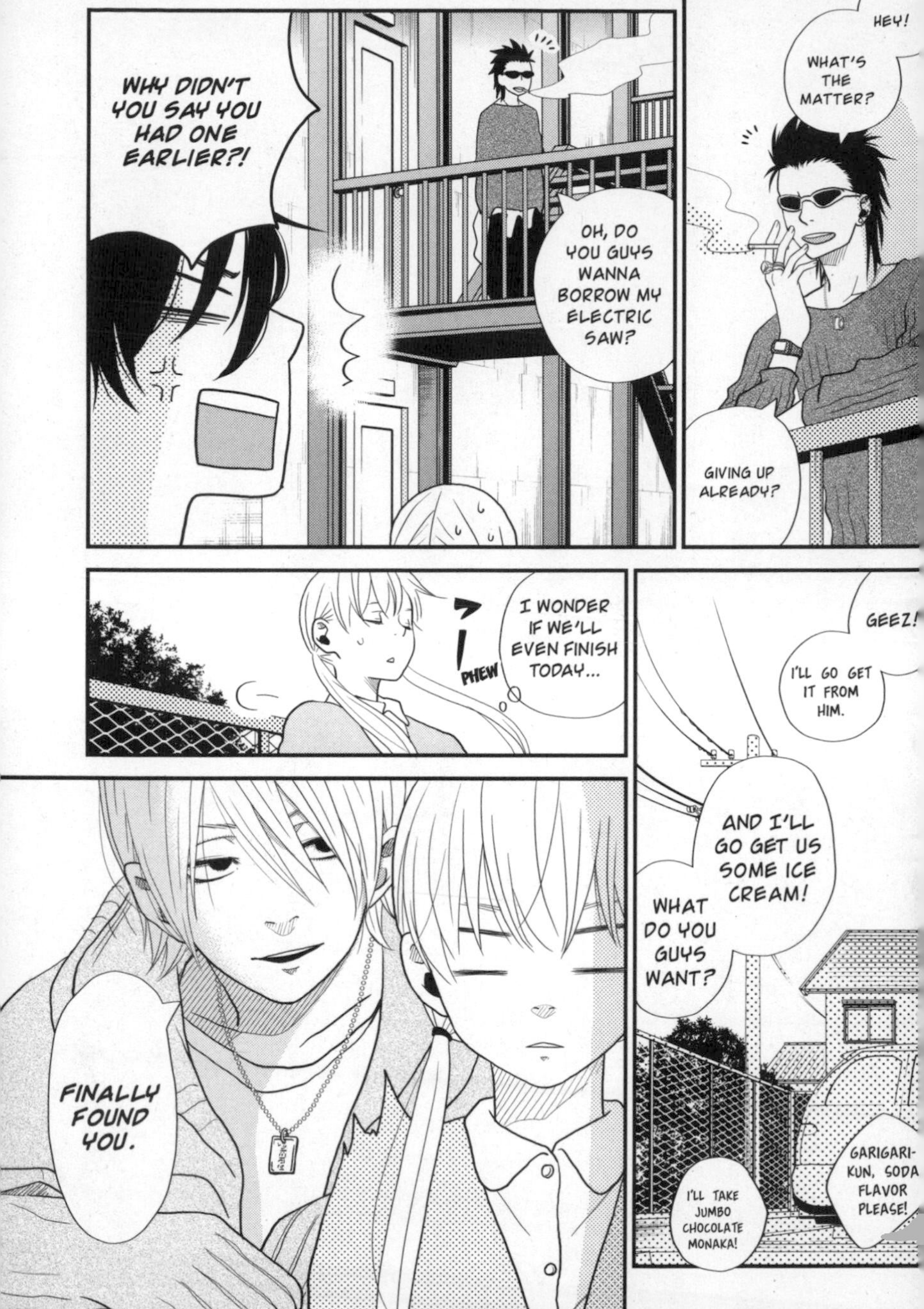
HEY!
WHAT'S THE MATTER?
GIVING UP ALREADY?
OH, DO YOU GUYS WANNA BORROW MY ELECTRIC SAW?
WHY DIDN'T YOU SAY YOU HAD ONE EARLIER?!
GEEZ!
I'LL GO GET IT FROM HIM.
AND I'LL GO GET US SOME ICE CREAM!
WHAT DO YOU GUYS WANT?
GARIGARI-KUN, SODA FLAVOR PLEASE!
I'LL TAKE JUMBO CHOCOLATE MONAKA!
PHEW
I WONDER IF WE'LL EVEN FINISH TODAY...
FINALLY FOUND YOU.

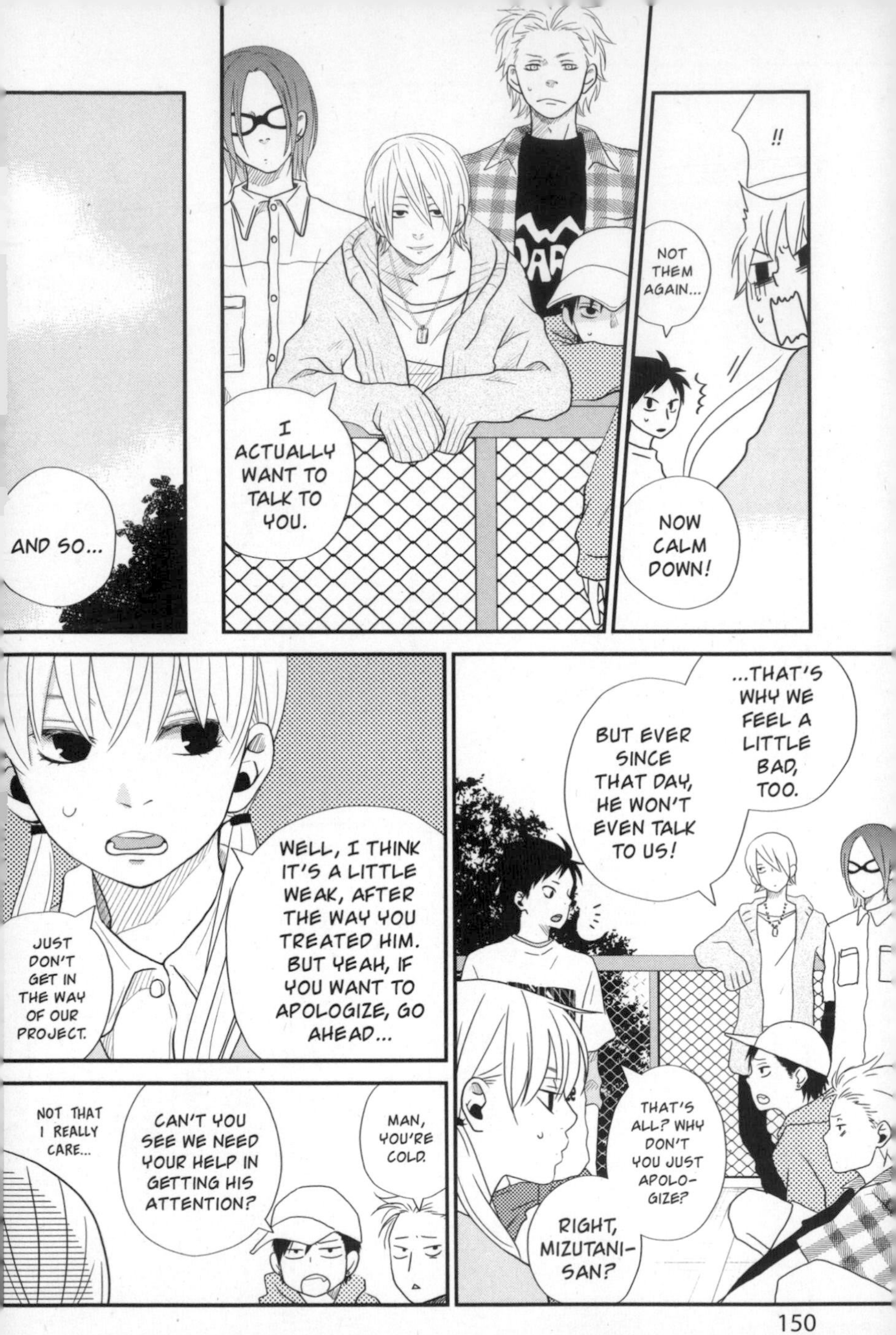
!!
NOT THEM AGAIN...
NOW CALM DOWN!
I ACTUALLY WANT TO TALK TO YOU.
AND SO...
...THAT'S WHY WE FEEL A LITTLE BAD, TOO.
BUT EVER SINCE THAT DAY, HE WON'T EVEN TALK TO US!
THAT'S ALL? WHY DON'T YOU JUST APOLO-GIZE?
RIGHT, MIZUTANI-SAN?
WELL, I THINK IT'S A LITTLE WEAK, AFTER THE WAY YOU TREATED HIM. BUT YEAH, IF YOU WANT TO APOLOGIZE, GO AHEAD...
JUST DON'T GET IN THE WAY OF OUR PROJECT.
MAN, YOU'RE COLD.
CAN'T YOU SEE WE NEED YOUR HELP IN GETTING HIS ATTENTION?
NOT THAT I REALLY CARE...

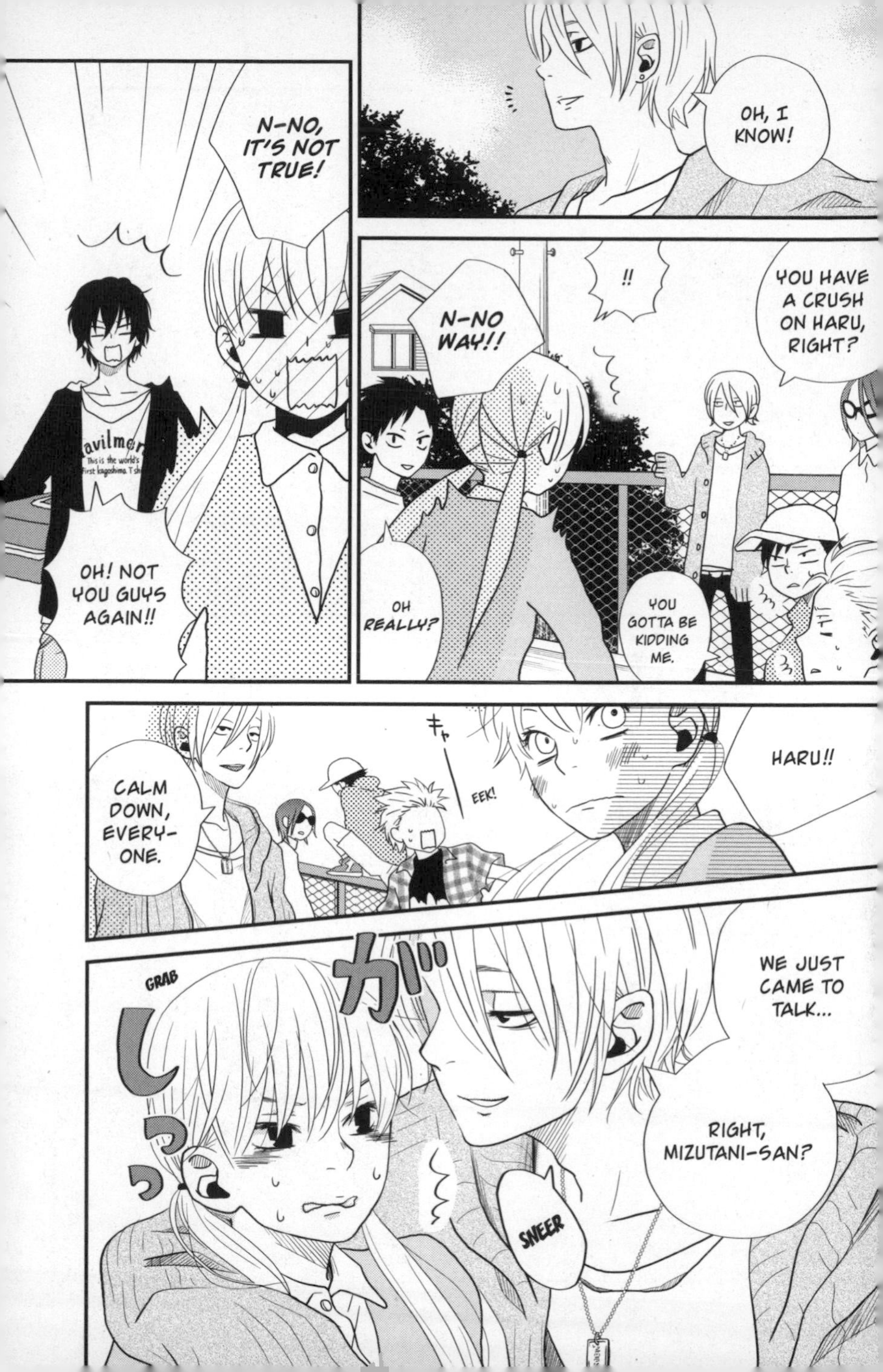
OH, I KNOW!
YOU HAVE A CRUSH ON HARU, RIGHT?
!!
N-NO WAY!!
YOU GOTTA BE KIDDING ME.
OH REALLY?
N-NO, IT'S NOT TRUE!
OH! NOT YOU GUYS AGAIN!!
HARU!!
キャー
EEK!
CALM DOWN, EVERY-ONE.
WE JUST CAME TO TALK...
ガしっっ
GRAB
RIGHT, MIZUTANI-SAN?
SNEER

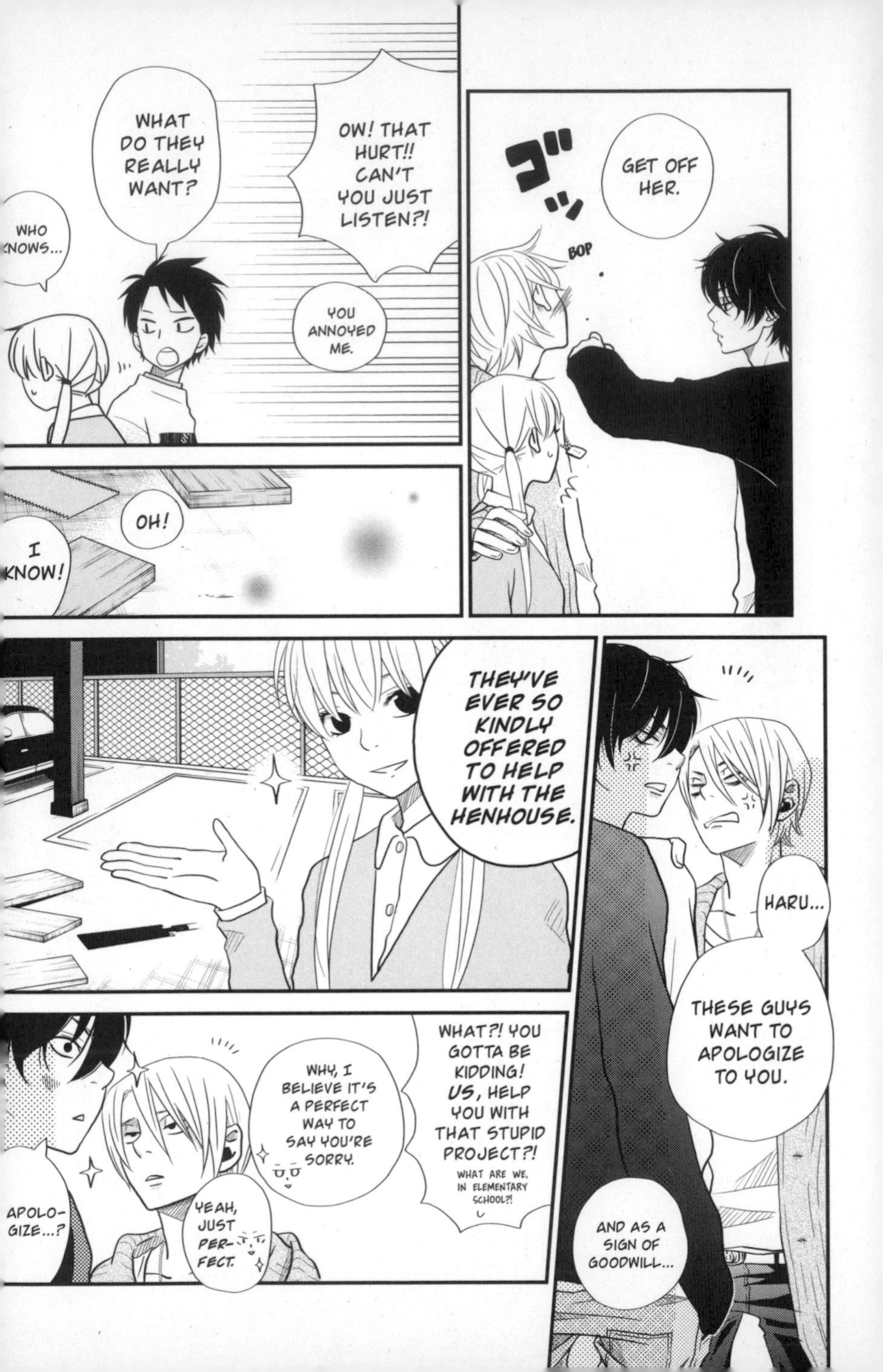
ゴッ
BOP
GET OFF HER.
OW! THAT HURT!! CAN'T YOU JUST LISTEN?!
YOU ANNOYED ME.
WHAT DO THEY REALLY WANT?
WHO KNOWS...
OH!
I KNOW!
HARU...
THESE GUYS WANT TO APOLOGIZE TO YOU.
AND AS A SIGN OF GOODWILL...
THEY'VE EVER SO KINDLY OFFERED TO HELP WITH THE HENHOUSE.
WHAT?! YOU GOTTA BE KIDDING! US, HELP YOU WITH THAT STUPID PROJECT?!
WHAT ARE WE, IN ELEMENTARY SCHOOL?!
WHY, I BELIEVE IT'S A PERFECT WAY TO SAY YOU'RE SORRY.
YEAH, JUST PER-FECT.
APOLO-GIZE...?

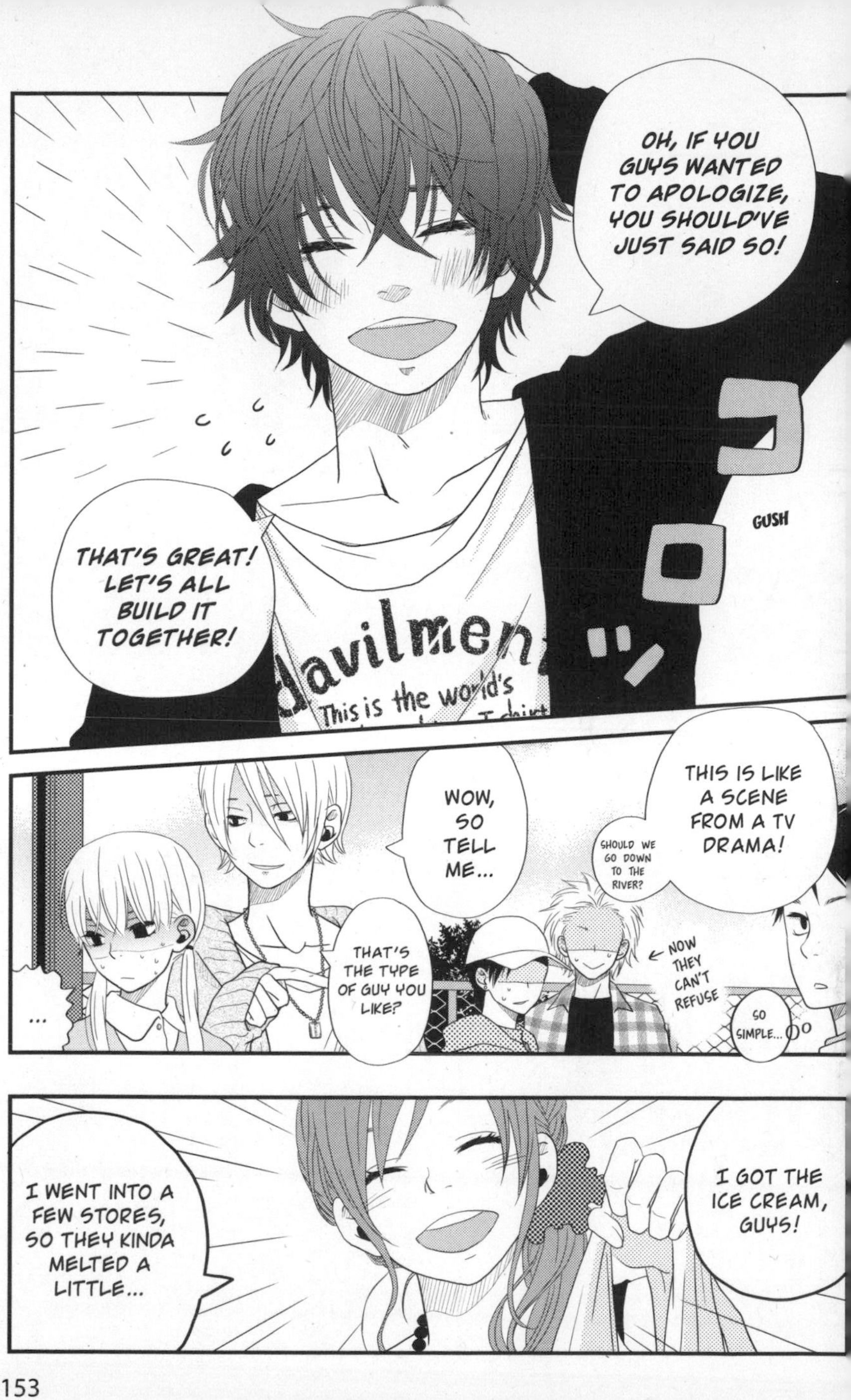
OH, IF YOU GUYS WANTED TO APOLOGIZE, YOU SHOULD'VE JUST SAID SO!
GUSH
THAT'S GREAT! LET'S ALL BUILD IT TOGETHER!
THIS IS LIKE A SCENE FROM A TV DRAMA!
SHOULD WE GO DOWN TO THE RIVER?
SO SIMPLE...
NOW THEY CAN'T REFUSE
WOW, SO TELL ME...
THAT'S THE TYPE OF GUY YOU LIKE?
...
I GOT THE ICE CREAM, GUYS!
I WENT INTO A FEW STORES, SO THEY KINDA MELTED A LITTLE...

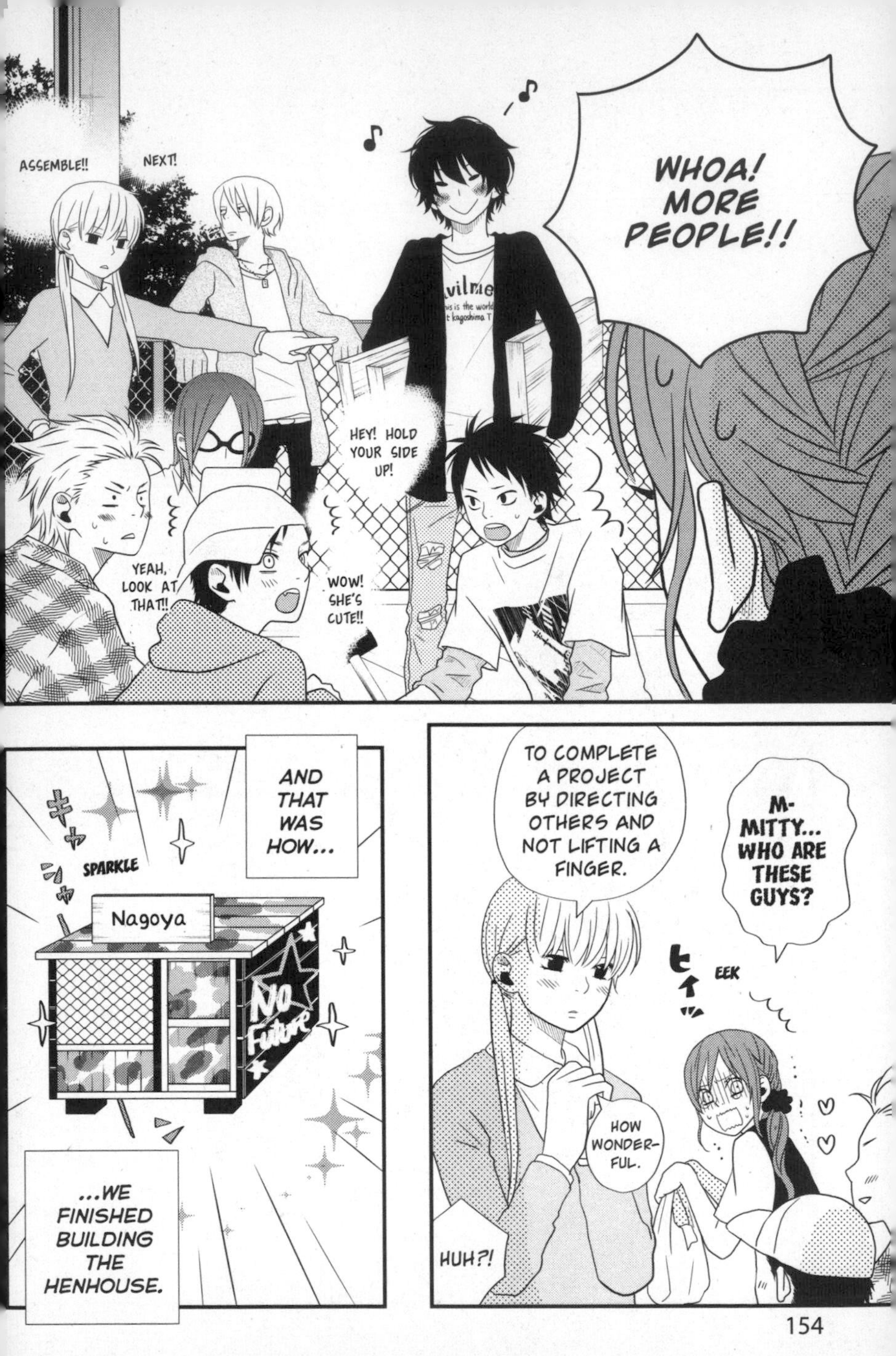

WHOA! MORE PEOPLE!!
HEY! HOLD YOUR SIDE UP!
NEXT!
ASSEMBLE!!
WOW! SHE'S CUTE!!
YEAH, LOOK AT THAT!!
M-MITTY... WHO ARE THESE GUYS?
TO COMPLETE A PROJECT BY DIRECTING OTHERS AND NOT LIFTING A FINGER.
EEK
HOW WONDERFUL.
HUH?!
AND THAT WAS HOW...
SPARKLE
Nagoya
No Future
...WE FINISHED BUILDING THE HENHOUSE.

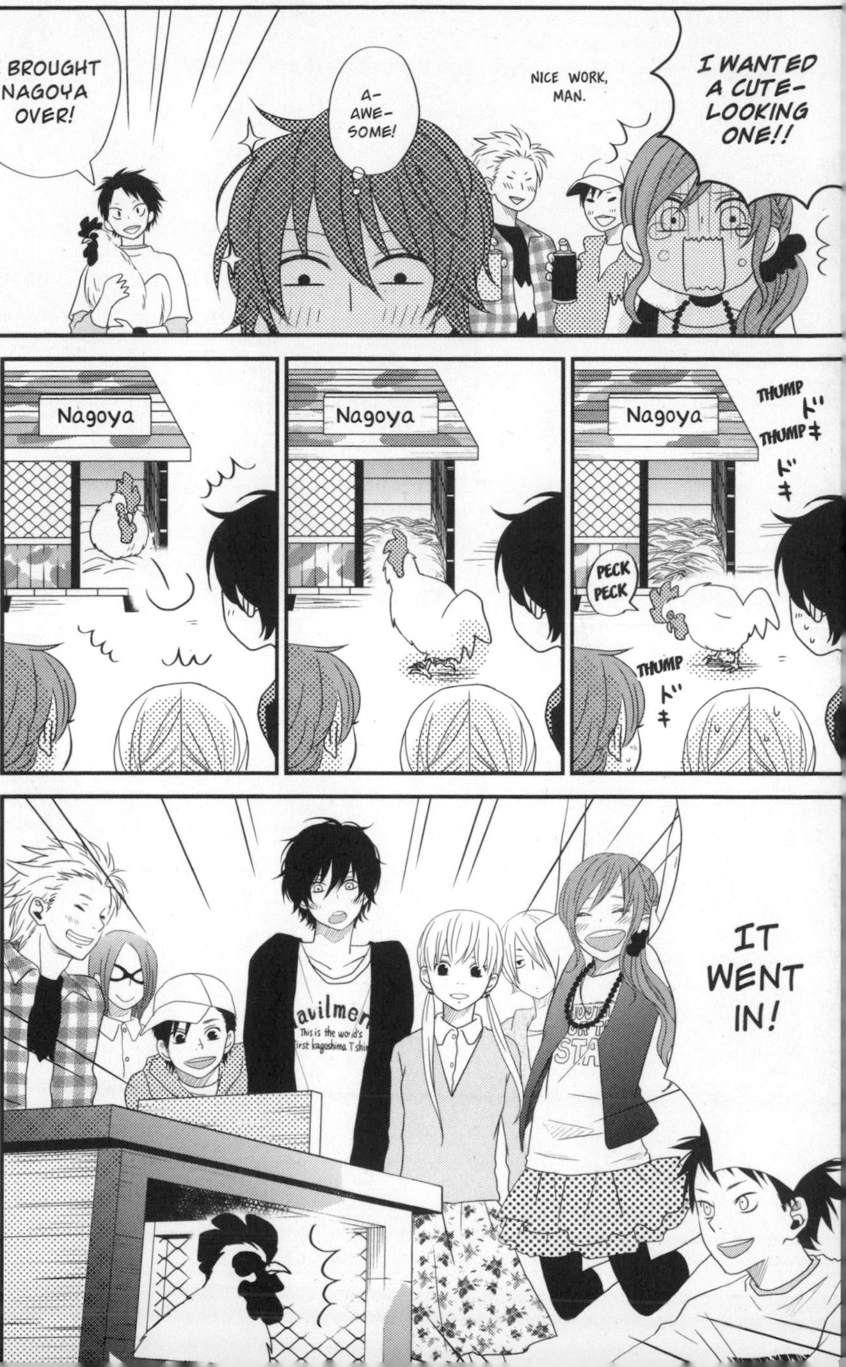
I WANTED A CUTE-LOOKING ONE!!
NICE WORK, MAN.
A-AWE-SOME!
I BROUGHT NAGOYA OVER!
Nagoya
THUMP ドキ
THUMP ドキ
PECK PECK
THUMP ドキ
Nagoya
Nagoya
IT WENT IN!

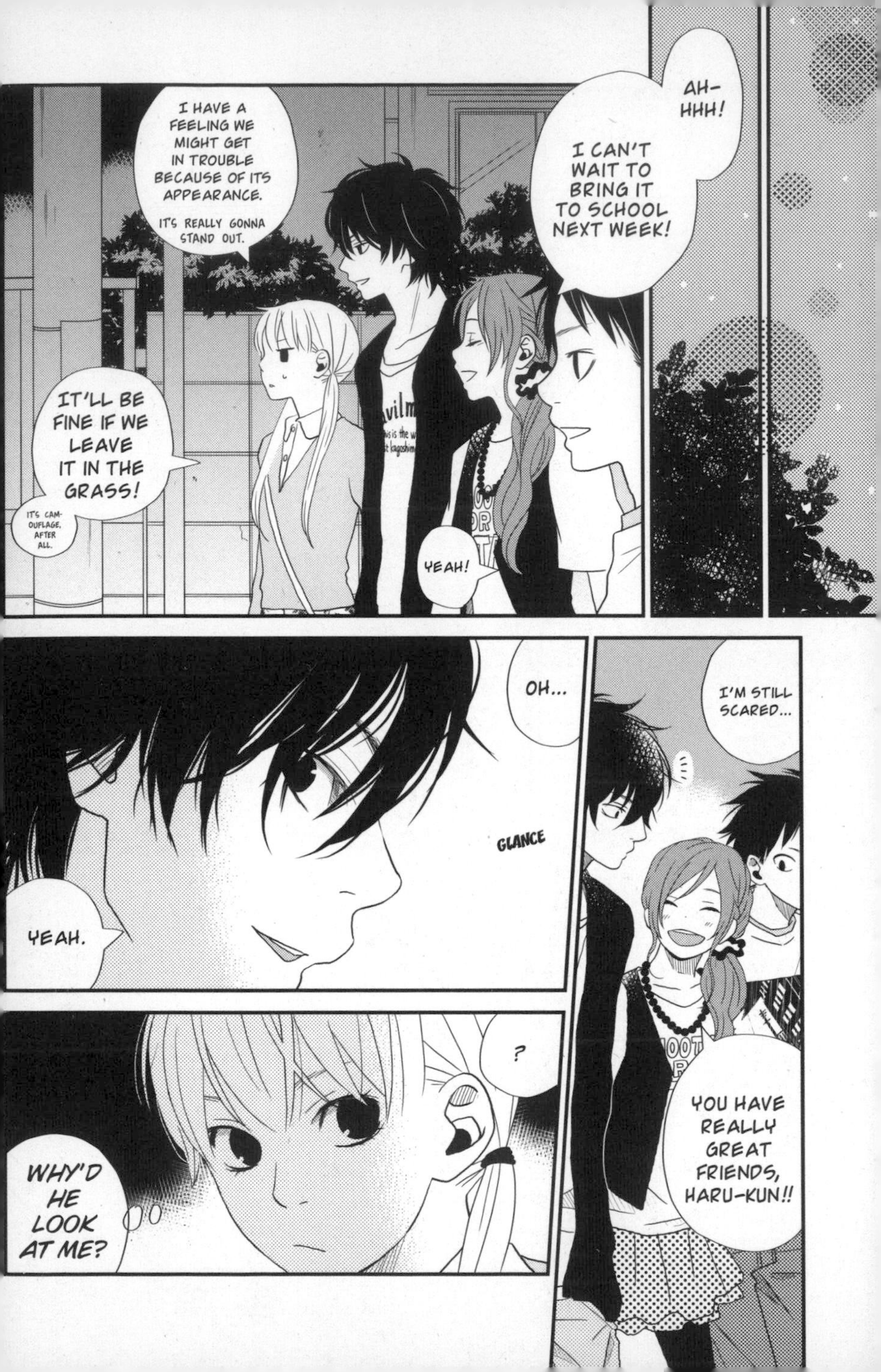
AH-HHH!
I CAN'T WAIT TO BRING IT TO SCHOOL NEXT WEEK!
I HAVE A FEELING WE MIGHT GET IN TROUBLE BECAUSE OF ITS APPEARANCE.
IT'S REALLY GONNA STAND OUT.
YEAH!
IT'LL BE FINE IF WE LEAVE IT IN THE GRASS!
IT'S CAM-OUFLAGE, AFTER ALL.
I'M STILL SCARED...
!
YOU HAVE REALLY GREAT FRIENDS, HARU-KUN!!
OH...
GLANCE
YEAH.
?
WHY'D HE LOOK AT ME?

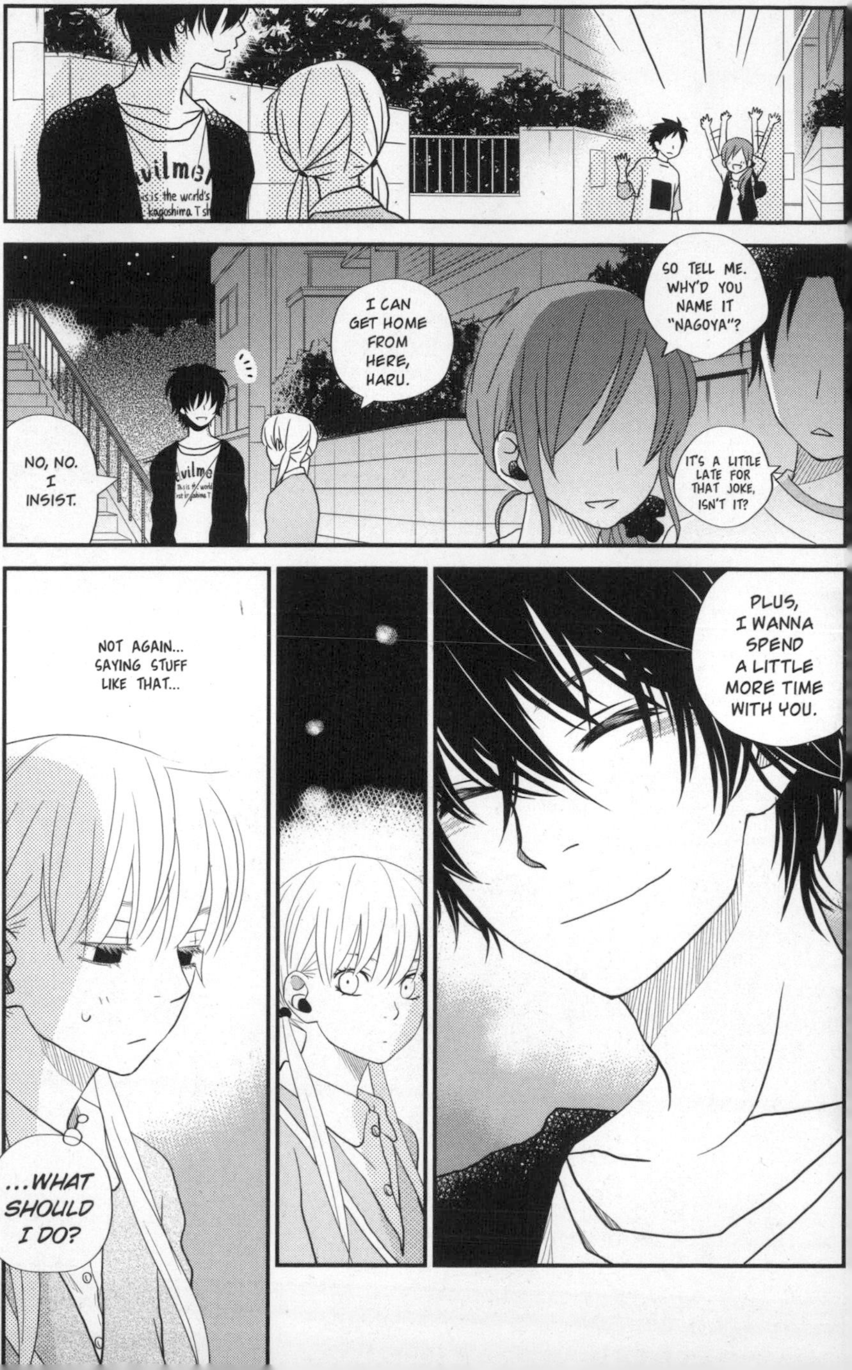
SO TELL ME. WHY'D YOU NAME IT "NAGOYA"?
IT'S A LITTLE LATE FOR THAT JOKE, ISN'T IT?
I CAN GET HOME FROM HERE, HARU.
NO, NO. I INSIST.
PLUS, I WANNA SPEND A LITTLE MORE TIME WITH YOU.
NOT AGAIN... SAYING STUFF LIKE THAT...
...WHAT SHOULD I DO?

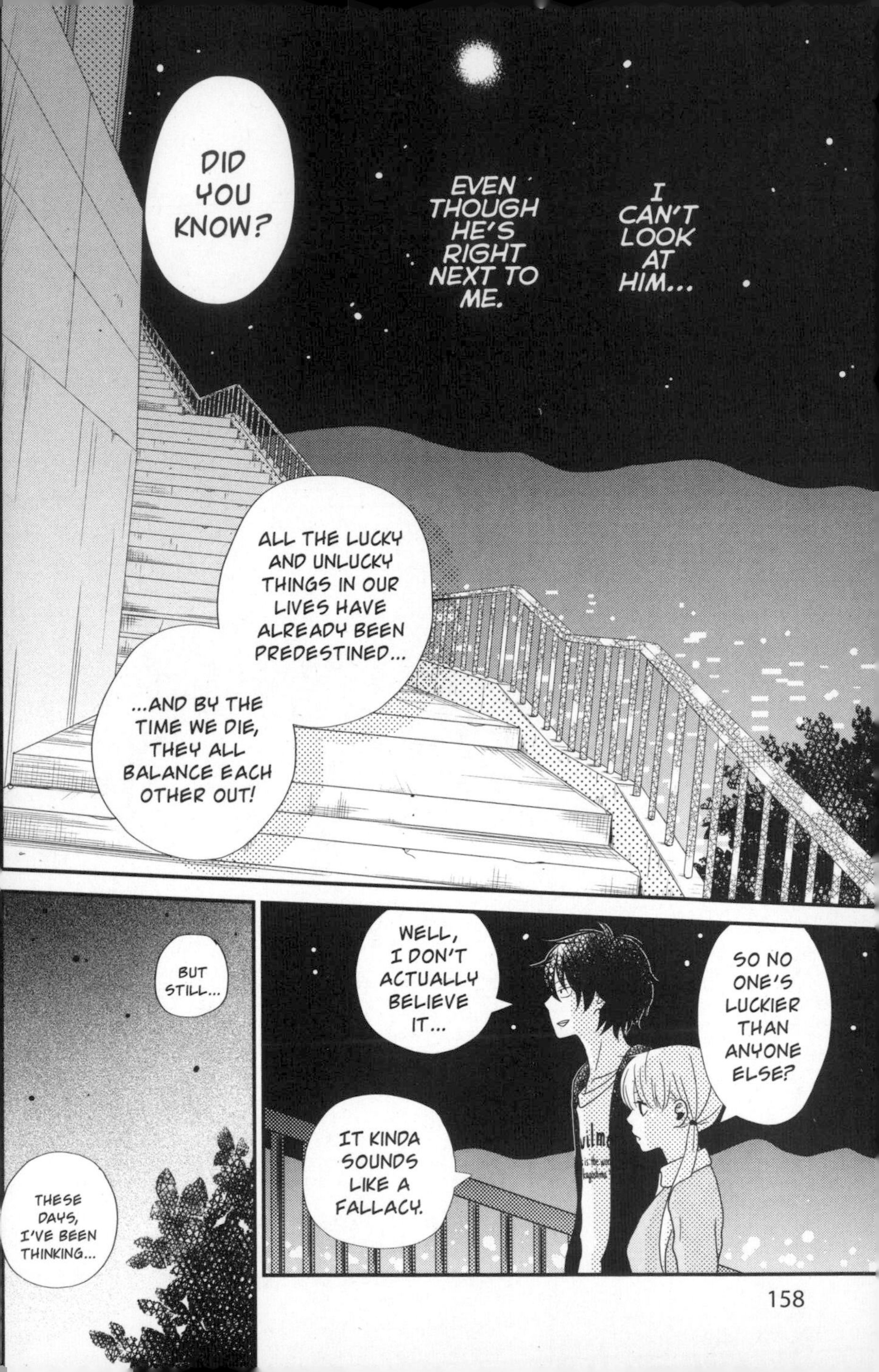
I CAN'T LOOK AT HIM...
EVEN THOUGH HE'S RIGHT NEXT TO ME.
DID YOU KNOW?
ALL THE LUCKY AND UNLUCKY THINGS IN OUR LIVES HAVE ALREADY BEEN PREDESTINED...
...AND BY THE TIME WE DIE, THEY ALL BALANCE EACH OTHER OUT!
SO NO ONE'S LUCKIER THAN ANYONE ELSE?
WELL, I DON'T ACTUALLY BELIEVE IT...
IT KINDA SOUNDS LIKE A FALLACY.
BUT STILL...
THESE DAYS, I'VE BEEN THINKING...

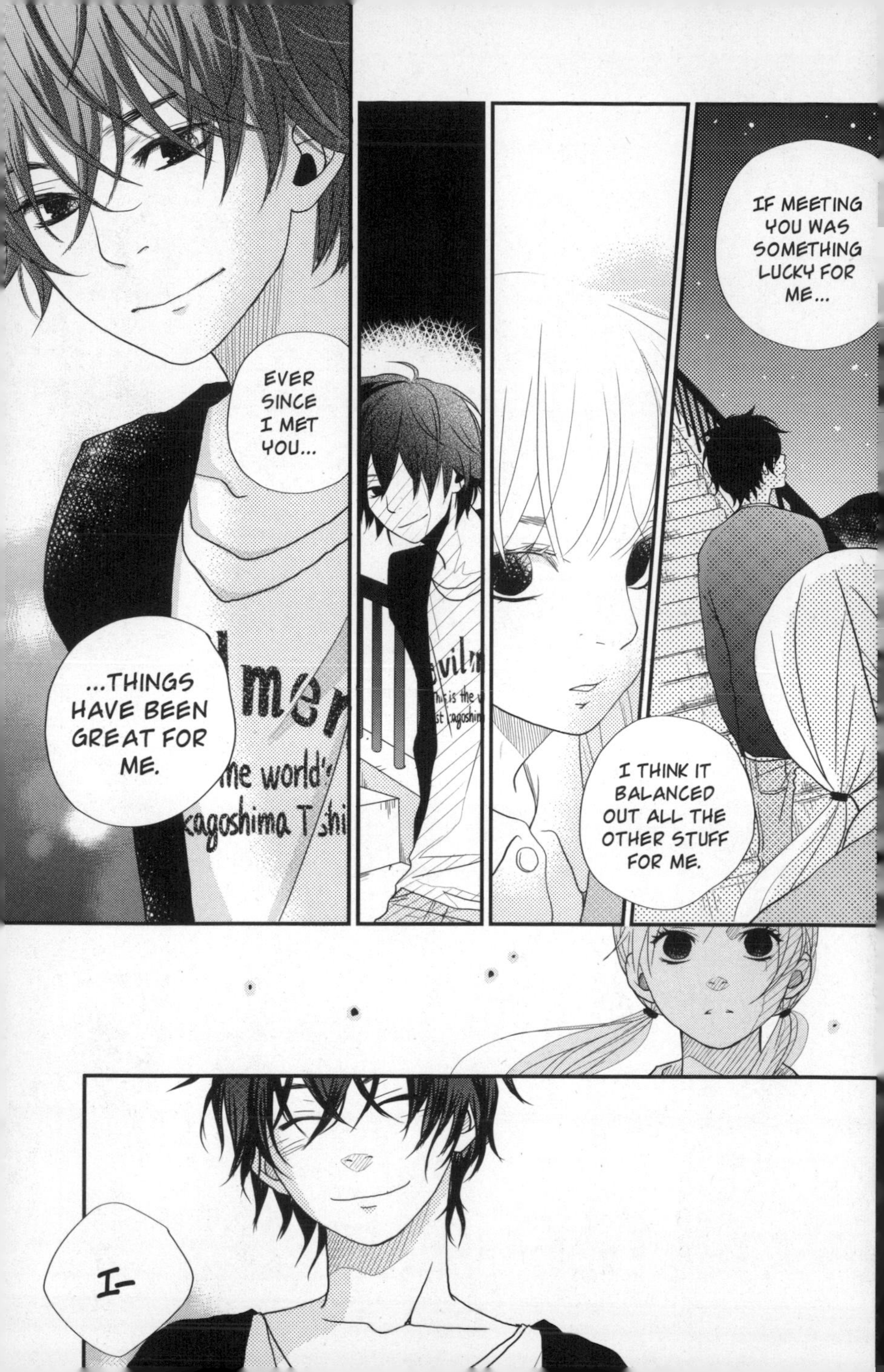
IF MEETING YOU WAS SOMETHING LUCKY FOR ME...
I THINK IT BALANCED OUT ALL THE OTHER STUFF FOR ME.
EVER SINCE I MET YOU...
...THINGS HAVE BEEN GREAT FOR ME.
I—

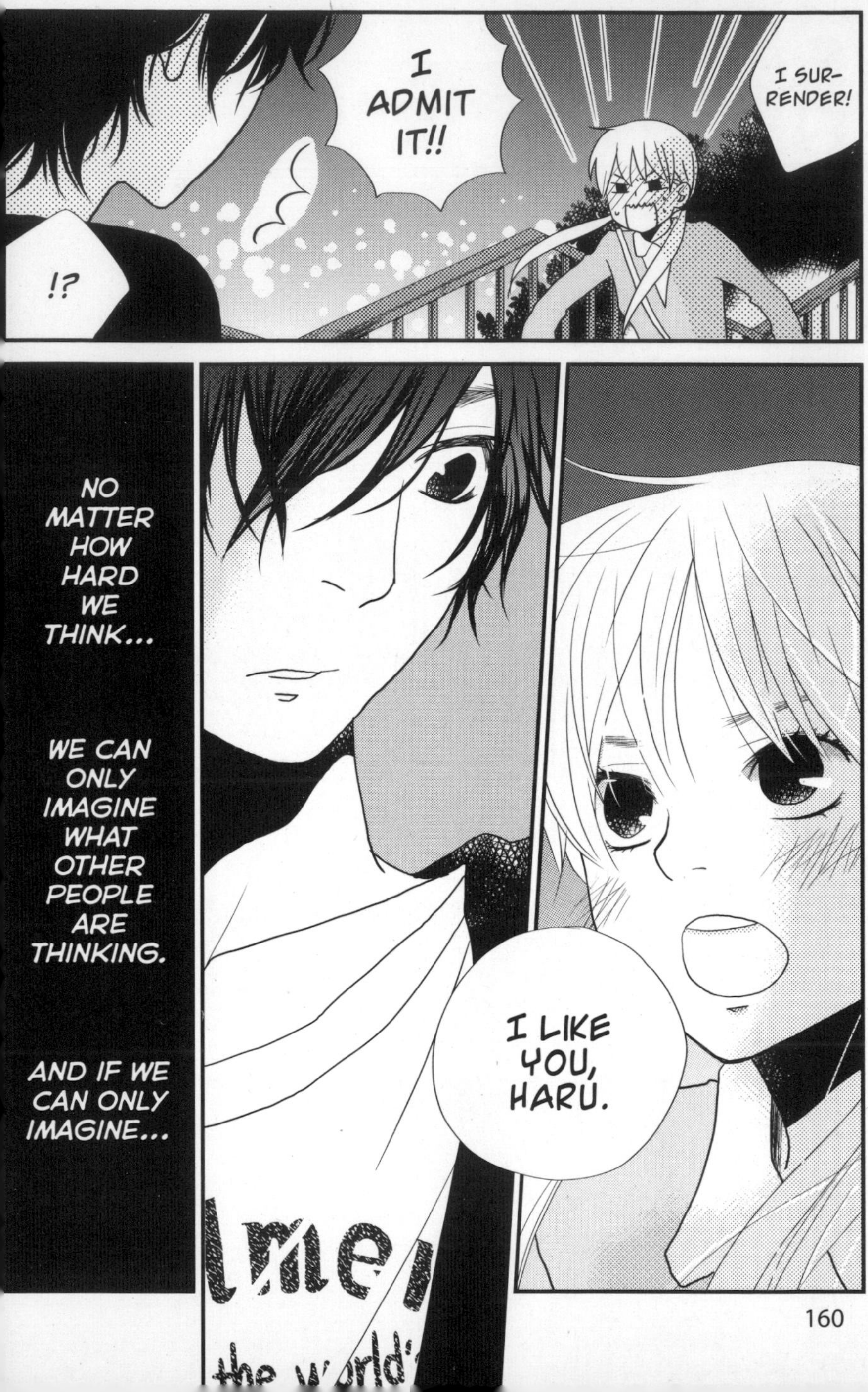
I SUR-RENDER!
I ADMIT IT!!
!?
I LIKE YOU, HARU.
NO MATTER HOW HARD WE THINK...
WE CAN ONLY IMAGINE WHAT OTHER PEOPLE ARE THINKING.
AND IF WE CAN ONLY IMAGINE...

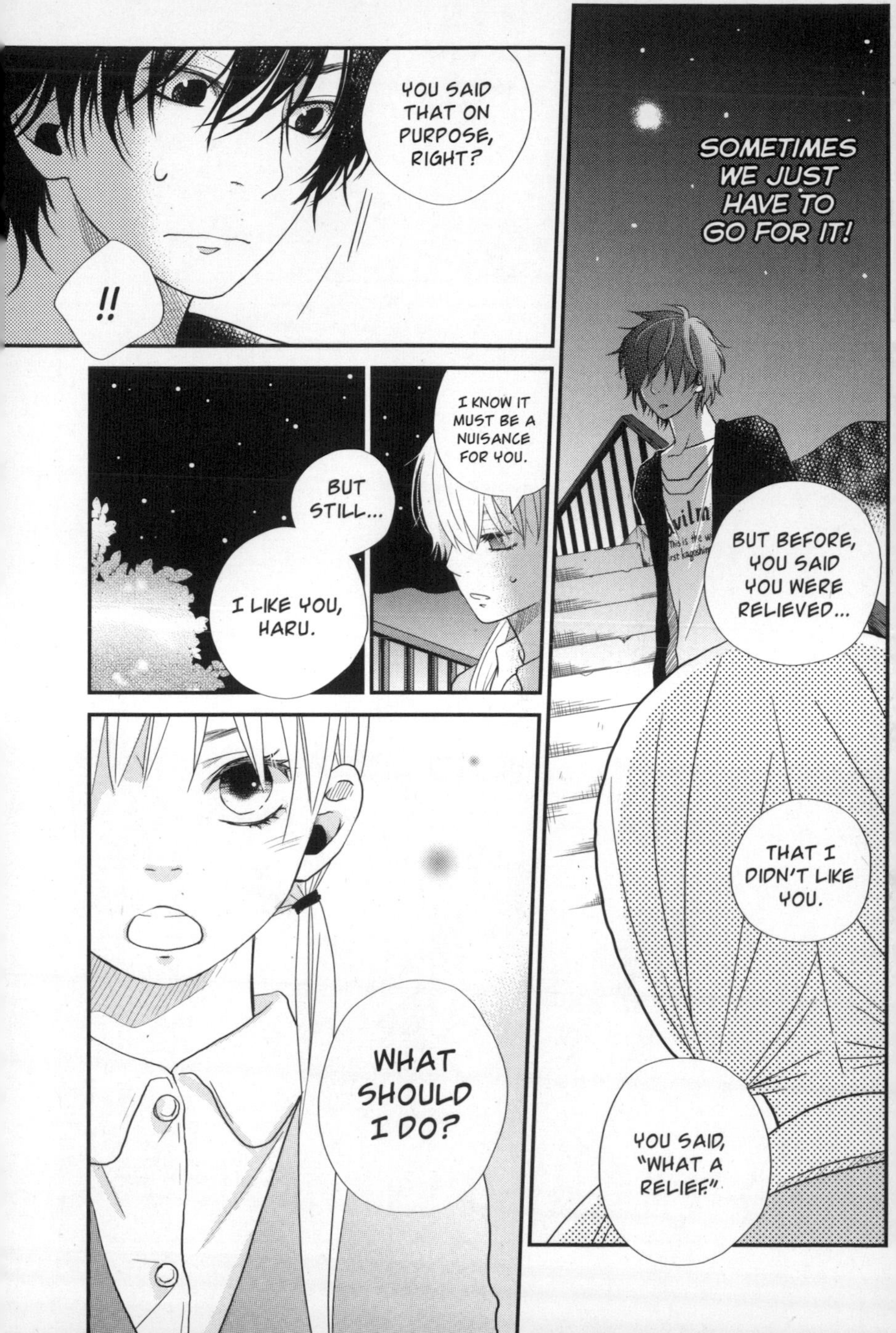
SOMETIMES WE JUST HAVE TO GO FOR IT!
BUT BEFORE, YOU SAID YOU WERE RELIEVED...
THAT I DIDN'T LIKE YOU.
YOU SAID, "WHAT A RELIEF."
YOU SAID THAT ON PURPOSE, RIGHT?
!!
I KNOW IT MUST BE A NUISANCE FOR YOU.
BUT STILL...
I LIKE YOU, HARU.
WHAT SHOULD I DO?

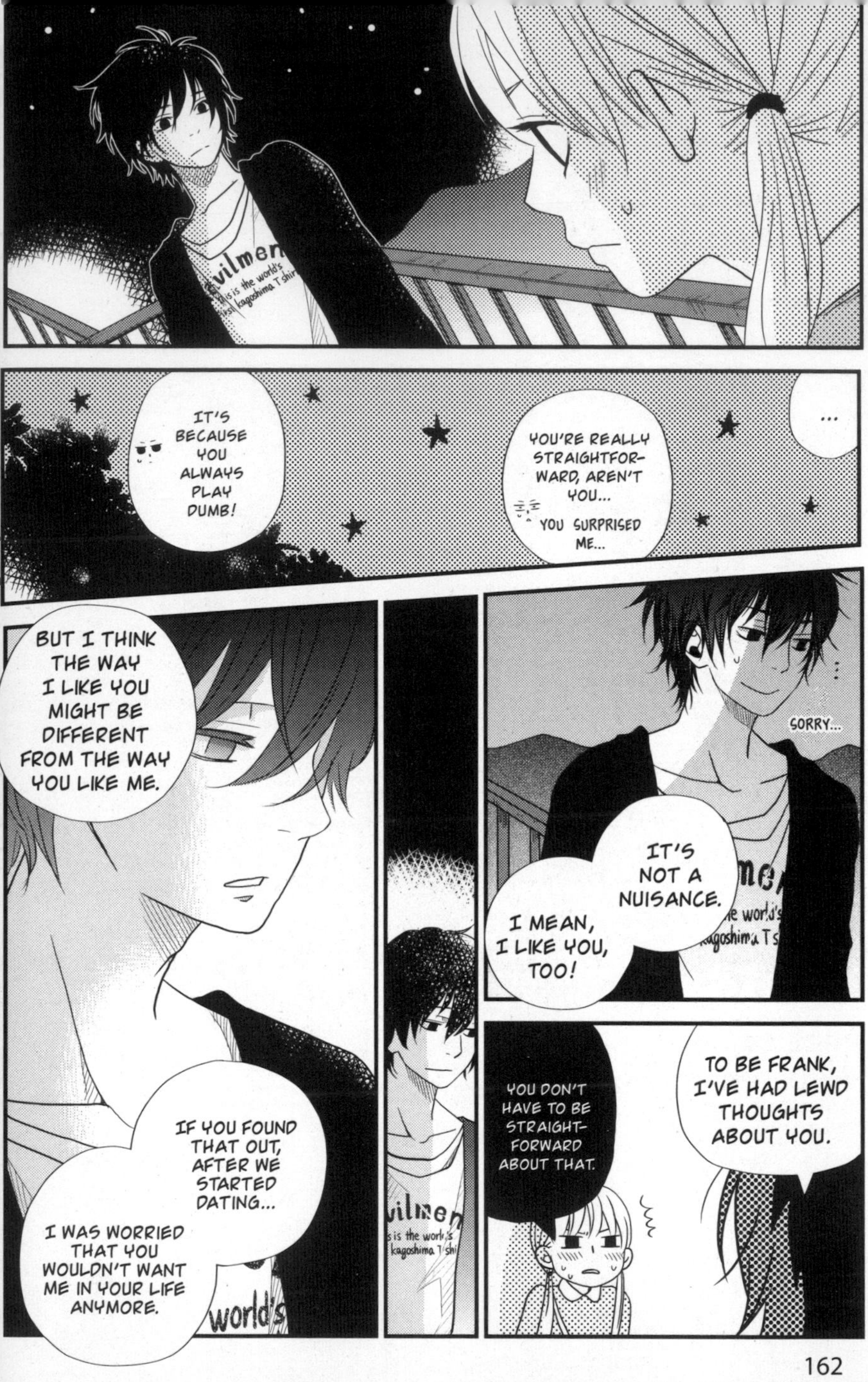
...
YOU'RE REALLY STRAIGHTFORWARD, AREN'T YOU...
YOU SURPRISED ME...
IT'S BECAUSE YOU ALWAYS PLAY DUMB!
SORRY...
IT'S NOT A NUISANCE.
I MEAN, I LIKE YOU, TOO!
TO BE FRANK, I'VE HAD LEWD THOUGHTS ABOUT YOU.
YOU DON'T HAVE TO BE STRAIGHTFORWARD ABOUT THAT.
BUT I THINK THE WAY I LIKE YOU MIGHT BE DIFFERENT FROM THE WAY YOU LIKE ME.
IF YOU FOUND THAT OUT, AFTER WE STARTED DATING...
I WAS WORRIED THAT YOU WOULDN'T WANT ME IN YOUR LIFE ANYMORE.

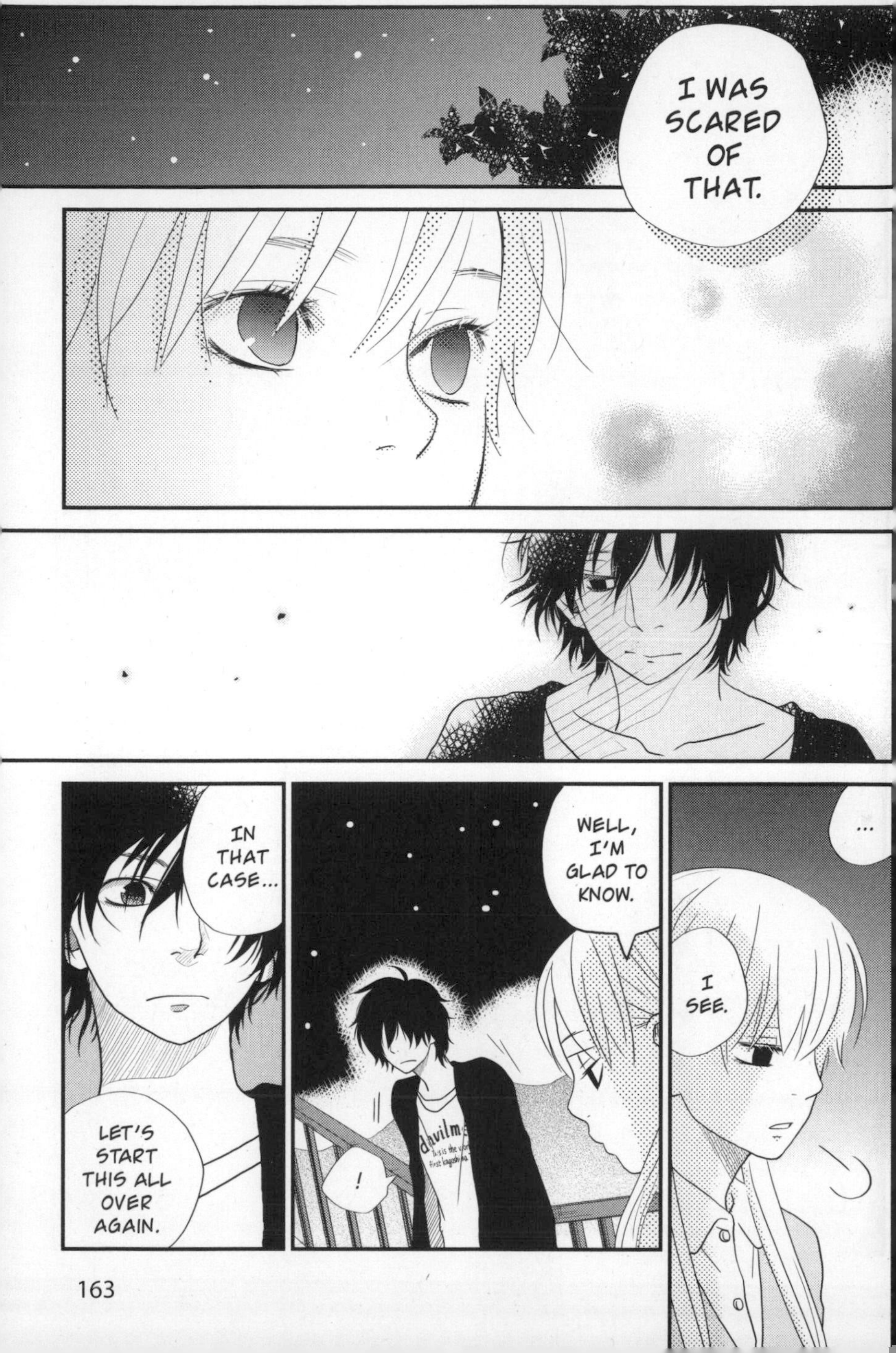
I WAS SCARED OF THAT.
...
I SEE.
WELL, I'M GLAD TO KNOW.
!
IN THAT CASE...
LET'S START THIS ALL OVER AGAIN.

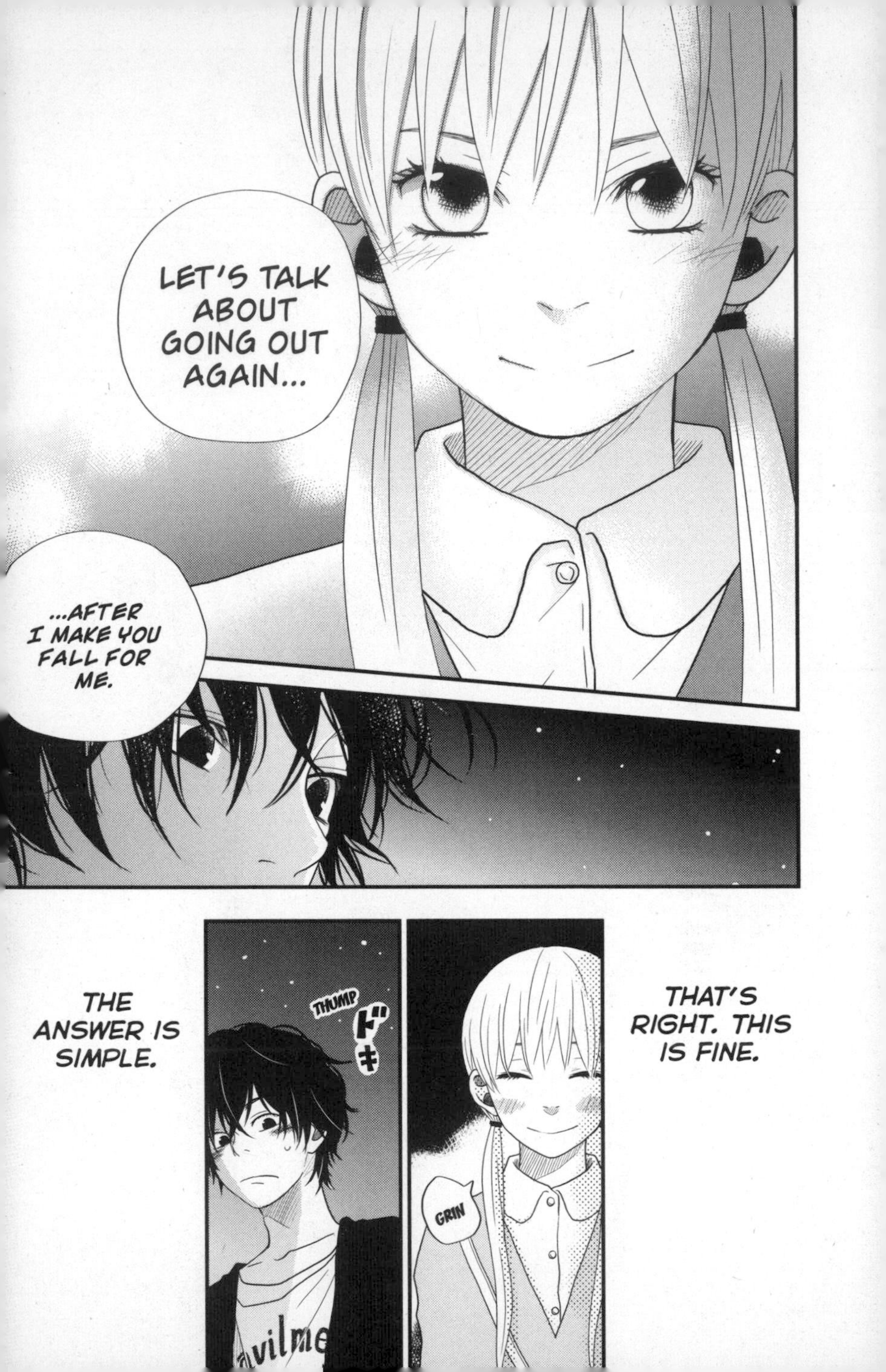
LET'S TALK ABOUT GOING OUT AGAIN...
...AFTER I MAKE YOU FALL FOR ME.
THAT'S RIGHT. THIS IS FINE.
GRIN
THE ANSWER IS SIMPLE.
THUMP
ドキ

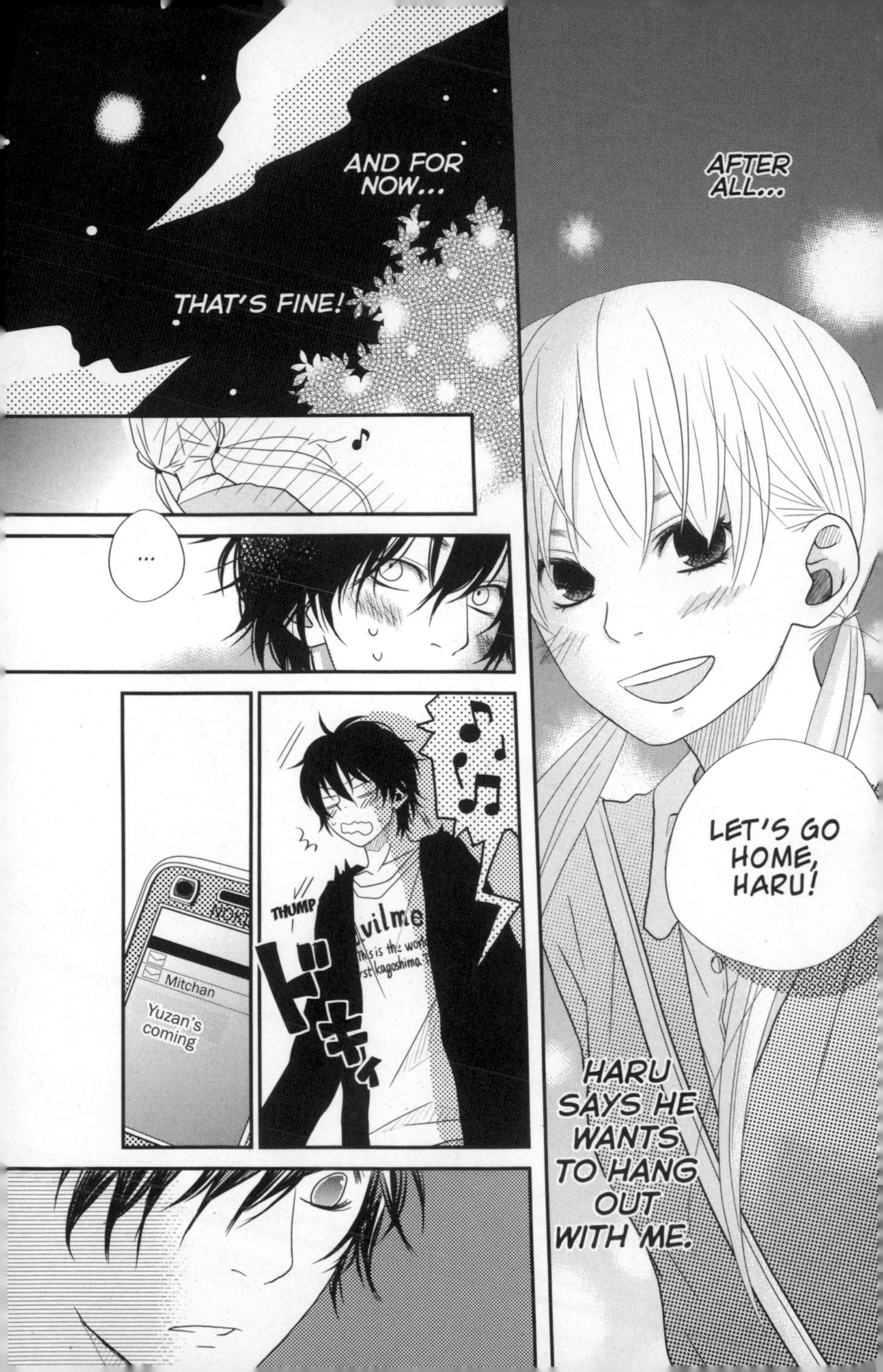
AFTER ALL...
LET'S GO HOME, HARU!
HARU SAYS HE WANTS TO HANG OUT WITH ME.
AND FOR NOW...
THAT'S FINE!
...
THUMP
ドキッ
Mitchan
Yuzan's coming

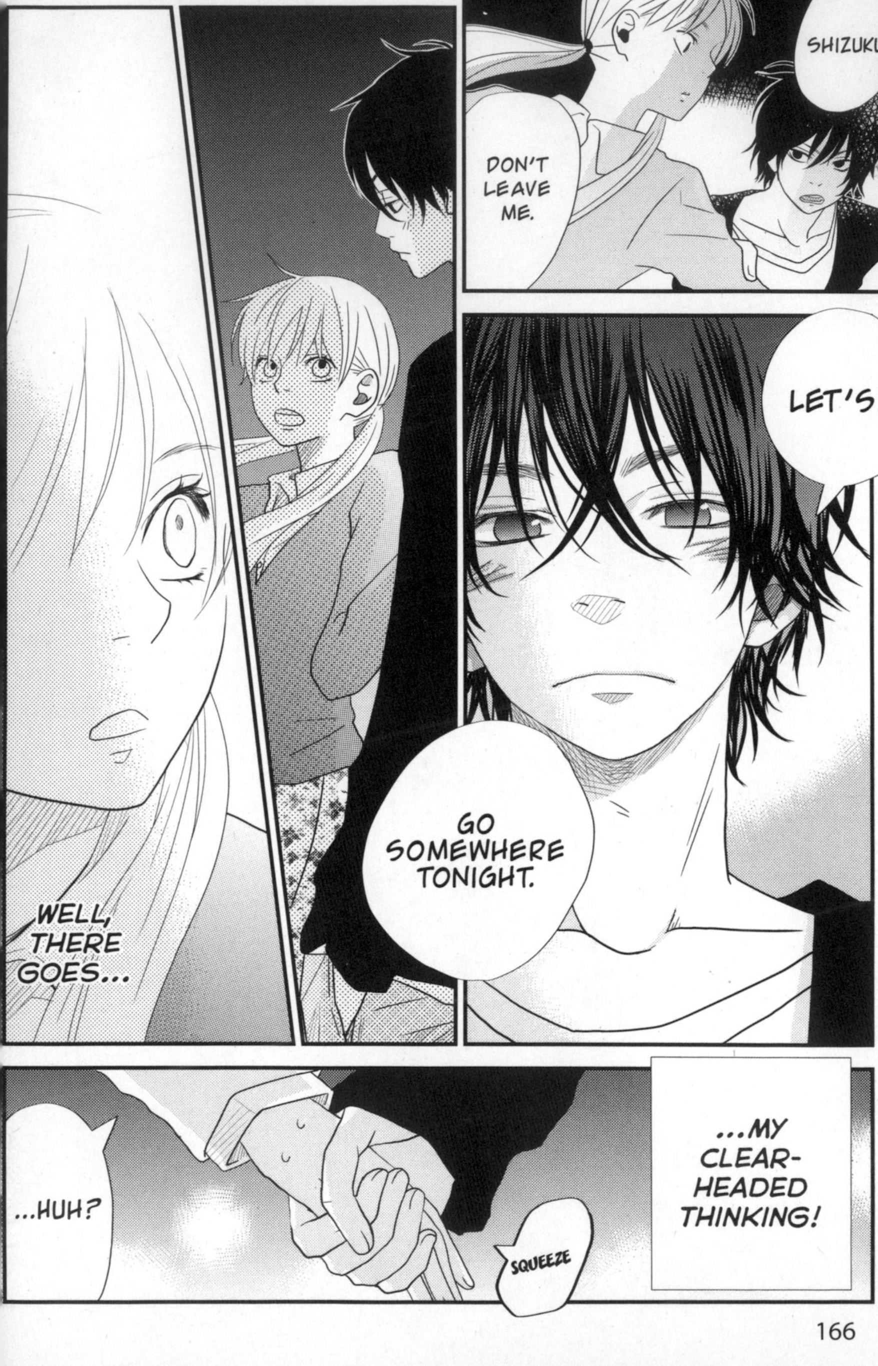
SHIZUKU.
DON'T LEAVE ME.
LET'S...
GO SOMEWHERE TONIGHT.
WELL, THERE GOES...
...MY CLEAR-HEADED THINKING!
SQUEEZE
...HUH?

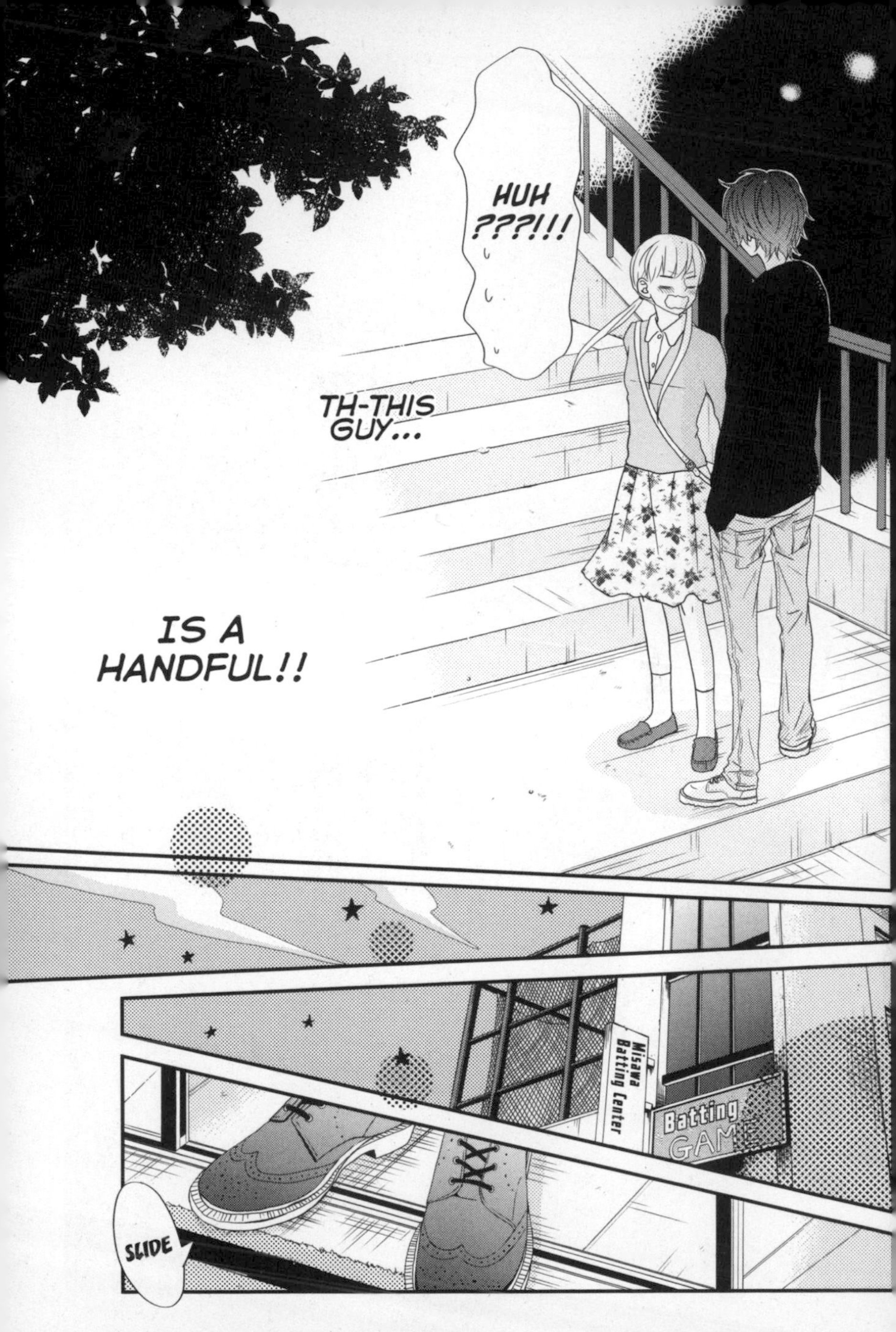
HUH ???!!!
TH-THIS GUY...
IS A HANDFUL!!
Misawa Batting Center
Batting GAM
SLIDE

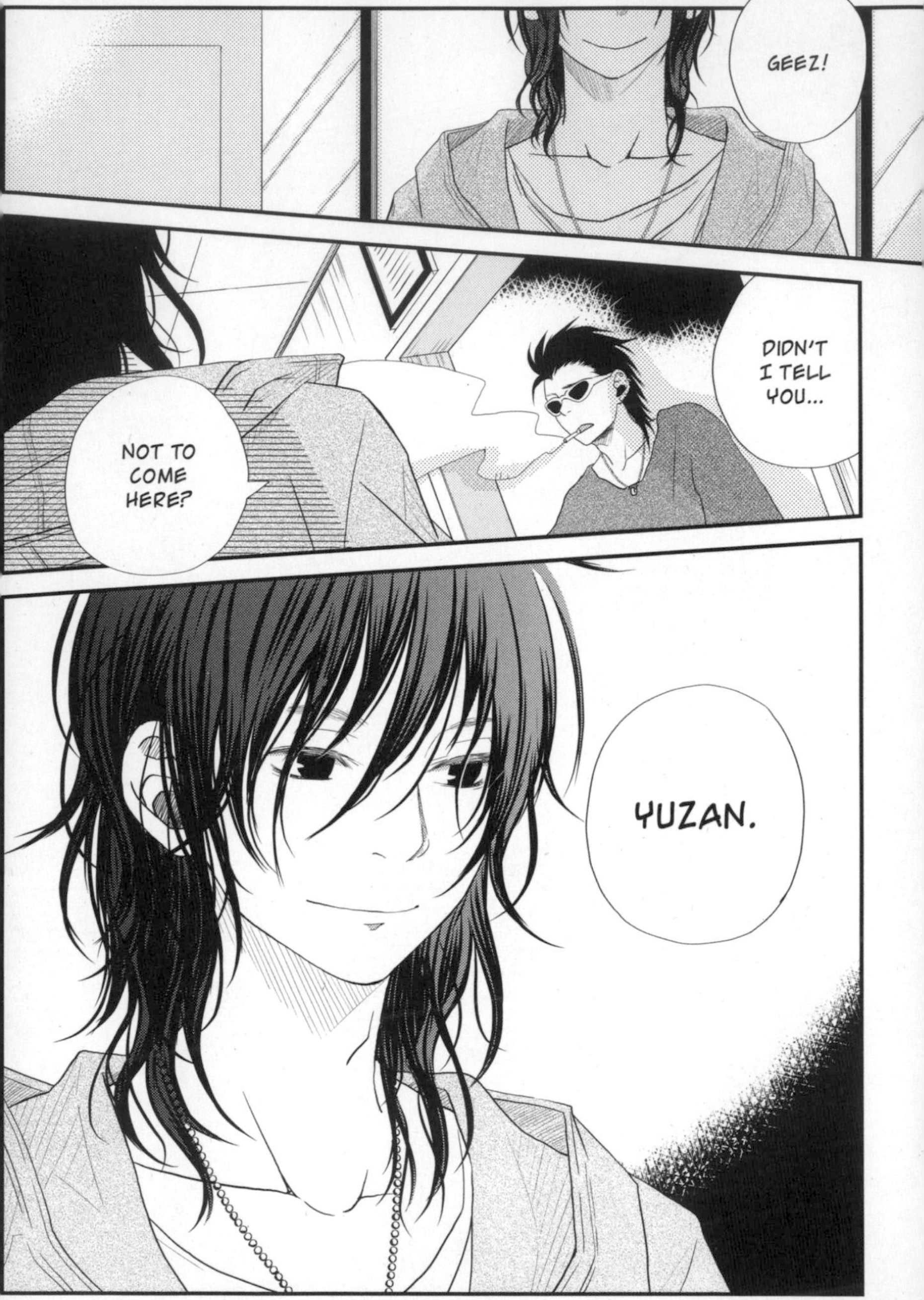
GEEZ!
DIDN'T I TELL YOU...
NOT TO COME HERE?
YUZAN.

Continued in Volume 2!!

JUST AS SHORT

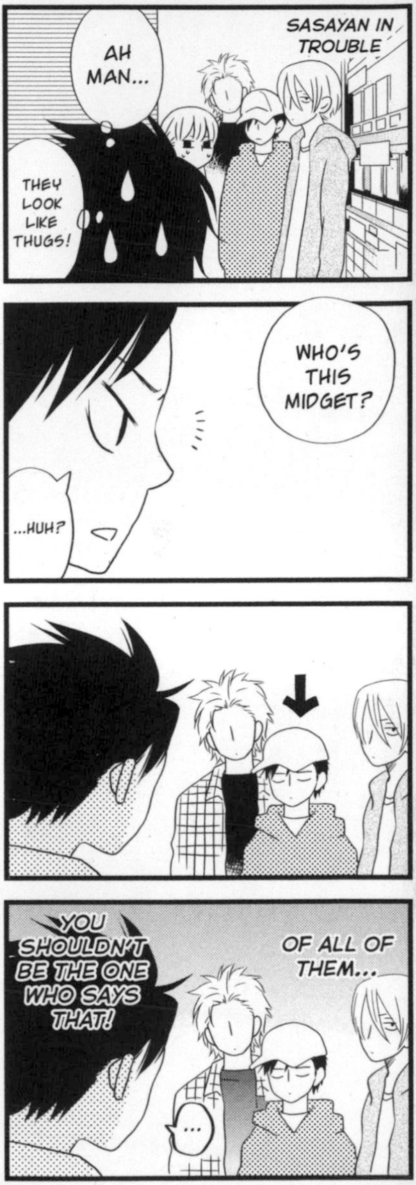
SASAYAN IN TROUBLE
AH MAN...
THEY LOOK LIKE THUGS!
WHO'S THIS MIDGET?
...HUH?
OF ALL OF THEM...
YOU SHOULDN'T BE THE ONE WHO SAYS THAT!
...

THAT GUY

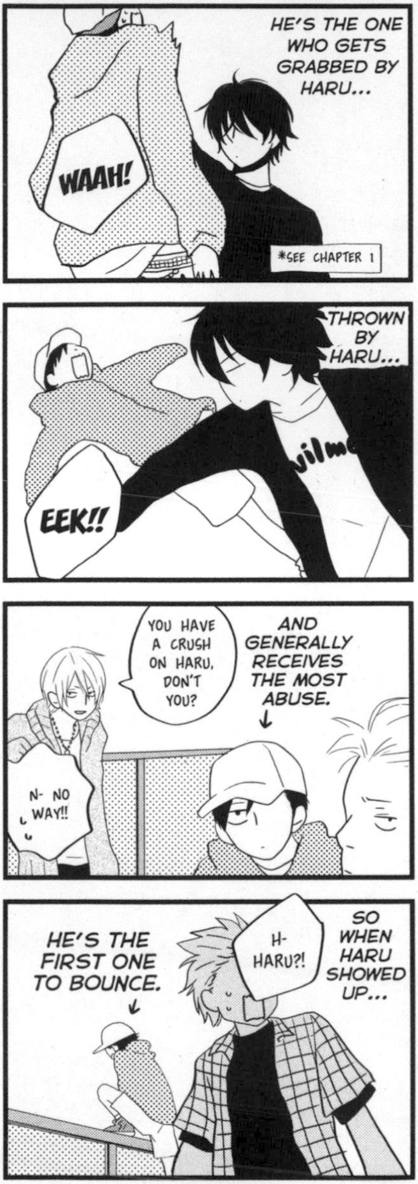
HE'S THE ONE WHO GETS GRABBED BY HARU...
WAAH!
*SEE CHAPTER 1
THROWN BY HARU...
EEK!!
AND GENERALLY RECEIVES THE MOST ABUSE.
YOU HAVE A CRUSH ON HARU, DON'T YOU?
N- NO WAY!!
SO WHEN HARU SHOWED UP...
H- HARU?!
HE'S THE FIRST ONE TO BOUNCE.

COMMENT

Robico

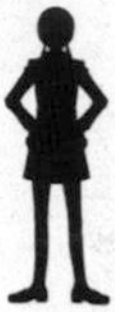

People often say, "the characters in my manga are like my own children!" But I don't feel this way at all. They're totally unrelated to me. I do hope we can get along, though. I'll do my best!

Translation Notes

Japanese is a tricky language for most Westerners, and translation is often more art than science. For your edificaiton and reading pleasure, here are note on some of the places where we could have gone in a different direction with our translation of this book, or where a Japanese cultural reference is used.

Monjayaki, pages 54 through 88
Monjayaki is a somewhat messy, pan-fried dish that combines batter with various other ingredients. It is similar to the better-known okonomiyaki, but is made with a more liquid batter, and is native to the Kanto region, as opposed to okonomiyaki, which is from Kansai. Two of the flavors Shizuku orders are "Baby Star," a ramen noodle-flavored crunchy snack, and mentai-mochi, marinated Pollock roe and rice cake.
In the mini comic on page 88, the joke is that monjayaki bears a resemblance to vomit, and that Haru is struggling not to point that out.

OOPArt, page 119
OOPArt, or "out-of-place artifact" is a term for an object of historical, archaeological, or paleontological interest found in a very unusual or seemingly impossible context.

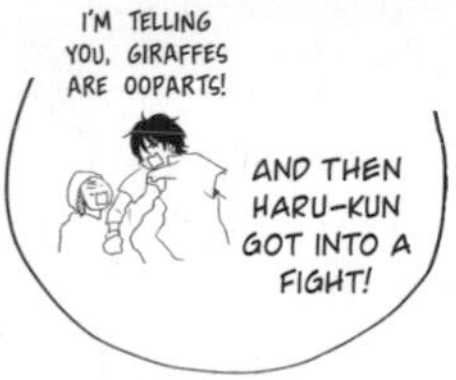
I'M TELLING YOU, GIRAFFES ARE OOPARTS!
AND THEN HARU-KUN GOT INTO A FIGHT!

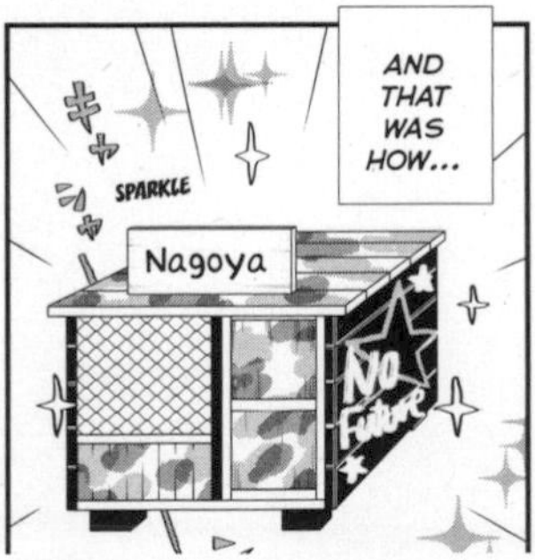
AND THAT WAS HOW...
SPARKLE
Nagoya
No Future

"Nagoya," page 137, 154
The name "Nagoya" (the third-largest city in Japan) for Haru's chicken is a play on "Nagoya Cochin," a famous chicken manufacturer near Nagoya, Japan.

Garigari-kun Soda, Chocolate Monaka, page 149

Garigari-kun and Chocolate Monaka are two popular ice cream brands in Japan. Garigari-kun is famous for a wide variety of flavors including corn potage and vegetable stew, although "soda" is the original and most popular flavor.

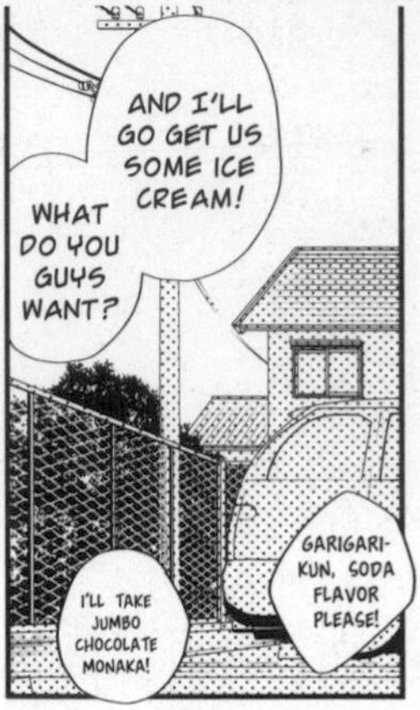
AND I'LL GO GET US SOME ICE CREAM!
WHAT DO YOU GUYS WANT?
GARIGARI-KUN, SODA FLAVOR PLEASE!
I'LL TAKE JUMBO CHOCOLATE MONAKA!

TV Drama, down to the river, page 153

Haru's comments about "going down to the river" are based on many Japanese TV dramas, where heartfelt scenes of reconciliation and other emotional watersheds are often staged along a riverside.

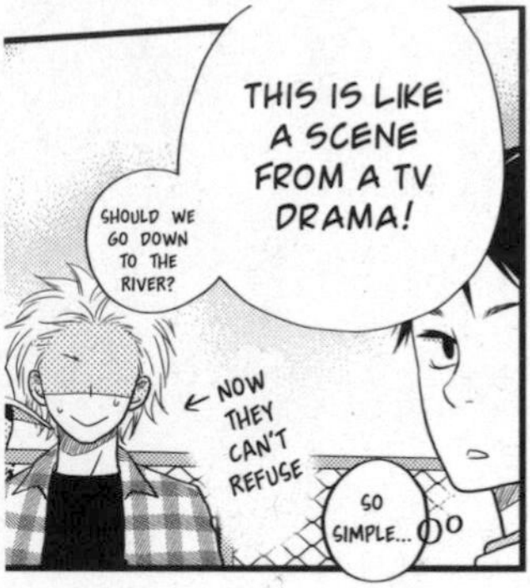
THIS IS LIKE A SCENE FROM A TV DRAMA!
SHOULD WE GO DOWN TO THE RIVER?
SO SIMPLE...
← NOW THEY CAN'T REFUSE

SANKAREA
undying love

"I ONLY LIKE ZOMBIE GIRLS."

Chihiro has an unusual connection to zombie movies. He doesn't feel bad for the survivors – he wants to comfort the undead girls they slaughter! When his pet passes away, he brews a resurrection potion. He's discovered by local heiress Sanka Rea, and she serves as his first test subject!

KC
KODANSHA
COMICS

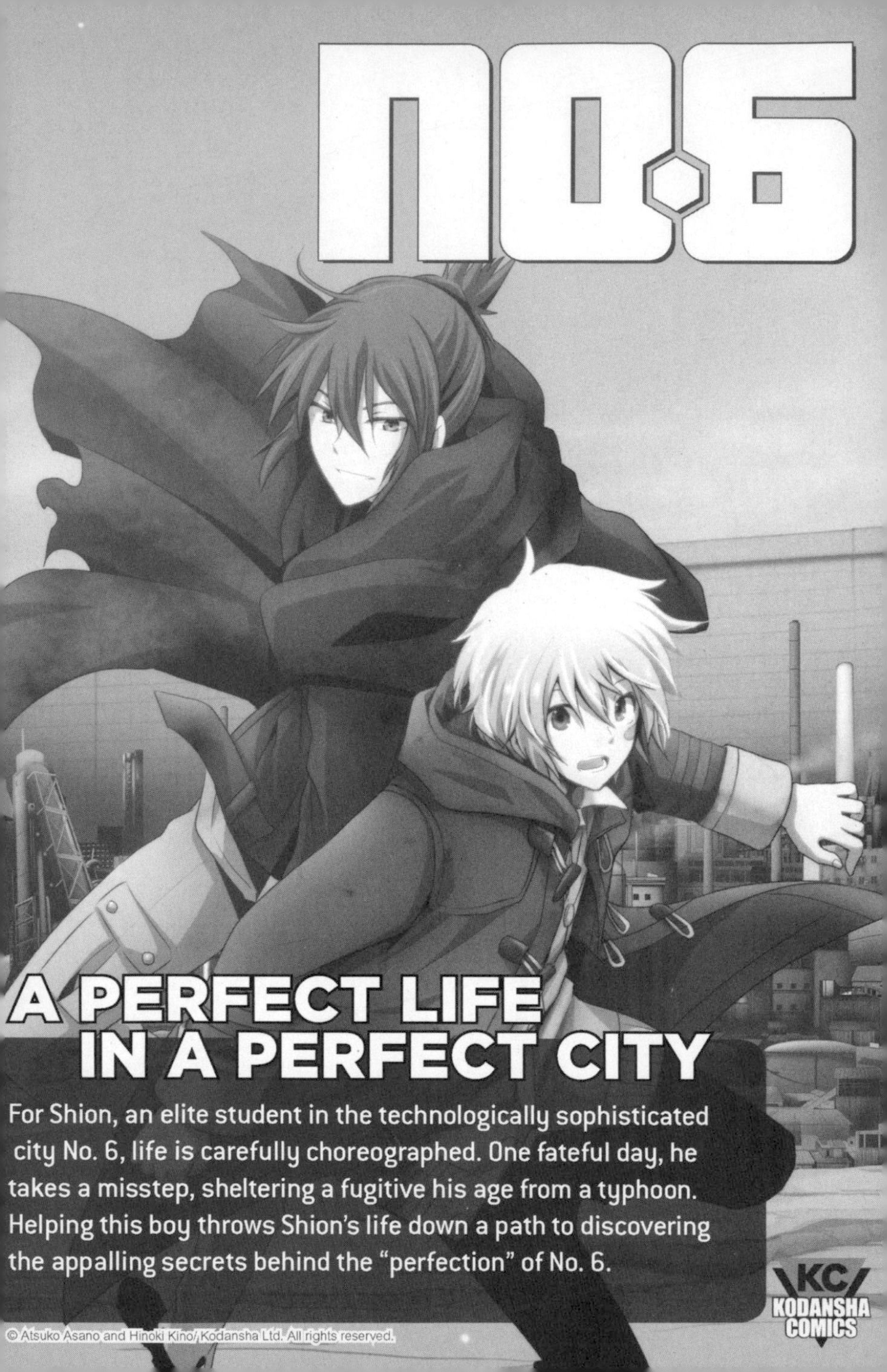
NO.6
A PERFECT LIFE
IN A PERFECT CITY
For Shion, an elite student in the technologically sophisticated city No. 6, life is carefully choreographed. One fateful day, he takes a misstep, sheltering a fugitive his age from a typhoon. Helping this boy throws Shion's life down a path to discovering the appalling secrets behind the "perfection" of No. 6.
KC
KODANSHA COMICS

A Kodansha Comics Trade Paperback Original.

Published in the United States by Kodansha Comics, an imprint of Kodansha USA Publishing, LLC, New York.

Publication rights for this English edition arranged through Kodansha Ltd., Tokyo.

First published in Japan in 2009 by Kodansha Ltd., Tokyo, as *Tonari no Kaibutsu-kun*, volume 1.

ISBN 978-1-61262-597-3

Printed and bound in Germany by GGP Media GmbH, Poessneck

www.kodanshacomics.com

12 11 10 9 8

Translator: Joshua Weeks
Lettering: Kiyoko Shiromasa & Mugwump Design

Stop

Japanese manga is written
and drawn from right to left,
which is the opposite of
the way American graphic
novels are composed.
To preserve the original
orientation of the art,
and maintain the proper
storytelling flow, this book
has retained the right to left
structure. Please go to what
would normally be the last
page and begin reading,
right to left, top to bottom.